Imago Dei: Man/Woman Created in the Image of God

Imago Dei: Man/Woman Created in the Image of God

Implications for Theology, Pastoral Care,
Eucharist, Apologetics, Aesthetics

George Hobson

Foreword by William Edgar

WIPF & STOCK · Eugene, Oregon

IMAGO DEI: MAN/WOMAN CREATED IN THE IMAGE OF GOD
Implications for Theology, Pastoral Care, Eucharist, Apologetics, Aesthetics

Copyright © 2019 George Hobson. All rights reserved. Except for brief quotations in critical publications or reviews, no part of this book may be reproduced in any manner without prior written permission from the publisher. Write: Permissions, Wipf and Stock Publishers, 199 W. 8th Ave. , Suite 3, Eugene, OR 97401.

Wipf & Stock
An Imprint of Wipf and Stock Publishers
199 W. 8th Ave. , Suite 3
Eugene, OR 97401

www. wipfandstock. com

PAPERBACK ISBN: 978-1-5326-8998-7
HARDCOVER ISBN: 978-1-5326-8999-4
EBOOK ISBN: 978-1-5326-9000-6

Manufactured in the U. S. A.   SEPTEMBER 18, 2019

Contents

Foreword by William Edgar | vii
Acknowledgments | xi
Introduction | xiii

Part I   Knowledge of God | 1
  The Explanatory Power of a Trinitarian Natural Theology | 3
  Resurrection and Life after Death | 17

Part II   The *Imago Dei* | 27
  Reflections on the *Imago Dei* in a Modern Context | 29

Part III   Pastoral Theology | 111
  Christian Identity: Who Do You Think You are? | 113
  Notes for Short Talk on the Holy Spirit | 142
  Notes for Talks on Pastoral Care and Counseling | 149
  Notes for Talks on Identity and Inner Healing | 155

Part IV   Eucharistic Theology | 173
  The Question of the Efficacy of the Eucharist | 175

Part V   Apologetics | 197
  Talks given at St. Michael's Anglican Church, Paris | 199

Part VI   Aesthetics | 235
  Beauty as the Radiance of Truth | 237
  Talk on Poetry | 277
  Notes for Short Talk on Beauty and Truth | 284

Bibliography | 289

Foreword

I WAS IN A clothing store, waiting for my wife to try on some shoes. To distract the consumer, the waiting room had a large bound copy of the *New York Times* with headlines and editorials dating back to the 1930s. I opened the volume at random and there, prominently displayed, was an op-ed article by the American theologian J. Gresham Machen. Whatever the merits of the particular article, it was clear that theological opinion was taken seriously by readers of this influential newspaper. Today believers still write for the *Times*, but more often than not the reader identifies, not a view that thought leaders need to reckon with as to how to change the world, but fascination, often condescending, with figuring out which tribe the author belongs to and moving on with life.

Coming from many corners, there is a nearly universal sense that the voice of Christian theology in public life is muted at best, harmful at worst. Standard reflections on secularization have measured the receding influence of religion in public and private life. Like the Cheshire Cat, less and less remains, until the only imprint is an enigmatic smile. The older, "standard" sociological model predicted (and often prescribed) the waning of Christian influence in decision-making. Not so long ago, political policy was filled with references to Reinhold Niebuhr's thoughts on sin, or Karl Barth's critique of statist idolatry, or even J. G. Machen's libertarian views. No longer.

It is true, however, that the standard secularization model has not proved enduring. One reason for that is the insistent way that *homo religious* refuses to sink beneath the waves. Even Enlightenment-based thinkers like Jürgen Habermas admit that there must be a place for Judeo-Christian convictions if society is to be sustained. French historian of jurisprudence Jacques Ellul has argued that while the Christian shape of religious life may have receded, new forms of *religion* have stood in the breach. Not everyone is convinced by the candidates he picks: hedonism, nation-building, and above all technology (or *technique* as he prefers it). But today there are only a few who still hold on to something like the standard model. *God is Back* as one book title has it.¹ Critics rightly ask whether he ever went away! It has simply taken us some time to notice what has been before our eyes all along. Has there been no real secularization? Of course there has. The return of religion is a bit more subtle, masking as spirituality and the like.

Most politicians are not riveted to Christian editorials in the *New York Times*. If they have faith, it is a rather private matter. In his powerful studies on the role of theology in public life, Miroslav Volf argues that theology has simply lost its audience.² He blames the audience, but he also blames academic theologians for becoming too in-house and specialized. "The general sense is that theology isn't producing any genuine knowledge that accomplishes anything, that it trades with the irrationality of faith and is useless."³ Is that all there is to the story? Not quite.

What is to be done? Retreat into a Benedict Option until the storm passes? Lash out with resentment? Is there a silver bullet? No, certainly not. The essays you hold in your hands by George Hobson are hopeful beyond many measures. The reason? They center, directly or indirectly, on one of the most needed doctrines for our times: mankind made in the image of God. The shorthand, *imago Dei,* is not only elegant and meaningful, but tells us that it has been believed from ancient times. The fundamental nature of human beings is a nonnegotiable answer to many of the challenges of our day. Hobson has written before on the dangers, as well as the opportunities, afforded by technology. As social media seeps in by osmosis, molding us into information-based machines, doomed to lose the control that is promised, the *imago* tells us not to look across, but to look upward. We have our primary identity in God himself, who conferred our nature on us.

The doctrine does far more. Instead of acrimonious denunciations of therapeutic abortions, it reminds us of the grandeur of even the most vulnerable human being. Instead of caving in to pragmatism, it reminds us we are capable of beauty from the ashes. Instead of empty defenses of the propositional value of the Bible (a value which it has, of course), it makes us ask why God revealed himself to a lost people and how it was possible for him to do so. Though it is not because the image makes us deserve him, when he does redeem us he restores us to a fuller image than we had even before. Instead of the rhetoric, "I have a plan," often heard from political candidates, it provides us with "I have a great God who leads us beyond plans into the house of the Lord forever, where goodness and love will follow us all the days of our lives" (Ps 23:6).

---

1. Micklethwait and Wooldridge, *God is Back.*
2. See Volf, *Public Faith*; Volf and Croasmun, *For the Life of the World.*
3. Volf and Croasmun, *For the Life of the World,* 44.

One of my mentors, the late Hans Rookmaaker, reveled in provocative statements. One of them was, "Christ did not come to make us more Christian, but more human." He knew, of course, that the statement was a redundancy. But his hope was to awaken his audience to what everyone today is talking about, but floundering to accomplish: human flourishing.

I don't think we are on the brink of a revival. Although these pages contain the marvelous answer of the gospel for our times, they risk being lost in the maelstrom of "*le cercle des bavards,*" lost in the chatter, but for two things. First, the prose here is crystal clear, compellingly lucid, and deeply persuasive. Hobson is a considerable poet, and his gifts for lyrics serve him admirably here. Thus, his great learning, far from making him mad (Acts 26:24), is translated into language we can all understand. This is a rarity. We need to listen, and then move into action. And second, most of these lectures, if not the three long essays, were delivered in local parishes. Here is Jesus's front line. Without denying the Kuyperian point that he is Lord in every sphere, there is something unique—dare I say, sacramental—about communicating directly with a church audience.

George Hobson is one of those rare human beings who has climbed what David Brooks has called the "second mountain."[4] The first mountain is one of achievement, accomplishment, success. It is a good place to be. But really to arrive at the place of true flourishing, one needs to ascend the second mountain, where selfish gains are shed in favor of selfless dedication to others, and to the worship of God. It is a better place to be. If I said more I would embarrass him. So I will say it this way: read these essays and enjoy the view from the second mountain.

WILLIAM EDGAR
Professor of Apologetics
Westminster Theological Seminary

---

4. Brooks, *Second Mountain*.

Acknowledgments

I owe a huge debt of thanks to a dear friend of forty-five years, Toni Contreras, whose stunning technical skill on the computer was exceeded only by his generosity in giving me, freely and graciously, of his own precious time. Without you, Toni, old friend, this book, for which even *you* found the formatting difficult, simply would not have seen publication. Thank you!

Introduction

THE TEXTS IN THIS book, with one exception, were written over the last fifteen years and vary widely in style and subject matter. I have updated them where this seemed necessary. Apart from the three long essays, they were given as talks in parish churches. All of them are rooted in one way or another in the seminal biblical text in Genesis 1:26–28. Verse 26 reads: "*So God created man in his own image, in the image of God he created him; man and woman he created them.*" This foundational Judeo-Christian anthropological principle is a revelation. It is not an inference from nature. One cannot read it off from the world around us. I believe it to be a fundamental God-given truth that Jews and Christians, in different ways, can use to bring theoretical coherence and practical responses to many of the challenges and baffling questions facing mankind in our day. How is it that lawful order and structure in the universe are, by a variety of means, apprehensible by human beings? Or how is it that what we call beauty is a reality eluding exact definition yet one that men and women perceive and cherish and seek tirelessly, in all cultures, to express in one form or another? What is this "beauty?" What does it signify? Or further: Is there a common human nature, an anthropological unity underlying the various ethnic and tribal expressions to be found on our planet, or is any such notion, or imagined commonality, necessarily a social construct, be it religious, philosophical, or juridical? (The relevance of this issue to current discussions about human dignity and rights cannot be exaggerated.) Or again: Whence comes the essentially religious nature of human beings, in the sense that we all experience a hunger for a transcendent reality, an inner longing for justice, peace, love, joy, freedom, and immortality, even within the existential reality of violence, cruelty, oppression, suffering, and death that characterizes human history? Whence comes this yearning for plenitude—for the absolute, for *dynamic perfection*—when the daily reality of human life falls far short of any such ideal or hope? How are we to understand the relation of this longing for a *supranatural truth and love* uniting human beings and indeed all creatures, with the intuition we also have of being *ontologically integrated* in an infinitely complex *earthly and cosmic natural environment* to which and, in a mysterious sense, *for* which we feel ourselves to be responsible?

The first two papers in this collection that make up Part One broach the question of our knowledge of God through natural theology on the one hand and—with specific reference to the resurrection—through divine action/revelation on the other. Emphasis is put in the first paper on a kind of natural theology based not on philosophical argument of the Thomistic sort, but rather on the *explanatory power* of theologically based insight into the natural world, even if such insight cannot actually give us *personal knowledge* of the Creator. By virtue of our being made in God's image, we have the capacity to intuit, discover, and explore the phenomenal *order* in every aspect of the universe. All of these aspects are integrated in a coherent unity which, upon reflection, makes nonsense of the notion that sheer chance has produced the cosmos and everything in it, including human life. It is not that chance is absent, but rather that it is to be discerned within an overall context of law, in a relationship that allows a creative balance of freedom and order in the deployment of energy and matter. I devote a number of pages to reflections on mathematics, cosmology, and evolution, and conclude with a few thoughts on beauty and mystery.

In the second paper what is underlined is the *impossibility*, in our finite and fallen state, of our knowing the *true* God without his self-revelation. The supreme moment of this divine self-revelation is the resurrection of Jesus Christ. But it must also be evident that if mankind were not made in God's image, we could not possibly either desire or receive this divine self-revelation. At the heart of Christ's resurrection is the revelation of the God who is life and love. This corresponds perfectly to the deepest desire in the heart of all of us, even in our alienated state. I consider at some length the theme of Christ's second coming as the necessary conclusion to his redemptive action on behalf of mankind, and I go on to reflect briefly on the nature of life after death and on the final judgment.

My underlying point in both essays in Part One is that we would not be able to know God in any way whatsoever—neither by reflection nor by intuition nor by revelation—if he had not created us in his image.

The lengthy essay on the *imago Dei* that follows in Part Two is an intensive discussion of this seminal anthropological revelation in Genesis 1 and serves as the centerpiece of the book and the thematic reference for all the other texts. It starts off with a discussion of genocide that leads into a sustained critique of the nihilistic side of modernity and postmodernity, of which, I suggest, the underlying cause is our progressive rejection of the Judeo-Christian God since the eighteenth-century Enlightenment and hence, logically, of man/woman as made in God's image. In no way do I presume to cover all aspects of what we may take the *imago Dei* to signify, but I do wish to underline the great importance, in our age of genocidal violence, technological revolution, genetic and genome manipulation, moral anarchy, and anthropological confusion, of recovering the basic truth about mankind provided by this biblical vision. Western society's retreat from God and from the *imago Dei* has opened up a black hole in our culture, sucking us into successive forms of ideological totalitarianism made possible by technological power and seeking, at bottom, to transform the ontological truth of man-made-in-God's image into its inversion, God-made-in-man's image.

My analysis of the *imago Dei* is to be seen against this dark historical backdrop. I argue that the core meaning of the *imago Dei* is relational, and that qualitative factors, such as our rationality and moral freedom, are to be understood within this relational context. We are ontologically bound to our Creator. Our rebellion against him entails an *inversion* of the *imago* but not an effacement of it, and we are seeing the ultimate outworking of this inversion in our day. We are *alienated* from our Creator but *not essentially separated* from him because our *very nature* is to be made *in his image*. Herein lies the explanation of all our idolatries but also of the *possibility* of our being redeemed by our merciful Creator. Jesus Christ, the Son of God, our Redeemer, is the very image of God (Col 1:15; Heb 1:3), who can identify with us and become man and save us *precisely because we are made in his image*, that is, in *God's image*.

I go on to discuss at length the nature of this Creator and Redeemer God in whose image we are made, as he has revealed himself in the Old and New Testaments. This leads on to cosmological and teleological issues, remarks about homosexuality, and finally to a concluding exploration of the *imago Dei* in relational terms, as noted above, showing how human dignity and unity, freedom, reason, and our human capacity to love, are all rooted in our nature as creatures made in God's image. It is, indeed, the ontological truth of this revelation, restored to the positive relational mode through the incarnation, passion, resurrection, and ascension of Jesus Christ, followed by the sending of the Holy Spirit, that accounts for the gradual emergence, in cultures shaped by the church, of concepts such as the unity of mankind, the essential value and dignity of all human beings (regardless of qualitative inequalities of whatever kind), the worth of the individual person and his/her vocation to be free and not enslaved, and the consequent belief in human rights.

I close with a few remarks recalling the earlier analysis of human rebellion as it moves in our day to eliminate God and replace him with man. By means of a technology-based ideology of individual autonomy and a false idea of freedom, we are trying to appropriate and exploit for our selfish purposes all the variety of gifts that God has given us in his creation and through his redemption in Jesus Christ. Blindly, violently, foolishly, we are pulling up the roots of the tree in which we have life. Having excluded, in the name of human freedom, all reference to a transcendent source of being, we have imprisoned ourselves. On the basis of an evolutionist understanding of human nature, we have confirmed a body/mind dualism that has us now presuming to dictate to material reality, including to biological structures and our own human bodies, whatever our subjective feelings and desires want it to be. Our minds rule, our bodies are mere matter. This is sheer illusion, a hubristic power-grab. Only sexual and social anarchy can result. Rebellion and self-hatred masquerading as a noble quest for freedom from constraints and limits for our "authentic self, " is leading to widespread despair and the loss of the very sense of identity we are straining to establish. The "man" I referred to above, whom we are intent on putting in God's place, is *inhuman*. Having cast the Creator aside, we are de-naturing his creature, man/woman, and damaging all the other creatures of the world it is our calling to care for. We are enslaving ourselves, while thinking we are doing just the opposite. It is tragic.

Part Three, which includes a short essay on the Holy Spirit, baptism, the new birth, and the charismatic gifts, is hands-on, practical material, and includes notes from parish seminars given by my wife Victoria and me on the subject of Christian identity, pastoral care and counselling, and inner healing through prayer. I have retained the repetitions in the material because they may be pedagogically useful by impressing on readers the principles and procedures under discussion. My aim is to provide basic scriptural and practical guidelines to equip Christians in local parishes, house churches, prayer groups, and other communal structures, with down-to-earth principles for living the Christian life and creating strong communities. I am convinced that these principles and procedures are essential for the building up of the body of Christ and are not adequately taught and deployed in the church today, either in theological colleges or in parishes—this is my reason for wanting to include these talks in this volume of essays. If we are to carry out our mission of evangelism in the revolutionary environment of today's world, we must be very clear as to who we are in Christ: sons and daughters of God the Father. We are *new creations* (Gal 6:5). It is our certainty about this identity that will enable us to be healed, trained, and anointed by the Holy Spirit in ways that go beyond what most Christians experienced in earlier generations.

This work of healing and training is not just the task of priests and pastors, though these ordained leaders should certainly have received the formation enabling them to train lay people in their communities to assist them in their pastoral care. The Christian believer, as a new creation in Christ through the work of the Holy Spirit, is called to be conformed to Jesus, who is himself the very image of God (Col 1:15; 2 Cor 4:4). The possibility of conformity to Jesus presupposes the essential nature of human beings as created in God's image. The doctrine of the *imago Dei* is therefore basic to all pastoral work in the church—hence, as I said above, the inclusion of these hands-on notes in this collection of theological essays. The seminar talks, which, deliberately, I have hardly altered, attempt to show from a variety of angles how this plays out—or can play out—in the practical daily life of a Christian believer as he or she enters more and more deeply into his/her new spiritual identity as a son or daughter of God that is God's gift through faith.

The essay in the next section, Part Four, is an in-depth study of the central sacrament of the church: the Eucharist. From a number of perspectives, including unity in the body of Christ, the Holy Spirit's action in the Eucharist, and the issue of sacrifice, I explore the meaning and efficacy of the Passover and the Eucharistic celebrations. How is Christ's body—crucified, sacramental, and ecclesial/mystical—present to us when we receive the bread and wine? While I do not explicitly develop the doctrine of the *imago Dei* in this piece, it must surely be evident that the spiritual efficacy of this central sacrament of the church, in which believers *participate* in the body and blood of Jesus, presupposes and depends on the prior ontological reality that the believers are created in God's image, that is, in the image of Jesus.

Part Five consists of four talks on apologetics given in a church in Paris, which, once again, are underpinned by the biblical revelation of the *imago Dei*. The aim is to provide a few basic apologetical tools for Christians as they share their faith with unbelievers or inquirers. The church is under attack today on all sides, and Christians must be better equipped conceptually than we have been in earlier centuries to carry out our mission of spreading the gospel. Our love for our neighbor and our social action must be complemented by a stronger grasp of the intellectual challenges we face. I touch on matters such as cosmology, Darwinism, secularism, Christ/truth/Scripture, and Islam, showing in outline how the truth about human nature revealed in Genesis 1:26–28 illuminates, challenges, or brings correctives to each of these subjects. Other subjects could be added, of course, but I chose to focus on these.

Part Six shifts the perspective to the subject of aesthetics. In the lengthy opening essay, beauty is understood to be the radiance of divine truth. Herein lies the mystery of its glory. Man/Woman made in God's image is called and gifted to apprehend this glory. Again, as in the essay on the *imago Dei*, I explore this biblical revelation and mount an in-depth critique of the reigning ideological "isms" of our day—materialism, productivism and the instrumentalization of nature it entails, consumerism, relativism, individualism (as distinct from individuality)—in an attempt to highlight our current alienation from nature and the impoverished sensitivity to beauty and truth that results from this. I cover some of the same ground as in the *Imago Dei* text in Part Two, and in talks three and four of Part Five, but from different angles. My hope is that what repetition there is will clarify further and reinforce the critique of late modernity that I am making.

Going on to consider certain aspects of Greek philosophical thought, I discuss the issue of *form* and contrast the Platonic intuition with the Hebraic and Christian vision. For the Greeks, the awareness of beauty arose from the contemplation of form, which was understood as the translation of *being itself*, and the rational order of the cosmos, into concrete manifestations; for the Hebrew and Christian mind, a beautiful form is an expression of God's creative word. In both cases, form reflects metaphysical reality and manifests rationality. Herein lies its beauty, in which we are called to participate. Such a vision is utterly remote from modernity's and postmodernity's positivistic perception of the physical world, which sees concrete things, including the human body, as mere disposable matter that human reason and will are called upon to control and manipulate for utilitarian purposes. Any notion of participation in metaphysical reality is totally absent; *reverence* before form, *wonder* before beauty, have disappeared.

Next, I underline strongly the *relational* dimension of our connection with other objects/creatures in the world, as over against the functionalist attitude of our productivist societies. This involves a discussion of naming—the task given by God to Adam in the garden of Eden (Gen 2:19-20)—as it may be applied to science and art. It is the *relational* dimension between us and the world, rooted in the *imago Dei* and in the stewardship of God's creatures that the *imago Dei* entails, that enables us to name creatures, to observe and know them, and that opens human beings to the perception and experience of the mystery of beauty. We are equipped by nature to *investigate* the world, scientifically and artistically. Our relation with creatures is the counterpart of our *imago Dei* relation with God. This means, of course, that our inversion of the *imago* through our rejection of the true God (original sin) has brought about a progressive alienation from nature and a ruinous exploitation of its bounty, culminating in the catastrophic ecological/environmental predicament mankind is facing today.

My concluding remarks in this paper speak again of beauty as the radiance of truth, a radiance that glorifies forms but also points beyond them to their Source, the Creator God who is love. A short disquisition on art and light closes the essay.

The autobiographical talk that follows examines the subject of poetry and art from the perspective of my own experience as a poet who, as a Christian, is faced with the challenge of communicating with a largely secular audience that is increasingly ignorant of and often hostile toward the Christian gospel. Moreover, regardless of the audience that he/she is addressing, writers who are new creations in Christ cannot write as they did before they were born again. My reflections on what I call true art are an effort to respond to these challenges.

Finally, a concluding short talk gathers together in summary form many of the points made earlier about the *imago Dei* and aesthetics in a final effort to show how, at a practical level, it is the truth of the *imago Dei* that inspires and makes possible the human quest, in particular through the arts, to express and give form to what is experienced—by all peoples everywhere—as *beauty*.

My hope is that the range and variety of the texts in this book will incite renewed reflection on the anthropological revelation in Genesis of the *imago Dei*, man/woman as created in the image of God. In our age of transhumanist ambition, which is rooted in the hubristic denial of a Creator God and in a corresponding refusal of the notion of a created and good God-given human nature—*twisted because of the Fall, yes, but good in its created essence*—it is of the greatest importance for the future of the church and for the well-being of our society to develop and defend this biblical revelation. The core of the modern project, as it takes ultimate shape in our technological age, is auto-salvation. For the transhumanist, though he/she wouldn't use salvation language, this objective is explicit and deliberate. The aim is not so much to augment the human being as to *replace* him/her with a technologically engineered, new and better model. This delusory enterprise—the definitive tower of Babel—is clearly a counterfeit of God's redemptive action through Christ to set right his sin-marred creation by opening for us the possibility of becoming new creations. There is no fixed, divinely created human nature, we are told. Man is a faulty organism and must be reconceived and reconstituted by himself. Such an objective is perceived to be the fulfillment of the process of evolutionary/historical progress, culminating in the kingdom of man, a simulacrum of the kingdom of God.

In the face of gnostic ambitions of this kind that both mock and mimic the creation and redemption of mankind through the Word of God, Jesus Christ, the truth of the *imago Dei*, in all its dimensions, is a tremendously powerful weapon in the hands of the church. As an anthropological principle, it is pertinent at every level of human reflection and action, in response to the moral and spiritual cacophony of modern life. My wish is that these texts, bouncing off each other in multiple directions, may illuminate for readers the truth and vital significance of this biblical revelation, by which is established *ontologically and forever* the true relation of human beings both to God their Creator and to the world—God's *good creation*—that they inhabit.

Part I

KNOWLEDGE OF GOD

The Explanatory Power of a Trinitarian Natural Theology

(Talk at the American Church, Paris)

I

THE PRACTICE OF NATURAL theology has traditionally been an effort to prove or demonstrate the existence of God by arguing from observed phenomena in nature on the basis of universal rational principles. It has been conducted separately from theological discussion of the God of *revelation*, the God revealed through the incarnation to be triune: Father, Son, and Holy Spirit. The perception that there is order within nature has always led to a felt need to explain this order. The classical Christian response shows the influence of the Greek notion of a universal logos, or cosmic order, and of Aristotelian cosmology, combined with Paul's insight in Romans 1:20 that God's power and nature have been understood and seen through the visible creation. Up until the twentieth century, this Christian response has been the rationalistic one of inference from nature to a first cause, on the assumption that God's existence is universally perceptible and philosophically demonstrable.

Let me describe briefly two quite different examples of this traditional approach to natural theology. In the thirteenth century, which saw the rise of scholasticism and an intense stress on reason, Thomas Aquinas set out his Five Ways, or Proofs, of God's existence, which involve tracing back to a First Principle the existence of motion, causality, contingency, degree of value—implying an ultimate perfection—and design or purpose. The basic argument for all Five Ways is that an infinite regress in any of these instances is rationally incoherent, and that in every case a First Cause, an Absolute Source, must be predicated. The existence of motion, for example, implies a Prime Mover; or, what exists might not have existed, so a Necessary Being must be predicated beyond the reach of contingency;

or, directionality—what appears to be purposefulness—is to be observed in nature, in organic growth and in human action, so an Original Designer must be inferred or deducted; or, at the ethical level, the existence of natural law and the human conscience which constrains us and yet which is clearly not the result of our own will or reason, points to a metaphysical source beyond ourselves. This kind of approach to the question of the existence of God, while strong philosophically and persuasive to a believer, is vulnerable to the criticism (in my view weak, but the determined unbeliever can make *anything* count as an objection) that it involves what critics call flat *assertion* on the basis of ignorance, and that the inference in each case to a personal primary being called God is arbitrary.

In the late eighteenth and early nineteenth centuries, arguing within the mechanistic cosmological framework of Newtonian thought as it had developed in the eighteenth century, William Paley saw the universe, and this world in particular, as a watch—that is, as a *mechanism*—from which he logically inferred a Watchmaker. He lived in the period of early industrialism and saw the apologetic potential of a mechanistic analogy to demonstrate the necessary existence of God. Paley adduced many other natural features to support his basic argument that contrivances in nature are inexplicable without reference to a Designer, but his mechanistic approach, in keeping with the tenor of his age, was vulnerable to the same criticism as Aquinas's arguments; moreover, with respect to the specific watch analogy, the atheist philosopher David Hume pointed out that the world could just as well be compared with a plant or some living organism for which a strict design argument was philosophically untenable. This last criticism became even more forceful later in the century when Darwin observed that an *appearance* of design arises naturally in the course of evolution.

In the twentieth century, the Swiss theologian Karl Barth objected strongly to the *independent* aspect of traditional natural theology, by which he meant the development of arguments for the existence and nature of God separately from the biblical revelation of God the Trinity. Not only could natural theology, so conceived, not give knowledge of the Trinitarian God, but it split discussion of the knowledge of God into two parts—the first concerned with the one God that reason was supposed to be able to demonstrate, and the other concerned with the triune God revealed through Jesus Christ. Barth perceived that this was theologically and methodologically unacceptable. It was not that Barth ruled out the possibility of seeing traces of the Creator God within nature, or that he saw no place for rational structure in our knowledge of God, but he insisted that such a structure must be coordinated with revelation if it was not to be misleading abstraction.

The approach to natural theology—to the question of how a Christian is to consider the relation of nature to God—depends on one's point of view, on what one *sees*. The modern world is very conscious of perspective, of point of view. It is evident that the fact that all human beings are rational does *not* mean we all see nature—the world out there—in the same way. Cultural context and religious experience fundamentally influence *what and how* we see. A converted Christian person will see evidence of God in nature, because he or she believes God is the Creator. A nonbeliever is not likely to see the same thing in the same way, obviously. This insight, common today, means that although the traditional approach to natural theology has been useful in its time, it is no longer really serviceable.

The main point to be made in this regard is that knowledge of the true God revealed in Scripture and supremely in Jesus Christ cannot be read off nature. One can sense—as Paul insists in the text from Romans that I mentioned a moment ago—God's reality in the power and order of nature, yes, but one cannot, by virtue of human reason, infer or deduce the Trinity from natural phenomena. In recent years, a new approach to natural theology has been emerging which takes its starting point from *within* the Trinitarian framework. Its aim is not to prove or even argue for the existence or nature of God, but to give evidence of the explanatory power of the specific Christian vision of reality based on revelation, with respect both to scientific discoveries and to everyday experience.

II

I want to look now at how the apostle Paul talked about nature when addressing a crowd of curious Greek intellectuals in Athens. The account is in Acts 17:22-34. Paul recognizes that the people are religious and worship a variety of objects. In his wanderings in the city he had seen an altar inscribed "To an unknown god," and he declares to his listeners that he will proclaim to them who God is. He does not proceed by using rationalistic arguments, as one might have expected in a Greek context. He refers immediately to the Creator of "the world and everything in it," and goes on to call this God Lord and to declare that God had given mortals life and breath and had set out times and spatial boundaries for nations so that humans would search for him and perhaps find him. The Greeks had no concept of such a personal Creator of all things—the Platonic notion of a demiurge was as close as they had come to such an idea—but a vague sort of pantheistic sense of a divine presence was clearly in the air, and it was to this religious intuition among his listeners that the apostle was appealing.

To support this approach he quotes two Greek poets, Epimenides and the Stoic, Aratus, to the effect that in God *"we live and move and have our being . . . for we too are his offspring"* (v. 28). He then makes his decisive move, which is to declare that this God, of whose existence the Greeks have an intuition but no knowledge, calls people to repent—that is, basically, to change their way of *seeing* reality, which will change the way they act—because he—this God—has fixed a day when he will judge mankind, and this judgment will be carried out by a *man* whom God has appointed and whom, as an assurance of this, he has raised from the dead.

What is interesting for our purposes here is that Paul, in making his case for the true identity of the deity whom the Greeks call *"the unknown god,"* puts his emphasis on the creation of the world by this God and on God's act to raise from the dead, in historical space/time, a man whom he has designated to be judge of the world. Paul does not speak explicitly here of this man as God—of the incarnation—but he does stress the *resurrection*. He does not use the rationalist tools of argument commonly used by the Greek philosophers when trying to take account of the religious impulse or to transcend it.

The God whom the Greeks have an intuition of, but who is very different from their ideas about him, is the Creator of nature and an actor in history. He is not to be *identified* with nature, but, as its Author, he is intimately *associated* with it. He is a personal deity who has dominion over the beginning and end of all things, over the destiny of mankind, over life and death. To speak *truly* of God, to identify the *true* God, one must speak of concrete nature, of the material world: God is the one who creates and orders nature and who acts within it to judge and redeem. His self-revelation happens in and through the material creation. Whether one accepts this argument or not—some Greeks did, some did not—it is evident that Paul's vision provides a kind of coherence to the material world and to man's destiny within it that neither the Greeks' religiosity nor their philosophizing could provide. It is my contention that Paul's vision, in its full-fledged Trinitarian shape, provides us too, living in the context of modern science, with a way of seeing all aspects of reality that gives them coherence and intelligibility.

III

Let me now approach this Trinitarian question from an anthropological angle. A philosophical stance adopted by the majority of the scientific community is what is called critical realism. It holds, in agreement with common sense, that there is an objective, external world out there separate from us, the observers, but also that we, as knowers, are subjectively involved in that world by virtue of our interpretation and appropriation of it; at the level of quantum phenomena, moreover, it is the case, the physicists tell us, that we actually *influence* that world out there by our experimental observation of it. Cognitive neuroscience of perception is showing that we exist in *relation* to the natural world, that our mental representations of it shape the way we see and understand it, and vice versa—in a word, that we are *participants* in nature, interactive with it; we do not create reality as such, but we do act creatively *upon* it—we are certainly not simply passive recipients of sensory data.

For our purposes, what I want to do here is to suggest the *theological ground* in Scripture for this relationality of mankind to nature, a relationality that philosophers at least since Kant have recognized and that neuroscience is confirming in our day. We are not so-called objective observers. Yes, our self-consciousness—unique in nature—gives us distance from the material world, but it does not separate us intrinsically from that world, in the manner of Cartesian dualism. The strict subject-object schema is transcended by the reality that we are integrated constitutionally into this material world that is God's handiwork. By referring to the Judeo-Christian Scriptures, we can gain the theological perspective that undergirds this reality.

Genesis 1 reveals that God is the Creator of all reality, the one who establishes order out of chaos, who brings light, energy, and all other creatures into being, where before was only darkness and void. Then verses 26–28 tell us that God has created mankind—man and woman—*in his image*, and that, as God's representatives on earth, we are to multiply and have dominion over the world, that is, to rule it wisely and tend it as we might a garden, not by exploiting it ruthlessly for profit but by cultivating it joyfully in the interest of sociability, culture, and human welfare.

Genesis 2 goes on to develop the *vocational* dimension of humankind by speaking of Adam's *naming* of the other creatures. Naming, which requires both authority and rationality, is accomplished through our linguistic gift and our tool-making capacity, which give rise to technology, science, and the various arts—in a word, to *culture*. By these means, we are enabled to carry out our vocation of exercising dominion.

From this double revelation of our being created in the image of God and of our having a cultural vocation, we may understand that men and women are ontologically—that is, in their very *being*—in *relation* to God and also to the created world. This insight provides a basic perspective on the Judeo-Christian doctrine of creation in its anthropological dimension, that is, as it relates to mankind. We are indefeasibly bound to both God and nature, and we are *responsible* to both. The insight illuminates the discoveries I just mentioned in the field of cognitive neuroscience, and we shall see shortly its explanatory power in regard to many human capacities and activities.

A proper anthropology that fits within a Trinitarian framework for natural theology requires us to go on and look at Genesis 3, which describes the seduction and corruption of mankind by Satan's wily appeal to human pride. This rebellion against the Creator leads not to a dissolution of our bond with God but to its *inversion*: it becomes a *negative* bond, rooted in fear instead of love, giving rise to unbelief, idolatry, competition with God, and finally atheism, expressed consummately in mankind's defiant ambition to *delete* God altogether by means of science/technology—I use a computer term here deliberately—and to make a new creation—*our own*—replacing the kingdom of God with the kingdom of man, as the satanic snake in Eden intimated we could do. Our bond with God being distorted, our bond with our fellow humans and with the rest of nature must necessarily be distorted too. Our God-given tool-making power is perverted to the end of self-aggrandizement and so becomes an ambivalent force as the human race uses it creatively on the one hand to make culture, thus reflecting God's creative power, and on the other hand deploys it to do evil by dominating and exploiting and destroying. Every period of human history gives evidence of both uses.

IV

Let me now return to the Trinitarian question as such, before listing areas of human experience that become more intelligible by being seen from within a Christian framework.

In the Genesis 1 narrative God is present and active in three expressions: first, God's *Wind, the Spirit,* sweeps over the face of the waters and the formless void; second, God imagines his creation and *speaks* into the void; third, by God's *Word,* creatures come into being, beginning with light, which is the energy that makes all other material reality possible. In the course of the Old Testament Scriptures that follow the Genesis text, there are countless explicit references to the Spirit and to the word of God interacting with human beings and the material world. A summary statement of this is to be found in Psalm 33:6–9, which says: *"By the word of the Lord the heavens were made, and all their host by the breath of his mouth. He gathered the waters of the sea as in a bottle; he put the deeps in storehouses. Let all the earth fear the Lord; let all the inhabitants of the world stand in awe of him. For he spoke, and it came to be; he commanded, and it stood firm."*

It is in the New Testament that the three forms-in-one of God's life and power, active in Hebrew history but not experienced yet as distinct divine persons, materially penetrate the creation by the incarnation of God's Son: God acts by his Spirit to speak his Word into flesh in the form of a man, who is the Messiah of the Jews and the full manifestation of God's grace. Within the framework of the Hebrew Scriptures, this incarnation of the Word of God is, of course, a pure miracle and quite unforeseen as such, as will be his bodily resurrection in the middle of space/time history after his crucifixion. But in fact both these events may be seen to be rooted in God's Triune act of creation and in his ongoing interaction with the natural world as recorded in the Old Testament narratives. The church recognizes here both continuity and discontinuity with the prior revelation of God in the Old Testament period; it sees in Christ a fulfillment of the inner meaning of that revelation, which is God's determination to save the creation that he has lovingly made and that mankind has so grievously distorted.

It is by the Logos of God—God's ordering Word—that the creation comes into being; and it is by that same Logos, the Word incarnate, that this creation, fallen into disorder through satanic and human rebellion, is redeemed. God is love, and he is omnipotent with respect to the achievement of what he wills to achieve, which means that his plan to share life with creatures, most notably with the creature made in his image, cannot be ultimately thwarted. Creation and incarnation—both the work of the Triune God—are inseparable as they are understood together within God's primordial intention. As the creation is an expression of divine love—the love between the divine Persons that has them choosing to *go out* from themselves, from the self-contained Godhead, toward a created *other*—so the incarnation is similarly an expression of divine love, as the incarnate Word chooses to *go out* from the security of the divine realm and to subject himself to the miserable human condition even unto death, for the sake of redeeming men and women from their sin and renewing the whole of nature.

Seeing nature through this double lens of creation and incarnation provides a way to understand both the good and the bad, the beautiful and the ugly, within the natural world we know. The *creation* is good, but has been spoiled and is under grave threat through the disobedience of the fallen angels and of mankind; the *incarnation* brings to fruition God's economy of salvation, his redeeming response to the disobedience.

Hope in the return of Christ in glory, a hope based on his promise and of which the gift of his Spirit provides us with a pledge, broadens still farther the conviction that God's eternal plan will be triumphantly consummated. There is somewhere in the human breast an inherent hope that life has meaning despite suffering and loss, and that death and dissolution are not the finality of being. Something in us—even in the modern age of skepticism and materialism—refuses to believe what I call the nihilistic gospel. Even those who resist God spin some kind of story that gives meaning to their lives, though that meaning and the hope it signifies will be necessarily reduced. Where does this ineradicable hope come from? I believe it is rooted first of all in the revelation that we are made in God's image; and secondly, in the incarnation of the Son of God, whereby Christ, the very image of God made man, has overcome on our behalf the forces that push toward despair—the devil, sin, and death—and so has opened a vision of eternal life. Certainly this ever-resurgent hope in the human heart is better explained by reference to the Trinitarian God than by the evolutionary mechanisms of mutation and natural selection understood in a materialistic way that excludes God from the process.

V

Let me try now, in my concluding section, to show the relevance of these remarks to various aspects of our lives, and especially to some recent advances in our scientific understanding of the material world. A Trinitarian natural theology enables us to *see* the world in a particular way, and my thesis is that this way of seeing throws a great deal of light on our experience and knowledge of reality. Limits of time and competence mean that my discussion can be only summary, but my hope is that it will provide you with food for further reflection.

A central issue in the philosophy of science is the *explicability* of the world. How is it that we human beings can actually read to a considerable extent the book of nature? This ability is in no way to be taken for granted. It requires explanation. Natural theology must seek a fundamental connection between experience and understanding, between perception and cognition.

The language by which scientists penetrate the secrets of the cosmos is mathematics. Cosmologists and physicists continue to be amazed by the effectiveness of mathematics to uncover the laws that govern the operations of the material universe. This purely abstract capacity of the human mind— a mind that has emerged from within nature itself—is able to elucidate to a considerable extent the way physical reality functions, in its macro- and micro-dimensions. Some scientists hold a Platonic view of the mathematical equations that correspond to objective reality: they believe that these are *discoveries* of preexisting mathematical structures, timelessly present in an ideal realm. Other scientists prefer to believe that they are human *constructions* that happen to correspond to cosmological reality. In either case, the correspondence is there: epistemology corresponds to ontology, what we can *know* corresponds to what *is*. How can this be? And how can we explain the remarkable fact that this mathematical ability has not come into existence to give our race greater survival value? It goes way beyond any basic survival requirements and clearly is not the product of a natural selection process, in the Darwinian sense. Its presence, apparently gratuitous, seems to point to a purpose that far outstrips the question of survival and fitness.

To such questions, the sketch I have given of the Triune God who creates and redeems should help us to provide an answer that has considerable explanatory power. What we know from our experience, and what scientists assume and then demonstrate in their labors, is that nature is ordered. It operates according to laws. Behavior is by and large predictable and dependable. Even what we may wish to call the strangeness of quantum or chaos theory is not beyond the reach of order, even if the nature of that order falls outside the ordinary connotations of that word and concept.

Heisenberg's Uncertainty Principle is instructive in this regard. It refers to the impossibility of measuring at once the momentum and the position of an electron on account of the fact that the act of measurement of one of these disturbs things sufficiently so as to make uncertain, indeed impossible, the measurement of the other. Heisenberg went on from this discovery to believe that this uncertainty was not a matter of human ignorance but of ontological indeterminacy in quantum systems themselves. This notion has since received experimental confirmation. We are left with a picture of the universe being indeterministic at its most basic level. But this does not mean that the universe is irrational or chaotic. Paul Davies points out that even if at the basic level of micro-reality intrinsic chance is operative,

> the relative probabilities of the different possible states are still determined . . . This statistical lawfulness implies that, on a macroscopic scale where quantum effects are usually not noticeable, nature seems to conform to deterministic laws.[1]

Epistemological uncertainty reflects the *ontological* uncertainty that is built into the universe. John Polkinghorne maintains that chance, in the quantum sphere as well as in the sphere of evolution, is evidence not of disorder but of freedom—the freedom given by the Creator to the natural order to create itself, developing as a process within the framework of the Creator's overall purpose. Chaos theory can be instanced as another theory

---

1. Davies, *Mind of God*, 31.

pointing in this direction. This theory, as I understand it, refers to immensely sensitive physical systems which are unpredictable in behavior because they cannot be insulated from even the tiniest events in the environment, and by "environment" one doesn't mean just the immediate planetary or even galactic locality but the entire universe.

Polkinghorne, in his *Quarks, Chaos, and Christianity*, gives the example of air and weather systems.[2] The recently posited theory of nonlocality shows that particles that have interacted at some point remain mysteriously linked even if physically separated by vast distances. Some tiny, even microscopic, event can affect an entire physical system such as the weather, in a manner that is altogether unpredictable. But chaos theory goes on to show that the range of possible behaviors is contained within certain bounds and that the randomness itself is contained within a patterned structure. Polkinghorne likes to call the pattern-forming propensity within nature "active information," and he suggests that the spontaneous generation of order emerging from indeterminate randomness points to a holistic level of reality deeper even than the concepts of energy and matter and not reducible to them.[3] He thinks that this concept of "information" will be a main focus of research for the rest of this century.

Where does all this order come from? How can we best explain the regularities and patterns within nature, which we call laws, and which, to a real extent, we can discover and elucidate by mathematics? How is it that even what we call chance occurrences at the quantum level are not manifestations of chaotic randomness but are events within a larger, apparently ordered framework? It would seem that there are only two explanations on offer today: the first is the existence of multiple parallel universes, perhaps infinite in number, of which ours, by chance, happened to turn out this way; the second is that an all-powerful creative mind—God—created the universe in just this way. The *first* possibility, without any basis in observation or experiment, seems, to many scientists, believers in God or not, to be a completely unscientific flight on mathematical wings into metaphysical fantasy in order to escape the *second* possibility—the one that points to God—which provides a far simpler and indeed much more probable metaphysical explanation of the order we find in the universe.

The biblical texts in the Old and New Testaments that I alluded to earlier, which speak of the Creator God and his creation, provide a plausible underpinning for the second hypothesis. The Triune God, who imagines, speaks, and breathes out the cosmos, is an inconceivably powerful,

---

2. Polkinghorne, *Quarks, Chaos, and Christianity*, 82–87.
3. Polkinghorne, *Science and the Trinity*, 82–85.

personal, rational mind, and the cosmos he created by his Word, the Logos, is therefore orderly and rational; man, because he is created in the image of this personal, rational God—of this Logos—and because he is given moreover the mandate to exercise dominion over the creation and is therefore designed to be able to *know* it, possesses in consequence the rational capacity, through mathematics, to do, among other things, what we call science, that is, to fruitfully investigate God's handiwork that we call nature and to discover its inner workings and laws.

The same explanatory strategy applies to the much-discussed Anthropic Principle, which refers to the nearly unbelievable fine-tuning of the initial cosmological conditions that would permit carbon-based life to eventually emerge. The universe, we now know—and this is a very recent discovery—has not always existed; the laws of this universe are contingent; the causal order we find is not a matter of logical necessity. This means that we cannot know this causal order by *a priori* rational deduction, as Aristotle believed; we must *observe* it. We can only know it through *a posteriori* empirical investigation.[4] It is this truth, revealed through sacred Scripture, that led Christian thinkers to the experimental method, which laid the basis for modern science. On the other hand, the convergence and intrinsic strength of certain fundamental constants (e.g., the four cosmic forces: gravity, the strong force, the weak force, and the electromagnetic force), and the incredibly specific numerical values of these constants with respect to electrical charge, density, and velocity that shaped the evolution of the universe starting an instant after the Big Bang, had to be, and were, of such precision that some astrophysicists can speak of the *virtual inevitability* not only of the formation of stars and of the heavier atomic elements necessary to carbon-based life, but also, subsequently, of the emergence of simple organisms followed by their increasing complexity all the way up the ladder to the human brain and the astonishing phenomena of self-consciousness and rationality.

The convergence of so many apparent coincidences among the primordial variables, all of them *a priori* independent of each other, demands an explanation other than chance. The presence of such precision had nothing to do with natural selection, obviously. The laws of nature that underlie the possibility of biological evolution were in place from the beginning of the universe, long before the mechanisms of biological evolution came into play; and it is becoming clear that they are still operative in the processes of biological development, though exactly how has yet to be discerned. But in themselves these basic laws, whose very existence to begin with remains

---

4. Pearcey and Thaxton, *Soul of Science*, 30–34.

an unfathomable mystery, cannot explain the emergence of life and the increasing *information* needed for the development of that life.

One of the many currents of thought in the ongoing debate in the scientific community about the mechanisms of evolution corresponds strikingly with the notion of directionality implicit in the Anthropic Principle. According to the biochemist and geneticist Michael Denton, there exist archetypal forms underlying proteins, similar to the structure underlying snow crystals.[5] This leads Denton to think that the evolutionary process is guided fundamentally by laws of nature—hence by the constants present since the Big Bang—and not just by chance mutation, adaptation, and natural selection. According to this understanding, the unity of a biological type would arise not just from a common ancestor and the laws of heredity but, beyond that, from rational criteria—for instance, all the legs of different terrestrial vertebrates obey a common principle. Such common morphologies, it is suggested, possess an internal logic and are not merely the result of blind processes following the rule of trial and error. This insight, strengthened by the fact that many organic forms are governed by mathematical laws (mathematical laws do not develop by chance!), provides, to my mind, a noteworthy parallel with the notion mentioned earlier that explanatory mathematical equations are actually discoveries of archetypal structures, ideas in the Platonic sense that exist beyond space and time and yet govern cosmological reality.

Notions like these lend plausibility to an associated contention, shared by a growing number of paleontologists, zoologists, and biologists, that the neo-Darwinian gradualist mechanisms used to describe microevolution are inadequate to account for macroevolution, i.e., the passage—sometimes occurring quite rapidly by a kind of leap—from one class or order to another. Large-scale shifts from one biological genre to another—macromutations such as that from reptiles to mammals—cannot, it is held by scientists such as Roberto Fundi, Jean Dorst, and Marcel-Paul Schützenberger, be the result of pure chance, but must arise by virtue of preexistent archetypes, comprehensive organizational schemas that are somehow potentially present and are triggered under opportune environmental conditions.[6] Denton observes moreover that many conditions such as the structure of the carbon atom, the nature of water as the liquid best adapted to carbon, the suitability for life of the light spectrum emanating from the sun, point, when gathered cumulatively, to a teleological orientation of the evolutionary process. As with the Anthropic Principle in relation to the initial conditions of the

---

5. Staune, *Notre Existence a-t-elle un Sens?*, 242–66.

6. Staune, *Notre Existence a-t-elle un Sens?*, 256–60.

cosmos, the features of our planet would appear to be optimally adapted to the emergence of life. Teleology, directionality, intentionality—all these are in evidence here, and they point logically to an infinitely powerful mind that created and ordered all things.

The order of the universe, and the special order peculiar to Earth, display a stunning particularity which manages to hold in a kind of equilibrium the rigidity of regimented structures and patterns such as crystals, with the random unpredictability of quantum activity. Law and chance operating together are required for the universe we know to have evolved the way it has done. There is constraint and there is openness; there is structure and there is freedom; there is stability and there is dynamism; there is necessity, in the sense of law, and there is contingency. But all these balancing features that structure reality are not inherently necessary to that reality; they are contingent; things could have been different. These features are imposed upon the universe by the free will of the Creator. Their order and rationality are not necessary in themselves, but are reflections of the rational nature of the God who willed them into being. And this order is intelligible to human beings because we are made in the image of that God. But, of course, our rational powers are limited; we are finite creatures, we cannot fathom everything. In what way, for instance, the astounding progressive complexification of life, involving evolutionary process and emergence, was contained potentially in the unimaginable release of energy at the Big Bang and in the initial cosmological conditions and forces that quickly channeled that energy, remains a mystery.

Such order, and the interconnectivity of all aspects of the universe, as illustrated again by the recently discovered phenomenon of nonlocality mentioned earlier—a phenomenon that seems to escape the constraints of cosmological law as presently understood—does appear to point in the direction of deliberate design by an omnipotent and infinite mind. It is the Triune God—three co-inherent, intimately related, divine Persons in one Godhead, as revealed in the incarnation and the Son's relation to the Father in the Spirit—that best accounts for such relationality, such interconnectivity, in the universe. Once again, a Creator, understood within a Christian Trinitarian natural theology, is the most plausible explanation available.

A natural theology so conceived can account for many other things as well, including, as I suggested earlier, the existence of evil, falsehood, and ugliness. These negative realities—linked with Satan and the perversity of men and women—are perceived and experienced against the backdrop of their opposites, i.e., goodness, truth, and beauty, which have their source in God. The economy of salvation, moving from the creation of morally free creatures made in God's image, through the fall, to incarnation, and finally to Christ's promised return and eschatological consummation, is the interpretive framework that makes the most sense of the order and splendor as well as the moral ambivalence of the natural world, including human nature as we experience it. The moral, rational, and aesthetic dimensions of reality that find consummate expression in human persons are mysteriously rooted in the physical creation we have been considering, in the order it displays and the unfolding complexity of its material structures.

Let me conclude with a brief comment on beauty. Beauty is inherent in all aspects of reality. It irradiates the universe. It is the aesthetic dimension of cosmological order, yet intimately related to the rational and moral dimensions as well. We speak, for example, of the beauty of a mathematical equation, or of a person who acts in self-sacrificing generosity; and we Christians speak of the beauty of Jesus, who manifests to us inexpressible love. Why is the natural world so beautiful? Why is mankind able to perceive and create beauty? Once again, as with our ability to read the book of the universe, here we find ourselves with the ability to appreciate its beauty. The universe is rationally and aesthetically intelligible to us. We are gifted to understand it and to be moved by its splendor. Perhaps we can call beauty the radiance of cosmic order, the radiance of truth, which itself may be understood as the manifestation of goodness, of the good, which is God. Why do the creatures that emerge through the processes of natural law, information, mutation, and natural selection turn out to be, each in a way quite beyond description, so beautiful? What always strikes me is that even the strangest biological creatures, like the ones discovered in the depths of the ocean, are oddly beautiful, though by some aesthetic criteria one might find them ugly. In themselves they are wondrous, amazing, stunning, and somehow the sheer wondrousness of them makes them beautiful.

It is all mysterious. And that is our final word: mystery. We are surrounded by mystery. And yet that mystery is not alien to us, nor utterly impenetrable. Even for the atheist, the cosmos is intelligible and beautiful. In a profound way, mankind is at home in the universe. And if by divine mercy we have come to know Jesus Christ, and to be in communion with our heavenly Father through the gift of the indwelling Spirit of God, we are filled with gratitude as we behold the natural world and see it as it truly is, God's splendidly ordered creation, groaning, yes, on account of man's rebellion, yet radiant still with beauty, and destined, when Christ returns, to be liberated from decay and restored to its full glory.[7] Considering all these things, we can confidently affirm that the gift to us of knowledge of the true God—of the Holy Trinity—has explanatory power beyond any competing worldview to make ultimate sense of all that we perceive and experience.

7. See Romans 8:18–25.

Resurrection and Life after Death

(Talk at St. Michael's Anglican Church, Paris)

I

WRITING TO THE GENTILE Christians in Ephesus, Paul says: "... *remember that formerly . . . you were separate from Christ, excluded from citizenship in Israel and foreigners to the covenants of the promise, without hope and without God in the world*" (Eph 2:11a–12). Both believing Jews and gentiles consider that the covenants of the promise are fulfilled in the Jewish Messiah, Jesus. Christ redeemed us, Paul wrote to the Galatians, "*in order that the blessing given to Abraham might come to the Gentiles through Christ Jesus, so that by faith we might receive the promise of the Spirit*" (Gal 3:14). Essentially, the covenanted promise is communion with God the Holy Trinity, Creator, and Redeemer. "*My dwelling place will be with them,*" says the Lord to his people through the prophet Ezekiel (37:27a). And near the end of the book of Revelation, as John sees in a vision the New Jerusalem—the renewed creation—coming down out of heaven from God (it is no man-made construction, no Babel) "*as,*" he writes, "*a bride beautifully dressed for her husband*"—at that very moment, writes John, "*I heard a loud voice from the throne saying, 'Now the dwelling of God is with men, and he will live with them. They will be his people, and God himself will be with them and be their God*" (Rev 21:23–24). And the prophet goes on: "*He will wipe away every tear from their eyes. There will be no more death or mourning or crying or pain, for the old order of things has passed away*" (Rev 21:4).

Life. This is what the covenantal promise is all about. God is life. God is life, and the form—the *heart*—of life is love. "*I am come that they may have life, and have it abundantly,*" says Jesus (John 10:10b). "*For God so loved the world,*" writes John, "*that he gave his one and only Son, that whoever believes in him shall not perish but have eternal life*" (John 3:16). And to Martha, before raising Lazarus from the dead, Jesus says: "*I am the resurrection and the life. He who believes in me shall live, even though he dies; and whoever lives and believes in me will never die. Do you believe this?"* he asks her (John 11:25–26). And yet another word from the Gospel of John: *"I tell you the truth,"* says Jesus, *"whoever hears my word and believes him who sent me has eternal life and will not be condemned; he has crossed over from death to life. I tell you the truth, a time is coming and has now come when the dead will hear the voice of the Son of God, and those who hear will live. For as the Father has life in himself, so he has granted the Son to have life in himself"* (John 5:24–26).

"Do you believe this?" Jesus asks Martha. It's the question we must ask ourselves. It's the key question. Do we believe that Jesus is the resurrection and the life? In him—in *himself*, in his *being*—is life, and as we are *in him* by grace through faith, and as he is *in us*, we have life—true life, everlasting life. Herein lies our hope, the hope that the world lacks and cannot give. *In him* who was raised from the dead, we shall be raised from the dead. This will be the consummate expression of God's love. *"For if the dead are not raised,"* writes Paul to some skeptics in Corinth, *"then Christ has not been raised either. And if Christ has not been raised, your faith is futile; you are still in your sins . . . If only for this life we have hope in Christ, we are to be pitied more than all men . . . If the dead are not raised, 'Let us eat and drink, for tomorrow we die'"* (1 Cor 15:16–17, 19, 32b). But of course Paul, who had encountered the risen Christ on the road to Damascus, and who, later, in Christ, had been caught up to the third heaven (2 Cor 12:2), was utterly convinced that Christ had been raised, and hence that those who belonged to him would be raised too: *"With that same spirit of faith,"* he writes to the Corinthians, *"we also believe and therefore speak, because we know that the one who raised the Lord Jesus from the dead will also raise us with Jesus and present us with you in his presence"* (2 Cor 4:13–14).

II

Resurrection life is what characterizes the kingdom of God. Where Jesus reigns, there is the kingdom of God. This kingdom is both present and future, hidden now in the hearts of those who believe and in the Spirit-filled lives they seek to lead (see Matthew 4:17, 23, 13:24; Luke 12:31–32, 17:20–21), and to be manifested fully in the future, when Christ returns to raise and judge the dead and renew the creation (see Mark 9:1; Luke 13:29, 22:30; John 6:40, 44; 1 Cor 6:9–10, 15:50). Eternal life and the kingdom of God are the same reality, as Jesus makes plain in his exchange with the rich young man (Mark 10:17–31). To enter it, we must die to the autonomous self—the rebel self that lives apart from the true God, according to its own dictates—and we must follow Jesus. We must humble ourselves and repent. We must decide to put to death our own *self-as-king* and receive in exchange, by faith, *Jesus as King*. This involves identifying with Jesus on the cross. The old man, the self-focused ego, dies with Jesus, and the new man rises with him. Neither for Jesus nor for us is resurrection possible without death. "*For you died*," writes Paul to the Colossian Christians, "*and your life is now hidden with Christ in God.*" And he exhorts them: "*Since, then, you have been raised with Christ, set your hearts on things above*" (Col 3:1). Paul uses the present tense. Because, by faith, we are in Christ and are indwelt by the Spirit of God, we have new life—eternal life—even now.

The Son of God, who is life, has overcome death: first by becoming one of us, then by living a sinless life of obedience to the Father, and then, at terrible cost, by laying down his life for us. He has defeated the devil, who holds the power of death (Heb 2:14–15). The evidence of this victory is Christ's resurrection and the establishment of his kingdom in the hearts of men and women down through the ages who, living in the shadow of death and conscious of the shadows in their own lives, have hungered for life and love and found hope and salvation in Jesus. The church is not the kingdom of God, but it is the vehicle for the kingdom to penetrate this fallen world. We who make up the church are sinners and have often failed to live the life Christ calls us to, but that does not alter the truth of the good news at the heart of the gospel we seek to proclaim. At his return, Christ the King will complete the victory won at Calvary by destroying Satan forever and renewing the creation (Rev 20:7–10).

Christ's return is a certainty of which Jesus himself and the apostles have a great deal to say. In no way should this biblical truth be considered myth, any more than our Lord's resurrection. Not only did Jesus promise it categorically (e.g., Mark 13:26–35; Matt 24:30–51; Luke 17:19–27; John 14:3–4; and see Acts 1:11; Phil 3:20–21; 1 Thess 4:13–18), his return in glory is, when you think logically about it, absolutely necessary to complete the work of salvation and new creation. The church knows that the divine invasion of earth has taken place and that Satan and death *have been defeated* by Christ at the cross (Luke 10:17–20, John 12:31, Col 2:15, Heb 2:14–16), but it is clear, as St. John puts it in his First Epistle, that the world still lies in the lap of the evil one (1 John 5:19). If Christ does not return to complete his victory at the cross, that victory would be stillborn. It would not be generally and conclusively effectual. Evil would still be effectively on the throne, and Satan triumphant. There would be no final judgment, justice would not prevail. God would not be God—he would not be the righteous and all-powerful Creator and Re-Creator.

The establishment of the kingdom of God within history happens in stages. There is first the period of Israel, when the true God reveals himself and calls out a people to make known his Name; this leads to the coming of the Jewish Messiah, the Son of God, who, by his incarnation and passion, accomplishes the work of salvation, making communion with the true God available not only to the people of Israel but to gentiles (pagans) as well; then there is the period of mission, when the good news of the kingdom is proclaimed far and wide by the church, so that those of the human race who desire truth may be able to turn to God and receive eternal life; and finally there is the time of fulfillment, when Christ the King will return in manifest power to complete his work of redemption, take back his creation, and definitively *destroy* the devil, the rebellious angelic forces, and death. Then God will be all in all, and his kingdom will be established forever (1 Cor 15:20–28).

The early church longed for the Lord's return, and so must we. And we must earnestly look out for the signs that point to his return (e.g., Matt 24; Luke 21; 1 Thess 5). In our day, they are everywhere, and it may well be the case that Christ's return is imminent. The modern spirit, with its materialism, its suspicion of transcendence, and its rejection of any objective divine reality beyond and behind the cosmos, has infected much of the Western church with skepticism as far as the Lord's return is concerned. The myth of progress has absorbed and virtually replaced the biblical understanding of the kingdom of God. In the last 100 years, this myth of progress has been basically shattered by world events, but it still hangs on, both in the popular mind and among elites, and is finding, to some extent, new strength in the prodigious advances of technology. But the hope and sense of purpose and direction that accompanied this myth in the eighteenth and nineteenth centuries—these are hardly to be found any more. Messianic political ideologies have been discredited. A sense of pointlessness, even despair, is now common currency, and corruption, fear, and violence of all kinds are overtaking every part of the world. Even the reigning god of technology and the economic structure of capitalism that expands technology's reach and power—and which is itself an expression of technology—is no longer looked upon, at least by reasonable people, as the source of salvation and the provider of ultimate meaning to human life.

And yet for all that, materialism and consumerism, sustained by technology, maintain their ideological grip on human society, even where nationalist or religious identity retains or asserts, often violently, a supposedly countervailing influence. While this state of affairs puts tremendous pressure on Christians who, along with Jews, are being scapegoated and attacked wherever they find themselves because, in principle, they follow a different—transcendent—star, it also provides a tremendous opportunity for the church to proclaim with boldness the good news of hope and eternal life in Jesus Christ. There is desperation and a great hunger for truth out there, underneath the apparent indifference to transcendent reality, and we Christians alone have truly good news to proclaim. The message of the return of the Messiah to set things right, of the final judgment of evil and the establishment of justice, and of the renewal of creation, even as we see the original creation being desecrated—this message, while it certainly stretches the mind and imagination and is in fact, for our finite minds, quite unimaginable in its realization (as were the incarnation and the resurrection before they actually happened in history), is an absolutely essential part of the good news we are called to proclaim, and it should be consciously at the heart of our personal and liturgical prayers, as it was in the early church.

Once again, it is Christ's resurrection that is the core of this proclamation. This, as I've been saying and as we know, is true dogmatically, with respect to sin, death, and salvation. But it is also true philosophically, in the following sense—and I think this is an important point. Christ's resurrection is the great reality within history that is *manifestly supernatural* (his incarnation was likewise supernatural, of course, but *not manifestly so*, not *publicly*—only to Mary and Joseph). His miracles are supernatural too, of course, and point to the reality of who he is, but they don't have the utter and absolute *strangeness* as has his own resurrection from the dead. His resurrection does not arise in any way from within historical conditions as such, or from natural law or causality. It is absolutely *sui generis*, a demonstration of power that is not human and so can only be divine. Those who deny it or who call it a myth cannot contest this, they can only claim—with no historical evidence whatsoever to support their claim—that it did not happen.

Here is not the place to develop this point, but it should be for believers a source of tremendous reassurance and hope: in Christ, God has manifestly penetrated our human sphere and has acted as nowhere else in the course of history, and the nature of that action being what it was, we have every reason to believe that what those who experienced it declared to be its significance—that is, redemption and the offer of eternal life to those who hunger for it—was and is *true*. Similarly, if such supernatural power has turned nature inside out once, we have every reason to believe—even if we cannot imagine how he will do it—that the Lord, at his return, will have the power to upturn and renew his entire fallen creation. Heaven will be joined to earth—to *this* earth, *our* earth. *"And I saw,"* writes John on the isle of Patmos, *"the holy city, new Jerusalem, coming down out of heaven from God, prepared as a bride adorned for her husband; and I heard a loud voice from the throne saying, 'Behold, the dwelling of God is with men. He will dwell* with them, and they shall be his people, and God himself will be with them; he will wipe away every tear from their eyes, and death shall be no more, neither shall there be mourning nor crying anymore, for the former things have passed away'" (Rev 21:2–4).

III

Let me now bring to your attention some of the peculiarities of what the Bible does tell us about life after death. The subject is vast, so I can only touch on a few points. When a believer dies, he/she goes to be with the Lord. Paul longed for this. *"Now we know,"* he writes to the Corinthians, *"that if the earthly tent we live in is destroyed, we have a building from God, an eternal house in heaven, not built by human hands. Meanwhile we groan, longing to be clothed with our heavenly dwelling . . . so that what is mortal may be swallowed up by life . . . We live by faith, not by sight. We are confident, I say, and would prefer to be away from the body and at home with the Lord"* (2 Cor 5:1–2, 4b, 7–8). And to the Philippians he writes: *"For me to live is Christ and to die is gain . . . I desire to depart and be with Christ, which is better by far; but it is more necessary for you that I remain in the body"* (Phil 1:21, 23b–24). The state referred to here—the state of "being with Christ"—appears not to be that of resurrection. The general resurrection will happen at the Lord's return, not before. It would seem that the state being referred to here—and the *place* being referred to—is what is called elsewhere "paradise," or the "third heaven," where Paul at one point was transported in the Spirit (2 Cor 12:2–4). The word has the connotation of a garden, a place of bliss and rest in God's presence, as in the words of the risen Lord to the church in Ephesus reported in the book of Revelation: *"To him who overcomes, I will give the right to eat from the tree of life, which is the paradise of God"* (Rev 2:7b). It is presumably the paradise where Jesus went immediately upon his death, and where the believing thief on the cross would go to join him (Luke 23:43).

In this state, the mortal body has been left behind, the incorruptible body has yet to be given. The human spirit, inbreathed by God, is the soul—the *form*, if you will—of the body, its vital structure and animating principle. At death it has been separated from the body, which has now become a cadaver—"I" am gone from what was my body, that decaying flesh is no longer "me." This bodiless state of the human person is impossible for us to imagine, yet Scripture does seem to reveal that it is a stage *between* our physical death and our ultimate state, our resurrection, when we will be clothed with a *spiritual body*. Personal identity is retained and recognizable, and communion in love—with the Lord and with those who are his—characterizes this new form of reality; but the *plenitude* of redemption, the *fullness of our hope*, when, as Paul writes to the Romans, *"the creation itself will be liberated from the bondage to decay and brought into the glorious freedom of the children of God"* (Rom 8:21)—this plenitude is not yet present. *"Our citizenship is in heaven,"* Paul declares to the Christians in Philippi. "Already—even now," he might have added, and surely after our death, when the soul is released from our earthly body. But the plenitude is still to come. "And," he writes, *"we eagerly await a Savior from there, the Lord Jesus Christ, who, by the power that enables him to bring everything under his control, will transform our lowly bodies so that they will be like his glorious body"* (Phil 3:20–21).

For the Christian, eternal life cannot properly be conceived without a body, for the body is an essential part of God's good creation, the means by which the soul—the body's inner life—expresses itself. Material and spiritual reality are not to be disconnected in a Cartesian manner and set in opposition, as the modernist mindset insists on doing. They are interlocked as a single reality. God, who is Spirit, has created and sustains a material cosmos, and he is immanent within every particle of it, even while being absolutely transcendent to it. Spirit animates materiality and, from a Christian point of view, materiality cannot be properly conceived apart from Spirit. The *plenitude* of created human being cannot be imagined apart from corporeality, but it must be a corporeality that is *incorruptible*, not subject to decay, animated entirely by the life-giving Spirit that is God. In a word, the ultimate perfection—the complete realization—of a human person is not an immaterial immortal soul but a *spiritual body*, as Paul describes it in 1 Corinthians 15.

This transformation will be wrought by the power of God at the moment of Christ's return. Paul longs for this, it is the source of his hope, that for which he *"presses on toward the goal to win the prize for which God has called me heavenwards in Christ Jesus"* (Phil 3:14). *"We ourselves,"* he writes elsewhere, *"who have the first fruits of the Spirit, groan inwardly as we wait eagerly for our adoption as sons, the redemption of our bodies. For in this hope we were saved"* (Rom 8:23–24a). And finally, in 1 Corinthians 15, Paul's extended treatise on the resurrection, he declares: *"So will it be with the resurrection of the dead. The body that is sown is perishable, it is raised imperishable; it is sown in dishonor, it is raised in glory; it is sown in weakness, it is raised in power; it is sown a natural body, it is raised a spiritual body"* (1 Cor 15:42–44). The perishable, he insists, cannot inherit the kingdom of God: *"For the trumpet will sound, the dead will be raised imperishable, and we will be changed. For the perishable must clothe itself with the imperishable, and the mortal with immortality . . . then the saying that is written will come* true (here he quotes from Hosea 13:14): 'Death has been swallowed up in victory'" (1 Cor 15:52a, 53, 54b).

IV

To conclude, a brief word on the final judgment. *"A time is coming,"* says Jesus in John's Gospel, *"when all who are in their graves will hear his—the Son of Man's—voice and come forth, those who have done good, unto the resurrection of life, and those who have done evil, unto the resurrection of damnation"* (John 5:28b-29). Jesus, echoing a text in Daniel 12:1-3, is presenting himself here as the eschatological Judge entrusted by the Father with the authority to exercise judgment at the time of the end, that is, when he returns in glory. All human beings will be raised up and judged according to what they have done. *Christians*—let us say all those who have believed in Christ or whose hearts will have been disposed to believe in him—are not under condemnation, because they have received Christ and the benefits of his atoning work on the cross (Rom 8:1). Jesus took our judgment upon himself, in our place. But our *works* will be judged. The apostle Paul writes: *"For we must all appear before the judgment seat of Christ, that each one may receive what is due to him for the things done while in the body, whether good or bad"* (2 Cor 5:10). *"You, then,"* he scolds the Romans, *"why do you judge your brother? Or why do you look down on your brother? For we all will stand before God's judgment seat . . . So then, each of us will give an account of himself to God"* (Rom 14:10, 12). And similarly, to the Christians in Corinth:

> But each one should be careful how he builds. For no one can lay any foundation other than the one already laid, which is Jesus Christ. If any man builds on this foundation using gold, silver, costly stones, wood, hay or straw, his work will be shown for what it is, because the Day will bring it to light. It will be revealed with fire, and the fire will test the quality of each man's work. If what he has built survives, he will receive his reward. If it is burned up, he will suffer loss; he himself will be saved, but only as one escaping through the flames. (1 Cor 3:10b-15)

John takes up the same theme in the Book of Revelation, in his vision of the final judgment:

> Then I saw a great white throne and him who was seated on it. . . . And I saw the dead, great and small, standing before the throne, and books were opened. Another book was opened, which is the book of life. The dead were judged according to what they had

done as recorded in the books . . . Then death and Hades were thrown into the lake of fire. The lake of fire is the second death. If anyone's name was not found written in the book of life, he was thrown into the lake of fire. (Rev 20:11a, 12, 13b, 14–15)

We are not *saved* by our works—we are justified entirely by grace through faith, in accordance with God's mercy in Christ; but our works on this earth have great importance, for we will be judged and rewarded according to them. What was godly in them will be retained, what was not will be burnt up. Our daily choices and actions have eternal significance. This a sobering thought. Not just our faith in Christ, but the way we live out that faith in historical time, from day to day, with the moral freedom God has given us, will impact the shape of our lives in eternity (Jas 2:14–17). We are making a sketch now, in this earthly life, of the full portrait we will someday be.

V

Let me finish by asking: What does one's soul, resting in heaven after death, separated temporarily from the old body ("temporarily" is an inapt word, since the nature of time in this state is unclear to us), actually do during this period of waiting? Reflection on that will have to await another occasion, but let me drop this thought in your minds: Might this be a sanctifying time, not for sin to be punished—Christians are fully justified in this life by grace through faith in Jesus, so there is no punishment for them to undergo after death—but rather for our lives to be considered and examined, including the sin—but examined as from outside those lives, with a detachment impossible on this earth, to achieve a kind of rereading of our lives and so a really full understanding of ourselves, both the good and the bad, bringing a kind of completion and, with it, a kind of in-depth washing of our minds and an even greater appreciation of Christ's redemptive work? The notion of purgatory, rightly conceived, might correspond to something like this. Perhaps this sanctifying work, involving the assessment and judgment of our acts and the final burning up of all that was sinful, is accomplished altogether at the final judgment, as Paul suggests in the texts I've quoted. But perhaps some kind of sanctifying and edifying work is accomplished by the Spirit in the soul as it waits restfully in paradise for the Lord Jesus Christ to return to earth triumphantly, when he will resurrect and judge the living and the dead and transfigure believers into the fullness of his image. On this point, it seems, the Bible gives us no conclusive illumination.

Part II

THE *IMAGO DEI*

Reflections on the *Imago Dei* in a Modern Context

I

Genocide and Racism

IF WE PEER BEHIND the unspeakable wars and genocides of the last century, we invariably find ideological forces at work. These break down into terms of race or class, with, in every case, one group claiming inherent superiority over another group. The tragedies of the twentieth century, rooted in the convulsions of the Industrial Revolution and their ideological consequences, in the decimation of native peoples in Africa and Asia by the European powers in the nineteenth century coupled with the competitive mercantilism of the occupying colonial administrations, and in racist thinking linked with chauvinistic nationalism and social Darwinism, combined to deal a terrible blow to three convictions central to the modern Western tradition: the unity of the human race, the spiritual/moral equality and dignity of all human beings, and the inherent value of the individual person as created in the image of God.[1] These convictions had been shaped over time, painstakingly, through the interwoven, competing, often competing influences of the ancient Hebraic biblical texts, Greek philosophy, Roman jurisprudence and political acumen, and Christian theology. Seventeenth- and eighteenth-century European philosophers, under the sway of the new scientific/rationalistic paradigm, succeeded (by entirely secularizing these several influences) in giving the convictions a political focus that found its concrete fulfillment in the founding of the American Republic and in the ringing declarations

---

1. Bernard Bruneteau, in the first chapter of his *Siècle des Génocides*, sketches an appalling picture of the ravages of European colonialism, both military and commercial. The near-destruction of many native peoples in Asia and Africa was a replay of the sixteenth-century decimation of South American native peoples by the Spanish and Portuguese, and a mirror-image of the brutal suppression of the indigenous peoples in America in the nineteenth century.

of the French Revolution; but the gradual extrusion of supernatural features from the new paradigm and from its political application, and the relegation to the status of irrelevancy of belief in the transcendent and immanent God of the Judeo-Christian tradition, sowed the seeds of the horrors that were to bloom malevolently in the next centuries, by leaving modern man stranded in what he perceived to be an empty universe, with no compass but his easily corrupted reason to guide the orientations of his will.

These foundational convictions of the Western tradition were then tested in the first half of the nineteenth century by the great question of chattel slavery and the African slave trade, and by the chronologically parallel question of the relation of North American natives to the white immigrants from Europe. If the ruthless treatment by the whites of the indigenous Americans and Canadians was a moral and political catastrophe, the success of the European nations and the United States in finally defeating the hideous institution of chattel black slavery after 300 years—a success spearheaded in England, France, and America by passionately committed Christians—was a moral triumph, though the existence of this institution in the first place, and its maintenance at the heart of a civilization calling itself Christian, was an unspeakable abomination for which the fact that the practice had originally been taken over in the sixteenth century from Muslim slave traders in Africa could offer no tenable moral justification.

Tragically, the racist snake still lay coiled in the European soul, and its poison infected the colonial experience in Africa and Asia for the next century, giving rise, in conjunction with economic exploitation, to barbarous actions that made a mockery of the Christian gospel and the enlightened civilization the European nations thought they represented.[2] Indigenous populations in the Congo, the Sudan, the Ivory Coast, Mozambique, German East Africa, and Oceania, to take just a few examples, were reduced by more than half in the course of the nineteenth century from the shock of military invasion and economic exploitation. Tens of millions of lives were lost. It has been estimated that the colonial famines of 1870–1890, directly connected with the integration of local economies into European economic

---

2. Bruneteau carefully exposes (29–37) the arrant racism of post-Darwinian thinkers such as Herbert Spencer, Alfred Wallace, Clémence Royer, Ernst Haeckel, and Ludwig Gumplowicz, among others, who used axioms drawn from social Darwinism to advocate the destruction of "inferior races" in the name of progress and civilization. First applied chiefly to the peoples of Africa and Oceania, it undoubtedly laid the ideological basis for the twentieth-century genocides, but it also contributed to the dehumanization of relationships between Europeans themselves that played out monstrously in the First World War, and, finally, in the wake of that catastrophe and intensified because of it, racist hatred produced the Shoah and the attempted annihilation of the Jews and Gypsies in Europe and the Soviet Union.

structures and the ruthless aggrandizement accompanying it, occasioned the death of at least 30 million people in Southeast Asia, India, and Africa.³ And as a more recent example, the Rwandan genocide, which claimed nearly 1 million victims in 1994, was not, as it has sometimes been alleged, merely a matter of African tribal warfare, but the direct fruit of European racist theory and in particular Belgian colonial and postcolonial policies confirmed by the French. While this certainly does not exonerate the Hutu Power government of responsibility for that great crime, it does place the tragedy in the larger historical context where it belongs. Such terrible realities as these constituted a travesty and subversion of the fundamental convictions on which the greatness of European and American civilization was based.

And the coiled snake also struck closer to home, at the very heart of Europe, with the planned decimation of the Jewish people, and along with them of the Gypsies, by the Nazis. Here a virulent pagan racism, allied to a militant nationalism, exploited the deepest and most shameful enmity in the Western tradition: that between Jew and Christian.⁴ With the tragedy of the Shoah, Western civilization amputated itself. It sliced off its two legs that together had enabled it to arise: the Hebraic (revelation) and the Greek (reason). The principles of the unity of mankind and the equality and dignity of all human beings were denied and trampled violently underfoot. This betrayal was a symptom of civilizational suicide.

3. Bruneteau, *Siècle des Génocides*, 23–29.

4. This enmity need never have developed if the church, which had the initiative after the destruction of Jerusalem in AD 70, had only heeded the apostle Paul's writings about Israel in Romans 9–11 and had trained its people to obey the Savior's command to show love toward all human beings, including their enemies and those who held convictions opposed to their own. It is clear from the New Testament writings that some Jews in the first century were persecutors of those of their Jewish brethren who followed Jesus, but this gave absolutely no warrant to Christians to reply in kind, either at the time or later. Neither is there any warrant in the New Testament for generalized anti-Jewish sentiment (the focus of any such sentiment in the New Testament—evident especially in the Gospels of Matthew and John—was the particular leadership of the Jewish community at the time that opposed the teaching of Jesus and that collaborated in his arrest and condemnation) or for a formal doctrine of supersession and a condescending theology of replacement of the people of Israel by the church in God's plan of salvation for the world. A proper Christian hermeneutic of the Hebrew Scriptures in this regard will make a careful distinction between the *fulfillment* of the Old Testament covenants by the New Covenant in the Jewish Messiah, Jesus, of which all the New Testament writings speak, and their *replacement*. It is notably Paul's writings that lay the groundwork for such a hermeneutic, and it is these which, in this respect, have been the most neglected by the church down through the centuries. That this is changing in our day, and that real dialogue between Jews and Christians is becoming common, is a fact of historic importance and cause for great rejoicing.

These frightful crimes of the last century, along with others produced by the even more widely destructive communist form of totalitarianism, provide the appropriate backdrop for our consideration of the biblical doctrine of the *imago Dei*, based on the text in Genesis 1:27, which declares that God created humankind in his own image. But before moving on to this subject, we need to make a few additional observations about these catastrophes. Along with the flouting and undermining of the two basic moral principles of Western civilization already mentioned, it is noteworthy that four of the seven major twentieth-century cataclysms that we have come to label genocides involved attacks on people who, as Jews or confessing Christians, were identified with what the Bible calls "the people of God": the Armenians, whom the Young Turk government sought to destroy utterly in 1915 and 1916, are the oldest Christian nation in the world, constituted as such in AD 301; the Jews are God's historic people, chosen by him to be the vehicle for bringing salvation, through the Messiah, to the whole world; the large majority of the tribes in Southern Sudan that have been methodically wiped out by the Islamist government in Khartoum in the last two decades are Christian (this genocidal project, to which the African Union, the European Union, and the UN have tried, with some success, to put a stop to, is not to be confused with its more widely reported and no less horrendous genocidal corollary in Darfour, in western Sudan, where the victims are Muslim and are made up mainly of black, non-Arab ethnic groups); and in Rwanda, almost all of both the Tutsis and the extremist Hutus who made a systematic effort to exterminate them in 1994 were baptized and bore the name "Christian," a deplorable fact that redounds to the shame of the Catholic Church on the one hand, which, notwithstanding noble exceptions in its ranks, had been largely seduced or silenced by racist propaganda over the decades, and of the Protestant churches on the other hand, which had failed for the most part to denounce the murderous racism that was taking over the country.[5]

5. The other three major genocides of the twentieth century were the destruction by Soviet agents, on orders from the Central Committee of the Communist Party in Moscow and using property expropriation and famine as tools, of an estimated 7 million Ukrainian Kulak peasants in 1931 and 1932; the slaughters orchestrated by the Khmer Rouge in the 1970s, which resulted in the systematic elimination of between 2 and 3 million Cambodians, mainly of urban origin and considered to be "foreign" elements; and the attempted annihilation of the Kurds in Iraq by Saddam Hussein after the first Gulf War in 1991. Both the annihilation of peasants in the first case and of city-dwellers in the second were generated by Communist ideology, augmented, in the Cambodian case, by a virulent strain of racism, in an attempt to cleanse the respective nations of those judged, for a variety of reasons, to be enemies of the party and the "truth" it incarnated (the party's incarnation of the truth is an obvious instance of the counterfeit of Christ and the Christian gospel that ideological systems always exemplify).

This terrible evidence of the irresponsibility of the church leadership and of the superficiality of the faith and commitment to Christ among the baptized

> It is to be noted here that the term "genocide" is much overworked. A distinction must be made between the countless massacres and wars—many of them civil wars—that, in addition to the two World Wars, marked the twentieth century in every part of the world (Biafra, Angola, Mozambique, Eritrea, Algeria, Burundi, Uganda, Congo, Sierra Leone, Liberia, Indonesia, China, Tibet, Burma, Pakistan, India, Sri Lanka, Chechnya, Afghanistan, Iran, Iraq, Israel, Lebanon, Syria, Serbia, Bosnia, Kosovo, Spain, Northern Ireland, Columbia, Argentina, Chile, Peru, Mexico, El Salvador, Guatemala, and Nicaragua, to name the best-known locations), and genocide. Genocide is deliberate, State-organized, systematic murder on a massive scale, using modern bureaucratic and technological means, of a national, ethnic, racial, or religious group, with the planned intent to obliterate it physically, to the extent possible, as a group (and for no other reason than that its members belong to this particular group). Its comprehensive and State-orchestrated total nature causes it to differ in scale from ethnic cleansing or crimes against humanity, even if the inner dynamic of both phenomena, prophylactic in nature, is the same, as was again demonstrated in the last decade in Serbia and Bosnia, a case where the line between genocide and ethnic cleansing is almost impossible to draw (exemplified in Sbrenika), and where deportations, as a common characteristic of ethnic cleansing, often degenerated into mass murder, even if this was not necessarily the initial intention. Likewise, the horrific massacres in East Timor orchestrated by the Indonesian government in the late 1970s, and the slow destruction in Burma over the last two decades of the Karen, Karenni, and Shan ethnic minorities, are "pure" examples of ethnic cleansing and clearly had and have genocidal characteristics. The appalling slaughters by Mao's Cultural Revolution and later by his Red Guards in the 1960s and 1970s—little remembered today in the West despite the colossal number of victims—unquestionably had genocidal dimensions and were aimed to cleanse the land of undesirable bourgeois elements, but they lacked a single, focused target and are therefore hard to fit into any formal category. War crimes such as the massacres by Japanese troops of hundreds of thousands of Chinese during the 1930s are also difficult to categorize, being neither genocide exactly, nor ethnic cleansing, yet resembling both.
>
> The denial, concealment, and justification that always follow such an enterprise, and the effort to transfer the guilt to the innocent victim, is a continuation and an integral part of the genocide. The ongoing denial—utterly unfounded from an historical point of view and cynical to the highest degree—of the Armenian genocide by successive Turkish governments for the last 100 years is the most egregious and scandalous example of such negationism. There are many reasons that explain why Turkey should wish to maintain this outrageous and irrational denial, but there can be no justification for this position. That so many Western governments should continue, for reasons of political and economic self-interest and expediency, to tolerate and condone such negationism, is perverse and cowardly and reflects the growing moral vacuity of Western societies. If European nations, prodded by America, should allow Turkey to become a member of the European Union without the requirement that that nation admit and take full responsibility for the systematic slaughter of a 1.5 million Armenians—Turkish citizens—between 1915 and 1916 (without even mentioning the horrific slaughters of 1895 under Abdul Hamid and again in 1906, 1909, and in the early twenties in the Caucasus, after Kamil Ataturk had taken power), they (and America) will not only have compromised their own political and social future, they will have sold their souls down the river and derogated definitively from the historic moral and cultural roles their Judeo-Christian foundation has bequeathed them.

members of the several churches brings to mind the words of Jesus in the parable of the sower: "*As for what was sown on rocky ground, this is he who hears the word and immediately receives it with joy; yet he has no root in himself, but endures for a while, and when tribulation or persecution arises on account of the word, immediately he falls away*" (Matt 13:20–21).

To this observation must be added two reminders: first, that the central principle of the Marxist-Leninist agenda, based on a historical analysis that presented itself effectively as a new gospel, was hatred of religion, especially the Christian religion with its Jewish roots—the very religion that had produced the culture of which Marx was a product—and that this dogma has inspired relentless persecution of Christians around the world for the last 100 years, most notoriously, of course, in the Soviet Union, China, and Southeast Asia (such persecution is now also increasingly to be found in Muslim states where extremist Islamism is on the rise); and second, that World Wars I and II, which brought to a head the national antagonisms and racist phobias noted earlier, were both fought primarily, if not exclusively, among European nations rooted in a 3,800-year-old Judeo-Christian tradition, the very tradition that, combined with its Greco-Roman counterpart, had given rise to the moral principles we have highlighted, principles that in turn have contributed to the emergence of political freedom and democracy, surely one of the great achievements of mankind.

II

The Wars of Religion in Europe; Divine Judgment; the Human Project of the New Man

Any visitor from another planet witnessing all this would be obliged to conclude that Western civilization as a whole, in Europe and beyond, is tearing out its own guts and committing suicide by implosion, cutting itself from and crushing its Hebraic taproot and utterly rejecting, in practice and in theory, the Christian gospel that has shaped and nourished it. To the persecution of Jews and Christians perpetrated by adversaries coming from outside the Christian sphere, such as is represented by many communist assaults across the world and by the murder at the hands of the Ottoman Turks of millions of Christian Armenians, Greeks, Arameans, and Assyrians between 1895 and 1923, has been added subversion, corruption, and persecution coming from within. While the twentieth-century genocides, totalitarian ideologies, and two World Wars involved many peoples from traditions other than Christian ones, it is clear that for the most part the protagonists were cultural brothers who had lost any sense of sharing the vital religious heritage whose center is Jesus Christ, the Prince of Peace, Reconciler of man to God and of man to man. The ever-growing rejection of the church and of the Christian gospel in Europe since the seventeenth century, entailing the loss among the European peoples of a common transcendental and moral vision, led finally to the most horrendous conflicts the world has ever known. The ironies here are sickening.

Undoubtedly the religious wars of the sixteenth and seventeenth centuries, which arose in response to the Reformation and its intention to reform the decadent late medieval church, were responsible for the first major breach in the basic cultural unity of Europe in the Middle Ages. The church, if not the gospel itself, has much to answer for in making Europe a battleground in these centuries and beyond. It is undeniable that the subsequent gradual disaffection from Christian faith of a large portion of the European population, especially among the intellectual elite, coupled with internal strife centered on questions of religious belief, of the nature and place of the now-divided church, and of the kind of political institutions needed to replace the church-throne alliance, profoundly destabilized European identity. This state of affairs quite naturally gave rise to a contentious, revolutionary spirit which, in the context of the industrial, scientific, and technological developments from the eighteenth century on, nurtured the hostilities and resentments that finally exploded two centuries later.

What is harder, perhaps, for secularized modern people in the West to see or assess adequately is the evidence that the tragic events of the twentieth century, and the unraveling of much that we hold valuable and noble in the Western tradition, are refractions—in some sense, *reflections*—of the cracks and splits in the Western church and the weakening and distortion of Christian faith over the last centuries. That is to say, they are intimately tied up with the condition of the church in Western society. As suggested above, the fractures of the late medieval church have causal links with what followed. The church's hunger for worldly power and its frequent substitution, in the course of its history, of political agendas or religious trappings for vital Christian life and witness, and its no less frequent disobedience to its Lord's commands to love and honor all men and women and to play the role of humble servant, explain, it seems to me, some if not all of the rejection and opposition it has experienced since the seventeenth century and continues to experience in our day. Current liberal efforts to sanitize Christ's call to repentance and spiritual rebirth, for example, or, in some cases of interreligious dialogue, to play down the uniqueness of Christ and to flatten out, in obedience to the foolish and dangerous doctrine of political correctness, the fundamental differences between, for instance, Islam and

Christianity, are misguided enterprises and will not alter the unbelief and frequent contempt that accompany the almost total ignorance, shared by a large percentage of Western men and women in our day, of the real content of the Christian faith.[6] I believe that this patent repudiation of Christianity—uninformed though it often is about the true nature of the gospel—is, in part, a manifestation of God's judgment on his own people within the frame of world history, in the sense that it has arisen to some extent as a consequence of aberrant attitudes and behaviors among those representing Christ's church.

But there is more to be said here. The church and any society it may be part of are inter-dependent. Its faithfulness or unfaithfulness to the true gospel of Jesus Christ will, under God's providence, determine to a large extent the course and direction of a given society, whether the leaders of that society are conscious of this or not. Likewise, the society's treatment of the church and the gospel to which it bears witness will bring blessing or judgment on that society in the short or long term. Both the church and the societies that participated in those terrible events of the last century mentioned here must bear their share of blame.

This is obviously also true with respect to the period of the religious wars in Europe. At this point a caveat needs to be introduced, however, to balance what has been said about the church's share of responsibility for these wars. In a recent publication, William T. Cavanaugh presents a strong argument that the religious wars were not, as is commonly suggested, "the events that necessitated the birth of the modern state; they were in fact themselves the birth-pangs of the state."[7] That is to say, they were inseparable from the power politics of the age, at a time when the centralized monarchical state was coming into its own and seeking to gain control over the appointments, revenues, and remaining temporal power of the church. In France, the absolutist, bureaucratic state was already fairly well defined when the religious conflicts erupted in the middle of the sixteenth century.

---

6. Interreligious dialogue is praiseworthy in itself and a vital dimension of modern life, but its purpose is distorted and its usefulness vitiated when participants—usually in the Christian camp—play down fundamental differences between the religions in the interest of harmony and on the basis of some supposed "ultimate unity" behind and above all particular religious claims. This syncretistic tendency, which has roots in the same soil as new age spirituality, moral relativism, and political correctness, hinders authentic exchange, even between the three religions that claim Abraham as their common ancestor. Its generalities fly in the face of the particularities of the different religions, and its underlying pretension to arbitrate between them on the grounds that "basically they all believe the same thing," is arrogant and uninformed. Serious exponents of all the major religions repudiate such an approach.

7. Cavanaugh, *Theopolitical Imagination*, 22.

All across Europe, the distribution of power was in a state of flux. The royal houses, the nobility, and the bourgeoisie were all struggling for advantage, and used religion shamelessly to extend their influence. "For the main instigators of the carnage," writes Cavanaugh, "doctrinal loyalties were at best secondary to their stake in the rise or defeat of the centralized state."[8] The strife in France in the sixteenth century and the catastrophic violence of the Thirty Years' War in the Habsburg Empire in the seventeenth century were not primarily due to religious conviction as such but to rivalries between classes and states all using Christian doctrine and allegiance as a pretext and tool to gain power.

It is not fair to allege, therefore, that the subsequent recourse to the secular state as the source of civil order in Europe, replacing the church, was brought about and rendered necessary simply by the collapse of religious unity and the violence engendered by religious passions. The posture of the modern state as savior of civil society and generator of the peace that the late Medieval Church failed to maintain is a self-serving myth according to Cavanaugh. Far from being the messianic peacekeeper that finally brought order out of confessional strife with the Treaty of Westphalia in 1648, the state was in fact at the root of the religious wars and the source of their atrocious ferocity. Moreover, the idolatry of the state in modern times, coupled with the doctrine of the state's absolute sovereignty within a defined territory, has massively increased, not lessened, the use of war over the last centuries to expand and consolidate boundaries.[9] The decline of the church as a temporal power and its domestication by and subordination to the secular state, leading to what we call today the privatization of religion and its effectual removal from the political sphere, is by no means the unmixed blessing it is often presented as being, even if the doctrine of the separation of church and state that ultimately emerged from this development in the West has undoubtedly brought great benefits within the territorial confines of individual nation-states.

And now a last observation in this connection, before focusing more narrowly on the question of the *imago Dei*. It seems to me that the blatant assaults on Christian faith common in the West since the late nineteenth century, and the massacres and persecution of Christians and Jews that were a major factor in twentieth-century conflicts throughout the world, take us way *beyond* the matter of what may be construed, in some instances, as God's judgment on his own unfaithful people, Jewish and Christian alike, to a deeper level of reality concerning mankind as a whole and the basic thrust

---

8. Cavanaugh, *Theopolitical Imagination*, 27.
9. Cavanaugh, *Theopolitical Imagination*, 43.

of modernity and postmodernity. Modern man appears to be aiming, with ever greater boldness and often with full awareness of just what he is doing, at the deliberate rejection of the divine moral and material order as revealed in the Hebrew and Christian Scriptures and the replacement of it with a human order authored by man himself.

The twentieth-century cataclysms, and then the final failure of both national socialism and communism, may be interpreted as the first major evidence that this project, whatever form it take, will exact a terrible toll and must fall under God's judgment and be doomed ultimately to failure; yet with the technology developed in the course of that same century, which now is being extended into the uncharted territories of biochemistry, biogenetics, global electronic circuitry, and so-called artificial "intelligence" (algorithms are not intelligent; they are the *fruit* of intelligence, not expressions of it), a new phase of the project is clearly underway. Western society today, as it repudiates its Christian heritage and, increasingly, the best of its Enlightenment heritage as well, which rejected traditional Christian faith but still retained belief in the concept of truth and of universal moral principles, is riddled more than ever with doubts and uncertainties about human identity and the meaning of life; yet at the same time its revolutionary mindset and technological power are pushing it to sit down again at the gaming table and try once more to produce a new man. If, it is surmised, the political utopian visions of the last few centuries have not ushered in a new Eden, perhaps the technological/economic version—essentially materialistic—will. This attempt, too, is bound to lead to unimaginable catastrophes, both social and ecological, and is also doomed to failure, because the ontological understanding of man that underlies and motivates it is false. God's created order is malleable and open to enormous development as its structures and constituent elements are discovered by the divinely designated caretaker of this order, mankind; but its malleability is not infinite and its indefeasible reality—its *being as God's order*—must in the end always reassert itself against human usurpation and manipulation. Man can, in his power and freedom, warp the creation order, though only at great cost; but he cannot destroy or replace it without destroying himself.

III

The Ideology of Individualism; Absolute Relativism; the Undermining of the Grounds for Affirming the Dignity of Man

I want to argue in this essay—in a summary manner, necessarily—that a central cause of the twentieth-century cataclysms of the World Trade Center calamity on September 11, 2001, and of any catastrophes still to come arising out of similar utopian visions rooted in human hubris and racism, is a progressive weakening through the centuries of a proper understanding of and adherence to the foundational biblical doctrine of the *imago Dei*. This doctrine, I shall maintain, is the chief ground for the Western conviction concerning the unity of the human race and the moral equality and dignity of all human beings. As, over time, it has been partially misconstrued within the church itself, then secularized, and then, as in the case of the racism alluded to earlier, subverted and contested from outside the church, the great creative energies it has unleashed into human self-consciousness and action, productive of all that is best in Christian civilization, both Western and Eastern, have become increasingly detached from their divine ground and order, to the point of curving dangerously in upon themselves and generating the suicidal explosions of the last century. This has produced a loss of perspective and intelligibility in Western self-understanding, which in turn, in our period of late modernity, has led to a crisis of identity accompanied by nihilism, crippling relativism, self-hatred, rage, destruction, and death.

The contemporary French philosopher Chantal Delsol observes that the West today, seeking to get beyond the traumas of its recent past, methodically denounces terror and totalitarianism, yet refuses to question the ideological foundations that made them possible.[10] She argues that our civilization is caught in a bind: it clings in principle to its one remaining moral certitude—its belief in human dignity—and at the same time subverts that dignity by its subservience to an ideology of individualism sustained by a willful materialism and a vision of technological utopia. Human dignity is the basis of what in the West is the only shared moral conviction left to us—human rights (which itself, of course, is the basis for any genuine democracy)—but Delsol insightfully asks the question of whether, or for how long, the postulate of human dignity can be maintained when the religious grounds for it, and the cultural context that produced it, have been repudiated and worn away. She writes:

---

10. Delsol, *Éloge de la Singularité*, 20.

> The dignity of man as an incomparable and irreplaceable being is a postulate of faith and not a given of science. The course of history demonstrates its fragility. The collapse of just one portion of the immense architecture of which it is the heart is enough for its defence to be severely weakened. Personal dignity requires the existence of the person; it requires a conscious and responsible subject, witness of its own acts; it presupposes the moral unity of mankind and an awareness of the specificity of the human as over against the animal. It rests on an inherited cultural world, and it was in annihilating that heritage that Nazism and Communism pulverized it.[11]

As a philosopher without any explicit Jewish or Christian faith, Delsol is able to affirm the vital importance of the creation texts in the book of Genesis for the upholding of the postulates of human unity and dignity.[12] For all its reasonableness and demonstrability, such an affirmation by a philosopher in the West is unusual today, since the refusal and hatred among the majority of the intellectual classes of anything biblical has reached such irrational proportions that thoughtful reflection on a scriptural theme—on the supposition that this ancient fount of Western wisdom and civilization might have some truth to teach us—is ruled out as a matter of course without even a look-in. Peter Sloterdijk, for example, an important contemporary German thinker, assumes, with Nietzsche, that God is dead and with him the entire edifice of Judeo-Christian culture, so that we live henceforth in a world without limits, where anything is possible, and where the only constant is endless experimentation and self-creation.[13] He admits, whether ruefully or not it is hard to tell, that this "experimental" mode of living, involving what he calls a "self-intensification,"[14] is driven at least as much by a thrust toward self-annihilation as by a hopeful quest for new personal and social structures. But any recourse to biblical paradigms as a way of exploring this thesis or of orienting creative thought at a time of social crisis, appears to be unthinkable to him.

What we have here, it seems to me, is evidence that the memory of the biblical God among opinion-formers and indeed among the masses of Western society under forty years old, is, on the whole, totally lost today, and the traces of it willfully despised, especially by a substantial proportion of the elite in Western universities and media. The resultant existential *angst*

---

11. Delsol, *Éloge de la Singularité*, 21 (my translation).
12. Delsol, *Éloge de la Singularité*, 27.
13. Sloterdijk, *Essai d'Intoxication Volontaire*.
14. Sloterdijk, *Essai d'Intoxication Volontaire*, 15.

and moral confusion, and the huge burden of guilt, cynicism, and self-hatred underlying them and covered over by constant hammering on the theme of human rights and by ever-new technological gadgetry (offering constantly new forms of distraction) and an ever-growing GNP, are themselves being turned into a *new ideology*. This ideology is basically self-destructive in content but masquerades under the banner of the absolute freedom of the individual to create/invent (read *destroy*) his or her *self*. *Destruction is creation,* and vice versa. Suicide is experience and being truly alive. *Negation is positive.* Commitment to any kind of transcendental value or belief that would originate from outside the self is mocked as naïve folly, while skepticism at every level is lauded.

Absolute relativism has become, for the majority of people in Europe and North America, an uncriticized cultural presupposition, postmodernism's seminal idolatry. Logically, we may say, denial of God as the Source of life requires that whatever is *truly vital* be equally suppressed and opposed, in favor of those counterfeits of true vitality, the meretricious, the ephemeral, and the flashy. This, of course, will comprise most of what we call the "Western tradition," and will include not only the bathwater of that tradition, its many failures and perversions, but also the baby, consisting in the conjunction of human dignity, reason, freedom, and order. Death, then, on such a reading, is actually the operative principle behind the ever more vertiginous straining toward new "frontiers of experience," new "extremes" of every kind, new "paroxysms" and "orgasms."[15]

15. I offer a number of examples drawn from contemporary life, all of which are consequences of the near total collapse in Western societies of the publicly recognized traditional religious beliefs that provided the communal values underpinning a sense of loyalty and shared membership in a common culture: the increasing violence, destruction, and moral corruption in many films coming out of Hollywood and film studios in Europe or under Western influence; the greed, deceit, fraud, and contempt for truth now common at all levels of entrepreneurial and political life, coupled especially in America with a flagrant and totally un-Christian neglect of the poor and needy; the mesmerizing and isolating grip of TV and video games on a large percentage of the population in Western countries, occasioning a breakdown in personal relationships and sociability and a glorification of the virtual and the abstract, at the expense of authentic imagination; the shameless exploitation of children by commercial interests, and the manipulation of young audiences around the world by rapacious media moguls, whose only concern, as they dish out mindless, sex-soaked trash, is to make money; the rise in occultic, esoteric, and gnostic beliefs and practices (a salient recent example is the success of *The Da Vinci Code*, whose preposterous and unhistorical assertions about Jesus Christ and the church are found compelling and persuasive by a gullible international public totally ignorant of the biblical texts and of the gospel tradition based on them) and in the influence of Westernized versions of Eastern religions with their denial of the ultimate value and perdurability of the personal self; the huge market for horror films, fantasy, and the supernatural, and for extraterrestrial dramas and intergalactic conflict,

most of which, as contemporary predilections, may best be understood as surrogates for the transcendent, spiritual realm denied by the materialistic model of reality proposed by positivistic science; the popularity of daredevil, death-defying/courting extreme sports, undoubtedly to be explained in part as a response to the soul-deadening boredom and stress of much of modern life; the frightening expansion of drug use and the widespread dissemination of pornography in newsstands and on the internet and telephone circuits; nudity and sexually alluring imagery at every level of advertising, consequent on the depersonalization and commercialization of sexuality; the breakdown of the traditional family rooted in a religiously based ethic and understood in that context to be the primary social building block; the normalization of divorce and abortion-on-demand, along with the increase of domestic violence, sexual promiscuity, and perversions such as pedophilia, coupled with the pursuit of all kinds of alternative social/sexual contracts, including homosexuality conceived as a "sexual orientation" on a par with heterosexuality. All these and many other forms of experimental behavior reveal the self-destructive undertow in contemporary society. They are efforts to escape the boredom, moral void, and apparent pointlessness of modern existence, and they reflect a desperate search for meaning and depth through sensational and ecstatic experience, of which orgasm and release from the normal constraints of personal existence are the symbols and paradigms. In practically every case they magnify a depersonalized individual self and downplay the person-in-relationship; ironically, they are quests for individual fulfillment precisely through the loss of personhood—quests, it should be noted, that perversely counterfeit Jesus's word that "whoever wants to save his life will lose it, but whoever loses his life for me and for the gospel will save it" (Mark 8:35). Jesus's call is to self-giving love, through which human beings find true fulfillment; by contrast, the call behind these and other counterfeits is to a denial of love and, in a majority of cases, to a refusal of responsible, committed relationships.

We should point out here that contemporary neo-conservatism in America, insofar as it is a political movement fueled at its base by religious legalism, is an extremist reaction to this prevalent moral lawlessness in Western societies. Its efforts to resist the pro-choice and homosexual movements where these have become virtual ideologies excluding dialogue with more conservative positions, are laudatory in intent if not always in execution; but unfortunately, the language neo-conservatism speaks is often as individualistic, self-centered, and corrupt as that of its extremist opponents, despite its claim to represent Christian moral values. Neo-conservatism is an ideology. Its corporatist mentality, self-serving contempt for the poor, and scorn for the notion of a just distribution of wealth; its greed and wanton exploitation of nature and the resources of the earth; its deceit, dishonesty, and constant recourse to lies, cover-ups, and deception; its willful repression or distortion of truth and its systematic policy of disinformation; its ruthless and abusive quest for more and more power in order to impose its thought-system, and its rejection and punishment in some form or other of critics and reputable whistle-blowers and of anyone who tries to speak truth; its fondness for calumny, smear tactics, and character assassination as a political method; its willingness to sanction torture and to thumb its nose at international law; its swaggering militarism; its blatant hypocrisy, arrogance, and self-righteousness, and, as far as the rest of the world is concerned, its imperialistic nationalism in the service of political and economic aggrandizement—all of this, clothed as it often is in the pious-sounding language of values and democracy, makes of it, even when this language corresponds to sincere impulses, little more than a sectarian movement armed with the tools of State power. Neo-conservatism— politicized, power-hungry, and merciless—is very far from being what its religious supporters present it as being: the upholder of the authentic

Technological innovation, with its appearance of unlimited power, potential, and possibility, is the fuel for this boundless propulsion. But underneath the propulsion, which gives people the feeling of being authentic and passionate because they are living in a pastless and futureless instant, there is boredom and a blasé sentiment that everything, at bottom, is pointless. In the place of meaning, there is either exhaustive scientific or pseudoscientific description—an infinite piling up of words and signs and numbers (data) in a quest for total control—or what might be called irrational self-detonation of one kind or another. Outside of the self's will to experiment (which, at another level, is being coopted increasingly by unbridled commercialism—the word "totalitarian" would not be out of place here—and becoming simply the self's will to make money), the propulsion does not seem to have any ultimate aim whatsoever, either in the sense of an objective and determining reality or reference over against the "self-subject," or in the sense of a finality/end.

I hear in all this an ironic echo, in the new guise of individualism in the context of technological utopianism, of earlier totalitarian proclamations of the new man, proclamations that the actual new men in the West today, those "neutronized autonomous individuals,"[16] would, at least in principle, most heatedly oppose. And what is striking is that, just like its communist and nationalist-racist predecessors, this new ideology is a counterfeit of biblical revelation. (We shall look at this matter more specifically in our later discussion of the doctrine of the *imago Dei*.) Ideologies are modern names for cultural idolatries, for human—and therefore finite and fallible—conceptions that become invested with ultimacy.

It is no accident, therefore, that, wearing the lineaments of divinity in the sense of ultimacy, they should invariably turn out to be secular imitations of divinely revealed truth. Revolution, progress, science, such and such racist myth, communist man, the classless society, capitalist man, history, the new man/creation (whether he/she/it be the product of political, economic, or genetic manipulation), the autonomous individual, self-reinvention, sexual liberation, technology-as-salvation, transhumanist man—all these

---

Christian gospel and enemy of the materialistic worldview that characterizes secular modernity. Quite the contrary—at its worst, to the extent that it is religiously driven, it is better understood as idolatry and a species of heresy, a misguided expression of the very materialism its Christian reference might be supposed to resist, shamelessly (and piously) masquerading, under the form of a robber-baron sort of capitalism, as the bearer of Christian values even while moving perilously close to a form of what might be termed plutocratic fascism.

16. Sloterdijk, *Essai d'Intoxication Volontaire*, 31. "Neutronized," of course, is even more extreme than "atomized," as a way of describing modern human beings as free-wheeling particles.

and others, as ideologies or as varieties of utopia aiming at human freedom, are, in the final analysis, biblical counterfeits or distortions, arising in the framework of a Judeo-Christian civilization that has willed and continues to will, for a host of reasons, to destroy its own foundations and then finds itself left with the impossible and dispiriting task of shoring up the tottering edifice while striving to build new foundations *using the wreckage of the old*. Obviously, despair, cynicism, consumerist materialism, and the thousand escapes through sensory intoxication must tempt many today, and the more so now as it begins to dawn on thoughtful people that technology is, as a matter of fact, no magic wand or panacea, and cannot possibly, masquerading as a man-made version of God's creative Word in the book of Genesis, produce a new Eden to replace the old.

IV

The Ultimate Danger that the Skeptical Doctrine of Perspectival Relativism Poses for Human Rights

The priestly account in *Genesis* of the creation of man reads as follows: *"Then God said, 'Let us make man [humankind] in our image, in our likeness, and let them rule over the fish of the sea and the birds of the air, over the livestock, over all the earth, and over all the creatures that move along the ground.' So God created man in his own image, in the image of God he created him; male and female, he created them. God blessed them and said to them, 'Be fruitful and increase in number; fill the earth and subdue it. Rule over the fish of the sea and the birds of the air and over every living creature that moves on the ground.'"*[17]

Counterfeits are full of pretense. They are proud. They *pretend* to be something they are not. Like evil of any sort, they can only arise in correlation with a prior reality, a prior good, of which they are a perverse imitation and distortion. The world that has been emerging in the West in the last centuries, with analytical science as its root and technological innovation as its trunk, branches, and foliage, is at once a logical and proper development from the creation story and man's place in it as set forth in Genesis 1 and 2, and a counterfeit of that story. Its excellences and accomplishments, its political, scientific, and economic achievements, its productive transformations of the matter of the world, its medical wizardry, its improvement of the quality of life for millions of people around the world, are in keeping with what a close examination of the creation story might lead one to expect.

---

17. Genesis 1:26–28 (Biblical citations are from the New International Version).

Man (man and woman) is fashioned in the image of God, and so is gifted with reason, moral freedom, and, as a corollary to that freedom, conscience; consequently, and as the practical dimension of the *imago Dei*, humankind is given a mandate to care for and develop the creation and to represent in its midst the generous and loving lordship of God; and both authority and power are bestowed on man and woman to carry out that mandate. Surely much in the modern age is a fulfillment of this biblical revelation, presented under the form of myth.

Indeed it is. Western civilization has a great deal to be justly proud of. Its achievement of democracy and political freedom and representation, along with a widely generalized concern with and possibility of economic advancement and social well-being, is, though incomplete and flawed to a considerable extent in practice, unique in human history and rightly the wonder and envy of the world. But simultaneously, alongside this modern growth, a counterfeit has grown up, a lookalike weed whose seed may be found by inverting my last formulation (". . . a fulfillment of this biblical revelation, presented under the form of myth.") to read: ". . . a fulfillment of this biblical myth, presented under the form of revelation." The modern mind considers divine revelation to be a mythical category, using the word "mythical" in a nontechnical sense as meaning simply "untrue." But the grounds for ruling out the possibility and reality of divine revelation are *rationalistic*, not rational. It is not the brief or competence of science to evaluate what Christian theology calls revelation, but science's own counterfeit, *scientism*, has presumed to do just this and has judged revelation to be a specious and outdated religious category.

Western philosophy since Hume and Kant has had the same presumption.[18] It works from within a subject-object schema that gives absolute

---

18. Although it is well known that Kant's doctrines of the thing-in-itself and of *a priori* synthetic judgments were the cornerstone of his effort to overcome the solipsistic implications of Hume's skepticism, it is less well known that Kant took over uncritically Hume's belief that we can only know representations and that what reaches us in perception are successions of particular data intrinsically unconnected by any causal necessity. The presupposition of both thinkers was an identification of perception with sensation. Though Kant "overcame" Hume's skepticism by positing his "synthetical unity of consciousness," which enabled him to say that we could know "things-out-there," he was unable to say that those "things" were the "things themselves": they were only "appearances," "phenomena." From the Cartesian starting point of the isolated ego, it is simply impossible for the subject to have direct perception of the external world. See Mascall, *Whatever Happened to the Human Mind?*, for a discussion of Hume, and Whitehead, *Symbolism*, for a decisive philosophical critique of Humean—and Kantian—skepticism, through the twin doctrines of presentational immediacy and causal efficacy. Whitehead's and, later, Michael Polanyi's relational epistemologies are massive counterweights to the postmodernist form of skepticism—relativism—as represented,

priority to the subject; while disallowing or at least severely limiting the possibility of objective knowledge, it sees the subject as able nevertheless, *from within its own finitude,* to posit the nature of reality—including that ultimate reality which, we are told, it is actually impossible for him to know. The fountain of Cartesian thought, which characterizes the thinking subject as the epistemological starting point and sets it over against and basically disconnected from the physical world, became, with Kant's *a priori* categories, a powerful river that romanticism and the relativizing forces of historicism subsequently extended across a wide valley floor, ending in the submersion of the whole land under modern subjectivism.

But Kant's disproof, through his antinomies, of the possibility of obtaining metaphysical knowledge by theoretical reason—a disproof that ever since has cast a shadow on Christian faith and made it seem unlikely that the personal God Christians believe in is anything more than a speculative projection—has in fact nothing whatsoever to say about the possibility of *divine revelation* being given to man, if a personal God exists who wishes to reveal himself. Ironically, Kant's arguments are actually a philosophical equivalent to theological arguments against natural theology and the pretension that finite and unholy man, by himself, can rise up to a knowledge of the true, infinite, and holy God without that God having first to come down to him in revelation.

The locus of philosophical activity today is no longer the question of whether it is possible to have knowledge of objects outside the self, but rather the position of absolute perspectivalism, according to which all perceptions and assertions (apart from mathematical, logical, and scientifically demonstrable statements), being made by a subject and being therefore necessarily subjective and under the constraint of arbitrary signs/words (which cannot correspond in any objective sense to the objects they stand for), are unable to make contact with truth external to the perceiving, asserting subject. The conclusion is not far behind, of course, that no such truth exists. Hermeneutics has taken over epistemology. Relativistic perspectivalism is the latest form of skepticism. It is my conviction that a renewed appreciation of the biblical teaching about the *imago Dei* can be a powerful response to the dangers facing Western society today, and provide an underpinning to the doctrine of human rights we seek rightly to apply more widely, while at the same time keeping this doctrine from becoming itself an exploited and exploiting ideology.

---

for example, by the language-oriented philosophers Jacques Derrida and Richard Rorty. Whitehead's and Polanyi's realist formulations (within a prior relational framework) are basically in keeping with the anthropological understanding inherent in the *imago Dei* doctrine.

V

Imago Dei: Man is a Creature Ontologically Related to God; M. Behe: Irreducibly Complex Systems; C. Tresmontant: Human Beings as Substances/Psychic Entities/Persons; the Irrational Human Project of Self-creation

"*So God created man* [humankind] *in his own image, in the image of God he created him; male and female, he created them*" (Gen 1:27). In the short space of this essay, we cannot possibly deal with all the complexities and implications of this foundational biblical affirmation. We shall merely touch on a number of key aspects that seem especially pertinent in light of the foregoing reflections about the critical situation of humanity at the start of the twenty-first century.

This statement, without equivalent in any other culture, is understood within the Judeo-Christian context as the basic revelation from God of the truth about human beings. What is given as revelation must, of course, be considered and evaluated by reason, but reason must not overstep its limits by arbitrarily positing its superiority to revelation. Such a move will only lead reason into contradiction with itself when it rules out the possibility of revelation simply because it repudiates the possibility of certain knowledge being gained through metaphysical speculation. The two modes of knowing, or of knowing about, unmeasurable reality—divine revelation and human metaphysical speculation—are in no way equivalent. The exclusion by reason of the possibility of revelation is *unreasonable* and cannot be defended on rational grounds.

The core of the truth about man revealed here is that he (male and female) is a *creature ontologically related to God*. To say that a man or woman *is*, is to say that he or she *is in relation to God*. This is primary, ontological; qualitative descriptions of men and women made in the effort to articulate an adequate anthropology and that describe human beings as creatures having ontic qualities like rationality and freedom are secondary and properly *follow* this primordial affirmation. It is these qualities that make possible the *expression* of the relation of men to God, but the relation itself is prior.

Man is a *creature*. He is *created*. This is the first aspect of the doctrine of the *imago Dei* that we must examine. However the mystery of his evolution is to be understood, humankind, according to the Judeo-Christian Scriptures, owes its existence to a Creator, a personal God, and not to chance, chance being understood here as the negation of an organizing intelligence. To posit chance as the ultimate source of all reality is to assert that the constituent elements necessary to the existence of beings have appeared randomly and come together over time and then produced *living* beings that have subsequently evolved through the mechanism of natural selection. The efficacy of natural selection as the operative force of evolution can, logically, have only two possible sources: a primordial organizing intelligence that has willed this to be the case, or chance. The assertion that chance *must* be the source of all form, order, and life in the universe, including the very process of natural selection operative in the evolution of living forms, begs the question of how natural selection itself came to be. Merely to assert that natural selection is the result of chance cannot even begin to address the obvious fact that natural selection has a teleological orientation that logically points to intentionality, not to chance.

The recent work of the biochemist Michael Behe seeks to show that irreducibly complex systems at the biochemical level—and, by extension, at higher levels—cannot have evolved gradually, by incremental mutations.[19] The complexity of just one cell, without even mentioning biological structures involving more than one cell, involves webs of different, identifiable, immensely complex systems. An irreducibly complex system, Behe writes, is "a single system composed of several well-matched, interacting parts that contribute to the basic function, wherein the removal of any of the parts causes the system to effectively cease functioning."[20]

Behe argues that traditional Darwinian theory which, to use a commercial image, deals in wholesale and not in retail goods, cannot account adequately for such systems, where every single protein has a definable role to play that is adapted to that of every other protein, all the roles being necessary to the operation of the system. A system must have a "minimal function" to be a candidate for natural selection, and in the case of an irreducibly complex system, this requires that all the parts be present at once and able to perform at a level suitable to their purpose.[21]

Behe concludes, logically, that irreducibly complex systems point to intelligent design as their cause. I say "logically" because ultimately there is no other logical conclusion possible, though materialists will continue to make appeal to some causal third force, neither a Creator/Designer nor Chance-plus-Time but some unthinkable Other Process. Such prevarication shows well how subjectivist ideology, with its materialist presupposition, has taken captive sections of the scientific establishment. Behe himself, discreetly, does not go on to plead for a Creator as the Intelligent Designer

---

19. Behe, *Darwin's Black Box*, 39–42.
20. Behe, *Darwin's Black Box*, 39.
21. Behe, *Darwin's Black Box*, 45.

behind the intelligent design, but his scientific work opens the way for metaphysicians and theologians to do so.

Behe's thesis has been challenged scientifically, however. Michael Ruse, in his book entitled *Darwin and Design*, takes issue with Behe by citing a number of examples of complex processes that appear to have come about over time, incrementally, through the process of natural selection. Instancing the case of the Krebs cycle, whereby energy from food is converted into a form that can be used by cells, he makes the important point that intermediate stages, or subprocesses, of the cycle, which initially had no fitness functionality with respect to the complex final product, started off their existence doing something quite different and were subsequently coopted by the cells and put to a new use. Ruse insists that this re-deployment by natural selection of material that already exists is the answer to the problem of irreducibly complex systems and explains how it is possible for such systems to emerge progressively. No intelligent design, he affirms, is necessary to explain their existence; natural selection performs the operation.[22]

While Ruse's argument is cogent and may indeed point to the evolutionary process that *normally* may make possible the emergence of irreducibly complex systems (though of course this is unproven), it still leaves unanswered the fundamental question of how the mechanism of natural selection itself emerged in the first place. Undoubtedly natural selection is evolution's principle if not exclusive method, but to imagine that such an efficacious method simply happened and is itself the result of . . . natural selection (!), is metaphysically jejune.

Equally odd, even disingenuous, is the argument of the traditional Darwinian that what he is expecting to find by virtue of natural selection—and does find—is not design but the *appearance* of design. "The question," writes Ruse, "is not whether design demands design. All can grant that. The question is whether design-like demands design, or if selection can do the job instead."[23] The same question is begged. Whether we are speaking of design or of the appearance of design, we are confronted by order that appears to arise, as far as we can determine at present, through the remarkably efficient mechanism of natural selection. But how did such an order-producing mechanism arise?

One thinker who has given much thought to the metaphysics involved in these issues is the Frenchman Claude Tresmontant, who observes that there are two kinds of metaphysics: a woolly, speculative type, arbitrary and imaginary, constructing castles in the air, which is what most scientists

---

22. Ruse, *Darwin and Design*, 319–25.
23. Ruse, *Darwin and Design*, 325.

think metaphysics *is* and what most scientists who engage in speculation outside their field—usually on *origins*, cosmological and biological—*do*; and a responsible type, founded on the experimental sciences, which pushes the rational analysis of reality to its utmost limits.[24]

Tresmontant finds scandalous the contemporary divorce of science and metaphysics, unknown before Kant, which has major philosophers being untrained in the sciences and oblivious to their findings, so caught up in their existentialism or their linguistic analysis or their pragmatism that the metaphysical and cosmological implications of paradigm-shattering recent discoveries such as that the cosmos is evolving and so had a beginning and will have an end, go virtually unnoticed, as if philosophical reflection need not concern itself with experimental science. (Ironically, the same philosophers, untrained in hard science or in traditional metaphysics, are usually materialists who, while presuming that science provides the only kind of knowledge we can have, yet unaccountably refuse to probe the implications of its discoveries.)[25]

Tresmontant, in discussing Chance-plus-Time as the possible source of the emergence of life and its astonishing orderly complexity, reminds us that modern materialists, as distinct from the Greek pre-Socratic philosophers such as Parmenides, no longer have available to them the categories of infinite time and space and an infinite quantity of matter, when they consider cosmic and biological existence.[26] Most thinkers (such as the eminent American geneticist Theodosius Dobzhansky, the biologist Pierre Lecomte du Noüy, and the astronomer Arthur Eddington) who have given any attention to the issue are aware that the statistical probability that life as we know it has emerged by undirected chance, through incremental mutations and natural selection, is effectively nil.[27] The fact that the implications of this

---

24. Tresmontant, *Sciences de l'Univers*, 99–100.

25. Tresmontant, *Sciences de l'Univers*, 7–10.

26. Greek philosophers, of course, were not trying to figure out the origins of the universe, since they assumed it was eternal. This, in fact, was the general assumption of philosophers until the twentieth century since, as even Aquinas admitted, a beginning of the world was impossible to prove metaphysically.

27. See Tresmontant, *Sciences de l'Univers*, 103. Eddington, who certainly had no Christian faith, wrote in a discourse on time: "I am simply stating the dilemma to which our present fundamental conception of physical law leads us . . . .the dilemma is this: Surveying our surroundings, we find them to be far from a 'fortuitous concourse of atoms.' The picture of the world, as drawn in existing physical theories, shows arrangement of the individual elements for which the odds are multimillions to 1 against an origin by chance." Quoted in Danielson, *Book of the Cosmos*, 403.

observation are rarely faced up to by materialistic evolutionists[28] is another disturbing commentary on the level of thinking in this discipline.

Michael Ruse maintains, however, that Richard Dawkins has "scotched" this argument according to which random mutation cannot of itself ever produce adaptation or design-like effects.[29] There is a big difference, Ruse points out, citing Dawkins, between a computer program operating by cumulative selection, where the program is jigged so that a successful move toward adaptation is *remembered* and built upon, and a program using single-step selection of the sort referred to above, where every new attempt to work toward a target is a fresh one. The obvious objection, acknowledged by Dawkins, is that in nature there is no ascertainable prior goal, as there is with the computer program. To this point Dawkins replies simply that *if* selection is factored into an evolutionary process, one has an entirely different trajectory—a very effective one, in fact—from that of the infinite randomness that, he admits, cannot possibly produce a design-like effect. This is certainly true, but it solves nothing, since the question remains as to how selection could ever come to be factored into the process in the first place.

Tresmontant, by metaphysical analysis, takes the discussion much further. Observing that living beings are not just more or less complex combinations of atoms, he draws on the concept of substance in the Aristotelian sense of a *form*, or identity (to be distinguished from a physical body), that subsists through the constant change of atomic matter (atoms in a living organism are continuously flowing in and out and being renewed) and that integrates, by its own proper activity, a huge number of elements and functions in a synthetic unity. He writes:

> Living beings are *substances*, beings that subsist even while their integrated matter is being constantly renewed; they are substances capable of action and reaction; they are psychic entities; and finally, with the last animal that has appeared [man] they are psychic entities capable of conscious reflection—what we call persons. . . . It is because they have not perceived the philosophical, metaphysical dimension of the problem that so many thinkers remain focused on the mathematical analysis of probabilities in connection with the composition of genetic messages. But again, a genetic message in itself is not enough to

---

28. I use this phrase to distinguish this sort of evolutionist not so much from fundamentalist creationists as from design evolutionists of the Behe type, who may or may not believe strictly in a Creator and in a personal creative providence guiding the cosmic and biological evolutionary processes.

29. Ruse, *Darwin and Design*, 325–26.

explain the existence of a substance that is a psychic entity and, finally, a person. This is of another order.[30]

An aggregate of elements, no matter how complex, does not make a living creature with its own proper activity capable of self-repair, assimilation, elimination, and reproduction. Along with the questions of the very *existence* of matter and of the *nature—energy—*of the matter that exists, there is the question of the *information* of matter, constantly increasing all the way up to the emergence of living beings and on to man. The passage from an aggregate of elements to a substance/subject is a mystery. A living being is constituted from its conception by a form, an idea, an organizing genetic message that is the *principle* of its activity and operations and that endures over time until the organism's death, whereupon it turns into the mere aggregate it never was while living, with the inevitable result that it disintegrates.[31] Where does this integrating principle of life come from? There can be no recourse here to random mutations as an explanation of such a radical novelty; and to give the cause as natural selection simply begs the question, as we have seen.

A correlative mystery involves the passage from a generic type, normatively coded—cat, say—to a particular individual cat. From an essence (cat) to an existent (*this* cat) is a move quite beyond our ken. *This* cat—and how much more so *this* man or *this* woman!—will be distinct, with unique peculiarities within its species-normative genetic code. The move from a fertilized human cell to the particular human individual it will become—from the *virtual* being, through the becoming, to the *actual* being—involves an inconceivably complex process of embryonic *information* of which the dynamic—the vital principle—remains utterly mysterious.

All this, then, and much more is involved when we say, with the inspired writer of the Genesis text, that "God *created* humankind, male and female he created them" (Gen 1:27). It is clear that if men and women are created beings, they are *essentially dependent* on their Creator, both for their existence and for their maintenance in being. God does not impose on us a conscious awareness of this reality, because he wills that our relation with him be one of freedom, with no trace of a master-slave dynamic. The human being-as-creature is changeable, vulnerable, mortal: as *created*, he/she is an

---

30. Tresmontant, *Sciences de l'Univers*, 105–6 (translation mine).

31. My discussion at this point is not concerned with the question of what happens to the soul of a human person after his or her physical death, or with the question of resurrection, which for Christian faith involves the clothing at Christ's return of the soul with a spiritual body. It should be clear, however, that the mystery of the integrating principle of life points beyond itself to a Source of Life other than chance and hence to the very real possibility—divinely ordained—of immortality.

absolutely different order of being from the eternal, omnipotent being who is the Creator of all that is. What is important to see is that both the *biological* life of human beings, *and* the *eternal* life that they are offered (by virtue of Christ's redemptive work) to share with their Creator, are *gifts*.

Man (man and woman) is not his own author; he is not and cannot be autonomous. Any creating he does, impressive and splendid though it may be, is derivative and secondary, using materials already at hand. Human beings cannot be *original* creators, since they themselves, and the world they inhabit, are already there as givens. *Everything we have, we have received,* as the apostle Paul puts it in 1 Corinthians 4:7 in an effort to show the members of the church he is writing to that pride has no place among Christians (and should have none among men and women in general), since our very existence, and our existence as individuals with particular qualities, talents, and vocations, are *gifts* and come from God in the first place.

At bottom, what theologians call original sin is a refusal of this truth and of the God behind it. As Creator, God is responsible for our existence; as creatures, we are responsible *to him* for our existence. And this sets moral and material limits to our being and our doing. It is these limits that we refuse, and it is this refusal that generates all our human counterfeits of the creation and the re-creation that God accomplishes through his word. These counterfeits are simply attempts at self-creation and self-salvation.

There is no *reason* for human rebellion; it is irrational. The pretension behind it, with the infinite suffering it has entailed in the course of human existence, is bewilderingly stupid, given the enormous intelligence human beings are equipped with and deploy in other areas of their existence. But precisely that fact points up sin's irrationality. Our will, much of the time, is not synchronized with our reason. By political and technological means (now including the possibilities offered by biogenetics, organ replacement, designer babies, reproductive cloning, and cryogenics), human beings, with mounting intensity and purpose (finding here, perhaps, the sense of purpose we have lost in losing sight of the providential God), seem determined to recreate their kind, to start, as it were, from scratch (obviously an impossibility), to do over God's original blueprint, deemed faulty (because we perceive it through the distorting lens of the refusal of our createdness and the catastrophic consequences of our rebellion). The ultimate aim of this enterprise, of course, must be to overcome death itself.

It is important to see that this determination is not, at bottom, properly therapeutic, though an exaggerated therapeutic concern can lead in the same direction. It is of quite another order. We are talking about a remake, a re-creation. Modern man, to the extent that he is captive to a triumphalist ideology patterned on an engineering model, proposes to save mankind by engendering a new man, invulnerable to the corruption of the first man, and by placing him in a new Eden environmentally controlled to the last degree and not subject to the dangers and unpredictabilities of the first Eden.

It is this monstrous pretension—rationalistic to an extreme, yet completely irrational—that I call a counterfeit of the mandate given to humankind by God to tend and develop the world, including his own human society. A correlative counterfeit, invariably operative in genocidal enterprises and, basically, an essential component of all ideologies, is the racist drive to create, in a given territory, *one homogenized people*, to the exclusion of all alien *others* (an exclusion that logically entails the destruction of these *others*, or at the very least their subservience). This is the counterfeit of the biblical revelation of the unity and ontological equality of the human race, a revelation that the counterfeit denies and seeks to replace. Like the vision of the new man, it subverts the truth of the *imago Dei* and opens the way for boundless manipulation and oppression.

As technological power has increased, so have such utopian projections; and ruthless human beings, incarnating humanity's drive to play God, have wreaked havoc as a consequence. The sequence of human cataclysms in the last century is evidence of this, each resulting from the perverse will to *make man over* in part by eliminating elements of humanity considered by the ideologues, according to self-serving criteria, to be subhuman. By claiming to be intrinsically superior, or by aspiring to be *super*human in the sense of *greater than the Adamic prototype*, the perpetrators of such abuses and atrocities become *in*human. The attempt by man to *make himself in his own image* is a misbegotten enterprise, a perverse use of the rationality with which he is gifted and in which he has put so much ideological stock since the Enlightenment; it is an enterprise fundamentally flawed because of the theological/ontological lie at its root that posits man as his own master; as such, it cannot but fall under God's judgment and be doomed inevitably to disaster.

VI

Imago Dei: Who is the God Who Created Man in His Own Image? Divine Revelation through the History of the Jews and Supremely in the Messiah

It is *God* who created humankind in his own image. Who is this God? This is the second aspect of the *imago Dei* doctrine that we shall examine. The question is entirely legitimate, and the misguided answers men give to it in the wake of our inner refusal to accept our status as creatures (that is, as *created* and *designed* by an Intelligence infinitely higher than ourselves) account for the atheological animus of modern society and the ever-increasing *hubris* accompanying our impressive technological achievements. It may perhaps be said that the yawning gap between these achievements, where we manifest such formidable control, and our shameful and flagrant incapacity to master our ethical behavior and social relations, serves as the chief driving engine of the totalitarian will to reinvent ourselves by political and technological domination and manipulation.

Through the egocentricity of sin, we are a fractured species, yet we hold in our heart, by virtue of our being created in God's image, a yearning for integrity, wholeness, and unity, in relation to our Creator and to the rest of his creation. But sin, in addition to causing our brokenness, also determines our response to it, which is to strive *by ourselves* to make things whole, unified, and harmonious. It is this striving that leads to totalitarianism at whatever social level it may manifest itself—to the assertion made by (self-)chosen elites of total control over others, using extreme force if necessary, to the point of turning men and women into objects, dehumanizing them, actually *destroying* them, in order to achieve the absolute domination and *ersatz* unity/wholeness/purity required by redemption. For, of course, the totalitarian/utopian enterprise (which always has a religious tenor because of its idolatrous belief in its own ultimacy) is invariably presented as a kind of redemption requiring purification and unification—and this, once again, as I have suggested, is an imitation of God's work, a diabolical counterfeit of God's saving plan for humankind through *his* chosen people, the Jews, and their (and the world's) Messiah, Jesus Christ.[32]

32. The Torah makes it very clear that the Hebrews are not chosen because of any intrinsic merit or superiority, but because God loves them and intends them to be, through the Messiah, the means of salvation for the whole world (see e.g., Gen 12:3b; 17:4; Deut 7:7–8, 9:4; John 4:21–26, 3:16–17; Rom 4:13–17). It should be obvious that the spiritual source of anti-Semitism (as distinct from political and sociological sources), supremely focused in Nazi ideology and surfacing again in our day, notably, if not exclusively, among radical Islamists, is hatred of the true God, the Creator and Lord of history, who has revealed himself through the Hebraic/Jewish people. That people, as a living witness to that God, must be obliterated, say the God-haters. This same hatred accounts, at bottom, for anti-Christian persecution, a phenomenon to be found in all cultures from the time of the Romans to the modern era, and one that is taking new forms in Western society today as well as elsewhere in the world, especially in Muslim countries and the few remaining communist States. The specific anti-Judaism that infected the church was the result of misguided theology and pride, as I have already suggested in note 4; anti-Judaism in Islam, which, as many of its texts make clear, is foundational to that religion, as is its hostility to biblical Christianity, is the result of qur'anic and post-qur'anic distortion of the biblical writings, both Old and New Testaments, and of jealousy of the Jews as the bearers, through Isaac and not Ishmael, of

It is here, precisely, in God's providential saving plan for humankind, revealed to successive generations through the scriptural narratives, that we discover *who God is.*

Unless God reveals himself to us, we cannot know him as he is. This is because we are finite and fallen (in rebellion against the true God and blind to his goodness), while he is infinite and holy. Through beholding the glory and order of the world—his creation—with wonder-filled eyes, we may intuit, even sense, his reality and presence, for he dwells here and the world is filled with his dynamic being; but nature itself is impersonal, so we cannot *know* the personal God, its Creator, simply by observing it. But providence is an implication of creation, and redemption is an implication of providence. Christians believe, with the historical witness of the New Testament narratives and apostolic letters as the ground for their faith, that Jesus Christ was the Word of God made flesh, the very utterance of God himself—one with him in being—become incarnate. God is personal and communicates; he *speaks*, whereas idols, as the prophets never tire of pointing out, are dumb (e.g., Jer 10:5); he *speaks*, and in Jesus that communication is made physically manifest to us. He is God's self-revelation—his *Word*—God who *comes down to us* (Isa 64:1; cf., John 1:11). *"No one has ever seen God,"* writes John, *"but God the One and Only, who is at the Father's side, has made him known"* (John 1:18). And Jesus himself says later in this gospel: *"I am the way and the truth and the life. No one comes to the Father except through me. If you really knew me, you would know my Father as well . . . Anyone who has seen me has seen the Father . . . "* (John 14:6–7a, 9b).

Jesus is presented in Scripture as the image—the *eikon* (*eīkōn*) and very representation—of God (Heb 1:3; 2 Cor 4:4; Col 1:15). Now we are considering a few aspects of the doctrine of *human beings as created in God's image*. It is proper and necessary, in doing this, to glance at the sweep of the scriptural revelation and not simply to remain in the book of Genesis, for

---

the Abrahamic promise of the offer of salvation to the whole world, by grace (not by law and merit, as both Judaism and Islam would have it). Ishmael, it must be remembered, was Abraham's natural son, his firstborn, conceived in unbelief by Abraham with Hagar, his wife Sarai's Egyptian maidservant; Isaac was his son by virtue of God's pure covenantal grace, the very image, therefore, of the gracious salvation God would offer mankind through the people of Israel and their Messiah, Jesus. While God did make a gracious promise to Ishmael and his descendants as well as to Isaac (see Gen 21:13, 18, 20), the two sons were not on the same covenantal plane (see e.g., Gen 21:12). The Muslim contention that the Hebrew Scriptures had been corrupted and that in fact Ishmael had priority over Isaac is an arbitrary and unjustifiable assertion without any historical evidence to back it up. The manifestation of God's sovereignty in his selection of Isaac to be the bearer of his covenantal promise, as reported in the Hebrew Scriptures, was intolerable to Muhammed and is therefore deliberately contradicted in the Qur'an and is still intolerable to his followers.

the full meaning of the text in Genesis 1 and 2 is only revealed in Christ. If Christ is God's image and we are made in that image, then we are created in *Christ's* image, and to find out *who human beings are* essentially, and to what they are called, we must look at Jesus. And similarly, we must look at this same Jesus—the One who is both God and Man—to *see who God is.*

Jesus Christ is unique. Yet the union in him of the divine and the human points to our human vocation, which is to be united with the Godhead, gathered up into eternal, dynamic communion with the Father through the Son in the Spirit. It is to this that human beings are called, for this that they were created. To refuse this vision after having first received it, as Western civilization is now doing, is to move inevitably, on the wings of technology-as-ideology and the infinite manipulations it makes possible, toward the sophisticated dehumanization of mankind. It is not that those who have faith in Christ, or those others who truly long for God (whatever their religious perspective), will be made divine, but rather that they will be taken up into the divine life, of which already here below faithful Christians have the vital deposit, the indwelling Holy Spirit, not because of any intrinsic merit of their own, but because they have been fortunate to hear the call and have been willing to open themselves to receive the gift and to bear witness in this life to the Giver.

But the call goes out to all men and women and is constitutive of true human identity; if we fail to heed it in our inner conscience, we alienate ourselves not only from our Creator but from each other. The result is the violence of human history, growing ever more intense as technology extends human means. The rejection by modern culture of Jesus Christ, the God-man who reveals in himself the glorious destiny to which all human beings are summoned, is the ultimate source of the alienation afflicting the West and wreaking such havoc across the world. We do not want to be what we are called to be by our Creator—the modern mind sees that call, falsely, as heteronomy and rejects it; we want to be what we will make ourselves to be, gods of our own manufacture. And this slavery to our own will we blindly call freedom.

VII

The God Revealed in Jesus Christ is Love; He is Righteous and Faithful

The God who destines us to union with himself is *love*. He *creates* in love (what greater love than the act of creation, when God goes out from himself to fashion an *other*, then calls that other to fellowship with himself?); he *redeems* in love (God in Christ humbles himself to become man, to pass unrecognized amongst his own, to bear opprobrium for our sake, to carry our sin, to suffer and die on a cross, all of this so that humanity-in-him—in him who is our representative and, for each of us, our substitute—might die with him on the cross to the egocentric nature and, forgiven, be raised with him, as a new creation, to newness of life, which means to a life of love); and he *glorifies* in love (by faith we are resurrected with Christ already, and abide already with him in the Father; and by hope we live in expectation of the fulfillment of this spiritual reality when, at his coming again, we shall be resurrected and clothed with spiritual bodies, and shall see him as he is and be like him (Eph 2:6; John 14:20; 1 John 3:2).

The revelation of the Word of God tells us all of this. This is the *gospel—the good news—*to which the whole Bible points. It hinges on God's incarnation in Jesus, the meaning and purpose of which are disclosed in his crucifixion and resurrection. Christ's resurrection, following on his crucifixion, is the pivot of revelation and hence lies at the heart of truth. Here, in this cross and empty tomb, we understand who God really is. The source and end of all reality—cosmic and historical—is *love*. This truth, revealed to us fully in Christ, is the essential meaning of Jesus's assertion in the Gospel of John that *he* is the truth. He shows us the true nature of reality. All is gift, all is grace, and these are expressions of love. In the person and life of Jesus of Nazareth, as he went about among men doing good, showing kindness and mercy, and dispensing wisdom and justice with great authority, we see what love means in practice: here we glimpse what God is like and how we are meant to be.

When we think of God's *righteousness,* we must think of it within the framework of love and grace. His righteousness combines *justice and mercy* and aims, with respect to mankind, to bring us back into an orderly relationship with himself and with each other. It involves *salvation* (e.g., Isa 46:13a: "*I am bringing my righteousness near, it is not far away; and my salvation will not be delayed.*"). This, precisely, is his supreme work of love, carried out effectively and definitively in Jesus. What God the Son suffered on the cross where he was *"bruised for our iniquities"* (Isa 53:5) expressed both God's just judgment upon human sin and his merciful forgiveness accomplished and offered to sinners, his beloved creatures made in his image, who had gone astray.

The doctrine of the *imago Dei* contains implicitly these comprehensive truths, as the genetic code in each cell contains the whole human being in its compass. The God who created us in his own image *loves* us. Furthermore, he is *faithful*. He is steadfast and dependable; we may rely on him; he will not lie. This is another part of what we mean when we speak of God as the truth revealed in Christ. We may abandon him—or try to—but he does not abandon us. To the contrary—he *remembers* us.[33] Discipline us he does, for that is part of love; but the ultimate judgment—death—due us for our rebellion against him who is life, he took upon himself in Christ, so as to make it possible for us to choose this life while we are on earth. If it were not so, there could be no possible hope for a race mired in endless war, capable of frightful sexual depravity, exploitation, genocide, and heartless terrorism. These great evils are *our* work, not God's. They arise out of man's refusal of him, not his of us. He remains faithful and available to us even in the midst of our depravity and degradation. We have only to humble ourselves and look to him to see what he offers us through his self-revelation in Christ. But in our human pride we almost invariably demand that he be present to us on our own terms, in the way that *we* see fit and appropriate and effectual. It is not thus that we will find him, either in our daily lives or at the heart of horrors like genocide and war.

VIII

Hatred of God and the Denial of Sin and Guilt are the Roots of Utopian Pretensions; Ideological Tribalism and the Totalitarian Impulse

On reflection, it is astonishingly foolish to think that such a race as ours, capable of what we have shown ourselves to be capable of, could save itself or change its own duplicitous heart. As *something* cannot arise out of *nothing*, so *good* cannot arise out of *perversity*. Human pride tries to get around this problem—a problem of moral logic—by denying our sinfulness and guilt, a denial that is achieved by blaming it on God, on society or institutions, on the unconscious, or on some other scapegoat like a different ethnic group or class, in order to shift the onus from humankind, collectively and individually (the phenomenon of *negationism*, as a corollary of genocide, is a local expression of this basic human deceit). The crowning tactic in this move—which modern human beings have deployed brazenly—is to deny outright the existence of God. Atheism is the ultimate end of human pride

---

33. The theme of God's remembrance is movingly developed by David Keck in his profound meditation on memory and time in the context of a reflection on the theological implications of Alzheimer's Disease. See Keck, *Forgetting Whose We are*, chapter 2. God's gracious remembrance of us is a pervasive theme throughout the Bible. See, for example, Genesis 30:22; Judges 16:28; Psalm 25:6–11; Jeremiah 15:15; Luke 1:54, 72, 23:42.

and faithlessness, which blinds us from seeing or even wanting to see the faithful Creator God. It is the ultimate negationism, whereby we deny our own creaturehood; and as such, it is the ultimate form of self-destruction.

Underneath the atheistic thrust, what we actually find is *hatred of God* masquerading as unbelief. The hatred arises from the experience of our own moral turpitude. We are not perfect, and we despise ourselves for it. Such imperfection is intolerable. In response, we accuse others, those who are different from us, and, in the modern period, we proclaim human perfectibility and passionately refuse divine intervention. Concomitantly, we deny original sin. Here indeed we find the root of modern utopian thought and the notion that *everything is possible*. Rebellion against God moves at this point into a new register, where moral fallibility and, eventually, finitude, are repudiated, in a virtual hijacking of divine omnipotence and perfection.

Everyone knows from personal experience how difficult it is for us to admit we are wrong. If we can point the finger at others and construct utopian systems promising perfection, we can, in appearance, avoid the onus of guilt and weakness. But of course the denial of sin does not lead to the disappearance of guilt. One of the fundamental aspects of man as made in God's image is conscience, by which an echo of the divine voice is ever present within us. Conscience can be repressed and hardened, but it cannot be destroyed. What the denial of sin does is remove the disposition to admit error and seek atonement and forgiveness. This in turn results in a massive transfer of guilt to the *other* and a constant inclination to accuse and avoid personal moral responsibility.

Thus the denial of original sin—sin as virtually inherent in human beings in their condition of moral freedom—leads inevitably to scapegoating and a totalitarian attitude, with the political consequences we are only too familiar with.[34] For if sin is not ubiquitous in all human beings, mixed with the good likewise to be found in all of us, then a Manichaean mindset begins to operate that has one group, understanding itself as guiltless, pure, and superior, pinning perversity on another group, perceived as wicked, guilty, impure, and inferior. That other group must then be destroyed, in one way or another. This is the distorted moral vision that underpins the totalitarian impulse we have been noting, and of which postmodernism's absolutist doctrine of tolerance—built, ironically, on ideological relativism—is the latest, soft (in appearance) variation.[35]

---

34. This insight is brilliantly developed in Delsol, *Éloge de la Singularité*, 217–25.

35. The doctrine of tolerance, which has become the cultural air breathed by postmodern man, is notoriously intolerant of any claims of absolute truth, whether moral or spiritual (political correctness is a good example of this). Its rhetoric of inclusivism, accompanied by its self-justifying ethic of individual preference, shows itself to be

One might call this phenomenon ideological tribalism, and it is the distinguishing negative mark of modernity, as well as of the current Islamist reaction *against* modernity, which takes the form of terrorism. Terrorism is another expression of the totalitarian impulse, and if it had the political and military means, it would produce another genocide, this time aimed at Western culture as a whole, of which America is perceived to be the current flag-bearer.[36] Ideological tribalism thinks in black and white, in absolutes.

rabidly exclusivist toward people who make such truth claims. The tolerance doctrine is especially virulent in its opposition to claims for biblical authority and revelation, and its resistance to the Christian view of the uniqueness of the Person and work of Jesus Christ, is itself absolute. Any society espousing this doctrine is bound to seek to curb, mock, marginalize, and, if possible, suppress genuine Christian faith, at both the public and private levels. As it works itself out, for instance, in ideological movements like political correctness, radical homosexuality, and radical feminism (all carrying within them the totalitarian, scapegoating impulse), the doctrine of tolerance bears striking resemblance, structurally, to the French Revolution's doctrine of (discriminatory) equality as it took shape in the fanatical revolutionary period. It is important not to confuse this modern doctrine with toleration, which emerged in the wake of the religious wars in Europe. Christian in inspiration, and arising in reaction to the travesty of the gospel represented by those wars and by the absolutist politico-religious ideology that motivated them, toleration naturally engenders an openness to all people, whatever their religious beliefs, even while avoiding the trap of relativism and its denial of the possibility of absolute truth and divine revelation. In principle, religious pluralism, as it takes its form in modern democracies, provides political legitimation to this attitude of toleration.

36. The attacks on September 11, 2001 against the World Trade Center towers and the Pentagon were a perfect example of this. No normal motive for war, such as territorial expansion, incites Islamist terrorists to perform barbaric acts like those; their inspiration is ideological/religious and aims at the total destruction of the infidel other, perceived to be the incarnation of evil and the ultimate menace with which there can be no negotiation or political compromise of any sort. This is the genocidal impulse, behind which lies a perceived injustice (which may or may not correspond to some reality in a given case), cultural and social alienation, deep bitterness, and jealousy coupled with a sense of moral superiority, all of which combine with fear to produce a consuming desire for vengeance and punishment. In the case of the attacks on the World Trade Center and subsequent acts of terrorism by Al-Qaeda or ISIS or similar groups, the motive is fundamentally related to resentment toward predatory Western foreign policies and triumphalist Western culture as a whole and toward the presence in particular of infidel foreign troops (especially American) in parts of the world considered to be sacred to Islam. This is coupled with resentment of repressive local regimes. But the move from such resentment—itself comprehensible under the circumstances—to a policy of systematic, hate-filled terrorism that even targets co-religionists judged to be collaborators with the West, goes beyond mere hostility and derives rather from the nihilistic impulse that inspires genocide and from the ideological mindset that orchestrates it. This genocidal impulse is blind and absolutist and lacks any sense of the unity of the human race and of the dignity of all human beings as they stand equally before God the Creator. It is the paroxysm of idolatry, where a group, convinced of its own eminent moral superiority and worshiping some false god, has invested itself with

It is fundamentalistic, and is governed by the quintuplet monsters of pride, fear, envy, jealousy, and resentment—all of which generate hatred. As with Islamist extremism, it often has, along with some legitimate grievances, an overtly religious reference, but its ferocity, heartlessness, and utter unreasonableness reveal its god to be an idol. Idolatry/ideology is always an expression of what is basically a perverted religious impulse.

The origins of ideological tribalism in the West are multiple. We have, first, the crusading and inquisitorial aberrations of the church, manifested occasionally in persecutions during the Constantinian Age and again later in the Middle Ages; and then the absolutist fanaticism of the religious wars of the late Medieval and early Modern periods (fruit of the subversion of the late medieval church by totalitarian pretensions), where, as in the earlier examples cited above, Christendom lurched into ideology and lost touch, to a considerable extent, with the gospel, thus betraying its own principles and bringing itself under God's judgment. The nationalist impulses that arose in the sixteenth century and governed Europe for the next 500 years also stoked the fires of tribalism, as did, indirectly and unintentionally, the philosophical conjectures of Enlightenment thinkers such as Hobbes, Locke, Hume, Rousseau, and Kant, who, in understandable reaction against the religious conflicts of the seventeenth century, were seeking a revised anthropology and a new (nonreligious) basis for social unity and stability, but who unwittingly laid the groundwork for the closed universe and narcissistic metaphysics that underpin the massive social engineering of the modern age, of which the utopian revolutionary vision of the French Revolution was the first major political and social expression.

It is prudent to remember that the French Revolution's slogans of liberty, fraternity, and equality were only applicable at first to the *pure and the good*, that is, to those who espoused the cause of the revolutionaries; but hatred and terror were reserved for opponents, i.e., the retrograde and the bad (Catholics and royalists), as demonstrated by the murderous fury visited by revolutionary troops on the royalist Catholic inhabitants of the Vendée region of France, a case of violence even more appalling than that of Robespierre's Terror in Paris. It should be evident that those massacres were an early form of ethnic cleansing, a harbinger of things to come and a precursor of the State-orchestrated genocidal phenomena of the twentieth century.

---

divine prerogatives and dares to assert that another group is worthy only of death.

IX

The Perfection and Holiness of the God Revealed in Jesus Christ; Modernity's Hatred of God Entails Hatred of Man

The hatred of God so current in the modern world, especially among those who think of themselves as avant-garde, liberal, even revolutionary, has another cause similar to the perception—and repudiation—of human moral turpitude mentioned above. This is the traditional belief in the *perfection* of God, as understood in the Judeo-Christian tradition. Along with his perfection we may speak of his *holiness*, the utter awesomeness and purity of his being, resplendent and immaculate beyond our conceiving, God uncreated, everlasting, essentially Other than his mortal creation. Obviously, by comparison, humanity comes off as inferior on every count.

For modern men and women, such a state of affairs, like the admission of original sin, is intolerable. Our response in the last two and a half centuries has taken two forms: we accuse God of evil, or we deny his existence. Both these solutions to the dilemma effectively remove the problem raised by the comparison of God's perfection and holiness with our own lack of them, thus clearing the way for the assertion of human perfectibility; motivated by a hatred that is rooted in pride, they amount in effect to the same thing. (Many people, for example, believe in God only to the extent that they can blame him for evil and pain—their own and that of others; clearly, this is not really very different from denying his existence.) In the West today, the innate call of human beings to know and love their Creator—who is eminently worthy of this devotion—is actually being inverted and turned into its opposite.

This is evident, once again, in the totalitarian impulse (both hard and soft): modernity refuses to believe in (to know) the biblical God or to love him, choosing instead, by denial of his existence or by indifference to his reality and commandments, to hate him. Since human beings are made in God's image, this can only result in similar attitudes toward their own kind—hence the gradual intensification in the last two centuries, alongside the remarkable achievements and manifestations of greatness during this period, of cynicism, hardheartedness, cruelty, and a kind of moral dullness and shallowness of character that shows itself in modern man's frenetic self-preoccupation, in his limitless deceit, dishonesty, and weak-minded fear of truth and difference, and in the superficiality of so many of his relationships.

This flatness and moral anemia is expressed in our day in the dogma of political correctness, which is the exact opposite of what one might expect and wish in a genuinely pluralistic society, and which inevitably, in reaction, gives rise to adversarial postures, the polarization of attitudes on issues, and the decline of rational debate. Rather than enabling harmony within a pluralistic society as is its supposed intention, this relativizing and sentimental dogma actually undercuts the self-expression and integrity of the different human groupings that make up the society and so creates frustrations that inevitably find other outlets and end up abetting tensions and confrontational positions. By regarding as of equal value all traditions and opinions, and by discouraging even cogent criticism of "the other" through a fatuous desire not to offend any party, political correctness and its academic twin, historicism, actually deplete the particular value and contribution of each grouping, shrinking its self-awareness and sense of its tradition and identity. The result is not the rainbow of vital diversity that characterizes a genuinely pluralistic society, where real dialogue and mutual give-and-take bring out the varied bands of color and encourage toleration, but a kind of indifferent gray wash across the social canvas, accompanied by heightened suspicion, fear, and ignorance. Historical depth and differentiation are sacrificed in favor of a bland and humorless homogeneity that conceals tension, ignorance, and mistrust under outward conformity. People who practice political correctness take themselves terribly seriously. Self-righteousness is their distinguishing trait. In certain religious circles that pride themselves on their tolerance, the equivalent of political correctness may take the form of a vapid inclusivism that passes for love. Jesus's call to repentance and a changed life for those who call him Lord will then be buried under a rhetoric of openness that turns the gospel into just another form of men-pleasing humanism.

X

Further Aspects of the God Revealed in Jesus Christ: He is Personal and Rational; Mysteriously Plural in His Unity; Transcendent and Omnipotent; Free, Immanent, Good; the Judge of Evil as Well as the Savior of Mankind

Returning to the Genesis narrative, we note that the God portrayed here is *personal*. It is clear that only a personal being can create, as only a personal being can love. Creation is an act of will and intelligence, not the result of random, impersonal forces. The category of the *personal*, of course, necessarily includes the category of the *rational*, of which it is the presupposition and substratum (a rational god that is impersonal cannot possibly be anything more than a human concept). The personal Creator God is *essentially* rational. Moreover, God speaks, and his creative speech is in the form of commands, e.g. "Let there be . . ." Rational speech—the power and will to communicate—is intrinsic to personal beings. The Creator God and his Word are identified here, as they are again later in the Gospel of John in relation to the Word of God incarnate in Jesus Christ (John 1:1-2). The incarnation is the supreme manifestation of the personalness of the living God, of which the essence is the will-to-communicate. Man and woman are personal beings—*persons*—precisely because they are made in the image of the personal God. Wherever the doctrine of the *imago Dei* is unknown, neglected, or subverted, different human tribes will see the other as an enemy and be inclined to treat each other as less than personal and, at the limit, as subhuman.

The God who speaks is, furthermore, *mysteriously plural* without being multiple. This is revealed in the self-address, "Let us," of Genesis 1:26, when God decides to make humankind in "our" image. Only personal beings have this self-reflexive capacity. The capacity to love—which always involves an exhalation and inhalation, a going out from the self to another distinct from the self as well as a welcoming reception of this other—depends on this prior ontological reality. God is not a lonely, opaque, remote Monad: he is a personal being-in-communion, in whom purpose and word and breath are distinctive yet one, not separate yet plural. In him who is the origin of all reality, each of these several divine expressions subsists as a particular absolute *hypostasis*, or personal mode of divinity, within the one divine being.

Moreover, throughout the Hebrew Scriptures, the one God, Yahweh, is constantly referred to in relation to his Spirit, his Word, his wisdom, and his *shekinah* glory, which are all ways of speaking about Israel's experience of the *transcendent* God who goes out from himself toward them to create and to save, who is also and always in their midst, *immanent, with them*. The Word reveals/expresses the primordial purpose/design, and the breath enables the Word to be manifest in effective power: a personal plurality-in-unity, without which neither *creation by God* nor *incarnation of God* nor *divine self-revelation* of any sort is actually conceivable. We have here, Christians believe, the adumbration in revelation of the mystery of God-as-Trinity, as Tri-Unity—the mystery that Jesus Christ, in his relation as Son to the Father in the one Spirit, and as God's Word and wisdom and presence come to be among men physically as a man, revealed in its fullness, and that the Holy Spirit was to make known subsequently to the church.[37]

---

37. The philosophical flaw in the qur'anic conception of God turns on the age-old problem of the relation of the one and the many. The Qur'an is supposed to be the dictation of the One God, Allah; but, whatever one may think of the truth of this claim, if the One God, Allah, has, by creating and then by speaking, gone out from himself toward

And, evidently, the creation narrative reveals God as *omnipotent* and *sovereign*. To say that God creates is to say that he is all-powerful. It is to say that he is transcendent, and thus of a different order from his creation. He is *free*, not dependent on or conditioned by what he has made, whereas creatures are necessarily and essentially dependent. This is precisely what galls people since, made in God's image, they are morally free, and yet as creatures they are ontologically dependent. They are both of these; and it is only as they live in communion with the free and good God, as they were made to do, that this paradox is resolved and the tension removed. Only then can persons become and be themselves, in fullness of life. For fallen humanity, existing in opposition to God, freedom is distorted to mean license and the pretension to autonomy. This is a caricature of freedom. The human creature can be truly free only when living in harmony with the Creator, who is life. Where death reigns, there can be no freedom. Only where God is, is death absent, overcome eternally by the divine power of being, and historically by the passion and resurrection of Christ.

As omnipotent and free, God has power over evil and all that opposes him. Evil, which arises out of self-will and issues in destruction, is derivative, not primary; it is a negation of being, hence dependent on the being it denies. It is a lie, and that which comes into its orbit is sucked into untruth and bondage. Sin, being a distortion of freedom, enslaves; it also deludes, so that the sinner is blinded and actually thinks himself free.

Only God, truly free and holy, can liberate and redeem those in the thrall of evil. This liberation involves *judgment*. God judges evil in his own time and way, with sovereign power, not only by condemning it—in individuals and in nations—but also by drawing good out of it, as with the crucifixion of Christ which, by divine determination, became the source of

---

the other-than-himself, he has entered into relation with the multiplicity of created reality, thus demonstrating complexity in his own being. As Creator and communicator, Allah cannot be the monadic or monistic God Islam claims him to be, for such a self-contained, absolutely transcendent deity could not nor would not create or communicate with creatures. The Allah who, according to the Qur'an, communicates with the prophet Muhammad is personal and relational, as the qur'anic dictation (whatever its truth content) demonstrates. In order to be this for creatures, he must already be this in himself. In this sense, the primordial paradigm of Purpose-Word-Breath—three movements or expressions in one divine being—holds as much for Allah and Islam as it does for Judaism and Christianity, even if what Christians believe to be the ultimate fulfillment of this paradigm in the incarnation of the Father's Word by his Spirit remains beyond Islam's horizon, as it remains beyond Judaism's, albeit to a lesser degree, since the God of the Hebrew Scriptures is already understood to be present to his people and in the world at large in a variety of ways. It is precisely in the incarnation that this presence is made fully manifest and is shown, through the acts of God in Christ, to be salvific.

mankind's salvation. He does not always prevent evil as we might wish him to do, for that would require him to impose himself on us coercively, and coercion, which is different from judgment, is against his nature. Those who trust in him are not thereby systematically spared evil's painful whiplash, for they live in a world enmeshed in sin, their own and that of others, and sin's concrete effects cannot easily be undone; but, penitent as they will be if they are in a relationship of obedience and trust with him, they stand under God's forgiveness and are saved from divine condemnation and undoubtedly protected from many of sin's effects as well, though this may not be readily discernible. The Holy Spirit deepens them as persons through their trials and keeps them from nihilism and despair, even while correcting them and changing patterns of behavior seen by God to be egocentric and destructive of love.

So the God revealed in Jesus Christ is *Judge* as well as *Savior*. These two dimensions of the divine being go together, and together they demonstrate God's omnipotence. Human sin is a failure of love and entails its own pernicious consequences. These consequences are stitched into the fabric of the world by its Creator, no less than the physical laws of the universe. However they may work themselves out, they constitute the inevitable judgment that falls upon any deviation from the norm of love.

Only the Creator of reality has the power and authority to intervene and amend that reality if, as has happened, one of its features—human freedom—has been distorted by sin, with deadly consequences for the whole of creation. Humanity's ambition to perform this salvage operation itself through utopian constructs of a political or technological nature is an extreme manifestation of the very evil it is intended to redress. God alone can alter what we call fate and undo the inevitable consequences of a bad attitude or action. He alone can forgive us our sins, deliver his human creatures from guilt and the judgment of slavery to sin and death, and create in us new hearts inclined to love him and love our fellow human beings. As *Creator*, he judges the sinner according to the moral logic he has built into the world; as *Redeemer*, he intervenes to pardon, save, and renew, according to his gracious mercy and his understanding of every individual human heart.

While in both these cases, as Creator and as Redeemer, God's omnipotence is operative, the ultimate expression of this power is present, paradoxically, in the complete abnegation of power in the worldly and temporal sense by Jesus, the Son of God incarnate, before his human judges, and in his acceptance to be crucified by them in absolute weakness. The power of sin and death, which in this world expresses itself in the power to dominate others by coercive force of one kind or another, is overcome by the greater power of love (John 14:30–31, 16:33): Jesus freely and humbly lays down his life for the world (John 10:17–18; Phil 2:5–8), gives himself up to God to be made sin for our sake (2 Cor 5:21), absorbs in his person the worst that man can do to man, and then is raised up by God through the power of the Spirit of holiness (Rom 1:4; Phil 2:9). Life, which is greater than death, works by the holiness of love, which is greater than material power. Life/Love/Holiness conquers death/power/corruption and *redeems*, just as, in the beginning, life/love overcame chaos and the formless void and *created*. This is the supreme manifestation of divine omnipotence and the definitive judgment of sin under the form of perverted human power.

If God did not judge sinners in this life and in the final judgment in the fullness of time of which the Scriptures speak, *justice* would be absent from the world and evil would triumph; and if he were not gracious, if he did not show mercy to the penitent—to those who hunger for mercy and who show mercy to others—*love* would be absent and evil would triumph. Both justice and mercy are present in the world, of course, woven into its structures; and they are present, ironically, in some of the actions of the same human beings who desecrate them.[38]

Made in God's image, we are not bereft of these qualities, though we regularly pervert both. But because of this moral doublemindedness we cannot redeem ourselves or fundamentally reform our behavior. In Christ, God's very image incarnate, who was like us in every way except that he was without sin and loved God and all his human neighbors with an undivided heart, the Lord God has undertaken to do this on our behalf. That is the meaning of the cross. The Messiah took upon himself freely the judgment and penalty for the sins of mankind, condemning condemnation itself to the grave and so manifesting supremely God's omnipotence and his essential nature of love and opening the way to resurrection and the triumph of life.

Two other aspects of omnipotence remain to be pointed out. We spoke above of God's immanence in connection with his mysterious plurality. Here I want to suggest that his *immanence* is an aspect of his omnipotence. He is *omnipotent as he is immanent* in his creatures since in some way every one of them, from the smallest particle upward, will reflect him, its Creator, and be sustained in being by him. Surprisingly to us, perhaps, God's omnipotence, in implying immanence, may thus be said to involve *intimacy* and

---

38. God, of course, does not act solely within the Judeo-Christian framework. His Spirit broods over the whole earth and moves on hearts open to righteousness, mercy, and kindness, whatever their cultural and religious traditions. Romans 2:14 is a basic text pointing to the "righteous Gentile," the pagan who—made in God's image—lives by the law of conscience and, accordingly, demonstrates moral sensitivity and responsibility, even while falling far short, as all of us do, of the demands of God's holiness.

intrinsic involvement with his world. This truth underlies the possibility of incarnation, where God in Christ comes amongst us as one of us and then sends the Holy Spirit actually to live within us, in what the Bible calls our hearts, in a real and not just symbolic sense.

Secondly, omnipotence must never be dissociated from *goodness*, inherent in God's love. God is limited by his character: as good, he cannot do or endure evil; as love, he cannot act unjustly or cruelly; as rational, he cannot act irrationally or arbitrarily; as faithful, he cannot break his word or alter his purpose; as merciful, he always seeks to give us grace. But these limitations in no way detract from divine omnipotence; rather, they qualify it and disclose its inner moral dynamic.

The concept of omnipotence is in itself impossible for finite mortals to grasp. The idea of the sheer act of creating *ex nihilo* or of raising another from the dead may give us a hint of what we designate by this concept, but even that idea is quite beyond our intellectual reach. All we can say about such an act is that the power to do it must be unlimited (except as suggested above), altogether beyond any analogy with power as we experience it *within* the creation. What we may be sure of, on the basis of revelation and of the structures of the natural world, is that the fruit of divine omnipotence is, as goodness, the opposite of chaos, and becomes manifest in order, beauty, and redemptive love.[39]

It is, finally, as noted above, God's redemption of mankind through the cross and resurrection of Jesus that provides the ultimate manifestation of omnipotence within the confines of history. The power to overcome death and bring forth a new creation *within* history—first Jesus the Christ, then those who long for him in their hearts (whether they know it or not) and so will be raised with him in the life to come—is equivalent to the power that brought forth light and matter out of nothingness "in the beginning." Creation and new creation—manifestations of sovereign love—are the work of the *omnipotent God*.

---

39. It is becoming apparent in our day that what seem to us at one level to be chaotic, disorderly, or haphazard phenomena, at another level may be seen to demonstrate patterns; at the very least, such a contingency is subordinate to and incorporated within the more inclusive horizon of order and coherent orientation. In the universe as we observe it, contingency is best understood as a constitutive aspect of law. The orderly shape of the whole logically points in the direction of intelligent design.

XI

The God Revealed in Jesus Christ—the Creator—is Purposeful; the Purposefulness of Organic Entities and Systems; Teleology in the Universe, as Focused in Humanity; Human Self-transcendence and its Perversion

God the Creator is also revealed to be *purposeful*. Obviously, purposefulness is implicit in the concept of creation, as its opposite is implicit in the concept of chance.[40] As, starting with the rise of deism in the seventeenth century, the concept of autonomous nature gradually displaced that of God-dependent creation, and as the Creator God, disconnected from his handiwork, receded from the human mind and finally disappeared over the horizon of unbelief, teleology was extruded from science and replaced entirely by the schema of cause and effect. Most unreasonably, yet wearing the mask of reason, impersonal chance (plus time) was called in to assume the mantle of the personal Creator God; as surrogate divinity, chance became the causal agent of the universe. The absurdity of this, in the light of the wondrous complexity and order of this universe, is only now beginning to be recognized by honest thinkers.

The biological and biochemical discoveries of the last century, combined with the astrophysical discovery of an evolving universe, should lead to a reconsideration of the place of teleology in the physical universe. Purpose is inherent in order and beauty. This affirmation which, empirically speaking, we may make initially on the basis of the phenomenon of life and, supremely, of *human* life, may be projected backward retrospectively and made with reference to the inorganic universe as a whole, in view of the fact that *life has emerged out of this universe and cannot therefore be altogether in discontinuity with its principles.* If purpose is to be found in living beings, we are entitled to infer that it is inherent in nonliving beings insofar as they are part of a larger, coherent context and are characterized respectively by their own forms of order.

Now, organic entities and systems are *intrinsically* purposeful and functional. With the increase of information in the universe and in particular in living organisms (for whose causality, it should be noted, no empirical explanation exists; we can only point to the obvious evidence for it in the process of cosmic evolution), the purposeful functions become ever more complex, culminating in the astounding complexity they assume in human

---

40. The existential implications of this fact are far reaching in light of the modern worldview based on chance, which, by implying a world without underlying purpose, must inevitably lead to a sense of meaninglessness.

beings. It is perfectly reasonable to argue, therefore, that the universe as a whole is indeed purposeful and that its purpose is focused in humanity—not in human beings alone *by themselves* (hardly a thinkable notion if one actually places humanity in the context of the evolving and interlocking universe that twentieth-century science has disclosed to us), but in humankind *as made by God for the purpose of fellowship with himself and stewardship over the rest of his creative handiwork.*

The astonishing capacity of human beings, acting purposefully, to study and comprehend to a considerable extent the structures of the objectively existing universe, is further evidence for the special relation of man to God, expressed in the *imago Dei*, and of both man and the universe to their common Creator. The concept of purpose, springing from the Creator's initial purpose in creating matter, is by far the most plausible tool in the effort to explain how it is that mankind, arising from within the context of the universe, should have the ability to examine and make sense of the structures of that very womb from which it (man/woman) emerged.

The same applies at the moral level, in connection with what might be termed the ethical dimension of cosmic order, i.e., natural law. The symbiosis of created beings—their fundamental mutuality and dependence—from photons to plants and animals and finally to humans, which together form an integral whole, can best be understood as the structural form love takes in the universe. This love, supremely fulfilled and manifest in Jesus Christ, the incarnate image of God, guarantees and sustains the order, solidarity, and creativity in the universe. It is this love that grounds the objective moral order of the world and that human beings, made in God's image, are hardwired to intuit both out there and within themselves, and then to reflect in their societies even if in their rebellion toward their Creator they often move in the opposite direction and manifest separateness, fear, and hatred. Even in our own day, when the ideology of the all-powerful individual and his/her personal desires reigns supreme, there is still, generally, a belief that some things are absolutely wrong and must not be done. This arises out of the human conscience and points to the reality of law, of order, that exists beyond ourselves and is not a matter of human convention or an invention of human reason and will. Only the *imago Dei*, pointing thus from within us to the God in whose image we are made, can account for this inherent apprehension of natural law and order, of an objective, transcendent, metaphysical reality that exists in the very nature of things and is in no way—intrinsically—a human construct.

Man (man/woman), like every other living and acting organism, does nothing without a purpose; but the purpose of his existence transcends him and cannot be discovered without revelation from the Creator. The book of

Genesis—whose promises are fulfilled in Christ—provides this revelation. The self-transcending thrust of human beings, our movement ever outward, beyond ourselves, toward infinity, the impossibility of our settling down in time and space, our dynamic openness to the ever-receding horizon of the future—all this bespeaks our inherent spiritual orientation, dissatisfied as we are with material reality alone and craving union with the personal Creator in whose image we are made.

It is precisely the rebellion against this vocation, through the misuse of the moral freedom that makes such rebellion possible, that leads to humanity's split personality and divided soul and to the tragic nature of human history. We want to make self-transcendence equivalent to divinization, so we transmogrify our God-given purpose of communion with our Creator into our self-assigned purpose of replacing God with humanity and of refashioning the human race and the whole creation in our own image. We thus refuse the limits imposed by God to the self-transcendence he himself has imparted to us. This condemns us to idolatry, to the investment of culture, necessarily finite, with ultimacy, to which we then cling as to God himself—for only in relation to an ultimate can we find meaning and identity. And the outworking of this is that anyone who differs from us becomes an enemy to be resisted and even destroyed. By immanentizing absolutes, which we are driven to do as we seek to put ourselves in God's place, we open ourselves to never-ending conflict and war and, in the modern age, to ideologically motivated genocide and terrorism.

XII

The Metaphysical Implications of the Twentieth-century Discovery that the Universe had a Beginning and Will have an End

One last point—a metaphysical one—needs to be made before we proceed to a consideration of the *imago Dei* itself.[41] Until the last century, most Western thinkers operating in the Greek tradition and, at least in their cosmological reflections, outside of the biblical orbit where a beginning and end of the natural order were explicitly posited, assumed that the universe—i.e., matter—had existed forever and, in the cosmic regions beyond our galaxy, was fixed and unchanging. Twentieth-century astrophysics has disproved this assumption and shown incontrovertibly that all empirical entities have a beginning, an evolution, and a death, or dissipation into disorder. The

---

41. For this discussion, see Tresmontant, *Sciences de l'Univers*, chapter 1.

known and projected evolution of our sun—a typical star—provides a kind of template of this state of affairs. The cosmos has a beginning; it evolves; it will have an end. Both the belief in the eternity of matter and the theory of continuous creation of matter, have been proven untenable by astrophysical observation. Whatever shape current thinking about the so-called Big Bang may take in future, the observed expansion and alteration of the universe is now an established fact of natural science.

The natural-historical question of the beginning of the physical universe is different from the metaphysical question concerning its origin. This latter is not amenable to scientific inquiry. Rational reflection shows that, since *nothing* cannot produce *something*, there must always necessarily have existed some absolute being. The question is, what is the nature of this being? Materialists have always posited that it is the material universe itself. But as we have seen, modern science has ruled out this possibility, since it is now evident that the material universe has a calculable age roughly in the order of fifteen billion years. The cosmos has not always existed. This means that it cannot be the necessary absolute being, since it is impossible for that which has not always existed to spring into being out of nothing. Some eternal being must be prior to the material universe and must be the source of its existence.

When we affirm, in the biblical tradition, that God created *out of nothing*,[42] we are not saying, of course, that before the creation there was nothing. Before the creation, God was/is. The creation is just that, a *creation*, and derives from a Creator who existed prior to it. It has, logically, no other possible source. The question, "What was before God?" is a pseudo-question, strictly unthinkable. Equally unthinkable, when one actually examines it, is the notion of absolute nothingness.[43] Just as the emergence of life and of irreducibly complex organic systems cannot reasonably be attributed to chance, but points to design and hence, by inference, to a Designer, so the appearance of *being* under the energetic forms of light and matter can neither reasonably be declared to have arisen by chance from nothing, nor, any longer (in light of twentieth-century astrophysics), be said to have existed forever. The evidence both of science and of careful metaphysical analysis points incontrovertibly in the direction of a Creator who, at some point, through the power of his creative Word (we will never be able to say more about the origin of the cosmos than that), brought the space-time universe into being. This leaves materialists with an insoluble dilemma, which goes

---

42. See 2 Maccabees 7:23, 28; Romans 4:17; Hebrews 11:3.

43. Tresmontant, *Sciences de l'Univers*, 40, points out that Henri Bergson argues this persuasively in the last part of his *Evolution Créatrice*.

far to explain why they prefer speculative fantasy—usually in broad-brush evolutionary mode, with scant attention to scientific detail or metaphysical logic—to serious reasoning.

XIII

That Man/Woman is Made in the Image of God—*imago Dei*—is an Ontological Affirmation, Given by Revelation and Not Empirically Demonstrable

God created humankind *in his own image* (Gen 1:27). We come now to the specific affirmation in Genesis about the nature of the human person-as-creature. The point made earlier must be stressed again: this is an ontological affirmation—given as revelation—before it is an anthropological one. That is to say, it refers to the very *being* of human persons and not just to qualities that define that being. While we may observe empirically many features in the human being, such as self-transcendence, which suggest that he is greater than his material environment and made for a reality beyond it, we cannot demonstrate that men and women are made in God's image and therefore have inherent and inalienable dignity. Without the word in the book of Genesis, fulfilled in Christ, we would not know this. Consequently, where we do not know this truth for want of access to the revelation of it in the Judeo-Christian Scriptures, or because of refusing to receive this revelation, we do not know ourselves in our essence, we do not and cannot really know who we are, which goes far to explain why, in our natural state, turned in upon ourselves rather than toward God, we so often treat each other with cruelty and contempt, unless we have reason for doing otherwise.

Likewise, without revelation of who the human person is as *imago Dei*, the traces of love, trust, and goodness found in society have no ultimate explanation or reference and are, in a profound sense, unintelligible, as is the capacity of human beings to comprehend the structures of the universe. The moral order of which we spoke above and the correspondence of the human mind to the rational order of reality make no sense. Even if we sense that love and rationality translate a spiritual reality to which we belong, that reality remains opaque. Just as humanity-in-rebellion-against-God cannot know God personally simply by looking at and embracing the natural world, even though, as the psalmist puts it, *"the heavens declare the glory of God"* (Ps 19:1), so human beings cannot know their true nature and vocation simply by self-analysis. They are lost in the forest of life, surrounded by wild animals. They will try to escape, understand, or dominate/manipulate, but without divine self-revelation, witnessed in Scripture, they cannot really know what is going on or what is at stake.

Divine revelation opens our eyes to reality. What we see is God's love and redemptive mercy, and, in the light of these, our high calling as well as our present brokenness. God comes to seek us out in the forest of life, to save us from our lostness, confusion, and spiritual death, and to lead us into the fullness of our being and calling. Revelation, as an act of love, is the disclosure of truth that we could not know by our own reason. We are reminded here, again, of the depth of meaning in Jesus's word about himself that he who is the plenitude of God's self-revelation as love is the "truth"; in him is the presence to us of being itself, who is life and love, to be known not by conceptualization but through the Father by the power of the Holy Spirit. *"Blessed are you, Simon Bar-Jona,"* cries Jesus to Peter after Peter has declared his Master to be the Christ. *"For flesh and blood has not revealed this to you, but my Father who is in heaven"* (Matt 15:17).

XIV

Revelation Must be Received by Faith; Trust, Not Doubt, is Primary, Since Knowledge can Only be Acquired within Some Kind of Prior Fiduciary Framework; Mistrust of God Leads to Mistrust of Man/Woman and to Violence

This revelation must be received by faith, which is our response of trust. Doubt, as the post-Cartesian epistemological principle of modernity, mistrusts trust as a vehicle for the acquisition of knowledge, and in fact, as we have seen, banishes it from the epistemological sphere altogether, not seeing that some kind of "fiduciary framework," as Michael Polanyi puts it, is the starting point for all knowledge, including scientific knowledge.[44] Much of our knowledge of reality is tacit, presupposing an extensive, unconscious investment in the world before we do any thinking or doubting at all. This presupposes trust as the basic human posture. Doubt, and the analytical power that accompanies it, is a secondary movement of the mind, necessarily following on a prior trust.

If we do not place trust in our self-revealing Creator, we will place it in some finite power or, as in much post-Nietzschean philosophy, in the glorification of power itself: physical strength, military prowess, religion, kingship, the nation-state, reason, history, the scientific method, the laws

---

44. Polanyi, *Personal Knowledge*, 267.

of science as we discern them at a point in time, art, technology, the will to achieve, our subjective feelings. These finite entities then risk becoming idols, which is why atheism is the most idolatrous of creeds. All of them are, of course, open to doubt, but—if we are operating this way—we may doubt them only by shifting our trust to something else. The modern age, following Descartes, has effectively done this by shifting its trust to the method of doubt itself.

Furthermore, since human nature and destiny are not merely finite, as the revelation of the *imago Dei* teaches us, confining the objects of our trust to finite entities forces us into Procrustean beds too small for us, and which are of our own making. Such an experience can only misshape us and lead to alienation and violence. The sequence of events in the Genesis narrative is telling. When, at the instigation of the snake, Adam and Eve (representative man and woman) distrusted—doubted—God's goodness, the object of their trust shifted from the Creator to a creature: to themselves first, their own emotions and reason; then, in addition to themselves, to an entity outside themselves—but still a creature—signified by the serpent.

By trusting themselves and then the snake, and then by doubting God, they came into the knowledge of good and evil, which means, in effect, that they became subject to evil as well as to good. The way was thus opened to endless variations on the theme of idolatry. In the last 200 years, the human presumption to be able to establish what is evil and what good, without reference to God or to natural law, has led to ever-growing violence and corruption, as idolatry has been magnified into ideology.

Having used their moral freedom to disobey, Adam and Eve and their progeny became enslaved to evil passions, which is the fate of man in his pretension to be autonomous. God, having been repudiated by their doubt, could no longer fully protect them from the consequences of their own sin. He remained with them, immanent in his creation, but his *fellowship* with them was broken and, to be restored, would have to await God's merciful plan of redemption through the Hebrews, culminating in the Messiah, Jesus.

XV

Mistrust of God and Rebellion Do Not Efface the *imago Dei,* but Invert it; Communion with God is Replaced by Alienation, Competition, Self-sufficiency; the Ideology of the Autonomous Individual; Man and Woman and Human Relationality

The *imago Dei* was not effaced, but it was *inversed*. Instead of the joy of communion with their Creator, men and women would henceforth know rather the misery of their alienation. They would be lost in the forest of life, moving in perpetual conflict toward death rather than enjoying the garden of the world and moving in peace toward life. The peace of creation would be replaced by the struggle for power, by which human history has been defined. Prayer, the natural, Spirit-taught first language of human beings created in God's image, would give way to religious practices of appeasement of the (unknown and feared) deity and, as human mastery of the world increased, to the defiance of the clenched fist and the indifference of agnosticism.

The evil that men and women now knew soon manifested itself in violence, when Cain, trusting only his own feelings and judgment and doubting God's goodness as his parents had done, killed Abel out of jealousy. This is the picture of the human condition, manifest in world history. The modern person, desperate and enraged at his moral impotence, but at the same time feeling his new power as *homo technicus*, wants to break out of finitude altogether, *but in his own strength*. He wants to change the Procrustean beds, the room, the whole house, the landscape itself, even his own nature—*but in his own strength*. And that is the rub. For if the infinite Creator God can accommodate the finite, having made it, the finite creature cannot *by itself and on its own terms* accommodate and appropriate the infinite. The dilemma is a logical one before it is a moral one. But in the sphere of human relations, it leads to tyranny.

As God is, mysteriously, plural in his unity, so also is humanity made in his image: "*male and female he created them.*" The plurality-in-unity of the one is reflected in the other, in such a way that the repudiation of the Trinitarian God revealed in Christ will eventually entail a repudiation of man/woman as made in God's image. When something of which something else is an image is repudiated and fades from consciousness, the image itself must surely soon be repudiated and fade from consciousness as well.

The relation of male and female in mankind is vastly more than what it is in the animal realm. The personhood of individual human beings arises out of their being in relationship, constitutively, just as the persons of the Trinity, while distinct, are and act as they are in relationship. It is, of course, the ontological relationship of human beings with God revealed in the *imago Dei* that grounds this primary resemblance. We are *social* beings. The individual-as-autonomous-unit is an abstraction and does not exist in reality.

The next step in understanding the inherent relationality of persons clearly involves our human sexuality. Primordially this relationality is made manifest in the relation between man and woman. Man and woman complement each other and so make a whole, and that whole is humanity.

They are called to multiply and fill the earth and, as (made in) God's image, represent to the rest of creation the Creator of life. The blessing that God gives them (Gen 1:28) is intrinsically associated with their fertility, through which they will be able to fulfill the mandate of stewardship given to them by God in the creation. This is one reason why the unisexual, androgynous vision, rooted in individualistic narcissism and working itself out in our day in homosexual ideology is, while appearing at first sight harmless compared with some other forms of social behavior, one of the most profound expressions of rebellion against God the Creator, though we must add immediately that particular *individuals* in today's disturbed and upside-down culture cannot necessarily be blamed for the directions their desires may have taken them from an early age or even from birth, for one reason or another. The cultural conditioning and social pressures at play here cannot be overestimated, and the matter is far too complicated to permit of quick judgment.

But by opposing sexual mutuality, it must be said that this way of thinking and acting flies in the face of God's created order and pattern for the human race—and for the *good* of the human race—as revealed in the Judeo-Christian Scriptures. As a result, any society that actually *promotes* it—beyond the rightful respect, compassion, and legal consideration toward individual persons involved in homosexual lifestyles—is bound to come under God's judgment in some way, whether one thinks of that judgment as direct or indirect.

Here the modern ideology of the autonomous individual, which views individuals not as persons-in-relation but as basically self-contained and self-sufficient units, reaches its culminating point, precisely for the reason that the paradigm for the traditional and universal understanding of individuals, formulated in the scriptural revelation and manifest in the natural instincts of human beings always and everywhere, is the complementary relationship of man and woman, manifesting itself primordially in the institution of the family and the blessing of children. It is in this complementary relationship that men and women, and the societies they constitute, may flourish and find the greatest happiness and fulfillment possible in this world. *Wilfully* to oppose and repudiate this foundational order of creation can only result in a steady increase of social discontent and hostility, gender confusion, tension between the sexes coupled with an unhealthy and misguided flattening out of differences between men and women, sexual confusion among children mirroring that of adults, massive identity problems, moral decline and promiscuity, and general disorder.

XVI

Reflections on Homosexuality

It is not the purpose of this essay to examine the many reasons for the rise of homosexuality in Western societies or to reflect on this issue in doctrinal and pastoral terms, though this certainly is a task the church must undertake far more boldly and systematically than it has done up till now. I refer interested readers to my own book, *The Episcopal Church, Homosexuality, and the Context of Technology*, which addresses these questions more extensively. In our day we are facing a novel situation, quite unprecedented. The wars of the last century; the pace of technological innovation; the perceived dissociation, ever since the introduction of the pill, of sexual expression and procreation; the exaltation of erotic pleasure and organismic ecstasy as things-in-themselves and as surrogates for spiritual transcendence and separable from the personal being of the sexual partner, with the result that the *other* becomes a manipulatable object; the rise of an individualistic understanding of freedom and self-fulfillment; massive social changes and the large-scale loss of religious faith, leading to the breakdown of the traditional normative family structure (more or less extended, depending on the culture and on social conditions) and to major shifts in the way men and women, fathers and mothers, relate to each other and to their children; and, not least, the jettisoning by much of the Western church, in practice if not necessarily in theory, of the moral teaching in the Scriptures on this issue, along with the theological grounding for this position—these are among the many interrelated factors contributing to this new situation. New understanding and fresh approaches are required.

Homosexual and gender radicalism, as an ideological movement, is only one facet of a widespread affirmation of homosexual activity in contemporary society. This development is part of the modern Western militancy in favor of individual rights and of an ethic based on no objective reference whatsoever but on personal preference and choice.[45] A supermarket mentality in a commercialist society of abundance can no longer conceive of or even be interested in an objective standard of the *good* or the *right* that might override personal preference. Moral discourse is no longer a matter of applying reason to ethical behavior; instead, sentiment, inclination, and impulse, informed and undergirded by what technology makes possible, govern ethical decisions. Consequentialism rules: this means that actions are considered in themselves to be morally neutral and to be bad or good solely in terms of their perceived consequences, evaluations of which are, at least initially, the prerogative of the individual agent and therefore necessarily subjective and short-sighted.[46] The laws of the state and judicial rulings, not divine revelation or moral reasoning, fix the only boundaries external to the individual that are generally recognized. The power to impose one's view through political, economic, juridical, and media pressure, divorced from any objective moral yardstick that might constrain it, becomes the determining fact in ethical issues. This makes inevitable the rise of increasingly bitter and polarized social and political ideologies.

The effort to end and correct hatred, injustice, and violence committed over the centuries toward homosexual persons is the positive and commendable aspect of what is happening today in Western societies. The biblically based Christian opposition to homosexual practice in no way condones the kind of treatment homosexual persons have often received in our society. Gay persons, though a small minority, must surely be guaranteed the same respect, dignity, and social rights that the heterosexual majority has a right to expect. But that does not mean or imply that the biblical injunctions against homosexual practice are to be dismissed as no longer relevant and set aside. The church must explore more deeply and make clearer to itself and to the public at large the theological meaning and social significance of the biblical prohibitions.

A complex of causes underlies the inclination some men and women have or the decision they make to embrace a homosexual way of life. Among contributing factors, there may be strains and emotional distortions in

---

45. An insightful analysis of this development as an aspect of what he calls "Liberalism transformed into a Tradition" is provided by Alasdair MacIntyre in his magisterial account of the several traditions of justice in Western civilization, entitled *Whose Justice? Which Rationality* (see especially 335–48)?

46. See Banner, *Christian Ethics*, chapter 9, for a penetrating theological discussion of homosexuality in contemporary society and its relation to Pelagianism and the modern ethical doctrine of consequentialism.

family relations, sometimes going back generations and exerting their influence even on unborn babies; there is no scientific evidence for the existence of a homosexual gene, but pre-natal influences upon the fetus can certainly occur; sexual abuse in early life is not uncommon; and, determinate in the contemporary context, there is the influence of the prevailing social and ideological climate, along with deep structural pressures and social constructs informing modern society as a whole. Such people are, needless to say, no better or worse than heterosexual persons and deserve no less of our compassion. Like other people who fall prey to what the church has traditionally considered illicit sexual practices not in line with God's perfect will and rooted in the disorder resulting from original sin, they are to be welcomed in our churches, exposed to the gospel, and encouraged to seek reconciliation with God through Christ and the consolation, soul-healing, and transformation that God the Holy Spirit can undoubtedly bring them, provided they are prepared—as others seeking reconciliation must be likewise—to let themselves be *loved* and *affirmed*, and also *disciplined*, by their heavenly Father. In this respect, the gay person is no different from the person naturally attracted to the opposite sex. Both, in their natural state, are self-focused sinners, alienated from God, psychologically disordered in many respects, and needing the redemption and restoration that can only come through Christ and that leads to the true inner fulfillment each longs for.

Self-hatred—often unrecognized or suppressed—is common to the homosexual condition, so that gay persons who find Christ and come out from under inner condemnation may experience a peace and a sense of well-being that they have never known before and that passes understanding. Frequently a lack of love and affirmation in early life underlies their emotional yearnings, which inclines them to identify their sexual *tendency* with their sexual *identity*. This inclination will be accentuated if there is a *denial* of the lack of affirmation in early life, when, as is so often the case, there *really was such a lack*. Repression of reality must be exposed if new life is to become possible. Those who receive Christ's love *find their true identity in him* and are affirmed as greatly valued sons or daughters of God the Father. At the sexual level, they may have to struggle to lay hold of that identity for themselves, but their inner disorientation and the wayward impulses arising from it will, in almost all cases, substantially diminish in their lives as they aim to follow Christ.

The fact that many homosexually active people are seeking, with another man or woman, precisely the kind of committed personal relationship they have failed to find or desire with the opposite sex (including, increasingly, the pleasure and responsibility of raising children), demonstrates the power of God's intention that human sexuality express, and make possible, completeness, *wholeness*. The fundamental human need and hunger for family is manifest here. But in light of the systematic analysis we are undertaking in this essay, it should be obvious that this attempt to find human wholeness in a homosexual relationship, laudatory though it may be in its intention (that is, in its quest for wholeness) and subject though it may often be to God's mercy as the partners truly do seek faithfulness and love, is intrinsically misguided, whatever satisfactions, even happiness, it may actually procure, at least for a time, for some of the individual persons involved. Existentially speaking, it must inevitably be a substitute, a *pis aller*. And here again I insist: it is through Christ and only through Christ that the plenitude of the love that gay persons are seeking in their relationships can be found, enjoyed, and sustained.

An individual success, it should be noted, cannot be generalized and made the basis for viewing heterosexual and homosexual relationships as equivalent. Far deeper theological issues must be taken into consideration, for which a judgment based on particular experiences and informed chiefly by the current ideology of individualism and the satisfaction of one's personal impulses and desires, whatever they may be, is utterly inadequate. Like cannot complement like, even if at the level of character traits there is wide differentiation and balance. The relationships, even if there is adoption and the building of surrogate family bonds, are biologically sterile by definition. They simply cannot be in conformity with the divine mandate given to man (male and female) to procreate as a species, to reflect the plurality-in-unity of the Trinity, and so to be a vital representation of God the Creator. Distortions in the perception of reality—personal, social, theological—must necessarily result from this and will become evident in the long run.

Such relationships cannot therefore be recommended as a sexual option *equivalent* to heterosexual relationships. They constitute an effectual denial that the basis of human reality and creativity is the relation of two sexes, two genders: male and female, man and woman (clearly, most gay persons engaging in such relationships have no notion of the spiritual significance of what they are doing and will object that such a denial is certainly not their intention—but their objection cannot alter the objective reality). This denial is a form of idolatry, a repudiation of God's created order and his holiness, which is why the Levitical law and New Testament texts condemn homosexual behavior so strongly (e.g., Lev 18:22–29, 19:1, 20:13; Rom 1:18–27). The inverted use of the sexual organs in homosexual practice is the manifest image of this repudiation. All forms of idolatry are sterile and cannot produce life. Homosexual practice exemplifies this at the biological level. It is a refusal to live in accordance with the physical design of one's body, thus setting in opposition one's biological and psychological identity. This is then justified by appeal to desires and urges, which are said to arise irresistibly from one's orientation even when that orientation runs counter to the physiology of the person. We have here another form of mind-body dualism, where the person's mind, feeling its peculiar urges and impulses, assumes against the physiological evidence that this designates the person's true and irrevocable identity. Mind and body are separated, and the disunity, despite the inner conflicts it creates, is taken as normal and right and in any case incorrigible. I am not denying for one moment here the existence of the urges and impulses of the orientation, but I am denying that it corresponds to the person's intrinsic sexual identity.

These considerations point to the *inner meaning* of homosexuality, regardless of the best intentions a gay couple may have, or of any temporary satisfactions such practice may procure to those indulging it. Undoubtedly there can be genuine *affection* between two gay persons living together, but to call their relationship a marriage, or their sexual engagement a union of *love*, is simply to distort the meaning of marriage and of sexual love. Both of these terms signify the being together of two opposite and complementary sexes. It is a manipulation of reality, a presumptuous artificialization of God's created order. The argument that one is born gay and that one has no choice but to give in to one's inclination because that is who one is, is a misconstrual of reality, a categorical repudiation of God the Creator. God creates *life*, not sterility.

The same-sex attracted person has the same choice as his/her heterosexual counterpart to engage or not in a sexual relationship. In our modern rationalistic—if not rational—world, irresponsible sentimentality, coupled with moral blindness, reigns over wide swaths of our social behavior. The quest, in the name of individual rights and "pleasure", to overcome all traditional moral limits and social distinctions—to legitimize, in effect, whatever one wants—is actually undermining our institutions, most notably marriage, and creating a virtually totalitarian conformism that stifles *true* difference and diversity while pretending to glorify them. The word "discriminatory" is wielded like a weapon to quash rational exchange over differences. The ideology of egalitarianism is undermining, not building up, our democracies. With regard to homosexuality, whatever the causes underlying same-sex attraction, such attraction arises within a *fallen* world, a world subjected to futility and, on account of our race's rebellion against our Creator, under the sign of death (Rom 8:19–21). This is why the *effectual* liberation from homosexual orientation and practice is to be found only in Christ who, as our substitute and representative, took our sin upon himself on the cross and whom God the Father, by the Holy Spirit, then raised from the dead, so that *in him* we might have *life*.

I am aware of the difficulties and the pain this view of things raises in our society. I recognize the struggles a gay person who has not found Christ and who yet does not want to enter the gay lifestyle will have, either singly or as joined to a partner, and yet who at the same time and quite naturally yearns for some kind of sexual experience. For a heterosexual person who in our day is encouraged to engage in sex quite independently of marriage, and who can marry and have children if he/she wants, to tell a gay person that he/she ought not to marry, or have sex, with a person of his/her same sex, sounds cruel and unfair. It is on the basis of this perceived injustice, of course, that same-sex marriage has been legally accepted in the West, along with the possibility of adopting children or arranging to have them through some kind of surrogacy.

But the church has much more to say than this to the person with same-sex attraction. We are not talking here about legalistic/moralistic decrees. What it has traditionally taught about homosexual practice is based on what it believes to be divine revelation in the sacred Scriptures of the Hebrews and Christians. On the strength of its conviction that God the Creator is good and knows what is good for his creatures, the church declares what it believes to be good for human beings and for society. It cannot impose this, nor ought it to try. It recognizes that to the ears of a secular modern person, gay or not, this declaration, with respect to homosexual practice, is perceived to be authoritarian and unjust. *But—and this is absolutely crucial—for the secular modern person to stop there is to miss the point and fail to see the good news that underlies the church's declaration.* For with its teaching, the church also declares that those gay persons who are unhappy with their estate and who choose to open themselves to receive Christ as Savior can, through God's power and love, be set free to a considerable extent, perhaps entirely, from their orientation, or at the least from the inordinate pressure of it, and can engage in what they will now consider, happily and gratefully, to be a "normal" lifestyle, as celibate or married persons.

The church as an institution has, like any institution, its own constitution, structure, and constraints which are peculiar to it and neither imposable on nor transferable to society at large. It does not today speak laws to society as it did in the age of Christendom. It speaks what it sees to be divine truth and grace, and argues (or should do) the theological rationality of its case as carefully as possible. As the spokesman, so to speak, for Christ, it challenges society, as Jesus did in his day—not to mock it, but to set it right in accordance with what it believes to be divine truth intended for mankind's good. *The declaration the church makes to society is not cruel or unjust when understood in this larger context, at the center of which is Christ the Savior of mankind.* Society is entirely free to accept or reject this declaration, of course. If Christ did not provide, through his passion and resurrection, a joyful plenitude of life impossible outside of his redemptive love, the church's stance in the midst of a secular society (a very different context from that of theocratic ancient Israel, where the whole population was subject to the Torah revealed by Yahweh to Moses) would understandably appear to be an instance of mere moralism, unrealistic and unjustifiable for that reason. Worse, it would misrepresent God by making him out to be a legalistic autocrat, a notion unthinkable in ancient Israel and utterly unbiblical. But—hallelujah!—Christ is risen, Christ is alive, and he pours out his grace on those who wish to receive it and become new creations in him.

On the basis of what I take to be the revelation of a righteous Creator, it is my conviction that the long-range deformations and fractures in a society that widely indulges and abets homosexual practices and unions and misplaces them, in the interests of a political ideal of equality and individual preference, on the same level, ethically and juridically, as normal heterosexual relationships between men and women, must be incalculable. Any such society, is, I believe, in the throes of illusion and decadence and vulnerable to increasing oppression from government, with the state assuming more and more importance as over against the family, if only to contain the rising social confusion generated by seemingly unlimited varieties of gender identity and sexual orientation and the rights being demanded on all sides. Expressive already of deeply strained relations between men and women, such practices can only exacerbate these in the long run and lead in the direction of moral anarchy and social disorder.

This is not to say for one moment that heterosexual relationships are always happier or more successful than homosexual ones, or that such relationships in countries with little tolerance for homosexuality are ideal or even better than those in Western societies. The Islamic world, with its traditional and often abusive subordination of women, is a case in point. Sin has radically perverted heterosexual relationships in every culture, as men and women have flouted their Creator and sunk as a result into disordered positions and attitudes with respect to each other, often marked by domination, fear, manipulation, and cruelty, both physical and psychological. *Precisely this reality in the West today, and elsewhere, is a major cause of the increase in homosexual practice.* Men and women, while having much in common, of course, are very different from each other, and a lifelong, happy marriage is difficult to achieve in any culture. Enormous adjustments are required by both partners. If it weren't for the promiscuity that characterizes the lifestyle of many homosexuals, one might be tempted to argue that homosexual bonds must be easier to sustain precisely because gender complementarity, with the challenge and tension this entails, is absent. It would seem to be the easier road to take, since, as far as gender is concerned, the other is the same, so that the effort needed to understand the other and adapt to him/her is far less arduous. On the other hand, boredom and the resulting contempt must also inevitably play a part in any relationship that is inclined to be narcissistic, be it between an individual focused on himself/herself or between two persons of the same sex. Long-lasting and monogamous gay relationships are rare, and surely God welcomes the good—the real affection—that may be found in them and in those persons who sustain them, as he welcomes good wherever it may be found; but that is no reason to argue that, as such, relationships of this sort involving sexual expression out of line with God's created order accord fully with the divine will and should be viewed, ethically speaking, as normative in the same sense as healthy heterosexual relationships.

Marriage between a man and a woman, normative by nature and tradition in every culture, is an institutional reality involving generation and filiation and insuring the future of a society. To call marriage just a contract between two persons of the same sex who simply want to live together and who cannot engender children of their own, is a subversive confusion of categories. Equality between these two relationships is impossible because they are two entirely different realities; each is what it is, they are not comparable; to call them equal is a deception, a verbal sleight of hand justified neither institutionally nor rationally, that can only have the long-range effect of undermining the institution of marriage, and with it the moral coherence, even survival, of a society. The meaning of what we call family is at stake here. In truth, there is no such thing as a homosexual marriage. Legal pronouncements will not make it otherwise.

I must insist again at this point that the quest by homosexual persons for full acceptance in society and for equal civil rights, for the democratic rights due to all minorities with respect to employment, housing, access to social services, legal protection, military service, sports, etc., is not for one moment being called into question here. In no way am I saying that such persons, as individuals, are inferior human beings or should be discriminated against by law or custom, as has often been the case in the past. But the issue of marriage is of another order, on another level. Marriage involves procreation, generation, filiation. The matter of *children* comes into play. One is not talking just about individual adult persons and their rights. One is talking about an *institution*, the most fundamental of all, in that it insures the continuance of society. All institutions have limits, definitions, constraints, as I indicated earlier, and are not to be watered down into incoherent mishmashes on the basis of the individual rights or desires or preferences of the persons who make them up. This is preeminently true of the institution of marriage.

It is not the place here to pursue these reflections further, but surely they merit more debate. We must conclude this discussion by saying simply that human relations between men and women, though sometimes admirable and wonderfully fulfilling, are on the whole very far from the complementary love and respect willed by God at creation, according to the revelation of the *imago Dei*. God's great gift of human sexuality is disordered; its expression is often unholy and needs to be redeemed through Christ quite as much as every other aspect of fallen, self-focused humanity. As to homosexuality, the Bible is clear from beginning to end that God the Creator is against homosexual practice, for the reasons I have suggested. In no way does that mean that he is against persons who experience same-sex attraction, whatever the cause may be. God loves us all. He created us in his image. He longs for our fellowship through his Son, Jesus Christ. Christians are called to proclaim this and to act accordingly with respect to gay persons. The church's welcome mat should be open to everyone. This has rarely been the case in the past, regrettably. Fear or contempt toward homosexual persons is unacceptable and should never be found in the church.

But that does not mean the acceptance of homosexual practice itself without demur, without a call to repentance and to changed life, just as the church is bound to make with regard to any other ethical behavior not in keeping with sacred Scripture. It does not mean what has come to be called inclusivism, which tends to put a sentimental gloss on gay unions and then takes the high moral ground by declaring the scriptural injunctions to be obsolete, even hateful. The Scriptures are not targeting same-sex attracted persons who obviously can be as admirable, kind, and charitable as normally constituted persons attracted to the opposite sex. The Scriptures are targeting homosexual *practice*, with its inversion of the normal, God-created use of the male and female sexual organs. It is the *theological significance of this inversion* that I have tried to elucidate. A misconstrued idea of justice and love on the basis of egalitarian ideology must not be allowed to override the word of God: "But just as he who called you is holy, so be holy in all you do; for it is written: 'Be holy, because I am holy'" (1 Pet 1:15–16). It is through the grace and power of Jesus Christ that gay persons and heterosexual persons both can become holy.

XVII

The Superiority of Human Beings to Other Animals is Obfuscated by the Ideology of Egalitarianism; the Loss of the Concept of the *imago Dei* Removes the Ontological Grounds for Affirming Human Rights and Abets the Now Common Practices of Euthanasia and Abortion; Egalitarianism Secularizes and Undercuts the Equality of All Human Beings before God

Both man (man and woman) and the animals, including the birds and fish, are characterized by fertility, and in this way the priestly writer of Genesis 1 conveys the proximity of human beings to other animals. Both are formed from the ground, as the Yahwist tells us (Gen 2:7, 19). But the distinction of man from animal, and the superiority of human beings to animals, is made absolutely clear, both by the priestly writer in chapter 1, through the *imago Dei* and the accompanying mandate to rule over the creation, and by the Yahwist in chapter 2, through his account of God bringing the animals to man *"to see what he would name them"* (Gen 2:19).

The power to name—the power of language—is the fundamental expression of the *reason* that characterizes man as made in God's image, that is, in the image of him who creates by his word. The Yahwist makes this distinction between man and animal even more decisive by showing, through his narrative method, that no animal could be the "suitable helper" Adam needed (Gen 2:20). The "woman," like the man but distinct, was brought forth from Adam's own side to be, quite exactly, *beside* him. In this way the Yahwist conveys the specialness of man, as a species and as an individual, and the mutuality of man and woman, generally and particularly.

The contemporary trend among animal rights advocates to place human beings and animals on the same moral level—a trend that overlaps disturbingly, if not surprisingly, with the advocacy of abortion, even live-birth killing, and of euthanasia, and with the tendency associated with these two practices to propose arbitrary criteria for what constitutes personhood on the one hand and a worthwhile life on the other—arises from the egalitarian ideology to which we have already alluded.[47] This ideology, linked closely

---

47. Advocates of euthanasia in the strict sense of mercy-killing, i.e., putting to death out of mercy, fail to recognize the ontic value of the human being (of which the true ground is the *imago Dei*), for whom death is a part of life essential to the completion of that life and over which God alone, the Creator, legitimately has power. Causing to die—euthanasia—is, whatever its motive, basically different from allowing to die, in which case the medical staff, seeing that no more therapeutic care can improve the

with the ethic of rights that is the dominant moral reference in the West today, parts company decisively with the Judeo-Christian vision of man as made in God's image, a vision that, as we have seen, places man in another spiritual and ontological category altogether from animals. To the extent that the animal rights movement seeks to eliminate cruelty to animals and treatment of them as mere exploitable material for human productivity, it is admirable and fully in keeping with our human vocation, as made in God's image, to oversee and care for the rest of creation. But when the movement veers into proclaiming the equivalence of moral human beings and other animals, it lands squarely in unreality and absurdity. That some animal rights advocates actually deny the right to life to unborn fetuses and to persons considered defective is a flagrant example of the perversions to which the rights ideology can lead.

The irony here is patent, and strikes to the heart of the current moral crisis of Western civilization: the dignity of the human person, and the equal dignity before God of all persons, is rooted in the *imago Dei* teaching of Scripture, and the human rights movement, admirable in its basic thrust, has ultimately no other ground than this teaching. If one abstracts the *imago Dei* revelation from anthropology, no sure ontological basis remains for affirming that human being and human life are sacred, or for arguing, in consequence, that all men and women have certain rights. The contemporary rights movement, unmoored from its ultimate anchorage, then becomes a free-floating entity, subject to arbitrary manipulation and open to special interest claims rooted in the ideology of individualism, such as, to give three examples, the moral equivalence of homosexual and heterosexual lifestyles, the equal rights of animals and human beings, and the right (subject to very few medical conditions) of a pregnant woman to have an abortion more or less on demand, quite apart from legitimate considerations arising from incest, rape, irremediable deformity of the fetus, or real and not trumped up threats to the mother's physical and mental health.

---

patient's condition and that death is inevitable, disallows medical procedures aimed simply at keeping the patient technically alive and allows the person to die naturally. Coupled with measures to alleviate pain, this is a true expression of mercy because it allows the dying person to experience his or her own death without presuming to short-circuit it by intervening in what is, with life itself, the greatest of all mysteries. At the other end of the spectrum from euthanasia is the technological manipulation of a patient for whom it is certain that no recovery is possible, in order to keep the patient alive at all costs. While masquerading as respect for life, this approach is in fact idolatry of life and arises from the unhealthy combination of pride in technical prowess and fear of death. It is as much a denial of God's sovereignty over the life and death of the patient as is euthanasia: in both cases, human beings are playing God.

This latter claim, widely used in contemporary society to serve as a birth control method and stopgap to deal with the consequences of irresponsible and hedonistic sexual behavior and to avoid the onerous responsibilities of raising a child, shows scant regard for the living fetus in the womb and, underlying that, betrays ignorance or contempt for the dignity of the human creature made in God's image, if that creature should happen to be in the way of the mother's and the father's personal comfort.[48] Nor does it take into consideration the proven psychological harm of an abortion to both mother and father, which assumes the form of guilt, lower self-esteem, and anxiety (though this may be repressed and denied), coupled sometimes with the bitter fruit for men of impotence and self-doubt about their right to be fathers,[49] and for women, the later difficulty, often experienced, of conceiving a *wanted* child. Rights claims such as these are specious and can only distort the principle of justice underlying the rights movement as a whole and lead to conflict and mistrust between competing groups all demanding their equal rights, and to a corresponding decline in the sense of citizenship and mutual responsibility.

What we see happening, in a word, is that the grounds for affirming human dignity are being undermined at the same time that the ethic of rights, which depends fundamentally on this very affirmation of human dignity, is being raised to the level of a moral absolute. Indeed, the emphasis on human rights, in itself commendable, is fast becoming in the West the dogmatic centerpiece of a kind of civil religion. Positively, this emphasis undergirds and makes possible the pluralism of democratic societies, even while serving as a unifying counterweight to that pluralism and a force for social stability, much as reason did in the eighteenth century. The danger is that it becomes a new form of idolatry and is subverted by special interest groups, precisely to that degree that its basis in the Christian revelation is rejected. This is what is happening. We are confronted here with an

---

48. The interminable discussion about when the fetus begins to be a human person worthy of consideration as a viable entity with a right to live has always seemed to me to be a massive red herring, revealing only the shameless contortions of people trying desperately to justify an indefensible biological and moral position. From the moment the zygote implants itself in the uterus, the human person is genetically present and on the way to fetal growth, birth, and extrauterine life in the world. There are no discontinuities, no moments when this material becomes a person. The search for such qualifications of personhood or viability perfectly demonstrates my thesis that the loss of the ontological understanding of the *imago Dei* leads to self-serving quibbling and prevarication in search of qualities that may provide an elusive and manipulatable definition of what it means to be a person.

49. The negative effect of an abortion on fathers is rarely discussed. A cogent analysis of this taboo subject is provided by Guy Condon and David Hazard in *Fatherhood Aborted*.

ideological tendency that bodes ill for the future, for a house divided against itself cannot stand.

The same holds true for the notion of human equality, which is being hijacked and distorted by ideologically driven egalitarianism. Human beings, if judged qualitatively on the basis of criteria such as intelligence, beauty, wealth, cultural inheritance, social standing, performance, manual dexterity, physical strength, or quality of life, are obviously not equal and never will be. Nothing in Scripture suggests that such equality was ever the divine intention. What Scripture does teach is that all men and women are made in God's image and are therefore of equal value in his eyes, whatever their qualities, accomplishments, or existential circumstances. This means that they are mutually responsible for each other and morally accountable to God for the way they treat each other. Egalitarian doctrine secularizes this teaching, severing man from his Creator, with the result that no reference remains for the equality being claimed other than the political power needed to enforce that claim and impose conformity to whatever arbitrary criteria the ascendant political power demands. This, a disguised form of fascism, is a recipe, once again, for totalitarianism and leads, as does fascism, to the loss of a sense of mutual accountability and responsibility. This loss can often be seen today in many areas of Western society, most obviously in government, business, and education. Power imposes some kind of equality; what doesn't fit is set aside, mocked, or suppressed.

XVIII

Love Brings Harmony because it Does Not Base its Judgment of the Other on the Criterion of Qualities; in Christ, Where He is Acknowledged and Followed as Lord, Ethnic and Gender Distinctions are Transcended and the Inverted *imago Dei* is Righted and Lived Out

In a world of equal human dignity and widely differing human abilities and conditions, the only cement capable of really holding people together in harmony is love. Love does not judge others on the basis of qualitative criteria. It recognizes all other beings, animate and inanimate, to be creatures bearing the Creator's imprint; and it recognizes human beings in particular to be made in the Creator's image and therefore to have inherent and inalienable dignity. Where the *imago Dei* is not recognized or honored, various man-devised criteria—such as intellectual acumen, ethnic, religious or class affiliation, wealth and social usefulness, and physical viability—will be imported to determine the relative value or worthlessness of human beings, as individuals and as groups. Those in a given society who do not fit these criteria will be marginalized, perhaps destroyed—one by one, as in the case of medical policies inspired by eugenics or by unconditional abortion on demand, or by entire groups, as in the case of genocide. Pride, jealousy, fear, and self-interest, working through power and manipulation, will increasingly take the place of love as the operative principles of human relations.

It is in this context that Jesus Christ, the image of God made flesh, who revealed to us God as he is and humanity as it should be, bequeathed us a gospel in which, for those who adhere to him truly, there is *"no Greek or Jew, circumcised or uncircumcised, barbarian, Scythian, slave or free, but Christ is all, and is in all"* (Col 3:11); or, as the apostle Paul puts it in another epistle, slightly differently: *"There is neither Jew nor Greek, slave nor free, male nor female, for you are all one in Jesus Christ"* (Gal 3:28). Only in Christ, who reveals and fulfills the transcendent goal of human life, are human beings able to live both within and beyond the differences and inequalities that define them in their existence on earth. Only in him and through him, by the power of the Holy Spirit, is it possible to live in the fullness of love within and across all human boundaries and natural identities. Whereas in social life as we know it, in a world not synchronized with God's will, differences of class, race, tribe, gender, or age are frequently a source of division, in God's kingdom, where Christ is acknowledged as Lord, they are experienced as complementary gifts and constitute a wellspring of diversity.

At its most exemplary, when it is really living out the gospel, the Christian church and those who live by its truth do actually manifest this reality of love, won for humanity by Jesus. The reversal of the *imago Dei* effected by human rebellion against the limits imposed on him by the Creator is here righted, and the social harmony possible between an infinite number of individuals, unequal in condition but equal in dignity as human creatures, is realized. Such social harmony is undoubtedly what our modern pluralistic democracies, based on reason and the rule of law, aim to demonstrate in a secular mode. But there is no other ultimate root than the Christian gospel for such an achievement—an achievement, that is, whose foundation and possibility depend on God's grace, faithfulness, and mercy, not on humanity's often perverse reason and inconstant behavior—and the question must be asked as to whether, or for how long, this admirable secular achievement can be sustained if its spiritual ground is eroded and finally denied.

XIX

Human Freedom and Reason, as Well as Human Dignity and Unity, also have Their Ultimate Basis in the *imago Dei*; True Freedom and Love are Indissolubly Linked; Jesus Christ Exemplifies and Demonstrates Both

It becomes clear from this discussion that the unity of human beings, as well as their dignity, have their ultimate basis in the *imago Dei*, and nowhere else. This is equally true of human freedom and reason, both of which have often been used in the past to define what is meant by the *imago Dei*, and serve frequently in the present as the chief points of reference in order to understand the nature of man.

Freedom, like human dignity, can properly be comprehended only in relation to love. It is not a quality but rather a state—a state of being open to and for others. *Relationality*, not independence, is its defining mark. Like reason, it is integral to the *imago Dei* understood not as a composite of qualities, but as an ontological, relational reality. While freedom from adverse constraints is indeed crucial to the exercise and hence to the meaning of freedom, this aspect of freedom is not its essential parameter. The true human person, created in God's image, is a person free to love, that is, free for a healthy love of self—which is the opposite of egocentricity—and so free for self-giving to others (including God), as God is free to love himself—Father and Son in one Spirit—and free to give himself to the other-than-himself, which is his creation. The true human person is free to love and serve others, as he or she is aware of being God's creation and *therefore beloved*. His or her identity as a free being is not something to be achieved or proved by an assertive will to power, but rather to be *received gratefully as a gift* from the Creator. It is through Christ that fallen humanity, shackled by self-centeredness, is set free to love fully—to love God, self, and others. Jesus takes upon himself the sin that holds man prisoner. *"If you hold to my teaching,"* he says to his disciples, *". . . you will know the truth, and the truth will set you free. . . . Everyone who sins is a slave to sin. . . . If the Son sets you free, you will be free indeed"* (John 8:31-32, 34, 36). This is not to say that a measure of freedom and love is never to be found outside of an effectual personal relationship to Christ. Of course not. The *imago Dei*, even if distorted in its manifestation, assures us of this. It is to say simply that the *fullness* of inner freedom and of the movement out of self toward others in love is to be found only in and through Christ and his work in the human heart, already in this earthly life and absolutely in the life to come.

The link, or union, of freedom and love is seen primordially in God. It is God's creation and redemption of the world, revealed to us by his word, that allow us to speak of his freedom, and it is precisely in these free acts that we see his love and perceive his nature to be love itself. Jesus Christ, God's image, shows us what freedom and love mean in and for human life, and how they wrap around each other as strands of a single rope; as God incarnate in a human being, he demonstrates how the Sovereign Lord intended man to be and to act as reflection and representative of his Creator. That person is least free, then, who thinks of himself as autonomous (this can only be a pretense, of course, since no individual can possibly be autonomous). Freedom manifests itself as solidarity, service, self-giving—all expressions of love—thus showing forth the life of the Trinitarian God.

XX

The Christian Gospel, Despite the Frequent Distortions of it by the Church, has Provided the Matrix in Western Society for the Vision of Human Dignity and Rights that is Beginning to Resonate in the Rest of the World

Fallen man could not possibly have come into this freedom—true freedom—without God's self-revelation to the Jews and supremely in the Jew, Jesus, Israel's Messiah and the Savior of the world. *"Salvation is from the Jews,"* Jesus said to the Samaritan woman in John 4:22a. As Jacques Ellul has persuasively shown in *Trahison de l'Occident*, political freedom as imagined by the Greeks, and institutional, civic freedom as imagined by the Romans, were basic acquisitions of Western culture,[50] but the matrix in which, over the next millennia, these freedoms were to take shape and slowly penetrate first European civilization and then the entire world—as being ideals proper to all men and women and basic to their fulfillment—was provided by the Christian gospel rooted in the Hebrew Scriptures, with its insistence on fundamental and universal human dignity as envisioned in the doctrine of the *imago Dei*. No matter that the church itself did not always perceive the

---

50. Ellul, *Trahison de l'Occident*, 31–35. Ellul makes the point that there is nothing natural about our modern notions of the free individual. Man is born with moral choice, as we have seen; he can choose against God and truth. But the political and social freedoms that he enjoys in the West today—and that the rest of the world fights to have—are altogether human constructs built up slowly in the West—and only in the West—on the basis of this primordial moral freedom revealed in the Judeo-Christian Scriptures and coupled with the power of reason that are constitutive capacities of man as made in God's image. They are not givens, and they may easily be lost.

link between this doctrine and what we today call human rights, or that the hierarchical churches, for theological as well as institutional reasons, were inclined to oppose the democratic right to self-determination that we tend to take for granted in the West today: it remains the case that the truth of the equal and fundamental dignity and worth of every individual human being was carried forward in Western society, century after century, in the womb of the church, by its Scripture-rooted proclamation and teaching and by the celebration of the sacraments, even if the behavior of Christians and their institutions did not always reflect the spiritual reality of which they were the bearers.

The thinkers of the eighteenth-century Enlightenment, in their quest for a social order based on a wider distribution of human rights and political freedom, may have thought themselves to be doing this in opposition to the Christian dispensation, but in fact the contrary was the case. In response to the religious wars of the previous centuries and to a reactionary church that in many parts of Europe was losing its way and failing to propagate the gospel of grace, in my view they were in fact—at least as regards this issue—instruments of the Holy Spirit, however imperfect, to bring to birth in Western society and then later across the world, after centuries of gestation, the concept of equal human dignity and freedom—along with some of the social consequences that the actual appearance of this idea entailed, an idea that had long been maturing in the body of Christ (i.e., the *church*). The fact that the birth of this new concept was perceived to be the fruit of secular and not of Christian thought changes nothing as to the truth of the matter. The French and English philosophes were, in this matter, the Holy Spirit's midwives, though certainly both they and the church would have found such a notion bizarre. Unbeknownst to themselves, they were used by God to work out his purposes in human history.

XXI

Reason and Love as the Bones and Blood of the One Humanity; Both Can be Distorted: Love into Possessiveness and Hate, Reason into Rationalism; Freedom and Reason, Operating Together in Love, Bring Coherence, Meaning, Direction to Human Life

Human reason may be understood essentially in similar terms. The unity of humankind—and indeed of the whole created order—arises from God's rational act of creation. Since this rational act is an act of love, as we have seen, it follows that for human beings created in God's image, those acts will be most rational—and most free—which are most loving. The bones and blood of the one body of humanity are reason and love.

Paul Avis speaks of "the mind's inherent power to discern and impose form, pattern, relations and analogies on the data presented by the senses."[51] Human beings are gifted by the Creator to establish coherence between what goes on in their minds, at the tacit and the conscious levels, and the world outside themselves. At the conscious level—the level of constructive reason—both intuition and inference operate with the given data of sensory experience, at one and the same time discovering and fashioning meaning and knowledge.[52] Neither subjective nor objective language is able fully to do justice to this astounding capacity. *Relational* language is necessary since, once again, the human being as made in God's image has been set by God in ontological relation with himself *and also with the world* in order for it to be possible for him/her to fulfil the Creator's mandate to be the earth's stewards. "Corresponding to the openness of experience," Avis writes, "there is the rational process by which we respond to its complexity, unpredictability and interrelatedness . . . the important thing . . . is to recognize that in perception the mind is actively engaged in a process of interpretation and construction."[53]

Language is reason's vehicle, as I have suggested. Reason and love together enable human flesh to dwell happily within the multiple relationships by which God has structured reality, and to live and thrive in freedom. Both are universal in scope, and both require a transcendent orientation, focused in God, to generate harmony among men and women. When either is appropriated by some local, tribal, or ideological interest, the two become separated; each is then distorted and can turn into its opposite. Love, for example, becomes possessiveness or idolatry and can degenerate into hate; reason becomes an end in itself, leading to a covetousness of knowledge for its own sake, or to analysis with no balancing sense of synthesis, or to

---

51. Avis, *Ecumenical Theology*, 14.

52. Avis's summary of intuition deserves to be quoted here: "Intuition is an essential component of every act of inference. All knowledge is inferential: there can be no by-passing the senses and the mind's work of interpretation and construction. But the process of inference is only made possible by the intuitive principles of causality, analogy, probability and so on. I use the word intuition for the directly and immediately apprehended rational principles presupposed in all thinking, and the word insight for those swift and subtle acts of reasoning, often loosely called intuitions, that employ subliminal or habitual inferences but that nevertheless can be distinguished from the more formal, explicit and disciplined processes of inference that are the prerogative of the trained mind" (Avis, *Ecumenical Theology*, 18).

53. Avis, *Ecumenical Theology*, 15.

materialistic/reductionistic positivism which, in its two-dimensionality, simply denies the existence of any reality that does not conform to its own arbitrary criteria for what is real.[54] In such cases, the resources of reason will be subverted and used to further basically irrational ends that will controvert and undermine freedom.

Freedom and reason, in a dynamic balance of creativity and self-mastery, are God's gifts to humanity, enabling men and women to establish coherence and meaning, to exercise self-criticism, and to go on continually reaching out beyond themselves. By virtue of them, human beings are able to live dynamically in time, always transcending their immediate condition, that is, always, *in the present*, going out from the past into the open future.

XXII

Perversion of the Freedom to Love into the Power to Dominate; Manipulation of History and Language; the Threat of Uniformity and Totalitarianism; Totalitarian Uniformity, Religious or Political, is a Counterfeit of True Unity in Christ; Murder Forbidden, Not Because of the Other's Qualities, but Because He/She is a Brother/Sister by Virtue of the *imago Dei*

When, in rebellion against finitude, human beings cut themselves off from the transcendent God in order to assert their own autonomous self-transcendence, they put themselves in the dangerous position of needing to achieve God-like control over reality—including, pre-eminently, over their

---

54. Positivism is a kind of negationism, and is by no means foreign to the specific negationism that always accompanies genocide. Its basis is the arbitrary exclusion of a reality that one is ideologically predisposed not to recognize. It is, at bottom, a covert form of the lie, essentially similar to the explicit lie constituted by the negationist's denial of genocide. To the extent that the whole structure of scientific/technological civilization is founded on the reductionistic principle of rationalism that only what is observable, quantifiable, provable, or mathematically determinable can constitute knowledge, thus excluding by definition the spiritual and moral realms as being beyond reach of what is knowable and, consequently, as being, at bottom, unreal, mere constructs of human imagination, it must be said that this structure is founded on an untruth and will therefore inevitably dehumanize man-made-in-God's-image by cutting him off from the divine and reducing him to a shadow of what he is. It is the burden of this essay to suggest that this is in fact what is happening as scientific/technological positivism takes possession of every aspect and detail of human life, imprisoning humankind in a narcissistic bubble. See, in this connection, Philip Sherrard's *Eclipse of Man and Nature*.

fellow human beings—in order to demonstrate, through a simulacrum of omnipotence, their divine vocation. Manipulation of the present, and hence of the past and future, becomes the norm. History is rewritten and in modern times man-made utopianism replaces God-ordained eschatology. The human being's freedom to love is perverted into power to dominate others, and a deviant exercise of rationality becomes the potential means to accomplish this end. Language itself, which is the chief vehicle of rational communication and the effectual means to human self-transcendence and achievement, is co-opted by ignoble political, commercial, or philosophical[55] ends and debased. God's creative Word, and the word of his human creatures who, fashioned in his image, are able to speak and act analogously to their Creator, are distorted and made the tools of manipulative propaganda.

What the modern revolutionary age has come to call ideology then becomes the characteristic orientation of politics, whatever shape such politics may take in a given culture. Since ideology—reductionist, exclusivist, and absolutist all at once—always partakes of some utopian ideal in imitation of the kingdom of God, history becomes a matter of domination and control by those who exercise power, not as God's representatives, legitimately, but in God's place, by usurpation. War and slavery in a variety of forms become the *basso continuo* of human social existence. Those who enslave are also enslaved, imprisoned in violence. And so we arrive at the modern political

---

55. It is not the place here to critique deconstructionist theory, but it should be obvious that the radical refusal of any posited coherence between thought, word, and object, and the rejection of any kind of correspondence between linguistic constructs and objective reality, in favor of a delirious hermeneutical subjectivism that makes of every human word and statement an arbitrary pronouncement subject to infinite modification and interpretation and lacking all objective reference—as if the determinations of linguistic convention, simply because of their being conventional, were therefore necessarily bereft of any kind of objective meaning—are themselves purely arbitrary gestures and forms of philosophical posturing that can move about in the arena of discourse solely on the basis of the reason they presume to denounce and discredit. It is precisely man's reason and his power to name that enable him to make of linguistic convention an effectual image of reality and system of correspondences that allow for transsubjective interhuman discourse and action. This is a kind of objective reality. Personalist thought, which is intrinsically relational, can account for it, but radical subjectivism, which is the reductionist perversion of this thought, can only deny it. What is pejoratively called arbitrary linguistic convention, far from being derisory and worthy only of ridicule and deconstruction, is a rational vehicle for achieving communication between persons and coherence between their thought and the world they inhabit. Deconstruction theory, with its metaphysical two-dimensionality and its entrenched disdain toward reason and language and their aspiration to both discern and posit some sort of objective reality, is another symptom of the wholesale loss of trust in Western civilization. Across the entire spectrum of human life, doubt rules. Ours is the Age of Suspicion. A healthy civilization cannot be sustained on such a basis.

aberration we call totalitarianism, which is the extreme form of the tyranny that is latent in the exercise of political power. The uniformity that totalitarian regimes always try to impose on their people is a caricature—another *counterfeit*—of, first, the fundamental unity of God-created humanity and, second, the unity of the new humanity in Christ, represented (not always faithfully, as we have seen) by the redeemed but still sinful people of God, the church, the "*Israel of God*" (Gal 6:16). Totalitarianism, where death and destruction are the rule, is the ultimate political perversion and, as such, the definitive manifestation of the kingdom of man and the diabolical counterfeit of the kingdom of God.

The remarkable text in Genesis 9:5–6 makes it clear that human dignity and the divine prohibition of murder consequent upon it, are founded on the *imago Dei*: "*For your lifeblood I will surely require a reckoning; of every beast I will require it and of man; of every man's brother I will require the life of man. Whoever sheds the blood of man, by man shall his blood be shed; for God made man in his own image.*" Murder destroys the unity and dignity of the human person and is a direct affront to God, in whose image the person is made. God's judgment is manifested through the vengeance taken upon the murderer, and the human desire for vengeance may in some sense be seen as perverted evidence of human value and dignity. Human systems of justice, again, are rooted in the ontological reality of the *imago Dei*. There is no mention in Scripture of qualitative or quantitative reasons as such for not slaying one's brother; rather, we are not to slay him precisely because he is our brother, a co-member with us of the one family of man created by God in the divine image and thereby possessing infinite worth.

In the Christian tradition, a dichotomous understanding of man (man/woman)—on the one hand, as a rational animal with an autonomous life of its own, and on the other hand, as a special creature called to communion with God—has a long history going as far back as the second century. It can be argued (though space does not allow me to develop this point here) that this view is the source of the dominant understanding, or misunderstanding, of the *imago Dei* within the church itself, which has tended to conceive of it qualitatively in terms of an ontic disposition, defined in particular and essentially by moral freedom and reason, rather than in terms of an ontological relation—of which freedom and reason are inherent aspects—of the whole human person to the personal Creator God. This distortion, due in no small measure to the influence on Christian theology of Greek philosophy and its equation of divinity and rationality, has had incalculable consequences, some of which we have glanced at in this essay.

The ontological relation of man to God is the source of the possibility of both incarnation (God becoming man) and resurrection (humanity being united with God). By this relation, we are by our created nature lifted toward God's love. Our longing for God is rooted in the *imago Dei*. By thinking of the *imago Dei* in qualitative terms, focused on the faculty of reason, the church has been inclined to formalize the relation of man to God, emphasizing—as the basis for articulating the restored communion between man and God achieved through Christ's saving work—liturgical acts and adherence to dogmatic propositions instead of the prior ontological reality posited at creation. The result has been either a sacramentalization or an intellectualization of the Christian faith, to the detriment of the personal relationship with God through Christ that has its ultimate ground in God's creation of humanity in his own image. Sacrament and dogma both obviously have a vital place in the Christian faith and life, but they cannot in themselves be the basis for our communion with God: they are *vehicles* of that communion, not the communion itself.

XXIII

All Creatures, as They Participate in Being, are Mysterious; the Mystery of Human Beings, Made in God's Image, is Deeper than that of Other Creatures, for We are Rooted in Eternity; this Gives Us Ground for Hope and Can Energize Us and Focus Our Sense of Responsibility for Each Other and Our Planet; Since All We have is Gift, Our True Vocation is to Give and Serve

All creatures, God-made, are mysterious, for they participate in *being* and cannot be comprehended or defined merely by enumerating their properties, even if this were possible. That a thing *is*, is a reality utterly beyond our ken. Prayerful contemplation and great art (in whatever medium) may lift us into the presence of this mystery inherent in an object and may establish between us and the object in question a connection. This connection will be founded in love, for only love allows us to make an authentic connection with an *other*. With our mind, through our senses, we will grasp the matter of the object; with our emotions we will embrace it; with our spirit we will sense the mystery of its being and sense the divine within it and beyond it. It will stand before us, autonomous, independent of our consideration, and yet at the same time, and by virtue of our own God-given powers and divine mandate, in mysterious relation to us and caught up with us in a kind of community.

The mystery of the human person is far deeper than that of other creatures. Made in God's image, we participate in his infinity. We are spiritual beings. Every man and woman is unfathomable, open in principle, through his or her spirit, to the Spirit of God, and so open also, in communion with the Author of all being, to range upon range, dimension upon dimension, of reality. This is the freedom we are made for, our *destiny*: our destiny lost through sin—that resistance to the infinite God which locks us into finitude, death, idolatry, and despair—then recovered by Jesus Christ, the infinite God who became mortal man for the sake of humanity and was raised to life by virtue of his obedience, in order to save us from narcissism and its infernal consequences. Man as *imago Dei* is rooted in eternity and called to praise and worship God his Creator and be with him forever. This is the source of the self-transcendence that drives us ever onward and upward. Our being and destiny, individually and corporately, are eschatological, that is, they go out beyond the frame of this space-time world and find their home in God. As mountains and stars and the vast reaches of space signal, emblematically, the eternal and the infinite, so God's whisper to our spirits actually brings into our presence the personal Creator of this matter, and we become aware that, though dust, we are eternal, and that, though yet far from home, we are loved. To speak of the *imago Dei* is to speak of our human destiny unto everlasting life in love.

And thus it is to speak of hope. For all its febrile agitation, ours is a despondent age. The West that has repudiated its religious heritage is sad. We have no real hope. This is to be expected, since we have jettisoned transcendence. We are thus fundamentally disoriented and without true vision. Hope placed in material/technological or political progress is not without value and significance, of course, but it is necessarily short-term and shallow. Authentic hope must be anchored in the eternal, which alone can provide ultimate meaning, impervious to the acids of mortality. If, irrationally, we refuse to believe in transcendent reality, we will be disinclined to open ourselves to the incarnation of the Son of God in Jesus of Nazareth. Yet true hope is to be found in him alone, whom God has raised from the dead. Through a change of heart, and by identifying ourselves with Christ by faith, we have the promise of forgiveness, resurrection, and eternal life, shared with others in communion with God.[56]

---

56. Men and women are saved by faith in Christ and his redemptive work, as this is followed by and evidenced in acts of love. But since God is the Author of all reality and his Holy Spirit indwells and sustains the cosmos, and since moreover he has revealed himself to be merciful, we are entitled to believe that those who, for one reason or another, have not known or believed in the Christ by whose blood they will still need to be cleansed if they are to stand before a holy God, will be judged according to their

True hope, more than anything else, will motivate and energize us to live lives worthy of God and of our fellow human beings. Fashioned as we are in our Creator's image, we are responsible to him. We may, in our freedom, respond positively or negatively, but we cannot elude our responsibility. Here hangs our eternal destiny. Like all human beings, we stand before him, whether we are conscious of this or not. This ontological truth, coupled with the mandate to rule as God's representative over his creation, implies an ethic, a way of life.

We are called, first, to worship our Creator and be thankful to him; second, to love our neighbor as ourselves; and third, to care for the world we live in, animals and plants and the rocks, soil, water, and air. Our ecological responsibility for the planet is rooted in a proper appreciation of the doctrine of the *imago Dei*, by which human beings are understood to be commissioned by the Creator as stewards of the created world, not in the sense of dominating it abusively, as some critics of the Genesis texts have mistakenly implied, but in the sense of exercising loving and effective dominion over it. We are social beings, persons in relation. We *are* our brother's keeper, as guilty Cain knew full well when he morosely questioned God after killing Abel.[57] And we *are* called to be the earth's keeper, not its destroyer. As God is love, mercy, justice, goodness, generosity, and kindness, so human beings are called to exemplify these qualities. We are called to respect the unity of humankind and the spiritual equality and dignity of every man and woman, as made in God's image and redeemed by Jesus Christ, in whom gender and social distinctions and tribal divisions of all kinds are transcended. Human beings are always to be treated as ends in themselves, never as means.

As God goes out toward others—supremely in Christ—so are we called to do likewise. As God serves, so we are called to serve too, and this, while frequently involving costly self-sacrifice, will prove to be the source of true fulfillment. He has made each of us a unique person, possessing particular talents and propensities. This means that our love and service to God, to our fellow human beings, and to the whole natural world, will run in the tracks of our peculiar giftedness, which we cannot alter. It is in our interest, then, and in the interest of our vocation in society, to discern in what our natural giftedness consists and to act accordingly, with the energy that will be supplied as we develop these capabilities and give expression to our in-built patterns of behavior.

---

acts and gathered into God's people if they have lived in truth according to the light they have received and, like their Creator and Redeemer, have shown mercy toward others when it was in their power to do so, manifesting thus, perhaps unbeknownst to themselves, an inner longing for the true God with its concomitant prevenient grace.

57. Genesis 4:9b.

All is *gift*, as we have emphasized. *"What do you have that you did not receive?"* asks the apostle Paul of the Christians at Corinth. *"And if you did receive it, why do you boast as though you did not"*? (1 Cor 4:7b) We cannot change this, or change the ontological truth about our nature as made in God's image (as postmodernity is trying to do), or change the peculiar giftings and motivations built into the persons we are. We are called to *manifest* these, in interaction with our world. What we *can* change, or allow to be changed by the Spirit of God—to a considerable extent at least, if not always entirely—are the self-focused attitudes and forms of *negative* behavior we have acquired and indulged, often in reaction, whether consciously or unconsciously, to harm done to us by others. Through Christ we have forgiveness and the possibility of new beginnings. As for the wounds we have suffered, God's love will heal them as we open our hearts to him. Our Creator, whom we know through Christ the Son to be our strong and faithful Father and who has for us a tender mother's love, will assuage our souls. We are made in God's image—*imago Dei*—and if we will turn back to him, we may be sure he will receive us as the father did the prodigal son in Jesus's parable, and wrap his wide arms around us in everlasting love.

XXIV

The Decadence of the West and Suffering of the World; Social Disorder and its Counterpart, the Totalitarian Quest for Absolute Control; Jesus Christ—the Very *Imago Dei*—the Hope of the World

The twenty-first century lies before us. We are already well into it. Its tone, already set, is shrill, clamorous, and violent. Accusations and demands fill the air. Lies, fraud, denials of wrong-doing, fierce self-justification, flagrant deceit, refusal to take responsibility, are seen at every turn. Religious ideologies and terrorism flourish. Greed, misery, and corruption are commonplace. Digital addiction is becoming endemic. Pornography is destroying marriages and perverting the sexuality of millions. Drugs and vicious gangs ravage entire countries. Human trafficking and new forms of slavery are on the rise. Millions struggle to survive in monstrous megalopolises. The rich grow richer and the gap between rich and poor, for individuals and for nations, grows wider. Ever-greater numbers of refugees and desperate migrants crisscross the planet. Vast refugee camps have become fixtures on the borders of numerous countries. Whole populations are shrinking catastrophically under the impact of periodic outbreaks of epidemics, various forms of tribal warfare, or ethnic cleansing. Malnutrition erodes the lives of countless children around the world. Climate change and damage to the ecosystems of the planet, with the potential for major meteorological disruptions, proceed apace as technological innovation opens the way for avaricious entrepreneurs, private and governmental, to develop (read "loot") the world, even as species of every kind become extinct each year. Overfishing and poaching threaten the existence of precious ocean creatures and wildlife. Globalized agribusiness depletes soils and impoverishes local populations. Mass tourism degrades precious sites, both natural and cultural. Biodiversity shrinks. Forests vanish. Deserts advance. Droughts increase. Usable water grows scarcer. Fires destroy vast tracts of forest every year. Vicious storms and flooding are more and more frequent and destructive, requiring heavy expenditures to rebuild or replant, way beyond what governments and insurance companies are able to provide. Air, land, and water pollution increase steadily around the world. Coral reefs die. Glaciers and ice-packs melt as the climate warms. Rising ocean levels threaten islands and coastal habitations everywhere. Plastic suffocates seas and shores.

At the political level, parochial self-focus and unhealthy forms of nationalism increase in reaction to the conforming pressures of globalization, to the detriment of the real harmony that could exist between distinctive cultures on the basis of our shared humanity as persons made in God's image. Rivalries between powerful nations are intensifying. Arms sales in every category of weaponry are multiplying. The possibility, even the likelihood, of nuclear confrontation, is mounting. The debt of governments, banks, and corporate entities is growing exponentially. Digital empires on the one hand and drug gangs and terrorists on the other hand are undermining the capacity of nation-states to maintain social order. In response, recourse by states to ubiquitous digital surveillance, with its potential for totalitarian control, is increasing and will soon be commonplace. Anti-Semitism is on the rise again in Europe and America, and Christians in every part of the world, including liberal Europe and America, are coming under attack; in many countries they are already undergoing severe persecution, and this will only get worse. Everywhere there is a sense of crisis, of danger looming. There are wars and rumors of wars. The political and economic policies and social adaptations needed to reverse or even stem all these disastrous trends in the world are so huge and costly as to seem simply impossible and beyond reach, leaving governments and leaders in every sphere overwhelmed by divisive tensions and conflicting imperatives.

The biblical revelation of the *imago Dei*, as we have tried to sketch it in this essay, contains the vision needed to offset the productivist ideology of unregulated capitalism, in both its liberal and its state-driven communist expressions, that is ruining the planet and threatening the survival of civilization. The Western nations that rose to greatness on the basis of their belief in this biblical truth are rejecting it now, out of a combination of arrogant willfulness and ignorance.[58] We must fight to recover this vision. The church must take the lead. It must challenge the reigning ideology at every level and stimulate the many positive forces in our society that are struggling to find answers to our predicament. The church must articulate for those forces the metaphysical and anthropological power of the *imago Dei* vision. As I have insisted in this essay, there is much great achievement and creativity in our age alongside the destruction, and a tremendous increase in scientific knowledge. To that knowledge must be added wisdom.[59] Man made in God's image, though fallen, does retain mighty capacities for good as well as for evil. The political, economic, judicial, scientific, technological, and artistic accomplishments of Western civilization, rooted in biblical truth, do not need to be vaunted; they should be obvious to anyone who observes and thinks. Let me reiterate some of the more recent ones. Since the close of the Second World War, serious efforts to extend the rule of law, promote human rights, end discrimination against minorities, and bring tyrants to justice have been made; huge progress has been made in improving the health and material lot of mankind and in extending the possibilities of human beings to have more fulfilling lives; many organizations, private and governmental, exist today, with the aim of assisting the downtrodden, improving education, and bringing aid in times of crisis; the lot of women is improving in many parts of the world despite ongoing atrocities like weaponized rape and trafficking; ecological awareness is growing—though far too slowly to

---

58. The biblical text from Deuteronomy, addressed by Moses to the Israelites as they were about to enter the Land, is apt here as a warning to the Western nations in our day: "Take heed lest you forget the Lord your God, by not keeping his commandments and his ordinances and his statutes, which I command you this day: lest, when you have eaten and are full, and have built goodly houses and live in them, and when your herds and flocks multiply, and your silver and gold is multiplied, and all that you have is multiplied, then your heart be lifted up, and you forget the Lord your God, who brought you out of the land of Egypt, out of the house of bondage, who led you through the great and terrible wilderness.... Beware lest you say in your heart, 'My power and the might of my hand have gotten me this wealth.' You shall remember the Lord your God, for it is he who gives you power to get wealth.... And if you forget the Lord your God and go after other gods and serve them and worship them, I solemnly warn you this day that you shall surely perish" (Deut 8:11–15a, 17–18a, 19 RSV).

59. One is reminded in this connection of the angel Gabriel's succinct and mysterious statement in Daniel 12:4b (RSV), with which he closes his long discourse to Daniel on "the time of the end" that will conclude with the final judgment and general resurrection: "Many shall run to and fro, and knowledge shall increase." In some versions, the Hebrew word translated here as "knowledge," is translated "iniquity" or "evil."

avert major crises in the offing—along with a concern to care for the planet and not simply to exploit it for profit; the transition from oil and coal to less-polluting sources of energy is gathering strength; initiatives—albeit desultory—on the part of rich nations to help poorer ones are being taken.

All this is admirable. There is tremendous innovative energy available today, stoked by what remains in our culture of a belief in human dignity and the goodness of creation. But despite this, I fear that without a renewal and restoration of the *imago Dei* vision, the dehumanizing forces at work today will continue to gain strength. Without a vision, the people perish. As Proverbs 29:18 puts it: *"Where there is no revelation, the people cast off restraint; but blessed is he who keeps the law."*

The light of Western civilization is becoming darkness. As I have argued in this essay, many of our finest contributions to the world, rooted in the Hebrew and Christian Scriptures, such as the notions of human dignity and the rights of the individual, are in process of being subverted by the lie of human autonomy and self-creation. That this is the case is becoming more evident with every passing year, though many well-meaning people are blind to it because, as mentioned above, gains in areas of justice and material well-being do continue to be made in some parts of the world. The mix of frivolity and frenzy that characterizes so much of modern life—its anomie, hedonism, selfishness, cynicism, and ubiquitous undertone of discord and aggression—is a sure sign of the *angst* and sense of meaninglessness that so many today experience. Addictions and distractions are the mark of the age. People are lonely, empty. Fear stalks. The lie of self-creation is destroying us.

Modern people—ironically, in our era of communication—are increasingly *disconnected* at the existential level: from the true God, from each other, from themselves individually, from the natural world. Nature, and behavior that is natural, are being subverted. Virtual experience in cyberspace is progressively encroaching on real, flesh-and-blood relationships. We live—and this is a major paradox in our materialistic age—more and more *abstractly*, less and less in contact with the concrete, tangible world. This is undoubtedly one of the chief reasons for the pervasiveness in our day of boredom, which itself is the source of so many behavioral excesses like those mentioned in this essay. Solidity, down-to-earthness, continuity—these elude us in our daily existence. Ephemerality, velocity, virtuality, and artificiality are our constants; images flashing by without meaning, sound-bites lacking substance, slogans, propaganda, fake news—these are our normal fare. Mountains of data are amassed, of which two of the chief purposes are to control minds and bodies and to make money. Mankind is living more and more in the realm of the lie and the unreal. Yet the irony should not be missed that the virtual violence on screens—horror movies, video games, etc.—is increasingly being translated into *actual* violence in the concrete world.

The obsession with sex in modern society translates a yearning for genuine physicality in a world of abstraction, but also reveals a surrender to evanescence and the cult of instant gratification, such that in the end it actually feeds the impersonal and the virtual that the focus on flesh and bodies may unconsciously be trying to offset and counter. The human body, as I have suggested in this essay, is increasingly seen as mere material, to be manipulated by the mind for the fulfillment of personal desires and ambitions. Language—at the heart of our humanity—is being co-opted and debased by commercial and political interests, leading to banality and flatness in human discourse. We are losing, even casting aside deliberately, that which, over the centuries, has rooted and nurtured our moral and aesthetic fiber, and this is happening at the very time when Western influence extends everywhere and determines, positively or negatively, the course of the world. *"If then the light within you is darkness,"* said Jesus, *"how great is that darkness"* (Matt 6:23b).

As a consequence, idolatrous aberrations, including the phenomenon of genocide with which we began this essay, are likely to undergo new permutations in the next stage of history. The totalitarian impulse appears to be inherent in technical/technological prowess as this is developed by self-focused human beings. But, to his dismay, modern man is discovering that transcendence cannot be blocked out of human vision with impunity. God will not be mocked. Nor will his creation. We transgress nature's limits at our peril. On every front across the world—politically, socially, ecologically—chickens are coming home to roost. Everywhere there is exhaustion, disillusionment, fear. Man is his own worst enemy, and so long as he excludes from his consideration the God of Israel and the atonement wrought for the human race and the entire cosmos by the Messiah of the Jews and of the whole world, Jesus of Nazareth, his promethean efforts to save himself and create a utopian kingdom on Earth and a new man must inevitably collapse in violence, disorder, and wretchedness. Such efforts, as we have suggested, are a counterfeit of Christ's redemptive work, an attempt to establish unity and peace by the sole exercise of human power.

Only Jesus Christ, God's very image, who is love and truth incarnate, can overcome ideological tribalism and the totalitarian impulse of fallen man. That impulse becomes more far-reaching and insistent as, on the one hand, technological know-how and the illusion of unlimited human power increase, even while, on the other hand, rising dissatisfaction and fear, anarchy, social chaos, and various forms of religious extremism threaten to engulf the human race.

This is what is taking place today. The modern drive to gain control over every aspect and detail of reality—indeed, to *alter* that reality fundamentally—is gaining momentum in proportion to the rising disorder of the planet. The totalitarian impulse is finding new forms of expression, both soft and hard, in an effort to contain the despair, suffering, and anarchy inherent in the ideology of materialism and godless individual autonomy. As I mentioned above, total digital surveillance of every aspect of our lives, along with the technological fundamentalism in the gnostic form of transhumanism—a manifestation of hubris that expresses both a hatred *and* a glorification of mankind—are extending their sway. This will continue, even as in the West we misguidedly trumpet a false vision of freedom. Communism, especially in its current Chinese expression, has much in common with transhumanism. The human race, in its vain effort to redeem itself, is, in a variety of political forms, enslaving itself. Most people are just struggling to cope and are too busy to notice or think about the *meaning* of what is happening, though they may feel in their bones that the times are out of joint and that something terrible is rising. Some few are like those animals near a coast who sense, well before the great wave appears on the horizon, that a tsunami is about to engulf them. The situation that man finds himself in today is tragic. Contending historical forces appear to be gathering to a head, moving toward some kind of cataclysm, in such a manner that authentic Christians—Old and New Testament Scriptures in hand—are noticing more and more the tumultuous signs of the times that will prevail before the return of Jesus Christ. The signs are all around us, for those with eyes to see. The demonic forces of the antichrist are now operating in broad daylight and gathering steam and velocity with every passing day.

This does not mean we must be silent and just stand by, watching as things get worse. Far from it. As I said above, the church must proclaim all the more ardently the Christian good news and the anthropological truth of the *imago Dei* that underpins it. The final phase of what the church calls the end times—the period between Christ's ascension and his second coming—may be approaching. We must evangelize, each of us in whatever way we can. Of course, at the political and social levels, the more genuine dialogue between contending forces that can be initiated and sustained the better, and this is certainly an objective the church should aim at and encourage. Rational discourse, as one of the great gifts the Creator has given to us who are created in his image, should be maximized as over against the ideological passions and sound-bite/Twitter idiocy running roughshod over reason in our day. But reason, even in its noblest manifestations, cannot save us from the forces of fear, pride, greed, self-aggrandizement, resentment, hatred, and sheer despair that fill the hearts of so many of today's men and women. We are fallen creatures, whether we like to think so or not. Reason alone cannot transform us, even if it has considerable power to orient our minds. And science/technology, as one of reason's finest achievements, is a double-edged sword, as we are discovering. When used wisely, it can bring great good, but it certainly cannot save us out of our spiritual desolation. Salvation, now and forever, lies only in the one who is the Image of God, the Messiah of Jews and pagans alike: Jesus Christ. Only he can overcome our alienation, turn us right side up, make of us new creations, and release into the world new streams of life and hope.

Part III

PASTORAL THEOLOGY

Christian Identity: Who Do You Think You are?

(Talks given at St. Michael's Anglican Church, Paris)

Introduction

THE ISSUE OF IDENTITY is very much to the fore in our day. There is a huge spiritual vacuum at the heart of the modern West, which atheistic secularism and militant Islam are working hard to fill. The social and economic chaos that many countries are experiencing, and the violent upheavals in every corner of the world, create a climate of fear and dismay in which these two ideologies—mutually hostile but united in their opposition to the Christian gospel—flourish. In the midst of these multiplying tensions, the sovereign God is judging our culture and purifying the church. He is challenging followers of the risen Christ to rise up and declare boldly, with accompanying works of mercy and spiritual power, the truth that has been revealed to us in Jesus, God's Word incarnate. And in all these ways, I believe, the Holy Spirit is preparing the church, the bride of Christ, for the Lord's return.

If we are to respond to God's call effectively, we must know who we are in Christ. If people ask us what it means to be a Christian, and the difference it makes in everyday life, we must know what to say. We want all aspects of our existence to come into line with God's word. We want *God's* life to enter into every corner of *our* lives, private and public. We want not just to know *about* God and the gospel and our salvation; we want, in St. Paul's words, *"to know this* [Christ's] *love that surpasses knowledge"* (Eph 3:19). In a word, we want to *know Christ*, to be conformed to his image, to live transfigured lives. We want to love and worship God with all our hearts and minds and strength. Doctrine and practice, knowledge and action, are inseparable. The spiritual and the material, the supernatural and the natural, are a whole, a unity, the creation of God; if we separate them, as Western civilization has been doing progressively for centuries and especially since the Enlightenment in the eighteenth century, we court disaster by losing sight of God's presence in the concrete world that we inhabit. *Transcendent* reality is cut off from *physical* reality, then access to it, by reason or faith, is declared illusory, and finally it is denied altogether. Once the conviction of God's *transcendence* disappears, as it has done in the West, the conviction of his *immanence* will disappear too, as it is doing. Eventually, as a consequence, the culture collapses into materialism, nihilism, self-focused individualism, hedonism, and hopelessness.

The ideology of progress, carried on the back of technological advance, has come to replace Christian eschatology, but it can't possibly fill the metaphysical and spiritual emptiness of the two-dimensional culture left behind after God has been banished effectually from public life—hence the rise of countless spiritual counterfeits and false religions, including the false religion called atheism. Hence also the rise of despair, moral numbness, spiritual indifference, drug addiction, and varieties of self-destructive behavior that characterize Western culture today, including suicide. Sometimes, in this dizzying and rootless environment, even Christians act like practical atheists, living a spiritual/material dualism, a worldless faith, where God, relegated to a sphere of pious ritualism, has effectively no place in the structure, orientation, and decisions of their daily lives. Their beliefs have not permeated their *being*, but remain more or less *external to their action*; their lives are compartmentalized; their identity as Christians has little or no impact on the way they actually think and feel and behave.

In our time, as the church of Jesus Christ is opposed more and more deliberately in our society and across the world, we who call ourselves Christians must strike our roots down deeper into the soil of faith, which means into the person of Jesus Christ himself. The aim, then, of these five talks is to sketch a *vision of life in Christ*. The vision is no more than a sketch, but it should open vistas for you. I want to help us, as Christians, to come to know our Lord, and *ourselves-as-we-are-in-Him*, more truly and intimately, and so to integrate more effectively our beliefs into our practical lives. We want to become more whole as persons, more permeated by the Holy Spirit—indeed, more *holy*. The more we abide in him and he in us, the more we will know his joy and bear fruit for his glory, even in the midst of worldwide confusion and strife (see John 15).

Let me add one more point. I'm hoping these talks will spawn new activities and new forms of outreach in our church, as well as a clearer sense among many of our personal and corporate vocations as members of the body of Christ. I'd love to see prayer groups arise, and our home groups become dynamic centers of spiritual formation and discipleship. I would rejoice to see the ministry of inner healing be more amply developed and made available to those among us struggling with wounds, fears, angers, debilitating anxiety, and unhealthy behavioral patterns they can't get the victory over, try as they might. People impacted this way by the power and tenderness of God become ardent witnesses for Christ in their public lives. Thus the body of Christ—the church—starts to walk, indeed *to run*! People take note. They listen. The body grows. That's what we're after.

So what I'm proposing in the next five weeks is to plough and disc lots of soil and sow lots of seeds. Some of the material will be difficult; it will stretch your intellectual and spiritual muscles. Don't be discouraged! Theology challenges the mind—a good thing in itself, as I'm sure you'll agree—but its ultimate aim is to help us to know and love God better. Read the course notes I'm handing out—they cover much more ground than I'll be able to do in the talks themselves; study the Bible texts *and their contexts*; think as hard as you can; and pray regularly and meditatively to the Holy Trinity, sometimes with words, sometimes in contemplative silence. If we can work hard to get a degree in law or biology or engineering or auto mechanics or nursing or medicine or plumbing or teaching, we can work hard to know our Lord better and to become more fruitful in his service.

I

Creation. The Trinity. Man/Woman Created in the Image of God: *Imago Dei*

(A) Reflections on the Creation

The cosmos, the world around us, is a *gift*, not a mere object. When we see it as a *creation* and not simply as a material reality, we understand it *sacramentally*, as *participating* in the Word of God, the personal Logos, the Maker and Orderer of all reality, who was before all things and who made all things; we understand it as shining forth with its Creator's beauty even while being, as a created and not self-generated reality, finite and essentially distinct from (and dependent upon) its infinite Creator. Our primary *posture* is to be one of *gratitude* to the Giver; our *vocation* is to be carers, governors, overseers of that which has been entrusted to us. This is obviously of immediate relevance in the context of the ecological crisis of our day. Because we see creation as a *gift*, because we understand it sacramentally, we value it highly, yet without assigning it *ultimate* value. Thus viewed, material reality will not be for us the source of *ultimate* meaning; it will not become an idol. We will rejoice in it and be grateful to God; we will see in the order and beauty of the cosmos the imprint of the Creator's hand; but we will refuse any pagan temptation to divinize nature. *Thanksgiving*, you will notice—a *eucharistic* attitude toward life—is a frequent theme in Scripture, especially in the Psalms and the Pauline Epistles (see e.g., Ps 26:7, 50:14, 23, 95:2, 100:4; Rom 1:21; Eph 5:20; Col 3:15–17; Rev 7:12); and you will notice in Romans 1:21 that the apostle explicitly stigmatizes the human race for its *lack* of gratitude: *"Although they knew God, they neither glorified him as God nor gave thanks to him, but their thinking became futile and their foolish hearts were darkened."*

The basic sense of sacrament designates a *physical* reality that points to and signifies a *spiritual* reality. The physical thus is understood as participating in the spiritual. It is more than a symbol, more than something standing for something else; the physical reality is actually inherent in the spiritual, and the spiritual in the physical. The supernatural and the natural are integrated, they make a whole. One can call this understanding of creation as sacramental ontology: the *being* of creation is sacramental; it is not self-subsistent, it points to the transcendent reality that is beyond it and also immanent within it, the Creator, who, as Creator, is *personal*.

Thus, to understand the created cosmos as participating in the Logos is to see it at once as created and ordered by the Word of God and as having its distinct being in freedom. Created freely by God who is altogether free, with no constraint upon him other than his own nature of love, the creation inherently bears God's imprint, as any work of art bears the mark of its creator; it is ordered by laws, but ordered to freedom, as a distinct reality called into being and sent forth to *be*, to be *itself*. God orders and sustains but does not manipulate his universe. This is a mystery, but we must affirm it forcefully. It is what his self-revelation in Israel and the incarnation reveal. God is not a dictator. He guides, but he does not coerce. Moreover, the creation is *one* creation, yet characterized by infinite *diversity*; in this, again, it carries an echo and reflection of its Creator, God the Trinity: one God in three persons.

The coherence that holds the infinite diversity of the creation together is the ordering presence of the Logos, of the Lord Jesus Christ. *"He is the image of the invisible God,"* writes St. Paul of Christ, *"the firstborn over all creation* ["firstborn" here is language in the biblical wisdom tradition, signifying preeminence, sovereignty. See Proverbs 8:22–30]. *For by him all things were created: things in heaven and on earth, visible and invisible, whether thrones or powers or rulers or authorities; all things were created by him and for him. He is before all things, and in him all things hold together"* (Col 1:15–17). The author of the Epistle to the Hebrews writes: *". . . in these last days he [God] has spoken to us by his Son, whom he appointed heir of all things, and through whom he made the universe. The Son is the radiance of God's glory and the exact representation of his being, sustaining all things by his powerful word*" (Heb 1:2–3a). And St. John in the beginning of his gospel writes of the Word, the Logos: *"Through him all things were made; without him nothing was made that has been made"* (John 1:3).

The incarnate Word is the Alpha and the Omega, as the risen Christ says in the Revelation 1:8. In the opening verses of Genesis, he is the Word by whom God spoke, even as the Spirit of God hovered over the void (Gen 1:1–3); and he is the end, the finality, to which the evolving cosmos and human history point: *"Jesus Christ, the same yesterday, today, and forever"* (Heb 13:8). It is by him and in him that we, individually and as the church, Christ's bride, may enter into God's eternity, which is communion with the Holy Trinity in the context of the new creation, God's kingdom, where the Trinity, in fellowship with redeemed mankind, reigns over a renewed cosmos (Matt 6:10; Rom 8:20–23; Rev 11:15, 22:5). In our day, when the created order has become unmoored from its origin in God, even as astrophysicists and cosmologists are probing the physical origin of the cosmos and scratching their heads about a Big Bang that seems to come out of nothing, it is vital that the church regain a Christocentric and Trinitarian understanding of reality, for which the eternal Word, who is not subject to the vagaries and vicissitudes of human history, provides stability and trustworthiness. Neither cosmology nor theology will ever *prove* God-as-Creator; but theology can give sense and purpose to cosmology and hence to all that the cosmos contains, most notably *life*—something cosmology alone can never do.

(B) Man/Woman Created in the Image of God (Imago Dei).

Genesis 1:26–27; 9; Colossians 1:15; 2 Corinthians 4:4. There are different approaches to the meaning of this wonderful revelation. Regrettably, time limits prevent me from developing the subject here, especially with respect to the matter of "naming" referred to in Genesis 2:19–20. I believe the essential meaning of the *imago Dei* is this: humans, as the summit of creation, are graced with an ontological relation to God the Creator (hence, necessarily, partaking in qualities like rationality, self-consciousness, and moral freedom). This relation is part of our *being*, of our very essence and structure. We are called to adore our Creator, to love him with all our heart and mind. Worship is inherent in our human constitution as created bearers of God's image. Furthermore, our man/woman complementarity-in-communion can be seen as an image of the Divine Trinity, three distinct persons in one divine nature. We are dust, but the spirit of life (all life comes from God) has been breathed into our clay (Gen 2:7). The statement that it is the Lord God who breathed life into our nostrils signifies our peculiar, personal, and ennobling relation with the Creator. Other creatures in Genesis are called *"living souls"* (Gen 1:20, 24, 9:10), but only of man (always to be understood as man/woman) is it said that the spirit of life was breathed into him (cf. Job 33:4, 34:14–15). But, being also of dust from the earth, we are earthy, physical, embodied, ontologically linked with material reality as well as with God. This is the basis for our God-given vocation to care for the earth, to have dominion (not domination) over it, to name the creatures (Gen 2:19–20), to create culture. As God the Creator cares providentially for his creation, so human beings created in his image are called to be stewards of his creation and to care for it as God's representatives.

The fall *inversed* mankind's original positive relation to the Creator, turning it into an alienation instead of a communion and opening our race to corruption, both moral and physical. God's grace through his word continues providentially to move through human history for *good* and to keep it from collapsing into chaos, but fear, jealousy, violence, deceit, and cruelty mark every age and every culture. Mankind's alienation from the Creator results in idolatry and what today we call ideologies (which are rationalized forms of idolatry). We worship man-made idols instead of the Creator. The depths of human sin are revealed in our rejection and crucifixion of Christ, the Son of God—not only pagans but even the leaders of Israel, the covenanted people of God, were blind to the person and works and message of Jesus of Nazareth, and actually went so far as to put him to death. We crucified the Word incarnate, the very Word who sustains the world. Alienation could find no deeper manifestation than this.

So, we fashion counterfeits where we play God. Nature is cut off from super-nature, from its transcendent source, and becomes merely an object for our manipulation. Because the relation of human beings to God is ontological, modern man can't eliminate God's presence from his life, try as he will (in the modern age, he does this *deliberately*)—he just substitutes himself for God (which is an unconscious form of acknowledgement of God's reality). Christ, the representative of mankind and the very image of God (2 Cor 4:4; Col 1:15; Heb 1:3), opens the way, by his incarnation (involving, of course, his birth, ministry, crucifixion, resurrection, and ascension), for man to reappropriate his original and essential identity. This restoration is a restoration of *relations*, with God first, then between man and woman, between man and nature, between neighbors, etc. Christian life consists in renewing and maintaining good relations, in bringing reconciliation where possible, and in establishing communion where there was hostility or alienation. In the coming talks, we shall explore several aspects of this restoration of the *imago Dei* that the Son of God's unspeakable and glorious self-sacrifice has won for us.

II

Christians, through Christ the Son, are Adopted Sons and Daughters of God the Father

We must be *"born again,"* say the writers of the New Testament (John 1:12–13, 3:3–6, 14:6–7, 20:11–18; Eph 1:5; Gal 3:23–29; Rom 8:12–17; 1 Pet 1:3, 23). If we know Jesus, as Jesus himself puts it in John 14:6–7, we will know his Father as well. We can only come to God the Father—we can only know God as *Father*—through the Son (John 14:6). Psychologically, we have a tendency to think of God the Father in terms of our earthly fathers, and this can cause problems of faith if we've had an unsatisfactory relationship with our own father. We should avoid doing that. We should look to Jesus, who reveals the true nature of God the Father. *"If you really knew me,"* says Jesus to Thomas, *"you would know my Father as well. From now on, you do know him and have seen him"* (John 14:7). We must be "born again" to enter into this relationship with God the Father. In our alienation as rebels who insist on our autonomy and refuse God's authority, we have to renounce and die to that false identity which separates us from our Creator and implants in us false images of God.

In the Old Testament, especially in Isaiah, God is sometimes called Father, but this is in the sense of his being the Father—the Redeemer and Creator—of the people/nation of Israel, not in the sense of his having a personal paternal relation to individuals (Exod 4:22; Isa 63:16, 64:8). The Old Testament reference to the name "Father" is maintained in the New Testament, but with the imperative of being born again, the understanding of redemption and creation take on new spiritual meaning. Not just deliverance from physical human enemies such as Pharaoh or Babylon is involved, but deliverance from the tyranny of Satan, sin, and death. But to be born again presupposes, of course, a prior death. It involves—indeed, it *requires*—our identifying, by faith, with Christ on the cross and in his resurrection; it involves death to the self-centered self and rebirth in Christ to new life in the kingdom of God. We die to our own lordship and come under Christ's.

The new birth, which makes of us a new creation (Gal 6:15; 2 Cor 5:17), is, like our original creation, a *gift*, as John makes clear in John 1:13. We receive the authority (*"exousia"*) to become children of God. We are "born of God," by the Spirit, not on the basis of will power or some moral achievement of our own. But we have our part to play. We are *"to receive Christ"* by faith (John 1:12–13). We *open ourselves* to the Spirit; we *humble ourselves;* we *receive* the word. Like a child, we *trust.*

The new birth is signified by baptism, which is not only a sacrament but a principle of Christian living. It involves dying to the old self, which is drowned in the baptismal waters, and rising to new life in Christ. This physical experience is the sacramental representation of the spiritual reality. This is as needful and valid for a child as for an adult, because the child, though it has not deliberately sinned, participates in the original sin of the human race. The notion of original sin is a doctrine of the church based on Adam and Eve's—*mankind's*—disobedience, as described in Genesis 3; its reality, while being a mystery, is massively and ubiquitously confirmed by the history of the human race. Baptism incorporates a person, child or adult, into the church, into a new, redeemed creation.

A child baptized is taken into the orbit of the church through the faith of the priest/pastor, the parents, and the godparents, but he or she must confirm the sacrament at a later point in life and lay hold of the faith for him- or herself. Assuming, then, that this has happened—that the sacrament, like a kind of grain, has yielded the fruit of faith—the baptized person is reconciled with God and at peace with him, has received the Holy Spirit and been revivified (Num 11:29; Isa 59:20–21; Joel 2:28–29; Acts 2:4, 10:44–46), is seated in/with Christ at the Father's right side, has access to God and may stand in his presence, forgiven and justified—made right before God—by the Messiah's shed blood (Rom 3:21–26, 4:23–25, 5:1–2; Eph 1:20, 2:6, 17, 18, 3:12; Heb 4:16). We are saved by grace through faith (Eph 2:8–10). Our faith does not save us—*Jesus* does; but we lay hold of him, and of salvation in him, by faith, which is itself a gift of grace. The Father sees us in Christ the eternal Son and *imputes* to us Christ's righteousness, but he also *imparts* to us, through the new birth and the gift of the Spirit, a new heart, a new *being,* so that an authentic Christian is *ontologically* a new creation. God the Father sees us as *adopted* sons and daughters come back to him through faith in his Son, and rejoices (Luke 15). *"In love,"* Paul writes in Ephesians, *"he predestined us to be adopted as his sons through Jesus Christ, in accordance with his pleasure and will—to the praise of his glorious grace, which he has freely given us in the One he loves"* (Eph l:5–6).

It is vital to understand that this is our *primary* identity, more fundamental than our cultural or even our sexual identity. Paul makes this clear in Galatians 3:26–29 (and see Colossians 3:9–11): *"You are all sons of God through faith in Christ Jesus, for all of you who are baptized into Christ have clothed yourselves with Christ. There is neither Jew nor Greek, slave nor free, male nor female, for you are all one in Christ Jesus. If you belong to Christ, then you are Abraham's seed, and heirs according to the promise."* These natural identities do not disappear, of course—they remain descriptive of who we are—but they are henceforth *secondary*. We have a new pedigree now: we are Abraham's seed incorporated, through Israel, into God's covenant with mankind. Our unity with others is henceforth in Christ—and this is *true* unity, not in some sort of what we might broadly call *tribal* or *ethnic* unity. In light of this truth, perhaps you can see why the disunity in the visible church is such a sin and scandal, and why it serves so perfectly the devil's purposes to mock the gospel.

Thus justified by God the Father through Christ's sacrifice (see especially Romans 3:21-26 and, as a prophetic echo, Zechariah 3), we are thus both clothed with Christ's righteousness as we stand before God, and graced with a *new heart* that inclines us to want to *act* righteously and, indeed, to become more and more holy, more and more like Jesus. This is the ground of our proper self-esteem, our proper self-love. The process of sanctification—of being made holy in attitude and behavior—builds, so to speak, on this ground. *"But just as he who called you is holy,"* writes the apostle Peter, *"so be holy in all you do; for it is written: 'Be holy, because I am holy.' Since you call on a Father who judges each man's work impartially, live your lives as strangers here in reverent fear"* (1 Pet 1:15-17). Our gradual transformation is a lifelong process that will at times be painful. Along with the glorious privilege of knowing God as our Father and having communion with him, comes the process of being disciplined by him so that we may become more and more like him as we are conformed to Christ, his very image (Prov 3:11-12; Heb 12:1-13; Rom 5:1-4, 8:15-17; Jas 1:2-4; Col 3:9-10). St. Paul writes to the Roman church: *"For you did not receive a spirit that makes you a slave again to fear, but you received the spirit of sonship. And by him we cry 'Abba, Father.' The Spirit himself testifies with our spirit that we are God's children. Now if we are children, then we are heirs—heirs of God and co-heirs with Christ, if indeed we share in his sufferings in order that we may also share in his glory"* (Rom 8:15-17). The issue of suffering and trials arises here, which we will touch on briefly in the next talk.

What I wish to emphasize now is that by baptism and new birth, the Holy Spirit, through the church, transfers to each believer, already in this present dispensation, the eschatological reality of his/her being and destiny. The Second Adam, Jesus Christ (Rom 5:12-17)—representative of the unity of mankind and of our common human nature—has, through his resurrection and ascension, opened the way for believers into life in the Spirit, into eternity. By the Spirit, by the power of his breath, God raised Jesus from Adam's state of *"living soul"* (Gen 2:7; cf. Rom 1:4; 1 Pet 3:18) to the state of *"life-giving spirit"* (1 Cor 15:45), the bodily element being changed from mortality and corruptibility to immortality and incorruptibility. In no way—and this is of the utmost importance—does this mean that the resurrection life in God's kingdom—the eschatological life—is incorporeal, for the ascended Christ or for us; rather, it means that the characteristics of bodily life under the regime of the fall, i.e., mortality and corruptibility, give way to *spiritual bodily life*, entailing immortality and incorruptibility (read 1 Corinthians 15 in its entirety). The Christian believer's identity as God's *adopted* son or daughter—that *gift* which we receive by faith as we enter into the body of God's *eternal* Son, Jesus Christ—will be fully realized at the resurrection when, as the apostle Paul puts it in Romans 8:23, we will receive *"the redemption of our bodies."*

It is important to see that between a believer's *first* and his/her *new* creation, there is both continuity and discontinuity. The key to understanding this mystery lies in the person's essential identity as *imago Dei*: the new creation is the redemption of a particular person's whole being—spirit, soul, body—which was created in the image of God, alienated through sin (the hunger for self-sufficient autonomy), and has been redeemed by Christ. The person's identity remains constant, but his or her relation to God moves from the negative to the positive mode, from alienation to communion, with the transformation this entails in this life and in the next. An immortal spiritual body—and it will be a *body*—will be given to the person at the resurrection, to replace the mortal material body he/she shed at death.

Let me conclude with a brief word about the Holy Trinity, about whom I shall be speaking more in coming talks. You will have noticed that the God we have been encountering from the beginning of our reflections is Trinitarian: Father, Son, Holy Spirit. The biblical God is triune, even if this truth is veiled in the Old Testament. It is veiled, yes, but to Christian believers the veil is lifted. The Holy Spirit opens our eyes to see God and his word and his Spirit/breath all present and active at creation, even if the three are not presented, as they will be later in the light of the incarnation of the Son of God, as three distinct divine Persons three mutually inherent and sustaining manifestations of the one Godhead. And we see the Three-in-One at work likewise in the history of Israel, as God the Creator and Father of Israel *speaks* through his prophets and *acts* through his Spirit in his effort to instruct, guide, and redeem his chosen people. This is not the place to develop a theology of the Trinity, but it is of the greatest importance for our practical Christian lives that we see God as the dynamic Trinity, as being-in-communion (this expression comes from an Orthodox theologian named John Zizioulas), and experience his creative and re-creative/redemptive work as being the grace of God the Father through the love of God the Son in the power of God the Holy Spirit.

III

New Creations. Life in the Spirit. Growing as the Father's Sons and Daughters

I said in the first talk that creation is God's gift. So, as we saw, is God's *new* creation, by which we, God's human creatures, alienated from our Creator since the fall, become God's adopted sons and daughters. God in Christ—the Word made flesh—*gave* himself to and for us by becoming man and dying on the cross. *"For the wages of sin is death,"* writes Paul to the Roman church, *"but the gift of God is eternal life in Christ Jesus our Lord"* (Rom 6:23). We are to see and celebrate the reality of *gift* everywhere—this is our eucharistic vocation, as I said earlier—a vocation focused by but by no means limited to our regular celebration of the sacrament of the Holy Eucharist (1 Cor 4:7). And this sense of the world as *gift*—this intuition of the nature of reality as *gift*—is a reflection of God himself, in his self-giving reality, both in himself as he is eternally and in what we might call his self-imparting movement out from himself in his acts of creation and redemption, acts that, in Trinitarian theology, are called the "economy." Each of the Persons of the Trinity is forever giving himself to the others and receiving the others, in a perpetual dance of love, of *self*-emptying and of what might be termed *other*-welcoming. Each, though distinct, inheres in the other in mutual love and oneness of will. We are to understand this mystery, which we only know of through the incarnation of the Son, as being the very nature of divine life: communion between a plurality, in one Spirit; mutual self-giving and in-dwelling, in love; diversity operating harmoniously, in unity. The incarnation itself—as the coordinated self-sacrificing action of the Father, Son, and Holy Spirit for the redemption of the human race—is the supreme demonstration of this self-giving that is the very nature of divine reality (see e.g., Luke 1:26–38; Phil 2:6–11; Acts 2:32, 4:10; Heb 9:14; Rom 8:11). This relationship of communion in the Godhead, in which it is our eschatological vocation to participate, pictures how we as Christians, created—and now renewed—in God's image, are called to live on earth.

We are to live a baptismal life. Key texts are Romans 6–8 and 12, Ephesians 4, Colossians 3, 1 Peter 1:13—2:3, where we are enjoined to *"die to self,"* *"put off the old man,"* *"put on the new man in Christ,"* and *"be transformed by the renewing of our mind"* (Rom 12:2). This is how the apostles, especially Paul, developed Christ's command to deny self and take up our cross (Matt 16:24; Mark 8:34; Luke 9:23). This is the shape that the practice of repentance and confession takes, and it is the basis of authentic Christian ethics (see e.g., Eph 4:20-25; Col 2:2—4:6; Romans 12—15:13). *"Since, then,"* writes Paul to the Colossians, *"you have been raised with Christ, set your hearts on things above, where Christ is seated at the right hand of God. Set your minds on things above, not on earthly things. For you died, and your life is now hidden with Christ in God. When Christ, who is your life, appears, then you also will appear with him in glory"* (Col 3:1–4). Learning to act this way can be very painful, because it involves surrendering, dying to many ways of thinking and acting in which, before we knew Christ, we placed our identity. It involves operating a certain violence upon ourselves—our old selves— and putting something to death is never pleasant, even if its aim and issue is new life. Through the Father's discipline (if we submit to it), through trials (if we experience them in faith), through biblical instruction and liturgical participation, through the Spirit's quiet work by all these means and others, the old self-life is put effectively to death and we are progressively transformed. About his own life and trials, but in a way that we can apply to ourselves and the baptismal life of any believer, the apostle Paul writes: *"We always carry around in our body the death of Jesus, so that the life of Jesus may also be revealed in our body. For we who are alive are always being given over to death for Jesus' sake, so that his life may be revealed in our mortal body. So then, death is at work in us, but life is at work in you"* (2 Cor 4:10–12).

Our personal relationships, starting in our families, are the main arena in which the Spirit does his work. The Spirit is in the business of reconciliation and the construction of community. Whatever work the Holy Spirit does in us will redound to the benefit of others, as Paul suggests in the text just cited. The "self" in question here is what Paul calls the "old man," the "carnal" self, the proud, self-righteous, fearful, cowardly, self-pitying, deceitful, resentful, unbelieving, rebellious, impure, covetous, self-justifying, often violent, *autonomous ego* that lives independently of God and that generates sinful attitudes and behavior and causes strife and division in our relationships. This "self"—the "carnal" self—is *not* our true being created in the image of God. It has been put to death in Christ, and the true self, the new creation, has been raised with him. On the strength of this wonderful truth, we are in a position to have our attitudes and behavior changed, and to lead a new life. *"Or don't you know,"* writes Paul, *"that all of us who were baptized into Christ Jesus were baptized into his death? We were therefore buried with him through baptism into death in order that, just as Christ was raised from the dead through the glory of the Father, we too may live a new life"* (Rom 6:3–4).

It is not, obviously, that we will never sin again (see 1 John 1:8–10); it is rather that *we will not continue to sin as a matter of nature and willfulness* (1 John 3:6). As we abide in Christ by virtue of our new nature and the presence of the Spirit within us, we will become increasingly sensitive and alert to that in us which is displeasing to God. We will begin to have real self-knowledge. Knowledge of God and self-knowledge grow together. Self-righteousness and self-sufficiency will begin to be revealed for the foolishness they are. When we discern bad thoughts or behavior, we will repent of them, confess them, and crucify them, by affirming that in Christ we are dead to them already and alive in the Spirit, clothed in Christ's righteousness (see Galatians 5:24–26; 6:14–15).

The *operative principle* in this sanctifying process—this process of being made holy by God—is explicated by Paul in Romans 6:1–12. Our identification by faith with Christ on the Cross, where God *"made him to be sin for us"* (2 Cor 5:21), means that our sinful nature *has been put to death*. We do not have to put it to death. We have to *recognize it as having been put to death*; we are *"to count ourselves dead to sin but alive to God in Christ Jesus"* (Rom 6:11). This truth is what enables us to put to death *practically* sinful attitudes and actions, as Paul frequently exhorts us to do (Col 3:5). We *are* dead to the "old man"; therefore, being alive in Christ, we *can* put to death the old man's behavioral patterns, developed when we were under his hegemony. Ethically speaking, this is what it means to live by faith and not by works. The essential work is Christ's; he *has done* it. We *are* new creations. We *appropriate by faith* his finished work. This is what makes concretely possible a life lived according to the Sermon on the Mount (Matt 5–7)—an eschatological life, where we live according to the new creation that God has made us.

The whole subject of grace and law arises here, which I can only touch on briefly. Jesus has fulfilled God's law of love of God, self, and neighbor, and has borne the penalty (death) for our human failure to live by this law; therefore those who receive him by faith and are clothed with his righteousness are no longer under condemnation but are actually *able* to obey the law of love, not through outward constraint but by virtue of its interiorization in our hearts by the Holy Spirit's action and presence (Rom 8:1–4; 1 John 2:5, 20–25; Jer 31:33–34; Ezek 36:24–27). I say again: we are *new creations* (2 Cor 5:17; Gal 6:15). Our identity—our ontological nature—has changed. This is a great truth, which few Christians really grasp. Once you lay hold of it and begin to apply it to daily life, your existence begins to change radically. Christ in us, who is our life (Gal 2:19–21), *obeys* the Law of love, as he did in his earthly life. We grow in the fruit of the Spirit (Gal 5:22–26) not principally by our own *willing* to be joyful or loving or patient or humble, but by our submitting consciously to Christ by the Spirit. It is by our faith—by the *obedience* that comes from faith (Rom 1:5)—that we conquer, not by our autonomous will power (1 John 5:1–5). I repeat: we conquer—we overcome sinful behavior—by *obedience*, by choosing freely to submit to our Lord. The moral law in the Old Testament, as well as the promptings of conscience and the determinations of moral reason, can point us to our duty before God and the path we are to follow, but they cannot *enable* us to obey God from the heart. The Christian who is trying to obey God by following rules and carrying out rituals in a legalistic manner has not understood the way of the cross, and can only fail. Our own striving to be good cannot make us good. From start to finish, it is by grace through faith that we are saved and sanctified (Rom 7:7–26).

Baptismal life is life in the Spirit, developed thematically by Paul in Romans 8 and instantiated in Romans 12:

> *Therefore, there is now no condemnation for those who are in Christ Jesus, because through Christ Jesus the law of the Spirit of life set me free from the law of sin and death. For what the law was powerless to do in that it was weakened by the sinful nature, God did by sending his own Son in the likeness of sinful man to be a sin offering. And so he condemned sin in sinful man, in order that the righteous requirements of the law might be fully met in us who do not live according to the sinful nature but according to the Spirit.* (Rom 8:1–4)

This is what it means to live as sons and daughters of the Father. We are no longer under the law's condemnation, because Christ has fulfilled the demands of that law for us, and as we, by faith, receive him, we enter into his redemptive death and risen life (Rom 5:18–21). Corporately and individually, Christians are the temple of the Holy Spirit (1 Cor 3:16, 6:19). This is the great mystery, the great truth: *Christ in us, the hope of glory* (Col 1:25–27). We are already incorporated into God's kingdom. The glory of eternal life is ours already and will be ours in fullness when we pass through death into the plenitude of communion with our Creator and Redeemer. This, not the moral law *as such*, is the foundation of Christian ethics. By virtue of the Holy Spirit dwelling in us, we have already a deposit and guarantee of eternal life in our heavenly dwelling (2 Cor 5:5). This establishes us in the hope that when Christ appears a second time, as John writes in his First Epistle, "*we shall be like him, for we shall see him as he is.*" And, John continues, "*everyone who has this hope in him purifies himself, just as he is pure*" (1 John 3:2b–3). The Spirit's indwelling presence, and our vision of Christ's return and eternal life in his presence, urges us to press on to grow in grace and purity. What we could not do for ourselves—to live a good and holy life, fully pleasing to our Creator—Christ has done for us, *making us capable, now,* to a considerable extent, of living according to the moral law.

CHRISTIAN IDENTITY: WHO DO YOU THINK YOU ARE?

We live out of a new heart, indwelt by the Holy Spirit, nourished by God's word, and so our conscience is alert and we readily respond to the Holy Spirit and are convicted, where necessary, of unholy behavior, and then are quick to repent and ask forgiveness or to forgive others, as the case may be (John 16:8; Matt 6:12). *"For through the law,"* declares the apostle Paul, *"I died to the law so that I might live for God. I have been crucified with Christ and I no longer live, but Christ lives in me. The life I live in the body, I live by faith in the Son of God, who loved me and gave himself for me"* (Gal 2:19–20).

It is important to see, as St. Paul declares in Romans 8:2, that we can do this—we can live like this—*because* we have been made free by Christ. The Christian starts from a position of freedom, of victory, of new God-given life, not from a position of moral failure and condemnation. By and through Christ, we have been justified and can stand before God with our heads high (Rom 3:21–26, 5:1). This truth is at the heart of Paul's teaching. The Christian is released not from effort but from *self*-effort. *Self*-effort to please God often leads to legalistic or ritualistic striving, which, at bottom, is rooted in pride, because it presupposes our capacity to please a holy God out of our own unholy resources. This is an illusion. The natural man is captive to the spirit of the world, which stands over against the true God (Gal 3:21–24; 1 Cor 2:10–16). Even those under the law—the Jews—or pagans who seek to live moral lives, cannot escape the centripetal pull of the ego, the self-centered principle that Paul calls "the flesh," which is not to be confused with the flesh that is the body. The law itself—the Mosaic law—was, according to Paul, given to the people of Israel in part precisely *to reveal* this bondage to sin, to the "self" and its attitudes and actions (Rom 3:20, 4:15, 5:20–21, 7:7–8; 8:3–4; Gal 3:19).

This does not mean that nothing that the natural man does is good, or that God does not see, encourage, and honor the good actions of those from all cultures and religions who do not know him as Father but who do strive according to their consciences to do what they consider to be the right thing; it means simply that the righteousness and holiness that God seeks in his creatures—the life of sustained love toward God and neighbor—is not achievable by fallen men and women, whatever their personal ideals may be. The fallen human nature of mankind is rebellious; we want self-sufficiency, autonomy, independence—indeed, *divinity*. We want to replace God with ourselves. For this reason, our race is under judgment. But God is our Creator, he loves us, and so he sent his Son, Jesus the Christ, to save us, to take our judgment upon himself. By God's mercy, many who for diverse reasons could not or did not know Christ in this life but whose hearts—*underneath* the idolatrous surrogates all human beings conjure and invoke, in one way or another—hungered for the true God and who sought to do good as they understood it, will surely find salvation at the last judgment. But this salvation will be in virtue fundamentally of *Christ's* righteousness, not their own (Rom 3:21–26), though their own actions that God considers laudable will surely be taken into account (Rev 20:12–13; Rom 2:6–7; 1 Pet 1:17; Jer 17:9–10; Ps 62:11–12).

As these texts show, God is not unjust or scornful of the efforts his fallen creatures, created in his own image (a truth distorted but not destroyed by our fall, as I have shown in an earlier essay), may make to act righteously according to their consciences and the moral lights they have (with or without knowledge of God's revealed law); but not for a moment can there be any question of our being saved through our own actions and moral aspirations, whatever these may be. *"Salvation is found in no one else,"* declared Peter to the rulers and elders of Israel, *"for there is no other name under heaven given to men by which we must be saved"* (Acts 4:12). All human beings are sinners and fall short of God's righteousness (Rom 3:23). The apostle Paul's position on this is radical. Whatever he may have achieved in his life before he knew Christ, and whatever pedigree he may have had in the Jewish hierarchy, he sets aside as being of no value as far as his standing with God is concerned. He writes of his achievements and pedigree:

> *I consider them rubbish that I may gain Christ and be found in him, not having a righteousness of my own that comes from the law, but that which is through faith in Christ—the righteousness that comes from God and is by faith. I want to know Christ and the power of his resurrection and the fellowship of sharing in his sufferings, becoming like him in his death, and so, somehow, to attain to the resurrection from the dead.* (Phil 3:9b–11)

For those who lay hold of this truth, it is wonderfully liberating. Living by faith, we are freed from the enslaving drive to justify ourselves and prove our worth by our performance and achievements.

Life in the Spirit involves dealing with sin, but it also involves being healed of wounds from the past. Forgiveness and healing—physical and psychological—are entwined in the ministry of Jesus. This is a large subject in itself, which I regret I haven't the time to develop here. Isaiah 53:4–6, cited by Peter in 1 Peter 2:23–25, is a basic source text in this connection. The etymological meaning of *"sozo,"* the Greek word translated "save," is to "make whole." There is a close link between holiness and wholeness. Our sinful behavior is rooted in our nature as fallen beings, but practically speaking it is invariably linked with wounds of all sorts that we have experienced in our lives, many of them not our fault, to which we have reacted in a variety of ways, often sinfully. Some of us are broken persons, divided within and against ourselves, often self-hating, resentful, fearful, angry, envious, bitter, licentious, or covetous. Alienated behavior, such as acting self-defensive and/or being aggressive, is commonly the result of suffering a person has endured, from brutality or rejection or contempt. It is hard to show love if we ourselves have not been loved.

As Christians, we are called to repent of responses to suffering that are hateful—hateful of ourselves or of others—but we also need to be healed, consoled, comforted. God wishes to make himself strong in our weakness (2 Cor 12:7–10); he wishes to redeem our pain and, as we progress into healing, to use our suffering to bless and encourage others who are in trouble, sorrow, or despair (2 Cor 1:3–7). It is as we pass through suffering and are healed that we become effective servants. We need to be *straightened* by the power of God the Father, but we need to know our heavenly Father's *tender love* as well.

Both the conviction of sin and the consolation for our pain are the work of the Holy Spirit. This may involve divine discipline, as when we are called up short before wrong behavior and urged by the Spirit to humble ourselves and go through the cross (1 Pet 5:6–7). We may have to undergo pain if pain suffered at some point produced immoral, unholy, or negative behavior patterns that need to be changed. *"God disciplines us for our good,"* writes the author of the Epistle to the Hebrews, *"that we may share in his holiness. No discipline seems pleasant at the time, but painful. Later on, however, it produces a harvest of righteousness and peace for those who have been trained by it"* (Heb 12:10b–11; also see Rev 3:19–20). God desires a humble heart (Pss 25:9, 147:6, 149:4), the heart of a servant who is willing to take the lowest place (Luke 18:9–14; Mark 9:33–35, 10:35–45; and, of course, Phil 2:5–8). We may need to pass through a valley of humiliation to find our way to humility. For the people of Israel, this is part of what their experience in the desert was intended to achieve, as the Deuteronomic text makes clear:

> *Remember how the Lord your God led you all the way in the desert these forty years, to humble you and to test you in order to know what was in your heart, whether or not you would keep his commands. He humbled you, causing you to hunger and then feeding you with manna, which neither you nor your fathers had known, to teach you that man does not live on bread alone but on every word that comes from the mouth of the Lord.* (Deut 8:2–3)

You will notice that these last words are those Jesus cites to Satan when he is tested in the desert (Matt 4:4). He resists the devil's temptation by citing the Word of God. Jesus is demonstrating his own instruction to the people of Israel.

A final word about trials, whatever form they may take. Trials, as we face them in trust, clinging to God's faithfulness and the certainty of his providential purposes, may be used by the Spirit to discipline, heal, and deepen us, all of which in turn will make us more compassionate and effective servants of others (2 Cor 1:3–7). James, the brother of Jesus, encourages us thusly: *"Consider it pure joy, my brothers, whenever you face trials of many kinds, because you know that the testing of your faith develops perseverance. Perseverance must finish its work so that you may be mature and complete, not lacking anything"* (Jas 1:2–4). In such ways are we gradually sanctified (made holy), made *whole*, unified in our person, renewed, transformed into the image of Christ. The Holy Spirit is in the business of shaping our *characters*, making us *mature* in every way (Rom 5:1–5). He is working *God's love* into every pore of our being: God's love for *us*, and *ours* for God and neighbor. As we are remodeled over time, our relationships and way of acting in society are progressively transformed as well. All of this is the process of a lifetime. This is the Christian life. *"Once you were alienated from God and were enemies in your minds because of your evil behavior. But now he has reconciled you by Christ's physical body through death to present you holy in his sight, without blemish and free from accusation—if you continue in your faith, established and firm, not moved from the hope held out in the gospel"* (Col 1:22–23a).

IV

Christians are Members of the Church, the One Body of Christ; We are Citizens of Heaven, Ambassadors, Witnesses

We are no longer to be defined basically as isolated individuals (modernity's self-understanding, with roots in Rousseau), or as members of this or that tribe, ethnic group, nation, or family. Our sexual identity is fundamental (contrary to the irrational pretentions of constructivist gender theory, which, ironically is deconstructing and fracturing American society), but in Christ even *that* is secondary to our identity as sons and daughters of the Father (Gal 3:26–29; Col 3:8–11). Our natural identity (in both the ontological and cultural senses) is real and important, and to be honored; but for Christians our spiritual identity as children of the Father and members of Christ's one body is primary, as we saw in my second talk. Natural tendencies for fallen men and women usually incline toward division; differences usually separate. Hence Paul constantly emphasizes *unity* in Christ and *diversity/complementarity* of persons, gifts, vocations (e.g., 1 Cor 12 and 14; Rom 12:1-8). He stresses distinctiveness and castigates divisiveness. *Individuality*, yes, insofar as we are unique persons; *individualism*, no. We are persons-in-relation, made in the image of God the Trinity, who is Persons-in-communion, in one being. Christians are members of one body, the universal church; while we are all different, we *belong* to each other (Rom 12:5). Our membership in this or that ecclesial confession or denomination is important, but secondary to our fundamental membership in Christ's body. We are sisters and brothers in the family of God, with one Father (Eph 4:3-6). Awareness of this truth is the basis for the Holy Spirit's call in our day to true ecumenism and mutual welcome between all those who name themselves Christians.

In his Epistle to the church in Ephesus, Paul highlights this truth by making the momentous proclamation that in Christ, Jew and Greek are one:

> *For he himself is our peace, who has made the two one and has destroyed the barrier, the dividing wall of hostility, by abolishing in his flesh the law with its commandments and regulations. His purpose was to create in himself one new man out of the two, thus making peace, and in this one body to reconcile both of them to God through the cross, by which he put to death their hostility. He came and preached peace to you who were far away and peace to those who were near. For through him we both have access to the Father by one Spirit.* (Eph 2:14-18)

That this great truth was lost sight of in succeeding centuries is one of the major tragedies of history (see Romans 9-11). But in our day God is moving to bring reconciliation and new understanding between Jews and the church, and centuries of hostility and mutual suspicion are being overcome (see Romans 11:17-24). The church has repented of its misguided anti-Judaism.[1] As this happens, the Holy Spirit is opening the eyes of more and more Jews to the truth that Jesus of Nazareth is their Messiah, the Christ. The church, for its part, as it seeks unity within its own ranks, is also rediscovering the enormous significance of Paul's momentous proclamation. The Spirit is using world events and rising opposition to both Jews and Christians to press the church toward the truth of its unity in Christ (see Ephesians 4:3-6, 11-13). This *"unity of the Spirit through the bond of peace"* is, like everything else from God, a *gift*, and Paul commands the Christians in Ephesus to *"make every effort to keep it."* Our witness in the world is effectual as we act *in unity* in our families, in our parishes, and in our wider ecclesial relationships. From the beginning of the church, Satan has always

---

1. See, notably, Vatican Council II, *Nostra Aetate*, 56-57.

worked to sow disunity and division, because these undercut the credibility of the gospel. Reclaiming our unity in and around the Jewish Messiah, Jesus, is a central task for the church in our time. And again, the more this true unity is realized, the more the first people of the covenant—the Jews—will be drawn to Jesus and see in him the promised Messiah.

Being members of Christ's body, we are citizens of heaven before we are citizens of some earthly nation or entity (Phil 3:20-21). Our heavenly citizenship is primary. We have been raised up with Christ and are seated with him in heavenly places (Eph 2:6). This statement evokes not only Christ's resurrection but also his ascension. As St. Paul declares in Ephesians 1:20-21, God exerted his power in Christ when *"he raised him from the dead and seated him at his right hand in the heavenly realms, far above all rule and authority, power and dominion, and every title that can be given, not only in the present age but also in the one to come."* The one who *ascended* was the Son of God who had *descended* and become man; it was *this human being*, who was *also* the incarnate Word, who returned to the Father and was made King and Lord of all. He rose in his risen spiritual *body*, the same body the disciples and 500 others had seen during the forty days after his resurrection. He did not discard his body. But this same human being was *also* the representative of the one human race, of mankind—he was the Second Adam—and we who believe *into* him, who identify with him *on his cross* where our "old sinful nature" died, and *in his resurrection* when we were raised with him into new life, also identify with him *in his ascended position*, in his *session* at the Father's right hand: we are seated there with him (Col 3:3).

All of this, of course, is by the Spirit. We who by faith are thus identified with Christ have not yet received the "redemption of our bodies," as we saw in Talk II (Rom 8:23). But this will come at the resurrection of the dead, when Christ returns. The apostle Paul writes: *"And if the Spirit of him who raised Jesus from the dead is living in you, he who raised Christ from the dead will also give life to your mortal bodies through his Spirit, who lives in you"* (Rom 8:11). And again, in his Epistle to the Philippians: *"But our citizenship is in heaven. And we eagerly await a Savior from there, the Lord Jesus Christ, who, by the power that enables him to bring everything under his control, will transform our lowly bodies so that they will be like his glorious body"* (Phil 3:20-21). And again, in his First Epistle to the Corinthians: *"But Christ has indeed been raised from the dead, the first fruits of those who have fallen asleep. For since death came through a man, the resurrection of the dead comes also through a man. For as in Adam all die, so in Christ all will be made alive"* (1 Cor 15:20-22).

It is important to mention here that this is not a universalist declaration. Paul is not saying that all will be saved, but that all will be *raised* to be judged according to their works. Jesus himself makes this quite clear in one of his discourses in the Gospel of John about judgment: *"For as the Father has life in himself, so he has granted the Son to have life in himself. And he has given him authority to judge because he is the Son of Man. Do not be amazed at this, for a time is coming when all who are in their graves will hear his voice and come out—those who have done good will rise to live, and those who have done evil will rise to be condemned."* (John 5:26-29) The judgment of evil and of evil-doers is a basic biblical teaching, and not for one moment should we yield to the sentimental temptation of universalism. That would be a denial both of human freedom and the real moral choice that God has given us (Gen 2:16), and of divine justice and holiness, as if, in the end, evil is acceptable and evil choices are of no great importance. To assert as much is grievous blasphemy.

The church lives by the Spirit, which means that it lives proleptically, eschatologically, in anticipation of the completion of Christ's work of redemption—that is, the resurrection of our bodies. Only in this way can we understand rightly our Christian identity. As new creations, our roots are in Christ as he suffered, died, and rose again 2,000 years ago; but the new life that is ours is bearing fruit *now* on this earth in the mortal lives that we are living presently in the Spirit; and at the same time—if I may use the word "time" here—by the Spirit we are seated in Christ at God's right hand, awaiting the Lord's return to earth and the resurrection of our immortal bodies.

The Eucharist sums this up and expresses it sacramentally, which is why it lies at the heart of Christian life. As we eat Christ's body sacramentally, we participate in his cross, in his risen life, and in his ascension and session at the right hand of God. We participate in the incarnational reality of the Son of God. Whatever liturgical form the Lord's Supper may take in our different ecclesial communities, this supper is at the heart of Christian identity. St. Paul's account of the Lord's Supper is as follows:

> *For I received from the Lord what I also passed on to you: The Lord Jesus, on the night he was betrayed, took bread, and when he had given thanks, he broke it and said, "This is my body, which is for you; do this in remembrance of me." In the same way, after supper he took the cup, saying, "This cup is the new covenant in my blood; do this, whenever you drink it, in remembrance of me." For whenever you eat this bread and drink this cup, you proclaim the Lord's death until he comes.* (1 Cor 11:23-26)

The context of this text is important. At this early stage of the church's history, the Lord's Supper was usually celebrated as part of a larger *agape* meal. Paul is admonishing the Corinthian believers for profaning the celebration by their gluttony and discrimination, the rich stuffing themselves and neglecting the poorer members in their midst. Far from uniting the church, he says, such reprehensible conduct perpetuates and amplifies divisions.

The church is the body of Christ, and unity is of its essence. It is God's redeemed community in time and space, the bride of Christ, united forever nuptially with God the Son. There is only one body. But it is important to see that in the eucharistic celebration, this *one body*, under the form of the bread and the wine, is present in *three* manners: the historical, human, physical body of Jesus Christ, broken for sinners, that is *remembered*; the eucharistic body that *re-presents sacramentally*, through the words of institution and the operation of the Holy Spirit, Christ's physical body and his sacrifice for our salvation; and the ecclesial body, the mystical body, the church, made up of those who, though many, *"partake of the one loaf,"* as Paul puts it in 1 Corinthians 10:17. In 1 Corinthians 10:16, Paul speaks first of "participating" in the blood and body of Christ, and then in the very next verse, he speaks of *"the one body"* that those who thus participate sacramentally in Christ's historical/physical body, constitute. And in 1 Corinthians 11:26, the apostle tells us that whenever we participate in Christ this way—that is, whenever we thus eat Christ's flesh and drink his blood sacramentally—we *"proclaim the Lord's death until he comes."*[2] We proclaim the Lord's death (and with it, of course, his risen life) precisely *by our participation in it*. The sacrament of the Eucharist is a memorial meal, yes; but it is also an eschatological meal, a foretaste now of the heavenly banquet in the kingdom of God in which, proleptically—by anticipation—we, as new creations, are already taking part. The Eucharist is a concentrated, sacramental expression of the church's proclamation and identity. In doing this, Christians are saying, all together and with one voice: *This is who we are.*

As citizens of heaven living presently in this fallen world, we are ambassadors of Christ on earth, workers in the embassy of the kingdom of God. Our mission is to represent our Lord and his government to "worldlings" (2 Cor 5:17–21). Being reconciled with God, we have, as Christians, the ministry of reconciliation. Our job description is to summon others to be reconciled to God through Christ, and, as far as possible, to act as reconcilers in our social and political relationships. We are called to make disciples (Matt 28:19–20), to announce fearlessly the mystery of the gospel

---

2. See Jesus's discourse on the bread of life in John 6:35–59.

(Eph 6:19-20; 1 Pet 2:9), to manifest Christ's life in such a way that people are drawn to him and wish to follow him. We are called to build loving and welcoming communities. The apostle Peter speaks of believers as *"being built into a spiritual house to be a holy priesthood, offering spiritual sacrifices acceptable to God through Jesus Christ"* (1 Pet 2:5). This is the fulfillment of a promise made by God to the Israelites at Mount Sinai (Exod 19:6). Christians have a priestly role to play in human society, as we represent the true God to men (men and women, needless to say) and, in prayer, men and women to the true God. In this sense we are light-bearers, reflectors of Jesus Christ, the light of the world (Matt 5:14-17; John 8:12; Eph 5:8-14). And as we act in this priestly manner, we are the salt of the earth, justice-seekers, pointers to the righteousness of God (Matt 5:13).

In all that we are and do, we are called, as disciples, to be witnesses for Christ and his kingdom. The more Christ-like we are, the more we are conformed to him, the more he lives out his life within us, the more we thus participate in the divine nature, as Peter puts it in his Second Epistle (2 Pet 1:3-4), the more effective and fruitful witnesses we will be in the various sectors and circumstances of our lives. This is the mission our Lord has given us. *"You did not choose me,"* says Jesus in his farewell discourse, *"but I chose you and appointed you to go and bear fruit—fruit that will last. Then the Father will give you whatever you ask in my name. This is my command: Love one another"* (John 15:16-17). And again: *"Abide in me, and I will abide in you. No branch can bear fruit by itself; it must abide in the vine. Neither can you bear fruit unless you abide in me"* (John 15:4).

Abiding in Jesus is at the heart of life in the Spirit, and prayer is the secret to abiding in Jesus. We cannot effectively be his ambassadors and witnesses unless we abide in him. This abiding is both personal and corporate, as our prayer is both personal and corporate. If we neglect either, we will find that our joy will wane, our fruit will diminish, and our sense of our distinctive Christian identity will weaken. We must cultivate intimacy and honesty with our Lord. With respect to knowledge of God, prayer and sacrament are the paths from our head to our heart; this movement will lead in turn to transformed character and godly action.

To use an image from photography: with respect to all we are and do, he is our *range finder*; by looking at reality through him, and focusing what we see in terms of his love, will, and sovereign purposes for our lives, the blurriness that often characterizes our vision—be it moral, spiritual, or practical—will give way to greater clarity. We will grow to be his friends, his intimates, and will bear the fruit he wishes us to bear. We will learn to hear, or sense, his voice; hearing it, we will learn to obey it; and obeying it, we will come to understand the true meaning of "freedom," namely, that we have been set free from slavery to our ego, to our "self," and to all the fears that drive us when our primal quest is self-preservation and self-aggrandizement and not love of God (Gen 2:16-17; Ps 19:7-13; Jas 1:25; Isa 61:3; Luke 4:18; John 8:31-36; 2 Cor 3:17). *"It is for freedom that Christ has set us free,"* writes Paul to the Galatians. *"Stand firm, then, and do not let yourselves be burdened again by the yoke of slavery"* (Gal 5:1). Learning to pray is a work of the Holy Spirit, coupled with personal discipline. As the Spirit leads us into intimacy with Jesus, so Jesus leads us into intimacy with the Father. We begin to reflect the Lord's glory. *"Now the Lord is the Spirit,"* declares the apostle to the Corinthian church, *"and where the Spirit of the Lord is, there is freedom. And we, who with unveiled faces all reflect the Lord's glory, are being transformed into his likeness with ever-increasing glory, which comes from the Lord, who is the Spirit"* (2 Cor 3:17-18). Such is the joy and power of prayer, whatever form the prayer may take. We find that we are carried by God. The grace by which we are saved becomes our *experience*, not just our head-knowledge.

V

Spiritual Combat: Christians are Soldiers in a War that Christ has Won; We are the Bride of Christ, Who Walk in Hope

In the Synoptic Gospels, the first event after Jesus is baptized is the temptation in the desert. This is of great significance. At his baptism he is anointed by the Holy Spirit for ministry, but before he can move into his mission, he must undergo a period of testing and demonstrate his holiness and power, the power of the word of God, of whom he is the incarnation. From start to finish of his earthly ministry, Jesus was tempted by the devil. This involved great suffering. The author of the Epistle to the Hebrews makes it clear that in order to atone for our sin, Jesus had to conquer the one who, through human sin, has the power of death, and this meant that he had to undergo and resist all the temptations human beings suffer. Only by sharing in our humanity to the very depths of our suffering—yet without sin, without rebellion—could Jesus become on our behalf *"a merciful and faithful high priest in service to God"* (Heb 2:17). And in order that his high priestly ministry might truly open the way to human freedom, *"it was fitting,"* as the author of Hebrews puts it, *"that God, for whom and through whom everything exists, should make the author of their salvation perfect through suffering"* (Heb 2:10). Thus, the writer adds a little later, *"Because he himself suffered when he was tempted, he is able to help those who are being tempted* (Heb 2:18).

Jesus has defeated Satan who, through our sin, has the power of death (1 Cor 15:54–57). As John writes in his First Epistle: *"The reason the Son of God appeared was to destroy the works of the devil"* (1 John 3:8b). But that victory is not available *existentially* to those who have not put their faith in Jesus. They are still under the power of the fallen nature and the fear of death, regardless of anything they may do to alleviate their plight, through religion or philosophy or technology. But the *completion* of Christ's victory will only come when he returns in glory and manifest power to destroy his enemies and assume his lordship over the world. In the *meantime*—in the time between his ascension and his second coming when, as Peter puts it in an early sermon, God *"will restore everything"* (Acts 3:21)—the church must declare Christ's victory and stand its ground. That is our task and challenge.

"I have told you these things," says Jesus to his disciples at the end of his farewell discourse, *"so that in me you may have peace. In this world you will have trouble. But take heart! I have overcome the world"* (John 16:33). Christians can fight and hold their ground because we have peace with God. We know that our sin has been forgiven, that Christ has borne our judgment, that we are not under condemnation, that death is not the last word for us, and that eternal life in its fullness awaits us beyond the grave. So John, in his First Epistle, adds to what Jesus says in his ospel: *"This is love for God: to obey his commands. And his commands are not burdensome, for everyone born of God overcomes the world. This is the victory that has overcome the world, even our faith. Who is it that overcomes the world? Only he who believes that Jesus is the Son of God"* (1 John 5:3–5).

We are in a battle, but the victory is already ours through faith in our Commander. We can only experience this victory in our daily lives by putting on the armor of God, which means nothing more nor less than *Jesus Christ himself*. The apostle Paul makes this clear in Ephesians 6:10–20. Our enemies are *heavenly powers*. This is not mythical language; these are real angelic powers and authorities that work through human beings and through political, ideological, religious, and economic structures. We must learn how to *put on Christ*, how to put on the armor of God, every piece of it: truth, righteousness, proclamation of the gospel of peace, faith, hope. And with that, we must learn to wield the *offensive* weapons, which are the word of God and prayer. *"Therefore put on the full armor of God, so that when the day of evil comes, you may be able to stand your ground, and after you have done everything, to stand"* (Eph 6:13). The satanic worm has infected humanity and blighted God's world. How it happened, we do not know; but Adam—mankind—*fell*. The fallen world—the world understood as an exploitative, self-serving system—is dark, cruel, ruthless; it is in rebellion; it is *against* the Creator and the Redeemer (John 1:10, 17:14; 1 John 2:15–17;

Jas 4:4). Practically speaking, it remains "in the lap of the evil one" (1 John 5:19), and will remain so until the Lord returns to defeat his enemies definitively and take back his creation.

But already, by his cross and resurrection, Christ has conquered sin and death and has been given all authority in heaven and earth by the Father (Matt 28:18)—and this authority has been given to his disciples—to the church—*in his name*. Already in his earthly ministry, when he sent out the twelve, Jesus had given them authority over evil spirits and disease (Mark 6:7–12 and parallels). But that was only a foretaste. Now the disciples have been anointed and indwelt by the Spirit, such that Christ's power is not just *upon* them for a time, as it was also upon the prophets—it is *in* them. Therefore, even in the midst of this dark world that is enslaved to the evil one and lives, to a considerable extent, in fear and violence, Christians, as citizens of heaven, are *free*—free *within themselves*, whatever their circumstances—because their final reference is not this world but *God*. They are *in* this world, but not, ultimately, *of* it, as we've seen in our earlier talks.

We have been set free by Christ and thus are *able to learn to love*—and to love even the unlovable. We have access in Christ's name to supernatural power and, as the Spirit leads, can cast out demons and speak healing; we can stand humbly and unpretentiously in the public square and show mercy and work for justice and resist corruption and denounce the manipulations of ideology; we can refuse to lie, whatever the cost; we can abjure vengeance and forgive our enemies and even learn to bless them, by committing them to God and refusing to curse them in our heart; we can face pain and mockery and even torture and death with dignity, knowing that death is not the last word and that God will be faithful to usher us into the joy of his kingdom (Luke 12:4–12; 32–34); and when we sin and fail—for sometimes we will sin and fail—we can repent and ask God for forgiveness in the name of Jesus, and, by so doing, we can resist the devil—the Accuser—by refusing to fall under condemnation and wallow in guilt. *"Be self-controlled and alert,"* writes Peter. *"Your enemy the devil prowls around like a roaring lion looking for someone to devour. Resist him, standing firm in the faith, because you know that your brothers throughout the world are undergoing the same kind of sufferings"* (1 Pet 5:8–9). Each Christian is part of the worldwide body of Christ in space and time. We are in solidarity, whether we always feel that or not. We depend on each other, and on our mutual aid and prayer. This is a truth we must take more seriously than we do.

In his Second Epistle to the Corinthians, the apostle Paul writes as follows: *"For though we live in the world, we do not wage war as the world does. The weapons we fight with are not the weapons of the world. On the contrary, they have divine power to demolish strongholds. We demolish arguments and every pretension that sets itself up against the knowledge of God, and we take captive every thought to make it obedient to Christ"* (2 Cor 10:3-5). This is the church's road map, one might say. Christ has done the hard work on the cross, as Paul sums it up in Colossians 2:13-15:

> *When you were dead in your sins and in the uncircumcision of your sinful nature, God made you alive with Christ. He forgave us all our sins, having cancelled the written code, with its regulations, that was against us and that stood opposed to us; he took it away, nailing it to the cross. And having disarmed the powers and authorities, he made a public spectacle of them, triumphing over them by the cross.*

This great work that Jesus accomplished is the ground we stand on. The church has been given the Spirit of the risen Christ to break apart the strongholds of the fallen world—namely ideologies, corruption, addictions of all kinds, and the recourse to violence to achieve ends. In so doing, we affirm *God's* reality, power, and faithfulness, and *man's* dignity—the dignity of man/woman made in the image of God. The church has often failed to do this, and has sometimes acted, as an institution, like a stronghold itself; but our failures notwithstanding, the gates of hell have not prevailed and will not prevail against Christ's church (Matt 16:18), and the truth of the gospel has profoundly influenced human culture in the direction of recognizing human dignity and extending mercy, even if human nature itself remains unchanged and rebellious and as much in need of redemption as it ever was.

The majestic Christ of the book of Revelation, appearing to the exiled John on the island of Patmos at a time when the young church was entering a period of persecution, declares: *"'I am the Alpha and the Omega,' says the Lord God, 'who is, and who was, and who is to come, the Almighty.'"* And he goes on a moment later to reassure the awestruck apostle: *"Then he placed his right hand on me and said: 'Do not be afraid. I am the First and the Last. I am the Living One; I was dead, and behold I am alive forever and ever! And I hold the keys of death and Hades'"* (Rev 1:8, 17b-18). This is our God. We are not to be afraid, even as we see violence erupting all around us, even as we see Christ's name being cursed and trodden underfoot by ignorant and rebellious men and women. But we are to fight in the Spirit, and stand our ground, and pay the price of our faith, whatever it may be. We are the soldiers of Christ. Our communities are his platoons and squadrons. We must build them up and make them strong. The church is the bride of Christ, and the Spirit is cleansing and purifying us to receive our Lord when he comes (Eph 5:3-14 and Rev 21). And perhaps he is coming soon, very soon. This is our hope. Ultimately, the church lives by that hope, the hope *"that the creation itself will be liberated from its bondage to decay and brought into the glorious freedom of the children of God"* (Rom 8:21). When Jesus Christ returns in glory to our world, he will set things right, judge the wicked, affirm his sovereignty, and establish his kingdom in a transformed earth.

This text in Paul's Epistle to the Romans is especially striking in our contemporary context of worldwide ecological crisis, due largely to our sinful mismanagement and selfish exploitation of God's creation. He writes:

> *We know that the whole creation has been groaning as in the pains of childbirth right up to the present time. Not only so, but we ourselves, who have the first fruits of the Spirit, groan inwardly as we wait eagerly for our adoption as sons, the redemption of our bodies. For in this hope we were saved. But hope that is seen is no hope at all. Who hopes for what he already has? But if we hope for what we do not yet have, we wait for it patiently.* (Rom 8:22–25)

The Christian lives by faith, but it is *hope* that anchors him or her, as the author of the Epistle to the Hebrews declares: *"we who have fled to take hold of the hope offered to us may be greatly encouraged. We have this hope as an anchor of the soul, firm and secure. It enters the inner sanctuary behind the curtain, where Jesus, who went before us, has entered on our behalf. He has become a high priest forever, in the order of Melchizadek"* (Heb 6:18b–20). The Christian lives by faith in Christ, *by whom we have hope* in the manifest and ultimate victory of goodness and truth and beauty. Paul writes: *"May the God of hope fill you with all joy and peace as you trust in him, so that you may overflow with hope by the power of the Holy Spirit"* (Rom 15:13). Christ has conquered, and in him we conquer. We conquer by the Holy Spirit, the Spirit of the Father and of the Son (Rom 8:9–11), who lives within us and gives shape, meaning, purpose, and power to our lives. As John writes in Revelation 12:11, "They overcame [the accuser of the brethren] *by the blood of the Lamb and by the word of their testimony; they did not love their lives so much as to shrink from death."*

Our Lord calls us to be his servants, then his friends (John 15:15), and gradually he transfigures us into his likeness, anointing us in this life for service and preparing us, as his Bride, for the eternal life of glorious communion in his kingdom. *"Dear friends,"* writes John in his First Letter, *"now we are children of God, and what we will be has not yet been made known. But we know that when he appears, we shall be like him, for we shall see him as he is. Everyone who has this hope in him purifies himself, just as he is pure"* (1 John 3:2–3).

Such is our hope, and the ultimate source of the Christian identity and ethic, as I suggested earlier. As Paul writes to the Philippians, he is *"confident* of this, that God who began a good work in you will carry it on to completion until the day of Christ Jesus" (Phil 1:6). We, who are heirs of Abraham (Gal 3:29, 4:7; Rom 8:28-30), walk by faith and hope, *"looking forward to the city with foundations, whose architect and builder is God"* (Heb 11:10). And hence, in the midst of this harsh world, we are able to love, even as we are loved. The power of this vision is splendidly expressed by John near the end of the book of Revelation:

> *Then I saw a new heaven and a new earth, for the first heaven and the first earth had passed away, and there was no longer any sea. I saw the Holy City, the new Jerusalem, coming down out of heaven from God, prepared as a bride beautifully dressed for her husband. And I heard a loud voice from the throne saying, "Now the dwelling of God is with men, and he will live with them. They will be his people, and God himself will be with them and be their God. He will wipe every tear from their eyes. There will be no more death or mourning or crying or pain, for the old order of things has passed away . . . I am making everything new!"* (Rev 21:1-5a)

Notes for Short Talk on the Holy Spirit

(St. Michael's Church, Paris)

John 7:37-39

The Holy Spirit cannot indwell unholy man. In the Old Testament, the Spirit "came upon" certain individuals with prophetic vocations, but did not indwell them or remain upon them. Luke 9:1-2 records a similar situation, when Jesus anointed the disciples temporarily with power and authority—that is, with the Spirit—for a particular mission, no doubt to give them a foretaste of what was to come after his departure.

In the Old Testament relation to the Spirit, we may see an analogy, in a sense, with annual atonement sacrifices of the Old Testament, which could "cover" sins, but could not definitively remove the guilt or expiate the sin and had to be repeated each year.

For believers to receive the Spirit, who would then flow out of them like living waters, Jesus had to be crucified and resurrected and had to ascend to the right hand of the Father. All these events together constitute his glorification. They are three elevations—the *cross* (see John 12:23-24): Jesus must *die*; the *resurrection*: Jesus must *live*; the *ascension*: Jesus must *reign*. The coming of the Spirit upon believers—upon the church—is the fruit of the cross. It is vital to hold these two realities together. The Holy Spirit can come to indwell believers because the atoning work of Jesus Christ has justified them—sanctified them in the sense of making them acceptable to a holy God—and so made them fit vessels for the Spirit to indwell (see John 14:15-17, 25-26, 15:26-27, 16:7-11, 19:30, 20:19-23; Luke 24:45-49; Acts 1:4-5, 8, 2:32-41, 8:4-8, 14-17, 9:17-20, 10:44-48).

The Spirit that the Father gives to the ascended Son to pour out on the disciples is the Spirit of God, the Spirit of the Father, and the Spirit of the Son, the same Spirit that the Father sent upon the Son at Jesus's baptism. It is the Spirit that Jesus gives up with his last breath.

The gift of the Spirit is the promise of the Father, sent from the Father by the Son. It is an act of the Holy Trinity. The promise was prophesied by Joel (2:28-32; Ezek 37:14) and proclaimed by John the Baptist, who declared that Jesus would baptize in the Holy Spirit (Luke 3:16; Matt 3:11–12; John 1:32–33). It is an eschatological gift, associated with the new era that begins with Christ's glorification and will continue until his return, when his glory will be manifest to all the world. It is understood by Paul as a guarantee, a kind of down-payment, of the fullness of eternal life that will come at the *parousia*, when the Lord returns (2 Cor 1:22, 5:5). The Spirit will convict of sin, of Christ's righteousness, and of the condemnation and ultimate defeat of Satan, the ruler of this world (John 16:7–11; 1 John 5:19; Heb 2:14–15). Without the gift of the Spirit, none of these truths would be evident, and nothing would change in the world, despite Christ's work. Without the Spirit, the church, although instituted by Christ, could not have been constituted. Without the gift of the Spirit, the New Testament would not have been written. Without the gift of the Spirit—the Spirit of truth who speaks to our hearts what is *true* (John 16:13)—we would not be able to recognize the man Jesus as the Son of God and would not be able to know that God is love and that the eternal life Jesus promised us and won for us is an *eternity of love* (Rom 5:5). In a word: to proclaim Jesus to be Lord, with all that this implies, is not possible for the natural man; it is a work of the Holy Spirit (1 Cor 12:3b).

The Spirit is given to equip the disciples and all believers with power—*dunamis* (Acts 1:8)—for mission, to go out as witnesses of the risen Christ into all the nations of the world, starting from Jerusalem, to tell the good news. Gentiles and Jews both must hear the gospel. The stories of the Samaritans, Cornelius, and Paul confirm this. Christ, empowered by the Spirit, died and was raised for all men and women; in like manner, his Spirit, now poured out on believers, will empower them to carry the truth of the gospel to all men and women. By the gift of the Spirit, confirming Christ's work, the barrier between Jews and gentiles is overcome (in *truth*, if not always in practice), and the promise first made to Abraham that all nations will be blessed through him, is fulfilled (Gen 12:1–4).

Receiving the Spirit is not just an inner spiritual experience. It is associated with proclamation and action. Proclamation of the good news is accompanied by signs and wonders, healings, deliverances, speaking in tongues, and prophetic utterances. These are manifestations of spiritual power. The gift of the Spirit is thus seen as a sovereign, mighty work of God, utterly beyond normal human capacity. The events reported in Acts give evidence of this.

John's account in John 20 of the gift of the Spirit is focused on the intimate circle of disciples, whereas the Pentecostal outpouring is for all who will believe, through the proclamation of the disciples as represented by Peter. The experience in John may be understood as a preview and preparation of the future apostles for the day of Pentecost itself. In both accounts, the disciples—and through them, all believers—are sent by Jesus into the world, as Jesus himself was sent by the Father into the world.

The basic pattern for receiving the Spirit is given by Peter in his proclamation at Pentecost. There is a welcoming of the message by many hearers, which we may take to be evidence of regeneration, of the new birth, of a mysterious, unconscious work by the Spirit to convince the heart of sin and of Christ's lordship and saving work; this is followed by conscious repentance and the receiving of forgiveness of sin; this is accompanied by baptism and the reception of the gift of the Spirit. The rite of baptism sacramentally gathers these elements together and formally incorporates the believer into the church, an act by which the person is publicly constituted and recognized as a Christian, a member of the body of Christ. There is no fixed formula or precise sequence for this entry into the life of Christ, as the variety of experiences of the Spirit as reported in Acts demonstrates; but all these elements are involved in becoming the new creation that is a Christian (2 Cor 5:17; Gal 6:15).

Baptism in the Spirit and water baptism into Christ are not two dissociated events, *theologically speaking*, though they may be separated in time, as has often been the case in the history of the church (the rites of infant baptism and subsequent confirmation, correctly considered to be aspects of *one* sacrament, are the evidence of this in the liturgical churches that baptize infants). A two-blessing theology misguidedly separates Christ and the Spirit. It is by the Spirit that Jesus Christ does his redemptive work on our behalf, obtaining for us the remission of sins; and it is this same Spirit whom Christ pours out and in whom he baptizes believers to empower them to proclaim the remission of sins and the hope of eternal life. He is both the *bearer* and the *giver* of the one Spirit.

The new life in Christ is an immersion in the Spirit that is sacramentally recognized by an immersion in water, which takes place at the rite of baptism. We must be born of water and the Spirit to enter the kingdom of God, Jesus tells Nicodemus in John 3:5. What is often missing in the historic churches is the *appropriation* of the fullness of what we have in Christ by the Spirit; but all that fullness is there in Christ *from the beginning*, and is *not added to* by the Spirit on the occasion of a second experience. *Theologically* speaking, this must be emphasized, for the sake of theological clarity; but *practically* speaking, the importance for individual Christians of appropriating for themselves, by faith, the fullness of the Spirit and the charismatic gifts that he dispenses (1 Cor 12), should be taught and stressed. Otherwise, the sacrament of initiation—baptism—may remain inefficacious and fruitless, confined to ritual and good intentions but lacking missionary motivation and transforming power—lacking, that is, the kind of reality that Jesus is talking about in John 7:38 when he speaks of *"rivers of living water flowing out of the heart."*

Jesus is our prototype. As it was in his life as a man, so it is to be in our lives as disciples. Jesus was born of the Spirit; so is a believer (Luke 1:35; John 1:12–13, 3:5, 8b). In both cases, a new humanity is generated. Interestingly, in John 1:12, the apostle says that the person who receives Christ, the "true light," is given *authority* to become a child of God, by which we may understand that our identity as sons and daughters of God, by virtue of the new birth, is the ground of our spiritual *authority* as Christians. Jesus was baptized in water and the Spirit and declared by the Father to be the Son of God; so is a believer (Matt 3:13–17; John 1:12–13). At the time of his baptism, Jesus was anointed by the Spirit and entered into his vocation and the fullness of his messianic call; so does a believer enter on his/her mission as a follower of the Messiah when the fullness of his/her identity as a baptized son or daughter of God is consciously recognized and appropriated (Rom 6:4, 8:14–16). This is our anointing, when we receive the *dunamis*—power—from on high.

As Jesus was led by the Spirit after his baptism into the wilderness and tempted by the devil (see Luke 4:1–2, 14), so are believers, albeit not in the same radical and destiny-determining way as Jesus, the Second Adam, was; as he was attacked by Satan, so will believers be, in countless ways, subtle and blatant; as he was anointed by the Spirit to do miracles of healing and to deliver people from demons, so are believers (Luke 4:18–19; Matt 11:2–6, 12:28; and numerous texts in Acts). Jesus the man, though the Son of God, did these works of power *as a man*—as a human being like us—*by virtue of the Spirit's anointing*, received at his baptism. We are summoned to do likewise, by the same Spirit: *"Very truly, I tell you, the one who believes in me will also do the works that I do and, in fact, will do greater works than these, because I am going to the Father"* (John 14:12). The fullness of God was in him (Col 2:9), and we are exhorted *"to come to the unity of the faith and of the knowledge of the Son of God, to maturity, to the measure of the full stature of Christ"* (Eph 4:13). Jesus was a man like us, but without sin. Yes, *he* was fathered by the Holy Spirit—but so are *we*, at regeneration. His power to do mighty works was given him at his baptism, when the Father anointed him with the Holy Spirit. So it is with us.

The Spirit first does a work in *Jesus* for us; then he does a work in *us* for Jesus. As Jesus mediates the *Spirit* to us, the Spirit mediates *Jesus* to us. Our redemption is a Trinitarian work: the Father sends the Son and anoints him by the Spirit, and the Son reveals the Father to us; Jesus gives up the Spirit at his death, and at Christ's ascension, the Father sends the Spirit by the Son upon humanity; the Spirit in turn reveals and glorifies the Son.

At Jesus's baptism, as at ours, the cross and the resurrection are both foreshadowed, as is the eschatological life to come, the fullness of life in the Spirit, in the communion of the Father and the Son. We are called to be conformed to Jesus Christ, who is the very image of God. Jesus suffered; so must we. This entails pain often of a different kind from what unbelievers suffer, who are not concerned with doing God's will; it entails suffering, bearing one's cross, dying to self, being subjected to attacks from the enemy—all this *along with* manifest blessings, joyous communion with God, freedom in the presence of the Trinity and progressive transformation into Christ's image (2 Cor 3:17–18), and the wonderful gifts of hope and of knowledge that through Christ the Son, we who believe are beloved sons and daughters of God the Father (Rom 5:1–5, 8:15–17). But it cannot be emphasized enough that there is nothing triumphalist about receiving the gift of the Spirit—the gift comes from the Lord seated in victory at the right hand of the Father, yes, but that victory was won at the cross, and its application in our own lives can likewise only be won at the cross.

In Christ by the Spirit we receive forgiveness of sins, sanctification, and the hope of salvation and resurrection from the dead. A keen awareness of eschatological reality and of the Lord's return comes upon us. We sense the presence of the Holy Trinity. The Bible comes alive as the word of God. We want to praise and exult in God, our Savior and Lord. We experience assurance of salvation and boldness in proclaiming Christ. We receive both the *fruit* of the Spirit, as we are progressively changed in our character and habits (Gal 5:22–23; 2 Cor 3:17–18), and the charismatic *gifts* of the Spirit, as we exercise faith to use them (1 Cor 12:4–11; Romans 12:6–8). We receive *authority, love,* and *power*. We need all three of these gifts to carry out the Spirit's mission of glorifying Christ on earth. The world, in its unbelief and rebellion against the true God, operates in terms of power, the power of violence and domination; Christians too must operate in terms of power, but it must be the power of the Holy Spirit, manifest in love and compassion—and *also* in mighty works.

It is by *grace* that we receive both the fruit and the gifts of the Spirit, and it is by *faith*—itself a gift of grace—that we appropriate these for ourselves. The Spirit of Christ grows his virtues—his fruit—within us over time, as we submit to him in faith; and he manifests himself charismatically through us, on particular occasions, as, again, we submit to him in faith. The charismatic gifts, including tongues, are called *"manifestations of the Spirit"* (1 Cor 12:7). They are specific gifts of grace given by the primary Gift, who is the Spirit. They are given to praise God or to declare his will or purposes or to carry out some specific ministerial task. They are for the building up of the body of Christ (1 Cor 14:3-4, 12), for developing and deepening its unity. Those who exercise them are not better than others, and boasting or self-satisfaction is uncalled for and must be resisted at all costs.

What we are *all* exhorted to do is to lay hold by faith of these "spirituals"—these *pneumatikon*, as Paul calls them in 1 Corinthians 12:1—and learn to exercise them appropriately, with sensitivity, love, humility.[1] We must *desire* the overflowing of the Spirit, in fruit and charismatic gifts; we must be *open* to the Spirit's sovereign activity; we must seek, thirst after, listen, receive, act. He is the subject, we the objects of his action; but we are not passive, we have our part to play, by trust, faith, and boldness. Paul's word in Philippians 2:12-13, generally applicable to the Christian life, also can be applied specifically to reception of the Spirit's charismatic power: *". . . work out your own salvation with fear and trembling, for it is God who is at work in you, enabling you both to will and to work for his good pleasure."*

What the French call the "effusion" of the Spirit—the "outpouring," as in John 7:38—may come by a sovereign act of God when we are alone in prayer, or in a large assembly where God is being worshipped, or through the laying on of hands by anointed ministers, whether ordained or lay. We are called to *keep being filled* with the Spirit, to keep seeking God for his presence and power (Acts 4:31; Eph 5:18). Doing this is like practicing a language. If you don't practice it, you begin to lose fluency and competence. We are speaking here, again, of *appropriation*. The Spirit of Christ is *with* us, *in* us (John 14:17), by virtue of our baptism or an initial experience of conversion later confirmed by baptism, but we must keep opening ourselves to him. *"Fan the flame of the gift of God that is in you by the laying on of my hands,"* writes Paul to Timothy; and he goes on: *"for God did not give us a spirit of cowardice, but rather a spirit of power and of love and of self-discipline* (2 Tim 1:6-7). We must keep *praying*—privately, in our marriages, in our assemblies. We must keep walking with God and exercising our gifts. The author of the Epistle to the Hebrews writes: *"Let us hold fast to the confession of our hope without wavering, for he who has promised is faithful. And let us consider how to provoke one another to love and good deeds, not neglecting to meet together, as is the habit of some, but encouraging one another, and all the more as you see the day approaching"* (Heb 10:23-25).

---

1. See 1 Corinthians 13, deliberately sandwiched between chapters 12 and 14.

Spiritual reality must become normal for us. It is easy for us to become deflated, especially in such an unbelieving society as the one we live in. We can fall into resigned passivity or fleshly striving. But that is the whole point of the baptism in the Spirit. The world has always been unbelieving. Our fallen race has always been mired in idolatry. Only the Holy Spirit can lift us out of unbelief. Only he can convince human beings that Jesus Christ is Lord, as he, the Spirit, touches hearts and manifests himself through love and gifts of power. The apostle Paul sums up the matter succinctly: "... *no one can say 'Jesus is Lord' except by the Holy Spirit*" (1 Cor 12:3b).

Notes for Talks on Pastoral Care and Counseling

(St. Michael's Anglican Church, Paris)

Talk I

CARERS AS ONES WHO *let themselves be cared for*. Christ calls *all* of us to progressive maturity and sanctification. Our concern today is not with technique and method, but with *who we are*.

I

Identity and Calling

a. *Election*. Ephesians 1:3-14. We were destined in Christ to be God's sons and daughters. 1 Peter 1:20-21. Christ was destined and made manifest *for us*; through him we have confidence in God and know him to be our Father.

b. *Vocation: Servants.* Luke 17:7-10 (service to God is our duty); Matthew 20:25-28 (called to service); John 13:14-17 (servants and their master); 1 Corinthians 6:19-20 (your body belongs to Christ, you are bought with a price).

We are able to be servants of God because the Son became a servant for our sake (Phil 2:1-11). We *are* servants, and as such are called to serve. Service is the Christian way of life.

But it is as *sons/daughters* and as *friends* of God that we are servants (John 15:12-17 [intimate relation to God]; and see John 20:17; Rom 8:15).

Our *mission of service*. John 17:15-19 (sent as Son was sent); Luke 9:1-6 (sending of first disciples); John 14:12-14 (doing works in Jesus's name—this text is in the context of the sending of the Holy Spirit, the

Paraclete); Matthew 28:18-20 (Christ's authority and ours: His presence and commission).

So: we are sons and daughters of the Father through Christ in the Spirit; and we are friends of the Son, with the vocation of servants. How do we serve? What do we do? How do we help?

II

Preparation for Service

Ephesians 2:8-10. He will lead us into works he has prepared for us. They will emerge out of what he does in us.

John 13:8. We must let ourselves be washed by our Lord if we are to do his works.

John 15:1-8. Abiding in him. Apart from him, we can do nothing that brings true life to the world. We do not have life in ourselves. We are branches in the vine, which is Christ (John 15:1-17). Our fruitfulness involves and requires pruning.

Pruning: this is the source of fruitfulness; through the process, we gain spiritual authority: 2 Corinthians 3:18, 4:12; Ephesians 4:22-23 (see Colossians 3:5-11); Romans 6:12-14; Galatians 2:20, 5:24. Identification with Christ on the cross and in his resurrection; our old man—our sinful nature—has been put to death in Christ, and, raised up with him, we have been given a new nature, we are a new creation; on this basis, we are in a position *to put to death our particular sins* as the Lord reveals them by his Spirit, because the generator of those sins, the old nature, is dead; death in *us* (the putting to death of sins, by the Holy Spirit) works life in *you*, says the apostle Paul, speaking for all Christians; our progressive sanctification redounds to the benefit others.

Transformation: conformity to his image; process of sanctification and healing, the coming into wholeness in ourselves and in our relationships. As we are changed and filled with him, we have life—*his* life—to give to others. The cross: *not reform, but death and new life.*

Colossians 2:6; 1 Peter 2:4-6; Philippians 2:12-13. As we are rooted by baptism in him, so let us walk in him, being built up. There is an active, conscious, deliberate side to this (Phil 2:12) and a passive side in the sense that the will sets itself simply to trust and let go (Phil 2:13). Thus are we built up, individually and corporately. This is the loving work of the Holy Spirit. He leads us into greater maturity and holiness.

III

Areas for Examination, as We Seek to Know Our Particular Calling and Sphere of Service

Principle: the particular state (married, single, parent, elderly, orphan, foreigner, education, etc.) and conditions of one's life (whether fortunate or unfortunate) are God's opportunity and are under his sovereignty. They are not to be seen, as such, as liabilities to be overcome in order to be able to serve God, but as providing the source and shape, broadly, of the ministry God wishes to give us.

Providence: Romans 8:28. We need to trust, believe, try to discern his leadings in our life, and respond creatively, boldly, to the features and persons that make up our daily existence and our heart's inclinations. Our effective service will then begin to emerge and happen. God is not limited by our limitations: he is strong precisely in our weakness, if we *accept* these weaknesses, whatever sort they may be, and *allow* God to be strong within them, whether to overcome, change, or simply work through them as they are (2 Cor 11:30, 12:9–10). It is not easy for any of us to accept or apply this—sometimes we don't even understand it—but it is a crucial principle for effective service.

Several areas for prayerful examination before God:

a. *Forgiveness and Judgment*: Matthew 7:1–5; 1 Corinthians 4:1–5; Romans 2:1–2; Matthew 18:21–35, 6:12–15.

b. *Self-image*. What image of ourselves do we present to God in prayer? Do we come just as we are, or with our best foot forward? The common combination of self-rejection and pride. The problem of self-condemnation, which often leads to condemnation/judgment of others. Loving ourselves as God loves us. The question of performance. The question of self-acceptance.

c. *Our image of God*. Is it two-tiered? Do we really believe God is a loving Father? Sovereign? Active in events and responsive to prayer?

d. *Relations with and attitudes toward others*. Parents, spouses, children, teachers, business colleagues, etc. Where are these out of joint? Do we speak truth in love? How real is our communion?

e. *Burden-bearing and listening*.

f. *Hospitality*. 1 Peter 4:9; Hebrews 13:2; 3 John 5–8; Romans 16:1–2; Luke 14:12–14 (guests to supper).

g. *Prayer.*

h. *Scripture.*

i. *Assembling together and eucharistic celebration.*

The last three are presupposed by all the others, and make them possible.

IV

Homework

1. Reflection and prayerful meditation on areas discussed.
2. Pray and, if possible, act to set things right where needed.
3. Meditate on our salvation through the blood of Jesus (Eph 1:3–8). This is a Trinitarian meditation: Father's unconditional love; Son's implementation of this and total identification with us; Spirit's outworking of this in our lives, as he lives in us and sanctifies us.

Talk II

I

Identity Question

Ephesians 1:5: *"He destined us in love to be his sons and daughters through Jesus Christ, according to the purpose of his will, to the praise of his glorious grace which he freely bestowed on us in the Beloved."*

To be sons and daughters is our destiny and inheritance in Christ. It is our *primary* identity, the fulfillment, through Christ, of our created nature as personal beings made in the image of God. This identity question is crucial.

Three texts to bring out its importance in Jesus's life:

1. *Matthew 3:16-17*. Baptism. Sonship confirmed.
2. *Matthew 4:5, 6, 9.* Satan's first attack is to question Christ's Being-as-Son; *only when he* can't get anywhere that way does Satan make a frontal attack and demand worship in exchange for wealth and power.
3. *John 13:3-4*. Sure identity as sons and daughters of the loving Father is *basis* for service. This was so for Jesus, it is so for us. We may

expect, then, from the model of Jesus's life, that our well-being and our useful service for God's Kingdom will depend on the firmness of our identity in Christ, with all that this means.

II

Biblical Anthropology: Spirit, Soul, Body

Romans 8:14–16. What Reformed doctrine calls the "inner witness of the Spirit," that we are saved, justified, loved, forgiven—in a word, fully adopted sons and daughters of God. This witness does not just drop on us out of the sky: it is a witness of the Holy Spirit in and with our spirit, as Romans 8:16 puts it (see 1 Corinthians 6:17).

What is our "spirit" (1 Thess 5:23; see Gen 2:7)? A human being is a *person*, made in God's image, that is, with the capacity (in distinction from all other animals) of *personal* relationship with his/her Creator. He/she is tri-partite, a *living soul*, constituted by virtue of God's breath breathed into matter. By virtue of God's breath, men and women have a *spirit*, and so can relate to God-who-is-Spirit. But because of sin, we were cut off from God and in this sense *"dead in transgressions and sins,"* as Paul puts it in Ephesians 2:1. The natural man's *spirit* is dead, he/she is *not* in personal communion with the living God, and cannot be, *until regenerated* through Christ. Such a person can think about God, have religious feelings, do meditation, practice rituals, etc., but cannot have *personal communion* with the true, living, holy God who is love. This is the condition of fallen human beings. Outside of Christ, we cannot truly love God or know that we are loved by him. We cannot *know* him. Made as we are in God's image, we may strive spiritually according to some religious impulse, seeking some kind of peace or sanctity before whatever we take to be God or the divine; but, alienated from God as our race is through the fall, we are functioning in the power of the *soul*, by our will, mind, emotions, imagination, under the direction of our own ego, and not through our *spirit* indwelt by and under the direction of God's Spirit. When, by grace through the word of God, our hearts are opened and Christ is revealed to us, then we humble ourselves and believe and receive him as risen Lord and Savior—and thus do we become a new creation, a son or daughter of God, as the Holy Spirit enters into our spirit and quickens it. It is here that the Spirit dwells within us, so that the apostle can speak of us as being *"the temple of the Holy Spirit"* (1 Cor 6:17, 19). It is by the presence of God's Spirit in *our* spirit that we can have communion with God, can pray, can worship *"in spirit and in truth"* (John 4:23).

The process of sanctification, accomplished in us progressively by the cross, consists in one area after another of our *soul* coming gradually under the dominion of the Holy Spirit working in us through *our quickened spirit*, whereby we are in communion with God and able to hear the voice of our Shepherd. As this happens, bringing with it healing and transformation, we become more and more *whole persons*, we enter more and more fully into our *salvation* here and now, as we are conformed to Christ's image and made ready, individually and as a corporate people, to meet the bridegroom. We become integrated, knit together. So Paul can write: *"May God himself, the God of peace, sanctify you through and through. May your whole spirit, soul and body be kept blameless at the coming of our Lord Jesus Christ. The one who calls you is faithful and He will do it"* (1 Thess 5:23–24).

Notes for Talks on Identity and Inner Healing

(St. Clement's Church, Oxford)

I

Theological Scene-setting

The crucial question of identity. There is great confusion in our secular age about what human beings are and about what they are called to. In order to stand firm and bear witness to Christ, we must know who we are.

It is as we know God that we know ourselves. We know God because we are known by him. Our knowledge of the true God is by divine self-revelation, through his word, written in Scripture and enfleshed in Jesus. And as we know God, as we believe in and receive his Word incarnate in Christ, we are given authority, as John 1:12 puts it, to become children—sons and daughters—of God. This is our *primary* identity as Christians, making *secondary* all other natural identities, whether gender, ethnic, tribal, or social.

To know God through Jesus—to know him as Father, through the Son, by revelation from the Holy Spirit—is to begin to know who *we* are, as humans and as this particular human each of us is. We cannot know otherwise that we are formed by God out of dust and created in his image as he breathed into us his life (Gen 2:7); that we are sinners who have left our true home, like the prodigal son, or who are self-righteous and judgmental of others, like the elder son (Luke 15:11–31); that we are loved of God, each one of us, despite our rebellion; that we are forgiven through the passion and the shed blood of Christ; that eternal life in God's joyous kingdom, not death, is our destiny, if we hold to our course in faith and love and persevere in hope; that we are called to reign with God—Father, Son, and Holy Spirit—in an everlasting communion of love. If we do not know these truths, we will be unable to know how to conduct ourselves in this life in a manner that pleases a holy God and sustains harmonious social relations. Neither moral philosophy nor scientific inquiry—worthy though both these activities are—can reveal these truths to us. Only God can. And this he has done through his revelation to Israel and through the incarnation of his Son in Jesus Christ.

"*All things have been handed over to me by my Father; and no one knows the Son except the Father, and no one knows the Father except the Son and anyone to whom the Son chooses to reveal him*" (Matt 11:27; Luke 10:22). This is a pivotal verse in Scripture. A correlative verse is 1 Corinthians 12:3b: "*. . . no one can say 'Jesus is Lord' except by the Holy Spirit.*" Only the Holy Spirit can reveal to us who Jesus truly is—the Son of God incarnate and Lord of all creation—and only the Son can reveal to us the Father. God the Father and God the Son are inseparable; each necessarily implies the other.

We know through the revelation of Christ that God is love and Spirit, *both* (1 John 4:7–12; John 4:24). To say God is love is to say *he is plural, relational*, more than one, for love is the free self-giving of one to another. It is also to say *he is personal*, for ideas and forces cannot love; only living beings can love, the highest creaturely form of which is conscious human persons. This confirms what is revealed to us in Genesis 1:26, namely, that *we are made in God's image*. On two counts, then, by inference from the creation account in Genesis 1, we may understand God to be personal: as Creator and as the One-in-Three in whose image mankind, made up of male and female *persons*, is created.

Father and Son constitute two Persons of the Triune God, the begetting Father and the eternally begotten Son, in an eternal mutuality of love. The Third Person of the Triune God is the expression of this mutuality, in the form of the Spirit of each given joyfully to the other in love: the Spirit of the Father and the Spirit of the Son in everlasting communion. The three Persons constitute one being who is differentiated Spirit, one divine being made up of three Persons-in-communion. God is One-in-Three and Three-in-One.

"*No one has ever seen God. It is God the only Son, who is close to the Father's heart, who has made him known*" (John 1:18). The incarnate Son Jesus cannot for one moment be thought of apart from his union in one Spirit with his Father. By his life, death, and resurrection, Jesus has won for us the privilege of entering into this union—indeed, into "the Father's heart." Adopted sons and daughters through Jesus, the Eternal Son, we who believe and receive this Jesus as Savior may also call God "Abba, Father." "*For in Christ Jesus you are all children of God through faith. . . . And because you are children, God has sent the Spirit of his Son into our hearts, crying, 'Abba! Father!' So you are no longer a slave but a child, and if a child then also an heir, through God"* (Gal 3:26, 4:6-7; see also Rom 8:12–17). This is confirmed most movingly in John 20:17b, where the risen Jesus speaks to Mary Magdalene as she stands weeping outside the empty tomb: *". . . go to my brothers and say to them, 'I am ascending to my Father and your Father, to my God and your God'"* (John 20:17b).

Abba is an Aramaic word meaning "Dear Father." It is intimate, but reverent. "Daddy" is too casual to convey its full sense. Every use by Jesus of the word *pater* carries the sense of *Abba* behind it, but it is salutary to note that the single actual use of the word *Abba* by Jesus occurs in Gethsemane: *"And going a little farther, he threw himself on the ground and prayed that, if it were possible, the hour might pass from him. He said, 'Abba, Father, for you all things are possible; remove this cup from me; yet, not what I want, but what you want'"* (Mark 14:35-36). What the Father wills is the salvation of humankind, and this requires the Son's (willing) self-sacrifice. To call God *Abba* entails a willingness to die to self if self-will conflicts with the Father's will. This is what Jesus is demonstrating in Gethsemane.

If we are *children*, it follows, as Paul puts it, that we are *heirs*, which implies conformity to the likeness of Christ. The heart of that likeness, as far as action is concerned, is obedience to the Father's will, and this will inevitably involve suffering for us, as it did for Jesus. Paul confirms this truth in a famous passage in Romans:

> . . . *if you live according to the flesh, you will die; but if by the Spirit you put to death the deeds of the body* [that is, the sinful deeds of the fallen nature], *you will live. For all who are led by the Spirit of God are children of God. For you did not receive a spirit of slavery to fall back into fear, but you have received a spirit of adoption. When we cry "Abba! Father!" it is that very Spirit bearing witness with our spirit that we are children of God, and if children, then heirs, heirs of God and joint-heirs with Christ—if, in fact, we suffer with him so that we may also be glorified with him.* (Rom 8:13–17)

As this obedience becomes natural to us through progressive healing and sanctification—progressive dying to the attitudes and habits of what Paul calls the "old man," coupled with healing from old wounds that often underlie these attitudes and habits—an authentic reflection of the life of Jesus will begin to appear in our own lives, freed from the striving and straining after righteousness and justification and worth and recognition and performance that characterize our natural self. We will know true inner freedom.

It is as this process moves forward that Jesus's words about his burden being light begin to take on meaning. *"Come to me, all you that are weary and are carrying heavy burdens, and I will give you rest. Take my yoke upon you and learn from me; for I am gentle and humble in heart, and you will find rest for your souls. For my yoke is easy, and my burden is light"* (Matt 11:28–30). It is vital to note that these famous words follow directly on the text from Matthew about the Son and the Father knowing each other that I quoted above. Jesus has taken upon himself the incalculable burden of our rebellion and the often-repressed weight of guilt and shame accompanying it that lies at the root of the insatiable drive of humankind, alluded to above, toward self-justification and self-salvation. The more we allow him to live his life through us (Gal 2:20) and to do in us individually by his Spirit what he has done for the whole race at Calvary (the process of dying to the old nature and rising to new life), the more we will find rest for our souls and know the peace that passes understanding.

The purpose of Christ's coming was to save us so that we might know the Father through the Son and, by extension, God's eternal plan for the human race and for each of us personally (see John 14:1–7, 17:3). Our self-understanding as adopted sons and daughters of God is essential if we are to have a fruitful life as Christians. This *sonship* is our *being*, our *spiritual identity*, out of which and on the basis of which we *act*. As we know the Father through the Son, we rest from our striving, our works-salvation—whatever form this may take—and we let the Spirit work through us to accomplish his will with the power and effectiveness that belong properly to him.

II

Inner Healing

I believe that the question of our identity in Christ as adopted sons and daughters of God is foundational for an adequate presentation of the subject of inner healing. The practice of inner healing is essential to the health and growth of any local fellowship of Christians. It is essential to the building up of a community in love and fruitfulness. The notes that follow provide basic guidelines on this theme, though the concrete examples that my wife Victoria and I provided in our talks are not included. Some of what I say here has already been touched on earlier, but, for pedagogical reasons, this is an area where repetition is important, even vital. My aim here is our *practice*, not just our theoretical understanding. We are seeking not just to learn more about the Christian life, but to *live it* more fully and to help others to do likewise.

Prayer counseling and inner healing are not adjuncts to Christian life and mission. They are central to the building up of the Body of Christ so that we may more effectively fulfill our mission in the world at all levels. We all suffer, we all have need of healing and greater wholeness. This is an aspect of the personal outworking of our faith in Christ and commitment to God. It is the work of the Holy Spirit, on the basis of Christ's atonement and redemption won at the Cross (Isa 53:1–6; 1 Pet 2:23–24; Rom 3:9b–26, 8:1–4; Eph 1:7, 2:8; Ps 103:1–14). *Sozo*, the Greek word usually translated "save," also means "heal." The primary context for this is the local parish, the local community of followers of Jesus, the local family of believers.

Healing and sanctification go together (1 Pet 1:16; 1 Thess 5:23; 1 Cor 1:30; Phil 2:12). Wholeness and holiness. As we appropriate our salvation and experience this work of the Holy Spirit, we become better and bolder witnesses for the gospel and more effective members of society. We are not doing psychological therapy, but healing of the *heart*, the inner man, involving spiritual conversion and growth in maturity. But the human *person*, as we saw earlier, is made up of spirit, soul, and body. The three make up the one unique personal identity, so the *pneuma* and *psuche* and *soma* are all involved. Spiritual discernment and psychological insight must go together and be integrated.

Wounds and sins are not the same thing, but almost always belong together. Underneath most sins—but not original sin itself—are wounds a person has suffered, which have induced, in reaction, patterns of sinful behavior. The source of the wounds will have been events that have befallen us, for which we were not responsible (such as natural disasters, war, prejudice, divorce of parents, accidents), and harm done directly to us by others. In prayer and counseling, we try to locate the root wound(s) needing healing, and to discern the sinful patterns needing acknowledgement, confession, repentance, and renunciation.

Healing of the inner person, like healing of the body, takes time. Emotions, repressed or avoided, often unconscious, must come to the surface and be expressed as the often painful truth of what one has experienced is faced and acknowledged. Sensitive, anointed prayer will always be effective, but we cannot predict or systematize the pace or manner of the Spirit's healing action in response to the prayer. Immediate results may or may not be evident.

III

Basic Principles of Inner Healing

We are all God's *creatures*; but original sin—our refusal to have our Creator be our Lord—has alienated us from God, and we are not God's *sons and daughters* until we have received Christ and entered into the reconciliation with God that he has won us. The experience of humbling ourselves and shifting our primary allegiance from ourselves and our works to God and his work, is what it means to be "born again" (John 1:11–12, 3:3, 6). We must become *new creations* (Gal 6:15; 2 Cor 5:17–19).

1. As *new creations*, we have a new fundamental identity as sons and daughters of God, and a new perspective on God, others, ourselves, the universe (2 Cor 5:16; Romans 6:11). Baptism—the putting to death of the sin principle, the ego-focus, the lordship of *self*, the old man—and the rising to new life as we emerge from the waters, signifies this (Rom 6:1–14). We must learn to see ourselves, by faith, as dead to the old darkness, the old wounds and sins, and alive to the light. The guilt, shame, and condemnation are past; grace, love, and hope are the new reality. We are no longer slaves to sin (Rom 6:12–14; 8:15), determined by fate, ruled by fear of death (Heb 2:14–15), and with a self-understanding of being victims. Christ, the voluntary victim on our behalf, our corporate representative (as Perfect Man) and individual substitute for each of us, has overcome all that for us. In love for us, he has set us free by his self-sacrifice from the curse of original sin, its unholy consequences, and the condemnation under which God's holy Law brought us (John 8:31–32, 36, 10:10; Rom 8:1–4). God the Father has sent Christ the Son and the Holy Spirit to give us life in abundance, to save us from alienation and violence and death.

2. *Forgiveness*. As we are forgiven, so we must forgive (Matt 6:9–15; Col 3:12–14). Asking forgiveness and granting forgiveness to those who have harmed us is fundamental to healing and growth in wholeness and holiness. As we grow in grace and maturity, such forgiveness, where necessary, should become instinctual with us, an integrated, regular, normal part of our lives. Through forgiveness, we are released from the offender, and the offender is released from us, into God's hands. Forgiveness is essentially a matter of the will, not the emotions. The emotions will follow eventually. For deep wounds, our act to forgive may have to penetrate down through layers of hurt,

over time. We must continue to stand in our basic position of forgiveness until the pain is dissipated, the sting withdrawn, the mine in our hearts defused. Forgiving is not a matter of forgetting or minimizing the offense and the pain, but of removing the sting and being set free from bitterness and the desire to be avenged. Those who do not forgive are captives of those who have offended them. Seeking revenge will bring neither justice nor peace. There is much misunderstanding of these issues. Forgiveness can perfectly well accompany the quest for penal justice, in a criminal case. But our hearts will be clear; our quest for justice will not be a quest for revenge; the possibility of ultimate reconciliation will be opened up. We forgive others in obedience to Christ's command, and by the power of his Spirit and example on the cross. Forgiveness of ourselves, where we recognize our sin and shame, is also very important. We must not hold onto our guilt, once we have repented and asked forgiveness of God. As God forgives us, so must we forgive ourselves and move on into the future and new life.

3. *False images of God.* These will have been implanted in us from various forms of rejection, unlove, abuse, the loss of a loved one, oppression, legalism, religious untruth, etc., suffered in childhood or later. All this negativity and the unbelief in God or in God's love that it generates must be discerned and corrected, according to the truth about God the Father revealed in Christ the Son (John 1:18, 14:6, 9; 1 John 4:16). Blaming God seems to be a natural human reaction to tragedy or disappointment, but in light of the incarnation of God in Jesus Christ, it is totally unwarranted and wrong. God is good, there is no darkness or injustice or indifference in him.

4. *False images of self.* The sources of these will be similar to the above. Abandonment in some form, rejection leading to self-rejection and a sense of unworthiness, even self-hatred, are common. Negative words spoken to us (put-downs, condemnations, insults, curses), especially when we were growing up, will have penetrated us like arrows and will need to be renounced and pulled out in prayer. They do not correspond to the truth about ourselves in Christ. The sorrow in our hearts, usually repressed and of which we may hardly be aware, must be brought to the light and healed. The counterpart to our inner self-denigration is a whole range of self-defensive and survival strategies developed over the years, usually unconsciously, leading to responses and inner attitudes like self-pity, seeing oneself as a victim, drawing attention to oneself through sickness or failure,

self-justification, perfectionism, arrogance and judgmentalism, legalism, workaholism, masks, manipulative obsequiousness, quest for power and domination, etc. These are all equally the bad fruit of false images of our true self in Christ and must be corrected and renounced. Both our spirits and our souls will have been wounded. Healing prayer and consolation will be needed.

5. *Self-acceptance.* This is essential, and often difficult. Suffering is hard to face. So is shame, when we see conduct in our past that we regret. We want to reject it as not part of ourselves, as something *un*acceptable. But we must resist this inclination and receive God's grace; we must stand in the new person that we are in Christ, loved and affirmed by God; and we must honestly accept the lives we have had, the events we have experienced that may have been destructive and painful, and the persons we have been and are, with our sins, limitations, regrets, gifts, failings, etc. Of course *this does not mean tolerating our sins*; rather, it is the path toward discerning them correctly, asking for forgiveness, and renouncing them. If we have not accepted ourselves for the persons we are, with the past that is ours, we will not/cannot truly hold ourselves responsible for our sins or really renounce them. Self-condemnation, self-pity, wallowing in guilt, blaming others, various forms of self-destructive behavior, self-justification, works-righteousness, etc., show that we have *not* fully taken responsibility for ourselves and our sinful behavior. We are still trying to hide from the reality, repress it, or get around it by justifying ourselves in some way. We are not facing it head-on and dealing with it in Christ. If we have not genuinely *owned* who we are and our pasts, we cannot genuinely surrender them to Christ and be made whole persons. Self-forgiveness follows from this and is vital, as indicated above. It is a matter of obedience to the Lord: if I have humbly accepted myself and my past, with the sin and shame it may contain, and if I have repented and asked for and received the Father's forgiveness through the Son, Jesus Christ, then I must forgive myself as God has forgiven me; to hold onto my sense of shame and guilt would be to do the opposite of what God has done and would in fact be a form of pride and disobedience.

6. *Soul-ties.* These are distorted relationships with other persons, where we are falsely bound to them, negatively or positively, through hatred, fear, obsequious deference, judgment, etc. Relations of this sort with the father or mother are common, and with siblings (envy, jealousy, competition, resentment, desire for vengeance). Such soul-ties can

lead to emotional transference, where a substitute/surrogate person receives the hatred and rebellion, say, that one is harboring toward a parent. A root of bitterness has become established and can lead to real devastation in families and whole communities (Heb 12:14-15). The workplace is often the scene for the expression of soul-ties, leading to the desire to control others, to obsequiousness on the part of an employee, or to unacceptable insubordination. Soul-ties involve false power or holds over another (suffocating and controlling mother, demanding and judgmental father, for example). A control freak is someone working out wounds that go back years and that may involve, for instance, the drive to please a parent, to succeed, or to show someone, perhaps a sibling, that one is capable and powerful. Marriages will be negatively affected by the wife's or the husband's soul-tie to a parent, hence the admonition in Genesis, which Jesus repeats, that in marriage, a man leaves father and mother and joins himself to his wife (Gen 2:24; Matt 19:5; Mark 10:7-8). The same applies for the wife, of course. Such soul-ties must be discerned, acknowledged, renounced, and cut by authoritative prayer in the name of Jesus Christ. They are a subtle form of idolatry. They lie behind Jesus's strong word that if we do not "hate" parents—in the sense of *hold at a proper psychological distance*—we cannot be free to be his disciples (Luke 14:25-27). Indeed, we cannot fully honor our parents, as we are commanded to do, if we have a false soul-tie to them.

7. *Generational sins and blessings.* A key text is Exodus 20:4-6. There is frequently a transmission down through the generations of a sin committed by a person's ancestor, as well as the transmission of blessings due to an ancestor's goodness or faithfulness. The person we are praying for will not inherit the *guilt* for the ancestor's sin (see Ezekiel 18), but may inherit the psychological, spiritual, or even physical *consequences* of the sin. There is frequently a demonic element in this transmission, so the helper must be ready to rebuke a demonic oppression and cut the person free from this influence, using the authority that we have in Christ and through his name (Matt 28:18-20; Luke 10:18-21; Acts 19:11-16). A particularly marked example of such transmission arises from any involvement in the occult on the part of an ancestor. The effect of this may be, for example, an attraction to occult practices. Any such involvement *must* be repented of and renounced, even if the person one is praying for engaged in the practices innocently, without really knowing what he/she was doing. The person must also forgive the ancestor who did the sin and stand

in as an intercessor for the family to ask God's mercy and liberation. Similar procedures should be followed if the person we are helping has been involved in New Age practices, which often have occult connections. These cloud the spirit and prevent the full penetration of Christ's light and truth.

8. *Healing of memories.* This involves praying for the painful, wounding events that surface in particular memories in the course of the counselling. We ask the Lord to enter into the memory, to be *present* in it (as he actually was, of course, in the event remembered, except that the person was unaware of it), and to bring consolation and healing through his Holy Spirit. The person being helped may be aided as well by visualizing the pain of the event lifted up and incorporated into the body of Christ on the cross, who bore in his own flesh our sorrows and pains and sins. Such prayer requires faith, sensitivity, and imagination.

9. *Spiritual gifts.* The key texts are 1 Corinthians 12 and 14, and Romans 12. The gifts are of all kinds, of course, including anointed teaching, preaching, administrations, helps, etc. Especially prophecy, the word of knowledge, and the word of wisdom, which may come through words in our minds, an impression, an image, or a dream, are extremely useful in the context of prayer ministry. This involves openness to the Holy Spirit and keen discernment of God's still small voice. The use of all spiritual gifts is for the healing and edification of persons and the upbuilding of the body of Christ as the biblical texts make clear. Submission to proper authority is vital. A primary place to exercise the gifts of revelation is the small prayer group where, by studying the Bible and sharing personal needs and praying for each other, people grow in trust and become willing to step out in faith and practice the *charismata* with mutual submission and discernment.

IV

Further Reflections on Our Image of God and on Self-image

Our images of God and self will develop primarily, if not exclusively, from our childhood experience of our parents and of our early relationships with other people, such as teachers and classmates. These experiences, resulting in *feelings* and, later, *concepts* about God, are more potent and formative than biblical instruction about God, though obviously such instruction from an early age is very important and can offset much harm that might come from, say, a bad parental image transferred unconsciously onto God. Negative examples include: God as tyrant, detective, unjust judge, mocker, philosopher's god, the Unmoved Mover, and taskmaster. Unhealthy personal relationships with parents and with other important persons in infancy, childhood, and adolescence will mainly determine our picture of God. Our soul will be misshapen, even our body may be bent or affected in various ways as a result. How then, regenerated by Christ, will we be able to witness with the Holy Spirit and, with our whole being, call God *Abba*—"loving Father"? There will be tension in us if we have had such negative images of God implanted in us when we were young: our spirits will pull one way, for God will whisper his love to our hearts; but our emotions, even our minds and wills, may pull in another, as the (probably) unconscious negative image of God resists the biblical picture of the loving Father whom we know through the Son.

All of this will have a big impact on our behavior and our Christian life. It will limit our joy and freedom in Christ, and dampen or restrain the development of our faith. If we are in a position such as this, we will need pastoral ministry and specific healing prayer, accompanied by the asking of forgiveness and the granting of it to others. Then God will rectify our image of him, reintegrate us, and assure us of his love. This is a *process*; it will take time, punctuated with sessions of specific prayer aimed at this end. As carers, we too may be damaged in certain areas of our lives and may need to be cared for in this way. This does not invalidate us for pastoral service; to the contrary, it *qualifies* us—on the condition, of course, that we have recognized our own neediness and have been willing—and continue to be willing—to receive prayer ourselves. This reveals a basic principle of Christian life, that God's power is made perfect in our weakness, provided we recognize our complete dependence on him and submit to his will (2 Cor 11:30–33, 12:7–10).

If we have difficulty, in our feelings and in the unconscious part of our soul, calling God *Abba*—"dear Father"—we will obviously also have difficulty calling ourselves sons and daughters (the biblical language—"sons"—is inclusive) of God. A negative God-image will almost always be accompanied by a negative self-image. The source in both cases is likely to be the same: early painful experience in family, compounded by subsequent painful experiences. Such feelings are usually buried and denied, unconscious, and do not just go away when a person becomes a Christian; nor are they simply eliminated from the soul if a person has been in Christ from early life. Indeed, in such a case, feelings like these may even be exacerbated and repression increased, on account of a felt need to please God and be good and serve others, to live up to a high standard of thought and behavior, when this is precisely what the person feels unable to do, because of the wounds, sins, guilt, and negative images of God and of self that she or he drags from the past. And yet there is the felt obligation to *try*, which can lead to moral striving, legalism, perfectionism, and so forth. The tension here is often at the root of anxiety and depression.

All these things will need looking into, as we care for people with such problems. We will often find them to be performance-oriented, resistant to receiving grace, living by the law according to a set of standards which they believe they must meet in order to be acceptable, to receive love, to be worthy. The concept and experience of unconditional love is virtually impossible for them to grasp until they receive healing, with the help of a priest or pastor, a counselor, or a caring, prayerful lay brother or sister. A sense of failure and guilt may accompany these things; a weak sense of gender identity; also, often, a self-righteousness and judgmentalism, of self and also of others; rage and anger, usually repressed in the compliant type, more openly expressed in the openly rebellious type; anxiety, legalism, perfectionism, often accompanied by manipulation and self-pity; drivenness, workaholism; sexual temptations or promiscuity, in search of love (to fill the deep, unmet-in-childhood inner need) but also in self-hatred and self-destruction; bitterness, inability to trust or surrender oneself, or to expect blessing from God's hand (or anyone else's).

Specific memories will lie at the root of these things, connected with particular relationships. There will be a need to forgive *specifically*, and to ask forgiveness *specifically*, as God opens up these areas by his Spirit. As mentioned above, there may be an involvement with the occult or some New Age esoteric oddity needing to be confessed and dealt with; or a hereditary sin going back a generation or more and never brought into the light. There will be a need for self-acceptance, in Christ, which will include an *acceptance* of one's life and parents as they *are*, not as we might wish they had been (acceptance is *essentially* different from either rebellion or resignation). There will be a need for healing prayer and a follow-up of loving fellowship, with regular eucharistic celebration, Scripture meditation, and prayer as new patterns of thought and behavior are developed.

V

The Helper/Carer; Authority and Compassion

Identity as son or daughter of God is the basis of our mission as servants. The helper is one who is being helped by God and who has been helped. He/She has authority and compassion because to some real extent she has opened herself to the Holy Spirit; she has acknowledged and faced at least to some degree her own anxieties, needs, and hang-ups, and the hurts and sins connected with them. She has gone to the cross with them and received new life in Christ in place of that old flesh life: and precisely here, in this *new life* received on the far side of the cross, lies her spiritual authority and her compassion.

Spiritual authority and compassion are the two basic qualities necessary to be an effective helper. It is presupposed, of course, that the carer is in a state of obedience and humility before the Lord, and that his/her conscience is clear. *All* Christians, redeemed and inhabited by the Spirit of God, have Christ's authority, they can speak *in his name* (Matt 28:18–20). The outworking and expression of this spiritual authority is associated with meekness, in the biblical sense of genuine humility before God and man (different from timidity, fear, self-deprecation, and false modesty). Compassion likewise, for it involves going down into the other's place, into his or her darkness, and suffering with him/her (this co-suffering must be done *in Christ*, however, not in one's own strength, through mere human empathy and emotional identification, otherwise we will get mired down in the same pit and be of no use in pulling the other out of it).

The carer must be living in the gospel dynamic of justification by grace through faith. He/She has "put on Christ" and wears the spiritual armor (Eph 6), knowing, as Paul puts it in 1 Corinthians 1:30, that *"He [God] is the source of your life in Christ Jesus, whom God made to be our wisdom, our righteousness and sanctification and redemption."* He/She is an effective burden-bearer because she knows herself—and experiences herself daily—to be borne by Christ, on the cross and in his resurrection. The carer abides in him, knowing that without him she can do nothing, that is, she cannot bring life (John 15:5); and she knows that God in three Persons—Father, Son, and Holy Spirit—abides in her, now and forever (John 14:23). This is the carer's strength and joy: the root of the Christian's faith, hope, and love, the source and power of compassionate service.

To bear another's burden and thus fulfill the law of Christ (Gal 6:2), is to take up one's cross; it is to share (not bear, but *share*) the sufferings of Christ on another's behalf, that Christ's work may be made effective in that person's life (Col 1:24; 2 Cor 4:10–11; Phil 3:10). (The two other aspects of cross-bearing are persecution for Christ's sake and inner crucifying of the old man, the sinful, self-centered nature the Bible calls the flesh, and by which, of course, is not meant the body but the sin-principle).

VI

Helper's Manner and Approach

1. *Listening and watching.* One ear open to the Spirit, other ear open to the person. Every person is different. Hear the words, be attentive to them; hear also what is behind them. What is the deep cry of the heart? What are the basic soul-structures? What are the key relationships?

2. *Remember as much of the details as you can.* If appropriate, take notes (explain what you are doing, if you do this). If time permits, you may be listening, questioning, explaining quite a while before actually praying. Seek for patterns, structures, relationships, root experiences.

3. *Your own manner is important.* Humble self-assurance; relaxed; attentive; facial expressions; eye contact. Always be respectful, clear, gentle, authoritative; never pushy, superior, or spouting clichés. Again: listen for what is *behind* the words, *behind* the symptoms that constitute the complaint. These are to be taken seriously; but they may be merely pointers. Example: in a hypochondriacal type, the affected organ may well represent the introjected parental relationship. The organ now does what the relationship did to the child: weakened it, exhausted it, emptied it of vitality. Before the symptomatic complaint can be healed, the relationship with the parents must be attended to in appropriate ways, *even if they have died and "reconciliation" can only be achieved through prayer.*

So: taking the symptoms seriously, the helper above all tries to attend to the structural/relational realities behind them. Often one has to deal with displaced—transferred—anger, bitterness, hatred, resentment (anger toward a parent transferred to a spouse, for example). The helper is mediating God's love: God the Father, who is also motherly; God the Creator; God the Redeemer, Friend, Savior. We are there to help the person get back into proper relatedness: with God, self, others. Our own loving and strong relatedness to the sufferer will be vital to achieving this. By "strong," I mean, again, in the Spirit, out of our weakness in which Christ's strength is made manifest. Burden-bearing, like Christ's work on the Cross, is always basically a ministry of reconciliation.

VII

Counseling and Prayer

Pastoral care must deal with the evils we have suffered as well as the sins we have committed, namely, wounds and sins (the sins often consist in reactions to the wounds). Our old man has been shaped by these (see Romans 6 and Colossians 3:5–11). Pastoral care of this sort involves bringing the person to Christ, so that he may dismantle the structures of the old man/flesh (dead with Christ but still effectual until dismantled) and raise up the person into greater psychological (and perhaps even physical) wholeness and new life.

The difference between this and psychological counseling as such is that, in Christian pastoral counseling and soul-healing, *Christ* is the healer, by the *Holy Spirit*, to whom we are presenting the whole person—spirit, soul, and body—in the light of scriptural revelation. Formal training of some kind is to be recommended, of course, but it must be coupled with on-the-job experience. Prayer of this sort is not a *technique* but a work of the Holy Spirit, in which we participate as intelligently and as sensitively as we can. If we walk in the Spirit and draw on scriptural truth, we'll have something to say, we'll be able to extend real help, as a brother or sister in Christ. We are not disqualified simply because we aren't experts with diplomas and years of training and experience. It goes without saying, of course, that study of good literature on the subject is important and that in a given parochial context, anyone praying—caring—for another in this sort of way should, if possible, be accompanied by another carer and should be under the authority of the incumbent priest or pastor and acting with his or her authorization. This is all the more true in our day when cases of sexual abuse are coming to light and protective measures, favoring total transparency and accountability in pastoral relationships, must be taken. This is not a ministry for lone wolves. Priests and pastors themselves would be wise, in counseling situations, to work with another carer if this can be arranged.

In a prayer session, there will be a listening-counseling phase and a praying phase. One might say that, broadly, there are three types of prayer of this sort: 1) a "peace-comfort" prayer, where time is limited or where nothing else is yet appropriate; 2) one or two sessions, with a single basic focus; or 3) long-term healing and restructuring, perhaps involving acts of restitution, which will involve comprehensive prayer across the whole range of the person's life, going all the way back to the fetus, if necessary.

Key elements that will almost always be involved in such prayer. Each of these is likely to involve specific memories. Self-images and God-images, as discussed above, will also frequently figure in healing prayer.

1. Asking and receiving forgiveness. This need not usually be accompanied by formal absolution by a priest or pastor (see James 5:16), but the person receiving the prayer, particularly if raised in the Catholic or Orthodox traditions, may feel that such a sacramental act is vital, especially in cases where the sins in question are very serious.

2. Granting forgiveness to those who have wronged us. We thereby release or unbind the other persons as well as ourselves, this already having been done by Jesus on the cross: we are hereby appropriating and entering into his finished work (see Matthew 16:19).

3. Self-acceptance, receiving from God proper self-love (the opposite of conceit and egotism). This, I repeat again, will involve accepting one's life circumstances, family situation, body, intellect, etc., as well as one's own being as such: obviously these are all inseparable.

4. Breaking of false bondages to persons; of imprisoning vows; or curses that may have come upon the sufferer through his or her own actions or by some channel or another.

Procedural approaches in prayer:

1. Invoke the Holy Spirit, the holy presence of God. It is he who will work: We are merely his assistants and the helpers of the sufferer.

2. Invite Christ into the person's past. He is already there, of course, since for him all time is present (a key concept in this kind of work) and since he has known the person from *"before the foundation of the world"* (Eph 1:4) and *"has formed us in our mother's womb"* (Ps 139:13). But it is important for the person to receive Christ's presence in his or her past by faith: this undercuts at the root the experienced agony of rejection, aloneness, loss, abandonment, etc. And of course where Christ is, there is the Father also, so that the proper relationship with God the Father can begin to be established as well.

3. The Holy Spirit, at various points, may bring an illuminating word of knowledge in the form of a word or a picture. If so, this should be brought out and submitted to the person for discernment, to see if it evokes something or leads somewhere in the discussion or prayer.

Be bold in sharing such words, but never force anything. If the word is from the Spirit of God, it will bear some kind of fruit; if it finds no echo, so to speak, it can simply be set aside. The Holy Spirit may also bring up specific painful memories in the mind of the person being prayed for, leading to prayers of comfort or the asking and giving of forgiveness.

4. We may need to speak declarative words of authority, in the name of Christ and spoken in faith. Breaking bondages to persons or habits, for example (assuming all the prior work of repentance, forgiveness, etc., has been done), will require this. Such a spoken act of authority is not remotely like waving a magic wand: it is acting in the name of the one who has all authority in heaven and on earth (Matt 28:18); and it is for the purpose of bringing release to the captives in accordance with what he, Jesus, has already accomplished on the cross. An act of authority of this kind is absolutely necessary in the case of liberation of a person from demonic oppression, external or internal, such as might have come through a wound, a behavioral excess, or from involvement in some occult practice, as mentioned above. The person's complete submission to Christ is crucial here, entailing repentance and deliberate renunciation of the evil spirit(s). Deliverance ministry is beyond the scope of these notes, but demonic oppression is not at all uncommon in our day and anyone engaged seriously in inner healing should study carefully what the Scriptures and the pastoral tradition and practice of the church have to say on the subject. A born-again Christian belongs to Christ and cannot be *possessed* by demons. But he/she can definitely be *oppressed* from the *outside* in the form of demonic pressure and attacks in some form, or, more seriously, on the *inside*, in which case deliverance is needed and the demon or demons must be cast out by the authoritative command of the person ministering. Evil spirits oppressing from the *outside* must also be commanded to leave in the name of Jesus. Anyone engaging in this ministry should definitely be accompanied by another spiritually mature and experienced person, ordained *or* lay. Once again, our authority in Christ, not our status in the church, is the key to our effectiveness in releasing people from such oppressions, once the prior actions of discernment, repentance, confession, and reception by the demonized person of forgiveness through the blood of Jesus have been accomplished. A grasp of the significance of the blood of Jesus, which is the very life of God shed for us, is vital in this ministry. Demons have a horror of the blood and will flee at its mention if the

necessary conditions of repentance, etc., have been met in the demonized person. *Sin is always at the root, somewhere and somehow, of any demonic oppression*, and it must be dealt with before a demon will leave. This is an area where the gift of "discernment of spirits" (1 Cor 12:10) is vital. People, Christians included, who think that demons do not exist and are no more than an outmoded way of talking about mental disease simply do not know what they are talking about.

5. Prayers of healing, comfort, consolation will be needed, where we ask the Spirit to regenerate, revivify, renew; to fill and empty places; to soothe the raw spots; to flow into the cleansed wounds.

6. Always keep in close touch with the person. What is he or she seeing? Experiencing? Feeling? Remembering? The person himself or herself may be the source of much of the discerning and guidance for the appropriate prayer.

7. Follow-up. The person is to learn to walk in newness of life, in respect to the areas in his or her life where God has done a work of sanctification and healing. This will involve, more or less rapidly, the development of new attitudes and behavior. Open, loving fellowship; eucharistic celebration; meditation on Scripture; prayer: all these are crucial to the person's entering fully into the wholeness that Christ offers him/her.

As more and more people in a parish or Christian community receive Christ's pastoral love by opening themselves to be touched and healed by him in specific areas of their lives, the congregation will be washed, built up, and empowered for service in new and exciting ways. Parish members will, as Christians, move outward with greater faith into the surrounding community to share Christ in word and deed (in their daily contacts, private and occupational; in the perspectives they bring to bear on their professions; in social action; or in deliberate evangelistic outreach); and people from outside will be drawn into the church. Liturgical celebration and worship will become richer, as God is glorified with greater joy and gratitude; Scripture will become more meaningful; and prayer will be deeper and more specific as people come to *expect* God to respond concretely in their personal lives.

Part IV

EUCHARISTIC THEOLOGY

The Question of the Efficacy of the Eucharist

To DISCUSS THE QUESTION of *how* the Eucharist may be said to have efficacy presupposes a positive answer to the prior question, "Does the Eucharist have efficacy?" It would normally be proper, therefore, to investigate the question of *that* (from the starting point of Christology) before tackling the question of *how* (from the starting point of sacramental theology). But since the answers to *both* questions do not depend on logical causality but rather on the person of Jesus Christ and his active will, it is arguable that they are at bottom one and the same answer and that ultimately this answer (both to the *how* as well as to the *that*) is christological before it is sacramental. Accordingly, I have chosen to subsume the *that* of the Eucharist's efficacy (including the nature or meaning of the efficacy, i.e., the *what*) under the *how*, in the hope that the centrality of Jesus Christ to the *whole issue* of sacramental efficacy will emerge in the course of discussion and that a few rays of light may thereby be shed on both these questions at once. The English translation of the Bible being used in this essay is the Revised Standard Version 1971.

I

Paul's discussion of the Eucharist in 1 Corinthians 10 and 11 is the only detailed record we have in the New Testament of the early church actually celebrating the Lord's Supper. The references to the Last Supper in Mark 14, Matthew 26, Luke 22, and John 13, though recorded later and doubtless with particular church situations in mind, lack the ecclesial context of the Epistle to the Corinthians. They are, strictly speaking, about the *Last Supper*, not about the Eucharist, since the cross, resurrection, ascension, and descent of the Spirit are yet to come (as far as the narrative is concerned). It is nevertheless clear that the same Christ and the same words and actions are at the center of both meals:[1] the *incarnate* Christ who in intention and anticipation offered himself unto death at the Last Supper is the *ascended* Christ who, seated in his glorified humanity at the right hand of the Father, offers himself at the Eucharist both as victim and high priest in and with the members of his body.

The centerpiece—if one may speak so—of the new covenant, and the earnest of the church's inheritance in the kingdom of God, is the coming of the Holy Spirit into hearts made new by virtue objectively of the sacrifice of Christ and subjectively (i.e., in relation to the particular subject) of the individual's baptism into his death and identification with him in his resurrection. If the evangelists do not explicitly mention the Spirit in the context of the Last Supper, the Lord's words in Mark and Matthew concerning the new covenant in his blood, and in Luke concerning the fulfillment of the Passover in the kingdom of God, contain such a reference implicitly, while Paul's entire discussion in his First Epistle to the Corinthians of the body of Christ and the Lord's Supper is dynamically intertwined with his discussion of the Spirit and capped—significantly—by his joyous rehearsal of the eschatological resurrection. In Paul, the implications of Jesus's words in the Synoptic accounts of the Last Supper have become *manifest*, since the apostle is writing in the postresurrection context of the church, the body of Christ, into which its members have all been baptized "in one Spirit" (1 Cor 12:13).

The union of fellowship at the Last Supper between Christ and his disciples (who are the nucleus of the church) is *established* by Jesus's invitation to them to partake in his body and blood, under the symbols of bread and wine; it is *sealed* by the sacrament of baptism, whereby Christians identify themselves with his crucified body, enter the eschatological community of the church, the body of Christ, and receive the Spirit, sign of the new covenant; and it is *celebrated and renewed* by the sacrament of the Eucharist, when the church, being one body because of the common identification of its members with the one Christ—being indeed for this reason *his* body—partakes sacramentally, through the bread and the wine, of his risen life. Christ's body-blood,[2] given *for* men on the cross and *to* men under the

1. Despite verbal disagreements in the several New Testament accounts of the Last Supper, there is real agreement as to basic procedure, emphasis, and meaning.

2. It is beyond my present purpose to go into the various ways in which theologians have discussed the distinction between Christ's body-bread and blood-wine. Body and blood are inseparable and constitute, for the Hebraic mind, different ways of talking about living beings. Life is in the blood, according to the Old Testament understanding, and life is expressed through the body. Body and soul are not separable parts of a whole; man is an ensouled body, whose biological life is in his blood. To say that Christ gave his body is to say he gave himself, the wholeness of his person; to say

material signs of bread and wine, may be said to be the vehicle of our communion with him, hence of our salvation; and it is the reality whose theological significance we must ascertain if we are to understand the continuity between Last Supper, cross, and Eucharist, upon which, in turn, hangs our understanding of how it is that the Eucharist, celebrated by the church, can make effective Christ's sacrifice.

II

As is well known, the Last Supper in the Synoptic Gospels coincides with the Feast of Passover, whereas in the Fourth Gospel it antedates Passover by twenty-four hours. Textual difficulties notwithstanding, it is admitted by many scholars that a Jewish festal meal—the *haburah*—provided the general form and structure of the supper and that the Feast of Passover, however it may have been related formally to the supper, was obviously in the forefront of the disciples' minds.[3] This context was important, even though the *fundamental* theological significance of the Last Supper cannot be derived from it. There is no doubt that one of the images for Jesus used by the early church and drawn from Jewish imagery of sacrifice was that of the Passover lamb (1 Cor 5:7; 1 Pet 1:19). John, moreover, by the chronology of his account of the Passion, is clearly concerned with synchronizing the death of Jesus with the time of the killing of the Passover lambs.[4] For the Jews, the whole meaning of Passover was derived from its relation to the exodus from Egypt. The feast spoke of deliverance from slavery, of freedom, and of God's faithfulness to his covenant with Abraham (Gen 15, 17, 22), a faithfulness sealed at Sinai by the making of a new covenant—the book of the law—through Moses (Exod 24). The explicit references in the New Testament to Jesus as the Passover lamb stress the newness of the situation in which the Christian finds himself (1 Cor 5:7) on account of the marvelous redemption Jesus has wrought (1 Pet 1:19). The Fourth Gospel, for its part, is marked by an emphasis on the *true* freedom and the *true* bread, the bread of life eternal, which Christ brings, in contrast with what Moses brought and which Jewish legalism has perverted (John 6, 8). This redemption, this freedom, this bread: all are to be had in Jesus *himself*, by whom we have fellowship with the Father through the Spirit (John 14–17).

---

he shed his blood is to say the same thing, but putting the stress on the sacrificial aspect of his death.

3. Clark, *Approach to the Theology*, 40–48. See Mascall, *Corpus Christi*, 88.

4. Ramsey, *Christian Concept of Sacrifice*, 4.

This brings us to the first theological point to be drawn out for our purposes from the Passover context of the Last Supper. Jesus uses Jewish tradition—the *haburah* meal and the Feast of Passover—as a frame, but what he does with it is altogether new.[5] By taking the bread and saying, *"This is my body,"* and by taking the cup and saying, *"This is the new covenant in my blood,"* Jesus applies to *himself* rather than to the paschal lamb the traditional interpretative words spoken by the presiding father at the Passover meal. He designates *himself* as the sacrificial victim associated with the deliverance of Israel from bondage, and indicates that henceforth, whenever the disciples gather to eat this bread and drink this cup, they will be recalling not the exodus from Egypt and, by extension, the Mosaic covenant of the law, but a *new* deliverance and a *new* covenant *in his blood*. Not until after the crucifixion and resurrection—indeed, not *fully* until after Pentecost—would the disciples grasp the meaning of Jesus's words and actions and understand how the Christ, by offering up his body to be broken for men, had brought a deliverance of a kind far beyond anything they could have imagined.

The context of Passover is thus a pointer both to the continuity of the Last Supper with past tradition and to the *dis*continuity. Continuity, however—and this is a second theological point—lay not only in the formal aspects of the meal so radically reinterpreted by Jesus, but also in the underlying meaning of the whole celebration. In Egypt, God *had acted* to deliver the children of Abraham. He had sent a man, Moses, through whose words and actions he saved his people. Jesus was the new Moses, the one "greater than Moses," the Messiah. Through him, not only would the children of Abraham by the flesh be saved, but all the children of Adam who hungered after God. For this Savior would effect a universal deliverance such as only God in his own person could effect: a deliverance from sin and death; and this deliverance would involve a sacrifice such as only God himself could offer. The self-offering of Jesus, symbolically figured in the bread and the wine *"given for many"* in the upper room, was the unthinkable, the utterly unforeseeable event of the Son of God incarnate dying for man as his substitute and representative; but it was also the culminating and decisive act in a series of acts expressive of God's constant redemptive purpose toward mankind, which he had determined in Christ from before the foundation of the world (1 Pet 1:20; Acts 2:23; Eph 1:4–5). The *way* in which God acted in Christ at Calvary to bring salvation to men was altogether new; but the redemptive purpose manifest there was continuous with all God's actions toward men in the past.

---

5. See Leenhardt, "This is My Body."

God acts to save men. Jesus acted at Calvary. But he *also* acted at the Last Supper, both to explain his imminent death and, by inviting his disciples to share in it symbolically by eating his body and drinking his blood, to show them how henceforth they would share in its benefits. *Because* he acted at the Last Supper and at Calvary the next day, he acts also in the Eucharist. Jesus's words over the bread and the cup in the upper room—*"This is my body"* and *"This is my blood of the new covenant"*—are united to his actions of taking the elements, giving thanks, and offering them to the disciples. The bread-body and the wine-blood given *for* the disciples are also given *to* them. The significance of this we shall explore shortly. The point here is that these material elements are *given*. There is a unity of word and action in a single *act*. In Hebrew thought, action belongs to the original native essence of the word.[6] Jesus, as the incarnate Son of God, is the man in whom word and action perfectly correspond: he is the Word made flesh. Himself the very image of God, he is very man, made in God's image; and for God—and also for man-in-his-image—to speak is to engage, to enter into purposeful activity. F. J. Leenhardt writes:

> The Hebrew does not see the things that are in the world for what they are, but for what they are called to be; he associates them with their end; he inserts them in a movement, in a history. . . . He is in the image of Yahweh, who, having created the world, ordered it by His word and continues to direct it by His word. *Dabar* is truly activity, power, historical agency, causality.[7]

We come now to the third theological point to be drawn out from the Passover context of the Last Supper. This point is connected with the significance and operation of ritual in space-time on behalf of men and of his whole creation. Leenhardt writes in relation to Passover:

> The Passover was not concerned only to recall or evoke this already distant event. It was necessary each year for the event to become again a present actuality for each generation throughout the ages. According to the Mishnah; "In every generation a man must so regard himself as if he came forth himself out of Egypt."[8]

Behind the different practices of the paschal ritual there was a single redemptive intention. The theological meaning of the ritual was that the acts of God for his people did not end with a particular event in the remote past.

---

6. Grainger, *Language of Rite*, 31.
7. Leenhardt, "This is My Body," 45.
8. Leenhardt, "This is My Body," 40.

God's acts do not cease to be contemporary and active. The "remembrance" of the exodus from Egypt involved in the Passover Feast was not only the grateful evocation of that specific historical event; it was the celebration of the *God who acts* and who, having acted, continues to act in the present and can be expected to act in the future. A recalling of the past event, it was most certainly; but, more wonderfully still, what generation after generation of Jews were doing at Passover was to appropriate the past event for themselves by virtue of their faith in and covenant relationship with the One who authored the event in the first place, and who was ever living and active to author other and even greater events like it.

Correlatively, as the Jew thus "remembered" God's acts in the past and expressed his hope and expectation that God would act again in the present and the future to save his people, he also was acknowledging God's sovereignty and God's *right* to sovereignty over his own acts and the direction of his will. In his monumental work on Israel and Hebrew culture, Johannes Pedersen writes illuminatingly:

> When man remembers God, he lets his being and his actions be determined by him. The Psalmist says: Seek Yahweh and his strength, seek his face ever more! Remember his marvelous works that he has done; his wonders, and the judgments of his mouth (Psalm 105:4-5). To remember the works of Yahweh and to seek him, i.e., to let one's acts be determined by his will, is in reality the same . . . the peculiarity about the Israelite is that he cannot at all imagine memory, unless at the same time an effect on the totality and its direction of will is taken for granted.[9]

Such was the way in which Jesus and his disciples understood the meaning, purpose, and efficacy of the Passover feast. The new rite which Jesus poured into the old form was to be understood in the same way. The focus of the new rite was the bread and cup, which Jesus declared to be his body and blood, given for many; but the heart of the sacrifice was the willingness of Jesus to do God's will, whatever the cost—and the cost was his life. Jesus's action in taking the bread and speaking over it the words, *"This is my body, which is for you,"* summed up the action of his entire life and ministry. He lived and died for others, willingly. The vital theological point here is that this which he did willingly was God's will. God's will was to be made flesh—to be embodied—and to sacrifice that body for men:

> *Consequently, when Christ came into the world, he said, "Sacrifices and offerings thou hast not desired, but a body hast thou*

---

9. Pedersen, *Israel*, 1:106–7.

> *prepared for me; in burnt offerings and sin offerings thou hast taken no pleasure." Then I said, "Lo, I have come to do thy will, O God, as it is written of me in the roll of the book."* (Heb 10:5–7, quoting Ps 40:6–8)

Therefore, when Jesus pronounced his words and performed his actions at the Last Supper, he was being the vehicle for God's consummate redemptive act of deliverance, prefigured by God's act at the exodus, of which the sacrificial lamb was rather more a sign than an effectual means. In Jesus's case the giving of his own body unto death was absolutely necessary (theologically, not logically) in order to bring about the supreme salvation which God in his love intended for men. The sacrificed body and shed blood were here no longer a type or symbol of another, greater reality; Jesus was the Incarnate Son, the Word made flesh: his body and blood were the very life of God, given for men in accordance with God's eternal and constant purpose.

It is in such theological and christological terms as these that it is appropriate to talk of the anamnesis in the Eucharist as an actualization or a re-presentation of Christ's death. The pattern for understanding the meaning of the word "remembrance" as used in the Last Supper and the Eucharist is to be found in the Jewish understanding of the Passover celebration and of God's purpose and action which this rite expresses. That which is remembered in the Eucharist is the supreme redemptive act of God; but what makes the commemorative words and actions effective is that God was in Jesus Christ reconciling the world to himself and that Jesus chose to perform this particular act at the Last Supper and *in this way* to link the sacrifice of his life given *for* them at Calvary with the sacrifice of his life given *to* them in the bread and the cup. The bread and the cup in themselves are merely objects; if, in the Eucharist, they become sacraments—that is, objects drawn from the secular and inserted into the sacred order—it is because Christ has chosen to *give* them, and what he gives is his body and blood, his life, his person. Speaking of Jesus's words at the Last Supper, Leenhardt writes:

> It is not because they are uttered that the bread is the body of Christ, but because Jesus intends to give this bread as His body. The bread is not the body of Christ by virtue of the repetition of certain words. The words uttered make explicit the will of Jesus; they make it known to the participants; they do not actualize it. It is in the action of giving that the ministerial will of Christ is realised.[10]

---

10. Leenhardt, "This is My Body," 55.

Between all other sign-objects used in liturgical action and the things they signify of a spiritual order, a gap necessarily exists, because the signifier and signified are not on the same level of reality. But because Jesus is the Christ, Creator, and Redeemer, the One whose word is truly creative, and because, as man, he chose to give himself under these particular elements to his disciples, in this unique case the reality of the bread and cup and the reality of Christ's presence with his followers in the communion are not incongruous. The spiritual reality signified is actually conveyed by the symbol. In partaking in faith of the bread and cup, we partake truly of his life, which he offered and offers to us under this form. Our communion with him is real, not symbolic. He is with us by his Spirit because it is his will to be with us and to give himself to us in this way. He is not physically, but sacramentally, present by his Spirit. E. L. Mascall, referring to Abbot Vonier's view of the eucharistic presence of Christ, writes persuasively in this connection:

> For Vonier, then, the Eucharistic presence of Christ is entirely real, but it is of an altogether different type from his presence on earth before his Ascension and his presence in heaven after it. Those presences are, so to speak, presences in their own right, while the Eucharistic presence exists because and only because Christ, by his institution and promise, has attached to it certain sensible signs. It exists simply because it has a sacramental sign ordained by God and through no other cause whatever.[11]

Outside the actual dialogue of Christ with believers, the bread is not the sacramental sign of Christ's presence to the church. Nor is there any intrinsic or logically necessary connection between bread and wine on the one hand and Christ's body and blood on the other. Food is not the basic issue, as Leenhardt points out.[12] It is only a means. What is basically at issue here is life. The bread is used purely symbolically: as we have physical life through bread, so we have spiritual life through the Bread of Life, which is Christ. And this is true because Jesus himself, in his body on the cross, took our sins upon him, in perfect obedience to God's will: *"And you . . . he has now reconciled in his body of flesh by his death, in order to present you holy and blameless and irreproachable before him."* (Col 1:22; see Eph 2:13, 16; Heb 10:20).

To deny the objectivity of Christ's presence in the elements is to misunderstand the unique kind of reality which the sacraments constitute, in virtue of the uniqueness of the One who instituted them; it is also to deny the objectivity of the divine action, both at the Last Supper and at Calvary,

---

11. Mascall, *Corpus Christi*, 95.
12. Leenhardt, "This is My Body," 84–85.

which it is the function of the sacraments to re-present.[13] God's presence to all men is never spatial or local; it is relational. It is in Christ that this relation to God becomes, on man's side, possible and personal. By his sacrificial death, which we commemorate in the eucharistic rite, Christ has opened the way of access to the Father, so that as we partake by faith of his body and blood, we have fellowship with the triune God, that is, we share with God in his life. This has been God's purpose of love from the beginning. "The Eucharistic Bread," writes William Temple, "is His Body for the purpose for which it is consecrated, which is communion, in exactly the same sense as that in which a physicochemical organism was once His Body; it is the vehicle—the effective symbol—of His personality."[14]

III

We must now explore the meaning of Paul's phrase, "the body of Christ," as he uses it to designate the church. We shall do this with particular reference to the Eucharist. Paul writes in 1 Corinthians 10:16–17, *"The cup of blessing which we bless, is it not a participation in the blood of Christ? The bread which we break, is it not a participation in the body of Christ? Because there is one loaf, we who are many are one body, for we are all partakers of the same loaf."* Our participation is in Christ's body and blood, in his life, given for us at Calvary. How do we do this? We do it sacramentally, by eating the bread and drinking the cup, declared by Christ to be his body and blood. Communion with him is certainly not limited to our participation in the sacraments; but sacramental communion is perhaps easier for us, in a sense, than communion in prayer or hymn or through the reading and exposition of the Scriptures.[15] For we are corporeal beings, and what we are participating in is the death and risen life of a corporeal being, Jesus Christ: as a man like us, he died nailed to a cross; as the perfectly obedient One, our Redeemer, he was raised from the dead and, in his glorified humanity, made to sit at God's right hand. His mode of being in his glorified body in heaven is different from his mode of being in the days of his flesh on earth—but he is the one Christ in both modes. His modes of being in the sacraments and in the mystical body which is his church are likewise different—but again it is the one Christ whom we encounter here. All of these modes of Christ's being have to do with his communion with us: they are different ways in which God in Christ goes about *realizing* this communion.

13. Baillie, *Theology of the Sacraments*, 97.
14. Temple, *Christus Veritas*, 252.
15. Temple, *Christus Veritas*, 241.

In the Corinthian text cited above, Paul both distinguishes and identifies the body of the man Jesus and the body of Christ which we, the church, constitute. The union between Christ and the body of Christ, the church, is not one of identity but of fellowship.[16] The key word is *koinonia*. In saying at the Last Supper, *"This is my body, which is for you,"* Jesus is saying in effect, "By eating this bread which I declare to be my body, you identify yourselves with me in the new covenant"; and by speaking of the church as the body of Christ, Paul is saying in effect, "We who are identified with Christ in his death have communion with him in his risen life." He is present in and with his people by his Spirit, and as the church gathers at his table, it both demonstrates and celebrates this spiritual oneness with its Lord. In this sense it is his mystical body. Because *he* is one, those who are baptized into him are one. It is into his *death* that Christians are baptized, and it is *because* they are baptized into his death that they have been raised with him into newness of life and are in a position to eat of his body and drink of his blood *"in remembrance"* of him, thereby proclaiming *"the Lord's death until he comes."*[17] It is by virtue of his death and of their identification, by faith and sacrament, with him in it, that they are in life; therefore, and by virtue of his life, it is his death that they proclaim.

Paul's use of prepositions and tenses in Romans 6:3–11 is instructive here: we *were* baptized *into* Christ, *into* his death; thus united *with* him in his death, we *shall be* united *with* him in a resurrection like his and *shall live with* him; hence we must reckon ourselves *now* to be dead to sin and alive *in* Christ Jesus. We identified ourselves with (*into*) him in baptism; therefore, we *are in* him now and *shall be with* him at the consummation, when we *"shall bear the likeness of the man from heaven"* (1 Cor 15:49) and our lowly bodies will be *"like his glorious body"* (Phil 3:21; see Rom 8:23). We are even now, in our identification with him, seated with him in heavenly places (Eph 2:6),[18] for we live by his life which he has given *to* us, having given it *for* us at Calvary. This life consists in our *knowing God*, in our being in communion—we, mere creatures—with the Creator-Redeemer God, Father, Son and Spirit (John 17:3). The mystical body of Christ is not identical with the ascended body of Christ, but it is *with* him even now in the Spirit and will be like him at the *parousia*; nor is it identical with the crucified or with the eucharistic body of Christ, though it is united sacramentally with both, by faith, through the Spirit.

---

16. Moule, *Sacrifice of Christ*, ch. 4.
17. See Romans 6:3–11 and 1 Corinthians 11:23–26.
18. This proximity is to be understood in relational, not spatial, terms.

Considerations such as these must rule out any materialistic, one-to-one identity, however formulated, of the bread and wine with the body and blood of Christ, of the sort implied in the doctrines of transubstantiation and consubstantiation, where the use of dualistic philosophical and spatial categories distorts the scriptural emphasis on personal communion;[19] and they rule out as well the doctrine that the church is an extension of the incarnation, where the failure to make clear theological distinctions leads to an unwarranted exaltation of the church and a misunderstanding of the gracious working of the Spirit in God's people and of the mode of Christ's presence on earth today.

All this being said, we must not lose sight of the one Christ whose incarnate body is mysteriously identified with the body of Christ, the church. The link between the two, as has already been suggested, can only be understood in terms of sacrament and Spirit. It is upon the eucharistic bread that Paul bases the unity of the church. *"Because there is one loaf,"* he argues, this loaf having been declared by Christ to be his body, *"we who are many are one body, for we all partake of the same loaf"* (1 Cor 10:17). The Eucharist does not *in itself* make us participants in the sacrificial death of Christ; but it shows symbolically how it is that by faith we *are* participants—Christ *gave* himself for and to us—and it enables us to express sacramentally the reality of our participation in our Lord's death and life and so to be nourished spiritually and renewed in our faith and fellowship with him.

The Eucharist is a corporate celebration because it is concerned with a reality at once corporeal and mystical, i.e., the body of Christ. We commune with Christ alone in prayer; we do not normally celebrate the Eucharist alone. Our communion with Christ, whether alone or with others at the Lord's Table, is always in the Spirit, by faith. Christ is one, the Spirit is one, and we are one body in Christ. This is the *objective* truth. But what we must ask ourselves is this: What is the *subjective* reality on any given occasion when we are celebrating together a communion of the body of Christ? The Eucharist cannot make fully effective the objective sacrifice of Christ if those participating in it are not united *between themselves* in one Spirit. *"Is Christ divided?"* Paul asks rhetorically in 1 Corinthians 1:13. Much of the content of this epistle bears on problems of division between the members of the

---

19. The formulations of Aquinas and Luther, of course, were not crudely materialistic—indeed, they were set out in part to rectify the popular, and very crude, medieval understanding of what happens to the bread and wine at the Eucharist. But the Aristotelian categories of substance and accidents which underlay these formulations nevertheless favored a materialistic-spatial type of conceptuality, philosophically sophisticated though it was. As a result, the undoubtedly spiritual intention of the theologians who worked with these categories was inevitably distorted and misconstrued.

Corinthian church. There were many causes of this division, e.g., sexual immorality, factionalism, boastfulness, competition, pride, inappropriate attitudes and public behavior of husbands and wives, contempt on the part of the richer and stronger for the weaker members, self-important posturing, an inclination to disdain the flesh even while indulging it, charismatic disorderliness, etc. Underlying all these causes was a lack of love: toward the Lord who had bought these people with the price of his life (1 Cor 6:20), and toward one another, all bought at the price of his body and all members equally, therefore, of his body the church. Paul says explicitly in 1 Corinthians 12:24–25 that the discord between them resulted from their failure to honor and care for the weaker members (in whatever sense) in their midst. The strife and division among them meant that they ate the bread and drank the cup in an unworthy manner and so were guilty of profaning the body and blood of the Lord (1 Cor 11:27). It was not the Lord's supper that they were eating (v. 20). They were not discerning the body (v. 29). The meaning of this was that they were not seeing the truth of or being committed to either the sacrificial body of Christ on the cross or the mystical body of Christ which, in its local manifestation at Corinth, they together constituted. As a consequence, what they were celebrating was not *koinonia*.

We see here how indissociable are the Lord's crucified body, his sacramental body, and his mystical body. There is only one Christ, therefore there is only one body.[20] Paul, in summoning the believers at Corinth to self-examination and repentance (1 Cor 11:28–33), is calling them to set their mutual relationships in order. The state of these is the gauge of the state of their relationship with the Lord. The apostle is saying in his distinctive way what John writes in his First Epistle:

> *We know that we have passed out of death into life, because we love the brethren. He who does not love his brother remains in death. . . . By this we know love, that he laid down his life for us; and we ought to lay down our lives for the brethren. . . . We love, because he first loved us. If anyone says, 'I love God,' and hates his brother, he is a liar; for he who does not love his brethren whom he has seen, cannot love God whom he has not seen. And this commandment we have from him, that he who loves God should love his brother also.* (1 John 3:14, 16, 4:19–21)

---

20. 1 Corinthians 10:17, 11:29, 12:12, 13, 20, 27; Romans 12:4–5; Ephesians 4:4–6.

IV

It is at this point that we may usefully introduce the question of sacrifice into our discussion. With respect to the Eucharist, it seems to me that there are three ways in which we may legitimately talk about sacrifice. The first refers to the willing self-sacrifice of Jesus on the cross. This is the basis of all other talk of sacrifice in connection with the Eucharist. It is with this particular sacrifice that the anamnesis has to do. Jesus's words, *"Do this in remembrance of me,"* are *strictly* associated with his actions of breaking the bread and offering the cup and with his accompanying interpretative words, *"This is my body which is for you"* and *"This cup is the new covenant in my blood."* Paul confirms the specificity of this remembrance when he declares that *"as often as you eat this bread and drink the cup, you proclaim the Lord's death until he comes."* The anamnesis has reference to the Lord's death on the cross. It does *not* refer to all that followed *from* and *after* that death. Its focus is precise: the Son of God gave up his life for us. We *do* the anamnesis as we perform the actions and speak the words that Christ performed and spoke at the Last Supper. It is not, as Cranmer realized,[21] a matter of our mentally calling to mind Christ's sacrifice by verbalizing "our remembrance." The anamnesis is liturgical, it is to be *done*: this is the force of Jesus's command, *"Do this. . . ."* By *doing*, we effect our unity with Christ's sacrificial *act*, as we cannot do merely by conceptualizing it in words. This is essential if the Eucharist is to make effective for us Christ's sacrifice on the cross.

The second way in which we may legitimately talk of sacrifice in connection with the Eucharist refers to the communion, in distinction from the institution/anamnesis. Here we *receive* Christ's body and blood, his self-sacrifice for us; here he offers himself *to* us. But this receiving *from* him necessarily involves our self-offering *to* him: the two movements are inseparable. D. M. Baillie writes:

> There is no other way of receiving Him except by giving ourselves to Him: and there is no way of giving ourselves to Him except by receiving Him. Both of these are happening in every single process, in every moment when we are worshipping God; and the supreme instrument and medium of that double movement, all in one, is the sacrament which we call the Eucharist, or the holy communion, or the Lord's supper.[22]

---

21. The 1552/1662 *Book of Common Prayer* does not include an anamnesis in the consecration prayer. Nothing intervenes between the recitation of the Lord's words and the communion.

22. Baillie, *Theology of the Sacraments*, 122.

William Temple expresses the same thought thusly:

> In the Eucharist . . . the distinction of subjective and objective is plainly a distinction of aspects only. In the experience itself, which is the spiritual reality of the service, there is a gift objectively offered by God and subjectively received by man; the gift is such that man's reception of it is identically his offering himself to God, for it is the very energy of self-sacrifice which is offered and received.[23]

This self-offering is both individual and corporate. *"I appeal to you therefore, brethren,"* writes Paul to the church at Rome, *"by the mercies of God, to present your bodies as a living sacrifice, holy and acceptable to God, which is your spiritual worship"* (Rom 12:1). This "living sacrifice" of ourselves in worship involves not only praise (Heb 13:15), tithes (Phil 4:18), and thanksgiving, but our whole lives. This is the force of Paul's use here of the word "bodies." Jesus, in giving his body for and to us, gave and gives us his whole self, his person; likewise, we, in presenting our bodies to him as a living sacrifice, give him all we are and have.

The reason this is called a sacrifice and not simply a gift is that it is costly and involves death. We hereby commit ourselves to love God and neighbor, and this means dying to self. We do this according to the pattern of Jesus's sacrifice and by the power of the new life obtained for us by this sacrifice—new life which we receive through the gift of the Holy Spirit. The communion in the Eucharist is a sharing in the poured-out sacrificial life of the Lord. Its being a liturgical, sacramental act and not merely a ceremony means that the activity going on here represents and demonstrates activity going on in our lives all the time: the benefits of Christ's self-sacrifice for and to us, and our self-sacrifice for and to him. This necessarily involves our self-offering directed outwards to men, starting with those who make up Christ's mystical body on earth, the church.

It is in this sense and obviously not in any expiatory sense that we are to understand Paul's words in Philippians 2:17, Colossians 1:24, and 2 Corinthians 4:7–12 about his own sufferings and sacrifice for the church, completing *"what is lacking in Christ's afflictions for the sake of his body, that is, the church"* (Col 1:24). "The body of his flesh," writes C. F. D. Moule of Jesus, "is so related to his Body the church that the church's afflictions are the implementing of his passion under Pontius Pilate."[24] To be a Christian is to follow the self-sacrificial way of the Master. The Christian can do this because he is baptized into Christ's death and lives by Christ's life: he

---

23. Temple, *Christus Veritas*, 243.
24. Moule, *Sacrifice of Christ*, 42.

is in Christ, seated with him in heavenly places, empowered by his Spirit. Therefore he is able, like Paul, knowing Christ and the power of his resurrection, to share Christ's sufferings, becoming like him in his death (Phil 3:10).

It is a matter, in John's words, of loving the brethren. Our participation in Christ's death, which we express and renew at the Eucharist, means that in Christ our self-centered life—our old man—has been put to death. As a result, living now by Christ's life, which is a self-sacrificial life, we live for God—and this entails living for others. That is the life of the new covenant, the life of love: *"For the love of Christ controls us, because we are convinced that one has died for all; therefore all have died. And he died for all, that those who live might live no longer for themselves but for him who for their sake died and was raised"* (2 Cor 4:14–15). And here we may profitably quote again John's words: *"By this we know love, that he laid down his life for us; and we ought to lay down our lives for the brethren. . . . We love, because he first loved us"* (1 John 3:16, 4:19).

We can now better understand the logic of Paul's train of thought in Romans 12, when he moves from his appeal to the brethren to offer their bodies as a living sacrifice to God, to an injunction to humility, and from there to a discussion of the body of Christ which together they make up, and of which each is a member with different gifts and functions. *"Let love be genuine,"* he goes on in verse 9; and in verse 10 he exhorts them: *"Love one another with brotherly affection,"* adding in verse 11: *". . . be aglow with the Spirit, serve the Lord."* Romans 12–14 form a parallel to 1 Corinthians 10–14, the major difference between them being that the Eucharist receives extensive treatment in the latter epistle, whereas in Romans 12:1 no reference is made, or perhaps even intended, to the Lord's Supper itself. It is clear in any case that the self-offering of the Christian to God which is involved in the eucharistic communion entails a radical reordering of his/her relationships with others, starting with his/her brethren in Christ. This will inevitably bring with it suffering and crucifying the flesh, since dying to self, forgiving others, putting them first, and serving and loving them with one's time, energy, and money are painful for naturally self-centered men and women.

Luke brings this out by following his account of the Last Supper in chapter 22 with an account of the dispute that arose between the disciples about which of them was to be regarded as the greatest. Such pretension is characteristic of *"the kings of the Gentiles,"* Jesus tells them (v. 25), a remark not calculated to make these staunch Jews proud of their conduct; it is incompatible with the Kingdom of God, where the greatest are those who serve; he is among them, Jesus concludes, *"as one who serves"* (v. 27). John makes the same point even more dramatically in his variant account of the Last Supper contained in chapter 13 of his Gospel. Jesus is shown washing the disciples' feet. *"If I then, your Lord and Teacher, have washed your feet,"* he says to them, *"you also ought to wash one another's feet. For I have given you an example, that you should do as I have done to you"* (vv. 14–15).

The Christians in the Corinthian church, divided and selfish, were not acting in love toward each other, which is why Paul is able to write to them; "When you meet together, it is not the Lord's supper that you eat" (1 Cor 11:20). They were not really receiving the life of Christ, given for and to them. Many were ill and weak as a consequence, and some had died (v. 30). If the Eucharist is to make effective for us Christ's sacrifice on the cross, those who partake of it together must do their utmost to honor each other and to live in harmony, mutually accepting, forgiving, and forbearing one another in love.

The third way in which we may legitimately talk of sacrifice in connection with the Eucharist has to do with an understanding of the sacrament as containing and communicating the whole redemptive activity of Christ. "The sacrificial character of the Mass," writes E. L. Mascall,

> does not consist in its being an event which happens to Christ after his Ascension and which in some way repeats or imitates his death, but in its being the means by which the whole sacrificial action of Christ, centered in the Cross and culminating in the Ascension, is made sacramentally present in his church. It is not a repetition of the sacrifice, nor is it the completion of the sacrifice; it is simply the sacrifice itself, present in the unique mode of a sacrament, present, that is, simply and solely because the sacramental species are the divinely ordained effective signs of it. The inner reality which the sacramental signs contain—namely, the whole redemptive act of Christ—does not *happen* historically and physically, in the Mass; it is simply *there*, sacramentally.[25]

Understood in this sense, the Eucharist as a sacramental whole speaks of the eternal sacrifice of Christ which begins and ends in heaven and expresses from start to finish God's will to redeem fallen men and have fellowship with them. It begins historically with the self-sacrifice of the incarnation, of which Bethlehem is the outward manifestation; it follows on with the self-giving life and ministry of Jesus; it finds its climax and fulfillment at Calvary and its effective sealing in the resurrection, ascension, and eternal session at God's right hand, from which position in glory Christ as

25. Mascall, *Corpus Christi*, 96.

high priest pleads before his Father the absolute efficacy of his shed blood.[26] In the Eucharist, we have communion with Jesus Christ, the self-offering One, the Alpha and the Omega, who is the same yesterday, today, and forever; with the One who is eternally both Priest and Victim, both King and Lamb, and who gave himself for us that we might have forgiveness of our sins, yet not only this but also new life in him and access to the Father's throne, where with the Son we shall reign forever. To view the Eucharist thusly is to stress the present efficaciousness of Christ's sacrifice, of which the Lord's Supper, as a sacrament, is both a representation and a channel. The redemptive action of God, culminating at Calvary, changed the condition of sinners once and for all; but the saving action of the sacrifice of Christ is renewed each time the believer calls for help and implores the grace of forgiveness. F. J. Leenhardt writes:

> The teaching which sets forth the Lord's Supper as a sacrifice illuminates this truth that the acts of God, although inserted into historical time by their contingent realization, escape it because the intentions which they reveal give them a permanence throughout their full duration. They preserve a perpetual actuality, because the intention which gave rise to them itself preserves an unchanged actuality. . . . The Lord's Supper is a Passover renewed as a function of the new redemptive action which God accomplishes in Jesus Christ. There is therefore more than a commemoration. The redemptive past becomes the present of faith. What God has done once, He continues to do.[27]

Such an interpretation is not to be taken as meaning that in the Eucharist the church is offering the sacrifice of Christ. The only sacrifice *we* offer is that of ourselves, as suggested above, in response to Christ's self-offering to us. In the Eucharist, the church makes present through the sacrament and appropriates for itself by faith the once-for-all sacrifice of Christ. What it "remembers" in the anamnesis is, strictly speaking, Christ's death. But its communion in his body and blood means that it is living even now in the new covenant which that death established and which the coming of the Holy Spirit sealed: it is living even now, that is to say, by the power of his resurrection life and in anticipation of the *parousia*. Here precisely we see how the Eucharist is fundamentally different from Passover. The sacrament is *more* than a remembrance, actualization, or commemoration of a past event, i.e., Christ's death on the cross. As our *communion* in his body and blood implies, it involves the totality of Christ's work on behalf of mankind

---

26. See Moule, *Sacrifice of Christ*, 47; see Clark, *Approach to the Theology*, 65.
27. Leenhardt, "This is My Body," 58.

and presupposes its *actual* efficacy. In the Eucharist, we celebrate Christ as Lord *now* and *forever*. We can make the commemorative act of Jesus's sacrificial death at Calvary, but we cannot do the same of his resurrection and ascension, since we do not relate to these events solely as events of the past.[28] This is demonstrated in our *communion* in his body and blood. The Eucharist makes effective Christ's sacrifice because Christ, having risen from the dead, is alive forever and seated at the Father's right hand in his glorified humanity, which is itself the eternal pledge of the absolute efficacy of the sacrifice the sacrament commemorates.

V

It is theologically appropriate that Paul, having written at length about the Lord's Supper and what it involves, should then proceed to a discussion of how the local members of the body of Christ are to function together charismatically in the Spirit. The Body is one, the Spirit is one, and the two are fundamentally linked (1 Cor 12:11–13). The body of Christ is the temple of the Spirit (1 Cor 3:16), as is each individual Christian's body (1 Cor 6:19). It is therefore normal that the Spirit should manifest himself in and through the body (1 Cor 12:7). The Spirit is the Spirit of God and also the Spirit of Christ, as Paul suggests by his parallel phrasing in 1 Corinthians 12:4–6, and makes explicit elsewhere, as in 2 Corinthians 3:17, Romans 8:9–11 and Philippians 1:19 (see also Acts 16:7). He is, as the apostle puts it in Romans 8:2, *"the Spirit of life in Christ."* It is by the Spirit that the life of Christ is imparted to believers. God's gift (charisma) to us, writes Paul in Romans 6:23, is *"eternal life through Jesus Christ our Lord."* This gift is given with the "promise" of the Father (Luke 24:49), in fulfillment of Old Testament prophesy in Joel (Joel 2:28–32; see Acts 2:16–21), and this promise is the Holy Spirit, received from the Father by the glorified Christ and poured out upon men (Acts 2:33). The Holy Spirit, like the life of Christ he imparts, is a *gift* to men (Acts 2:38). John's doctrine of the Spirit matches Paul's and Luke's insofar as for John it is the Spirit who gives life (John 6:63) and who is given to the disciples by the Father through the glorified Christ (John 14:16, 26, 7:39, 20:22–23).

The gift of the Spirit at Pentecost is associated by the apostles with the "last days" (Acts 2:17), in accordance with Joel's prophecy. Paul similarly writes of the Spirit in eschatological terms, as *"the guarantee of our inheritance until we acquire possession of it"* (Eph 1:14; see 2 Cor 1:22; Rom 8:23; Gal 5:5). Matthew and Luke both associate the Spirit explicitly with

---

28. See Gregg, *Anamnesis in the Eucharist*, 29–32.

the kingdom of God (e.g., Matt 12:28; Luke 11:20), and Luke in particular is concerned to show how Christ's coming involved the Holy Spirit's breaking into ordinary life. In like manner, the whole structure of the first chapter of Mark's gospel, for example, is calculated to demonstrate the relationship between Jesus Christ, the Spirit, and the gospel of the kingdom of God.

If the Spirit of Christ is the sign of the presence of the end in our midst, so is the body of Christ, in which he resides. Christ is not identical with the Spirit or with his body, the church, but the Spirit is the Spirit of *Christ* and the church is the body of *Christ*. The church is a new creation, an eschatological reality (2 Cor 5:17). It is the body of Christ in virtue of the new covenant in Christ's blood by which it lives and in which it is sealed by the Spirit. What is at issue here is *eternal life*, which has to do, as we have seen, with knowledge of God and communion with Him (John 17:3). We have that life in Christ's blood and by his Spirit, and we receive it by faith and enter experimentally into it by the sacraments of baptism and the Eucharist. To participate in Christ's death is to participate in his life. The Spirit who brings us this charisma of eternal life manifests himself in Christ's body charismatically, to encourage, admonish, and build up the church (1 Cor 12, 14; Rom 12); likewise, at the Eucharist, as we participate in Christ's body and blood, it is the Spirit living in us who ministers Christ's life to us and makes effective his sacrifice. All of this is in fulfillment of God's gracious purpose to us and in order that his glory may be seen among men in the humility and love exemplified by Christ's sacrifice on the cross and in the power of Christ's resurrection life (see John 17:10, 22; Rom 8:17–30; Phil 3:10).

As Christ, according to the Epistle to the Hebrews (Hebrews 9:12–14) offered himself *"through eternal Spirit"* without blemish *to God* (his life was lived in perfect obedience to the will of God and therefore was of the Spirit, of the eternal order), so equally the offering of his blood (life) which he made at Calvary, and which, as our heavenly high priest, he took into the holy place once and for all to secure our eternal redemption, is made real for us, is offered *to us*, by the Spirit. It is by the Spirit that we enter into all that Christ has obtained for us at the cross. This is the thrust of John's pneumatology, as developed in chapters 14–16 of the Fourth Gospel. The Spirit will teach us *all* things and lead us into *all* truth concerning Jesus Christ (John 14:26, 16:13). He will minister Christ to us and will glorify him (John 16:14). This means, in keeping with the same author's Christology, that he will illuminate us on the one hand, about the *glory* of Christ's *cross*, where God's love for men was consummated (John 12:27–33, 13:31–32); and on the other hand, about Christ's *glory* with the Father in *heaven* (John 17:3–5). It is his death on the cross that we remember in the Eucharist; and we proclaim that death until he comes, that is, until he comes in *glory* to establish God's kingdom. In this way, we may conclude the Spirit does work through the sacrament of the Eucharist to *glorify* Christ in his Body.

It is the Spirit, John tells us in his eucharistically oriented account of the feeding of the five thousand in chapter 6 of his Gospel, *"that gives life, the flesh is of no avail"* (v. 63). He goes on to add, *"The words that I have spoken to you are spirit and life."* In the Eucharist, as we do what Jesus did at the Last Supper and speak the words he spoke, the Spirit who was in him and is now in us makes the bread and cup, his body and blood, to be unto us eternal life, in communion with the Father and the Son. It is in this sense, perhaps, that we may understand the eschatological force of Jesus's words in John 17:10 and 22, when he speaks of being glorified in those whom the Father has given him. He goes so far as to say that *"the glory which thou hast given me I have given them."* The clause he then adds is surely significant for our purpose: *"that they may be one even as we are one."* We cannot help but be reminded here of Paul's eucharistic teaching in 1 Corinthians 10 and 11 about the one loaf, coupled with his subsequent discussion of the one body and the one Spirit. The glory which is in Christ's body is *Christ's* glory; yet this glory really has been shared with his *body,* the church, and is the basis of its unity—just as the unity is a reflection of the glory.

For this reason Paul can write in Romans 8:30: ". . . and those *whom he called he also justified; and those whom he justified he also glorified."* As we are *in Christ now,* seated with him in heavenly places, we are *in his glory now.* Identified with him in his death by baptism, we are also united with him in his risen life. This is true of us as individuals and as the church, a truth to which Paul points in his doctrine of the Spirit by teaching that the Spirit inhabits *both* our individual bodies and the body of Christ which we constitute corporately (1 Cor 6:19, 3:17). Together, the sacraments of baptism and Eucharist express this reality: by baptism, the individual is incorporated into Christ's body (crucified and mystical); by the Eucharist, he partakes, as a member of the church and in corporate communion with his brethren, of Christ's body and blood, and through Christ's body Christ's Spirit ministers life to him personally.

Yet despite all this we know that Christ's glorified humanity is still not ours, at least not in fullness. We are not yet *"like him"* (1 John 3:2). We see only in a mirror dimly (1 Cor 13:12). Although we have already received *"the Spirit of sonship"* (Rom 8:15), we have only *"the first fruits of the Spirit"* and still await our *"adoption as sons, the redemption of our bodies"* (Rom 8:23). Hence in the same chapter in which he tells us that God *has glorified* us in Christ, Paul can write: *"When we cry, 'Abba! Father!,' it is the Spirit himself bearing witness with our spirit that we are children of God, and if children, then heirs, heirs of God and fellow heirs with Christ, provided we suffer with him in order that we may also be glorified with him"* (Rom 8:15b–17). As Jesus's suffering and glorification go together, so do ours. If we would be united with Christ in his glory, we cannot avoid either his cross or ours (ours is not only grounded in his, it is also patterned on it, as we have seen, in the sense of involving self-sacrifice). At one and the same time we are glorified with Christ and not yet glorified. Thus shall it be *"until he comes."* The church lives eschatologically; it walks by faith, not by sight (2 Cor 5:7). We do not yet see Jesus *"as he is"* (1 John 3:2), *"face to face"* (1 Cor 13:12).

It is for this reason that the church needs the sacraments. Like a hyphen, they link Calvary and the *parousia* and so gather up the whole course of time into the present of God's eternal life given to us in Christ Jesus. "And in both baptism and the Lord's Supper," writes D. M. Baillie,

> the church looks back to the death and resurrection of Christ, which have to be reproduced in us, and forward to the full enjoyment of the Kingdom, of which the Holy Spirit given in baptism is an earnest and seal, and whose messianic banquet we rehearse and anticipate in the sacrament of the Lord's Supper.[29]

By grace through faith given us by the Holy Spirit we enter into these spiritual realities and participate in them sacramentally. In the Eucharist, God's eternal purpose toward us of love is focused, expressed, and actually offered to us in Christ's body and blood given for us. As, united together in one body and Spirit, we receive gratefully and with faithful hearts Christ's gift to us of himself, his sacrifice is made effective in our lives by his Spirit and we are renewed in our communion with him who is *"the resurrection and the life"* (John 11:25).

---

29. Baillie, *Theology of the Sacraments*, 70.

Part V

APOLOGETICS

Talks given at St. Michael's Anglican Church, Paris

Talk I

Glossary of Terms. Brief Synopsis of Worldviews Leading Up to Postmodernism

The Greeks. I am referring to ancient Greek culture, especially of the fourth century BC.

Plato and ideas. A Greek philosopher of the fourth century BC who posited a conceptual realm of Ideas that provided the eternal patterns for all existing things on earth, which were transient and subject to change. Plato, along with ancient Greek culture in general, considered that which changed and passed away to be essentially unreal, and he imagined an intelligible realm of ideas beyond the reach of transient material reality, which, in correspondence with the human faculty of reason, could provide, conceptually, a ground of permanence and therefore of meaning. In the natural world, the (apparently) fixed stars were thought to be divine because they were unchanging, and Plato saw them as images of the changeless intelligible realm.

Aristotle and causation. A Greek philosopher of the fourth century BC, and a student of Plato. He diverged from Plato's doctrine of ideas by asserting that such ideas do not have independent existence in an intelligible realm but that an idea or form has existence as it is united with matter. So, for example, the idea/form of "tree" has existence only as it is united with a material tree. His four senses of cause were posited to explain this doctrine: the *material* cause of something is the matter on which a form is imposed; the *formal* cause, in conjunction with matter, makes the thing a distinct entity; the *final* cause is the end which, in processes of growth or change, determines the course of development; and the *efficient* cause is the motive power that produces the event. Thus teleology (see below) was intrinsic to physical causation, a conception that prevailed until the seventeenth century. While not averse to empirical observation, Aristotle's philosophical method proceeded deductively from general *a priori* principles to expected factual particulars, rather than inductively from observed particulars to general laws. This was the fundamental reason why Greek science never developed in the manner that modern science has done.

Worldview. A comprehensive picture, held by individuals and cultures, of the way things are in reality. Such a worldview, which will shape the thought and beliefs of an age, will be structured by prevailing mythical, religious, or ideological convictions. The worldview of a given epoch is usually formed in reaction to the previous worldview, seen as false or oppressive by the pioneers of a new overarching vision of reality, both social and metaphysical.

Medieval worldview. The universe is a created, orderly, integrated, hierarchical whole, created by God for his glory. God is both transcendent to the created universe and immanent within it. The spiritual and material interpenetrate, and physical reality reveals God's beauty, majesty, and perfection, as in, for example, the splendor of the stars and the rotation of the planets. Divine purpose is manifest everywhere in the world of nature. He is omnipresent, most immediately in the sacraments of the church, and since, in Jesus Christ, he himself became manifest and visible in the incarnation, he may be represented in physical imagery.

Metaphysical. The origin of the word goes back to the ancient Greek philosopher, Aristotle. It means the philosophical study of principles or problems underlying the physical world, such as the origin, nature, and purpose of the universe, the connection of mind with matter, and the relationship of appearance and reality. Empirical science is deeply involved in such issues and may orient metaphysical insights, without however being able to provide answers to the issues themselves.

Ontology. The branch of metaphysics that deals with the nature of *being.*

Teleology. The branch of study dealing with the evidence of purpose in the physical world, based on a philosophical belief in final causes (Aristotle) or a Judeo-Christian belief in divine design.

Plausibility structure. A structure of belief and practice that provides a sense of credibility and assurance to those who adhere to it. The plausibility structure of a minority group in a given society will be much weaker than that of a majority group.

Copernicus, Kepler, Galileo, Newton. Four great mathematical physicists/astronomers whose work, extending successively from the late fifteenth century to the early eighteenth century, fundamentally altered the classical understanding of the structure of the solar system and the laws governing the motion and relation of material bodies (Copernicus argued, against the Greek Ptolemaic conception, that the sun, not the earth, was at the center of the solar system; Kepler discovered the laws of planetary motion; Galileo invented the telescope and, by applying empirical methods of observation, discovered the laws of dynamics and falling bodies and confirmed the Copernican theory; Newton formulated the law of gravitation and universal laws of motion, invented calculus, and theorized that light is composed of corpuscles). The concept of law-determined cause and effect definitively replaced the concept of purpose as the explanatory principle of physical phenomena, and the method of inductive reasoning, moving from particular observations to the formulation of hypotheses with experimental confirmation or disconfirmation, replaced the deductive reasoning from abstract first principles that had been in use since the development of the science of logic by Aristotle in the fourth century BC. These thinkers, along with the late-sixteenth-century-philosopher Francis Bacon, practiced empirical, observation-based methods by which to penetrate the secrets of nature and control natural phenomena, and thus laid the basis for the development of modern science. Purpose was henceforth seen as an irrelevant category, methodologically speaking, with respect to the workings of the physical universe, which could be explored and analyzed adequately without reference to God, whether one believed in God or not. The term "creation" gave way to the term "nature." With the rise of Darwinism in the nineteenth century, the exclusion of purpose from cosmology and physics was extended to the biological realm and finally to the human sphere as a whole, which atheists consider to be undirected, purposeless, and meaningless.

The Enlightenment. An historical period extending broadly from the late seventeenth century to the mid-twentieth century, of which the peak was the last quarter of the eighteenth century. It was an optimistic age that believed in the supremacy and universal potency of reason and the scientific method—consisting of empirical observation, hypothesis, and experimentation—to bring knowledge and progress in all spheres of human life. It proclaimed the autonomy of the individual as over against systems of ecclesiastical or political authority. While its scientific forerunners such as Copernicus, Kepler, Galileo, and Bacon were all theists (believers in God, though not necessarily in classical Christian orthodoxy), belief in God among the intellectual elite of Europe declined markedly in the eighteenth century, leading to open declarations of atheism in the nineteenth century.

With Emmanuel Kant in the late eighteenth century, the possibility of metaphysical knowledge through the use of pure reason on the basis of sense experience was denied. Furthermore, sense experience can give knowledge of the appearance of objects, but not to knowledge of the objects in themselves. Through formal categories existing in the mind—in particular space and time and a mental process enabling conceptualization—the autonomous self /mind, the free-standing individual, imposes order on the raw data of sensation and so in a real sense actively determines knowledge. The thinking self of the seventeenth-century-philosopher Rene Descartes, who had argued that the thinking self was the basis of the certain knowledge of one's existence ("I think, therefore I am"), was thus amplified by Kant and subtly exalted to become the world-creating self of nineteenth-century philosophy and, in another expression later, of the postmodern relativistic self (see below) whose personal perspective on reality determines its meaning and truth for him/her. Objective matter, including the human body, is mere material for subjective manipulation.

The sacred/secular dualism. While the medieval worldview had seen all reality as integrated and God as present everywhere in the natural world and daily life, most manifestly in the sacraments and institutions of the church, the sixteenth-century Reformers (Luther, Calvin, Zwingli, Cranmer), in reaction against instances of superstition, idolatry, and corruption in the late medieval church, stressed God's written word, the Bible. The Roman Church had underscored the real presence of Christ in the eucharistic elements to the point of insisting on the transubstantiation (change) of the wine and bread into Christ's actual body at the moment of consecration by the priest. The Reformers discarded this belief along with the Roman Catholic emphasis on images and the appeal to the senses, stressing instead the preaching of the word. The result, in part, was an increasing intellectualization of Christian faith, a weakened sense of sacrament (in particular in the Calvinist branch of the Reformation, less so among Lutherans and Anglicans), and the extrusion of God's presence and the sacred from secular reality. This was, unwittingly, a factor in preparing the way for the Enlightenment and the rise of atheism in the eighteenth century.

Deism. A movement of thought in the late seventeenth and eighteenth centuries that construed God as the Creator of the world who had disappeared over the horizon once his creative work was done and who no longer had any relation to it. It was easy to move from Deism, with its absent God, to atheism, where the absent God is declared simply not to exist.

The fact/value distinction. A dualistic understanding of reality that emerged in the eighteenth century, characteristic of the enlightenment worldview, which divided fact from value. *Fact* was understood as that which was thought to be objectively knowable by the scientific method of empirical observation and experiment; *values*, including all moral, religious, or aesthetical assertions, were mere opinion and could not count as knowledge. In this way Christian faith was gradually relegated to the private, subjective realm of feeling and opinion and lost credibility in Western culture.

Romanticism. A movement within the Enlightenment in the first half of the nineteenth century, both continuous with the Enlightenment worldview as far as the supremacy of the individual was concerned and in opposition to it as far as its emphasis on the centrality of objective reason was concerned. Subjectivity and the self began to take center stage, and the value of emotion began to overtake that of rationality. Along with this came a rising stress on nationality and particularity, and an emphasis on the virtues of beauty and nature. Romanticism can also partially be understood in opposition to industrialism as this was emerging in the second third of the nineteenth century. Alongside the romantic movement, the development of science proceeded apace, thus widening the fact/value split in Western culture.

Pluralism and plurality. Pluralism as an ideology—a set of ideas, necessarily partial and limited, yet held to be absolute—holds religious and social beliefs and ethnic groupings to be of equal value and truth. Plurality as a concept corresponds to the social reality of multiple religious and social groupings with different truth claims and values. It refers to the same reality as the word "diversity."

Postmodernism. The worldview that began to find expression in the 1930s and that has flourished in the last thirty years. In strong reaction to the Enlightenment, it repudiates knowledge as an ideal and denies the possibility of universal truth and objectivity. No universal theory of knowledge is possible. It stresses diversity as against uniformity and universality, cultural pluralism, and the fundamental importance of difference and perspective. Each person and culture has its own perspective, equal in value to any other. The way we think and act is embedded in our cultural context, and universal truth claims are illusory. There is no meta-narrative, no overarching vision of human purpose and meaning. Relativism and subjectivity rule, which makes problematical the evaluation and judgment of personal behavior. The individual reigns supreme and can act as he/she sees fit, as long as this does not impinge on another's freedom. The rights of the individual are the arbiter of the good, there being no objective moral referent. No universal ethical standards exist, even in a given society. This leads to political correctness on the one hand and inevitably, on the other hand, to power as the decisive factor in society. Ultimately, it tends to undermine democracy in favor of fiercely competing interest groups and the domination of the most vocal and influential. This can lead to increased state control and a kind of soft totalitarianism. Underneath the alleged respect for diversity exists a powerful thrust to conformity; a dissident from this ideology will be accused of discrimination and sanctioned.

Another fundamental aspect of postmodernism concerns the emphasis on language. Our access to the world is mediated by language, and language is a human construct, contextually conditioned and conventional. All language is interpretive, which means that all knowledge of reality is interpretation and variable according to time and place and cultural context. No objective reality exists beyond our speech and writing that might enable us to substantiate a claim that a statement is authentic and true. There are no objective meanings in texts, but only a free play of meaning with endless connections and correlations and analyses. Through language and concepts, we impose a sense of objective meaning on the flux of experience, but in fact this is an illusion, and no concepts, no universals, exist apart from the words attached to them. Language is merely self-referential. It is disconnected from its objects, which it designates by linguistic signs. But the signs—the signifiers—are not the things signified, hence language is characterized by the absence, not the presence, of the things signified. This theory denies the traditional correspondence theory of truth, since the essence of what is signified is not conveyed (made present) by the linguistic signifiers, the words. Any meaning of a discourse can only be found in the contextual network of linguistic relations, not in any objective reference.

Talk II

Cosmology. Darwinism

I

Background Reflections

> "The wrath of God is being revealed from heaven against all the godlessness and wickedness of men who suppress the truth by their wickedness, since what may be known about God is plain to them. For since the creation of the world God's invisible qualities—his eternal power and divine nature—have been clearly seen, being understood from what has been made, so that men are without excuse." (Rom 1:18–20)

It is still thought by many people that science and Christian faith are in conflict. This is only the case when science is made to rest on a materialistic/

naturalistic ideology, excluding any reality that is not observable and demonstrable, experimentally or mathematically, and when faith is construed as an irrational leap into the dark against all evidence.

In fact authentic science and biblical faith support each other. As there is only one God, and, from the scriptural perspective, he is the Creator of all that is, there can only be one truth. The Creator and his creation cannot be at odds with each other. His self-revelation to the Hebrews—both in Scripture and supremely in Christ—will be in harmony with the indirect revelation of his nature and power in the created cosmos.

Modern science has developed fully in the Christian West, nowhere else. Why?

On the basis of the Judeo-Christian revelation in the Bible, the world is a creation *ex nihilo*: it was created by the sovereign will of God out of nothing. Consequently, it is contingent and rational.

Contingent means that it could have been different and that it is not based on *necessary* laws that can be known by deduction from *a priori* principles, that is, from principles that exist in the inquirer's mind and from which truth can be deduced logically without recourse to empirical observation and experiment. Scientific truth about God's created cosmos can only be known by empirical observation, hypothesis, and experiment, using the language of mathematics.

Rational means that its structures and processes are ordered and constitute a coherent totality, a cosmos and not a chaos. Furthermore—and this is extremely important—these structures and processes are discoverable by rational minds. This fact underlies what is known as the correspondence theory of truth.

Contingency and lawfulness together allow the universe to take the shape it has and bring forth life. The order and stability are *dynamic*, not static, and chance plays an important role in it, as quantum theory, notably with Heisenberg's Uncertainty Principle and chaos theory, has shown. The Creator incorporates randomness into his overarching order and lawfulness, thus giving to contingency an ongoing role in opening out the universe to new possibilities.

Such a cosmos is the fruit of a rational mind, a personal being, all-powerful, eternal, timeless, and purposeful. He is outside of time. Space-time, matter, and energy are his creations and did not preexist him. He is Spirit. He is transcendent over his creation and ontologically distinct from it. He is also immanent in it to sustain and develop it according to his purpose in creating it.

This biblical revelation of God the Creator opens the way to scientific investigation of the world by human beings, who, we are told in Genesis

1:26-28, are created "in the image of God." Science as we know it did not develop fully in other cultures because the world was taken to be eternal and necessary, or divine, or illusory. In any case it was not open to analytical and empirical investigation by human beings. But according to the biblical revelation, human beings are creatures with a special ontological relation to the Creator and are endowed with reason. As creatures, they also have an ontological relation to other creatures; as made in God's image, however, they transcend all other creatures and have the rationality to investigate and know them. They are called by God to be stewards and caretakers of the creation, and to name the creatures. It is by this naming that they know the other creatures and may carry out their mandate. This is essential to caring for the creation, and it is the basis on which the vision and method of modern science eventually came into being.

Science is one chief way of naming. Another is art. Art is intuitive and is concerned with meaning and sense, with the spiritual aspect of the invisible and visible. Science is essentially analytical and seeks to understand the ontological structures and functional principles of material reality. Both are motivated by a desire for truth and are guided by the beauty—the order, economy, harmony, proportionality, and radiance—inherent in the created cosmos.

In this talk, we are concerned especially with science. Scientists marvel at the correspondence between their own rational powers and the rational order of the universe. We human beings have the capacity to discover objective truth about the way things are. The basis for this is, on the one hand, the contingent and rational nature of the universe, and on the other hand, the doctrine of the *imago Dei*, as suggested above. God has created the universe and us within it in such a way that we desire and are able to explore and develop his creation. God's purpose in this is that we may find his footprints there and seek to know him, the Creator.

At this point, we revert to Romans 1:18-20. Always, in looking at the world we live in, we must have bi-focal vision: there is the creation and there is original sin, the turning away from the Creator. We resist acknowledging the Creator, despite the natural evidence pointing to him. We want to use our rational powers to glorify ourselves instead of God.

The Enlightenment project demonstrated this in one way, by exalting reason and then reducing it to that which could be ascertained by the scientific method, then by excluding the possibility of knowledge of God, and finally by denying God's existence altogether and calling theistic belief a mere human projection and illusion. Postmodernism demonstrates this in another way by denying the reality of any overarching metaphysical truth and the possibility of objective knowledge of anything, including the material world, and by turning all truths into subjective perspectives and all discourses into relativistic language games, ever changing and ultimately meaningless.

II

Brief Notes on Issues in Cosmology

The origin of the universe. Until the twentieth century, it had always been assumed by most cultures, including ours, that the universe was eternal. It was just there, without explanation. Christians could believe otherwise on the basis of Genesis 1, but even Aquinas was unable to prove it, and creation *ex nihilo* was, at best, simply asserted as an article of faith without evidence to support it.

Theoretical and observational discoveries in the twentieth century have disproved this age-long assumption by showing that the universe has a beginning, is evolving, and, on the natural level, will have an end. Einstein's theory of general relativity does not allow for a static universe (1915); Hubble discovered the red-shift of light coming from distant stars and concluded that galaxies are moving away from us at ever-increasing velocities (1929); two scientists discovered cosmic background radiation, a vestige of an early dense state of the universe (1965). These and other discoveries point to a beginning of the universe—what is called a "singularity." This is the theory of the Big Bang.

Such a beginning raises the problem of a cause. Both logic and intuition tell us that everything that comes into existence must have a cause. This cause must be different from the universe itself, so it must be timeless, spaceless, immaterial, and personal, that is, the result of a personal will and not of initial conditions and natural laws. There are only two kinds of explanations for events: scientific and personal. A beginning to the universe cannot be explained scientifically, because precisely what is needed for a scientific explanation did not yet exist but came into existence. A personal creative will provides the only explanation possible.

Many physicists and cosmologists are searching for scientific explanations for this extraordinary and unexpected development in cosmology. Surely there is much more to be discovered about the Big Bang, but in any case it provides powerful support for the biblical affirmation that the universe came into being by an act of an unimaginably powerful Creator God.

Intelligent design and the anthropic principle (AP). In the last twenty-five years, scientists in every field have made huge advances in uncovering inherent order in the structures and processes of the universe. The AP arises from the ever-increasing knowledge about the fine-tuning of the universe that enables life to emerge and develop on our planet. The chemical and physical conditions for this to be possible had to have been—and were—almost unbelievably precise, such that the tiniest deviation from the actual values would have meant that life as we know it could not have developed.

Parameters like what is called the cosmological constant (which corresponds to the energy density of empty space), force of gravity, electromagnetic force, and strong nuclear force, are fine-tuned to magnitudes of one part in billions and billions which, if stronger or weaker, would prevent stars from forming, or cause the universe to collapse, or cause all atoms except hydrogen to be torn apart, making the emergence of life impossible.

Furthermore, the physical conditions of the earth, the moon, the sun, and our location in the Milky Way galaxy have been shown to be astoundingly complex and uniquely propitious for the development of life. The earth's biology and geology interact very tightly. Just the right chemicals have to be present, but environmental factors like geophysical and meteorological processes have to be just right also. As one scientist, Guillermo Gonzales, has said, "From the magnetic field to plate tectonics to the carbon dioxide cycle—ongoing life depends on a variety of very complicated interactions with the planet."[1]

Interestingly, some scientists have observed that our precise place in the universe not only provides the incredibly fine-tuned elements that make life possible, but also provides the best imaginable platform for observing the universe and penetrating its inner workings with our reason. There appears to be a relationship between habitability and measurability. This is evidence from a new angle in support of the so-called correspondence theory of truth alluded to earlier, for which theologically the basis is the doctrine of the *imago Dei*.

A related point arises from what might be termed the methodological importance of the criterion of beauty in scientific investigation. This comes out especially in mathematical equations and the search for theory. Beauty exists in the underlying world of physical laws and mathematics and cannot be accounted for purely in terms of subjectivity or by reference, in evolutionary theory, to the mechanism of natural selection.

The cumulative power of all this evidence is enormous. While of course it does not *prove* the existence of a Creator God or of deliberate design, it points powerfully in this direction and certainly suggests that the universe was made for humankind to live in.

---

1. Strobel, *Case for a Creator*, 106.

III

Brief Notes on Darwinism

Intelligent design and evolution. As with cosmology, a great deal of evidence is emerging in evolutionary and biological science that points to design in the development of life and life forms. The chance-plus-time formula, with natural selection as the mechanism that brings about the evolution of life, looks more and more unlikely as an adequate explanation.

The instance of irreducibly complex systems, of which each part is necessary for the functioning of the whole—the eye, or cilia on the surface of cells, are often given as examples—brings a powerful case against the fundamental Darwinian tenet that evolution must always proceed by small steps, through genetic mutations followed by natural selection. No single part in such a complex system has meaning or utility outside of the whole, which makes it very difficult to see how the whole could have evolved incrementally. A system must have a minimal function to be a candidate for natural selection, and in the case of an irreducibly complex system, this requires that all the parts be present at once and able to perform at a level suitable to their purpose.

One Darwinian response is to say that there exists in some cases a process of redeployment by natural selection of material originally developed for a different structure, such that a function that started off serving one purpose is co-opted to serve another one. This is supposed to explain how complex systems could emerge progressively. There seems to be no doubt that this is the case in many instances, as I observe in my discussion of intelligent design in chapter 1 of this book, but the concept of intentional design, which can *include* the above-noted insight regarding the incremental development of irreducibly complex organisms, seems a much more coherent and comprehensive *overall* explanation for the evolution of such organisms, unless ideological considerations rule it out arbitrarily from the start as impossible, as evolutionary fundamentalism insists on doing.

Among scientists who believe in a Creator God and in purposeful, God-guided evolution, there appear to be two main currents of thought about the operation of this divine guidance. Some, like the scientist-theologian John Polkinghorne, agree with the Darwinian thesis that evolution is incremental and that natural selection is the crucial mechanism, but insist that the divine impulse is mysteriously built into the fabric of created matter. This design, incorporated into matter, acts entirely naturally in such a way as to preclude any sort of extranatural intervention or influence, even while enabling evolutionary development to advance toward ever-more-complex forms. God has made the world free to develop by *creatio continua*, a concept similar to the classical concept of God's providential maintenance of the created universe. *Creatio continua* carries forward, by evolutionary means, the *creatio nihilo* of the beginning. There is purpose and direction to the process, leading intentionally to the creation of a *new creation* in and through Christ, which brings into existence the church and will ultimately bring into existence a transmutation of the present world, a "totally sacramental universe whose divine-infused 'matter' will be delivered from the transience and decay inherent in present physical processes." [2]

This first current in theistic evolutionary theory is usually represented by physicists. The other current, usually represented by biologists or chemists associated with the intelligent design movement, tends to repudiate the traditional Darwinian notion that all evolutionary advance is incremental, by means of random genetic mutations of which some are retained and taken forward by natural selection. Scientists of this persuasion argue first of all that no strict Darwinian has provided an *adequate* refutation of the challenge raised by irreducibly complex systems. The concept of self-organization, for example, which posits a property in biochemistry that encourages the parts of molecular machines to self-assemble, does not explain large-scale developments such as complex interactive systems. At the molecular level, it is no help whatsoever in accounting for the structure of the DNA molecule, which patently requires informational input from outside the system. No naturalistic explanation has been found that is able to account for the development of the genetic code and for the first living primitive organisms. The mantra of self-preservation as the driving force behind evolution—a mantra that functions, where Darwinian dogma has eliminated teleology from nature, as a *pseudo teleology* intended to explain the obvious directionality of all living organisms—is obviously irrelevant as a way of accounting for the emergence of the DNA molecule and living organisms, since it presupposes their existence in the first place. Only intelligent design provides a good match to the data. Even if natural selection on the basis of random variations in organisms could account for all biological development—which it can't in any case—at the chemical level it explains nothing, since it only operates on existent self-replicating organisms. The question remains as to how these organisms, and the material making them up, came into being in the first place. There is no such thing as prebiological natural selection. And the enigma about the chemical origin of life, and the *molecular information and organization* needed to achieve it, remains

---

2. Pulkinghorne, *Belief in God*, 22.

unexplained. The fundamental cosmological laws cannot in themselves account for this information.

Another argument against Darwinian gradualism as an *adequate* theory to explain evolution makes reference to what is called the Cambrian explosion, which began an estimated 530 million years ago and lasted approximately 5 million years, which in this context is a very short time span. Paleontologists, who study fossils, estimate that at least twenty and perhaps as many as thirty-five of the world's forty phyla (a "phylum" is a major division of organisms that contain one or more classes) came into existence with unique body plans during this period. This explosion of organisms represents an incredible quantum leap of biological complexity. Biologist Stephen Meyer has this to say about the phenomenon: "The big issue is where did the information come from to build all these new proteins, cells, and body plans? . . . This would require highly complex, specified genetic information of the sort that neither random chance nor natural selection, nor self-organization can produce."[3] No fossils in earlier strata have been found showing gradual evolutionary development. The phenomenon appears to be what Meyer calls "top-down," that is, major differences in form and body plan appear first, with no simpler transitions before them. Subsequent small-scale variations only come later. Meyer argues that the only available explanation for such a phenomenon is intelligent design.

Many other kinds of evidence are advanced today by theistic scientists to argue in favor of purposeful, deliberate design in nature that points to a Creator God who continues to be active in the development of his creation. How the Creator actually does this remains utterly mysterious and perhaps always will, and there is urgent need for scientists and theologians to continue to explore this issue.

In discussing these matters of cosmology and the theory of Darwinian evolution, Christians will want to underline the order, coherence, and complex organization in the world at every level, starting with the theory of the Big Bang. This theory itself, which has massive support from the scientific community, is a major apologetic point: the cosmos had a beginning for which known physical principles provide no explanation, since those principles themselves, which involve space-time, came into being with the Big Bang. As with much in the story of the evolution of life, by far the best explanation for this is that a Creator God willed the world into being and is guiding it toward fulfillment, just as the Bible says. The fact that we cannot figure out exactly how he is doing this within the physical processes he has created is not a valid reason for the critic of Christian faith to sidestep

---

3. Strobel, *Case for a Creator*, 240.

or rationalize away the overwhelming scientific evidence pointing in this direction.

Talk III

Christian Faith. Modernity and Secularism. Collapse of "Progress." Scripture

I

There are no scientific or even philosophical *proofs* of God or of the truth of the Christian faith. Personal experience of God's reality is important, as are evidences in Scripture of fulfilled prophecy. But these do not constitute proof. What we often fail to realize is that there are no proofs of alternate or opposing worldviews either. All worldviews, all metaphysical affirmations about *reality*, about *the way things are*, are matters of faith. This is as true of modernism and of postmodernism as it is of Christianity. We must remember this when we are challenged on a point of faith. The challenger will have no stronger basis for his or her challenge than the basis we have for our convictions. To the contrary: the Christian position, while not demonstrable in scientific terms, is a strong one. We stand on very solid ground.

One point, however, that we must always bear in mind: we who believe in Christ have died to the systems of the world—they do not define or constrain us ultimately any more—and our life is hid with Christ in God (Col 3:3). Our true citizenship is in heaven (Phil 3:20). This is incomprehensible to the nonbeliever, and the reality and significance of it will always encounter resistance, as it did with us before we knew Christ and surrendered our lives to him. The natural man does not understand the things of the Spirit and does not want God to be Lord of his life, even when the blessings and benefits and reasonableness of submitting to his Lordship are set out before him (1 Cor 2:14–16). We must understand this when talking to others. Their objections and challenges will often arise from spiritual resistance rooted in the natural man's rebellion against God's law and sovereignty, rather than in the specific objection or query at issue. We must be prepared to answer, respectfully and graciously, the particular objection or query, even while being conscious of the deeper spiritual resistance that may underlie it. The natural man or woman does not want to die to self, nor reach the point of recognizing and acknowledging that the worldview he/she has held, conditioned by their culture—the worldview in which the self finds its identity—is inadequate to provide the salvation and eternal life that the deep heart of every human being—made in the image of God—yearns for. Our witness to him or her, our responses to the questions they ask us or the challenges they throw at us, are crucial to opening them to the work of the Holy Spirit, but their willingness to die to self and to receive Christ as Savior is the Spirit's work and achievement, not ours:

> "When he—the Counselor, the Holy Spirit—comes, he will convict the world of guilt in regard to sin and righteousness and judgment: in regard to sin, because men do not believe in me; in regard to righteousness, because I am going to the Father, where you can see me no longer; and in regard to judgment, because the prince of this world now stands condemned." (John 16:8–11)

Such conviction of one's sinfulness, of Christ's righteousness, and of Satan's judgment, is altogether the work of the Holy Spirit operating through the revealed Word of God and the human conscience; rational argument is important and may well prepare the ground for the Spirit's action, but conversion of the natural man to faith in Christ and commitment to follow him is a miracle, quite beyond the reach of rational thought.

At the cross, we are all judged: the world, its systems and structures and worldviews, and each one of us. Every individual, every principality and political power, every ideology that asserts its autonomy as over against the Creator God, is found guilty and judged, as these are represented by the myriad forces arrayed against Jesus in Jerusalem. Humankind nailed Jesus to the cross. The defeat of these forces, and the defeat of any claim to absolute truth or reality they may have made or may make, is displayed at the resurrection, when the one who made the world and came to redeem it by bearing its rebellion in his own body down into death is raised to new life.

This is the great revolution in human history. Ever since, the world has been in crisis because its own structures and metaphysical and political systems have been challenged and defeated insofar as they have been taken to be absolute, changeless, and ultimately determinate of human reality. The fallen world has always been in crisis, of course, in that rebellious man derailed God's plan for mankind from the beginning. But with the resurrection, a new dynamic—a revolutionary dynamic—enters human culture that opposes the traditional static systems of political power and domination. Change and hope enter the human equation. Through the proclamation of the gospel that death has been defeated, sin forgiven, and guilt cleansed, a vision of new life, of a new man, appears in human culture—a vision, based on affirmations about the mercy of God in Christ and about the dignity of individuals and the unity of mankind, that will henceforth progressively and profoundly transform human life.

This vision takes root in Christendom. Where its influence spreads, however, religious and political counterfeits and ideologies arise that imitate or appropriate the hope in Christ and distort its meaning. The powers of this world are defeated at the cross, but they are not destroyed and will not be until Christ returns in glory. The human rebellion against God continues to gather its forces and oppose the revealed face of God, Jesus Christ. This involves persecution of the church, Christ's body and witness on earth, and a sustained effort in every domain of life to undercut and pervert this witness so that God's truth will not be heard and the human systems of power and domination may continue to hold sway.

Up until the seventeenth century, the major external challenges to the church in those parts of the world where the gospel was proclaimed were the early christological heresies (such as docetism, ebionism, and arianism, which, in one way or another, reduced or denied the divine or the human nature of Christ), gnosticism (which declared the material world evil and Jesus a kind of divine avatar providing secret knowledge of otherworldly salvation to a favored few), and Islam. All these, to a greater or lesser extent, are religious systems that distort the Hebrew and New Testament Scriptures and orthodox Christology as rooted in those Scriptures and set forth in the Apostles', the Nicene, and the Athanasian Creeds of the fourth century.

The rise of modernity in the seventeenth century brought a new challenge: that of secularism. The power of science and the technological development it engendered, based on reason and the empirical scientific method as these are applied to the observation and investigation of material reality, arose in Christian Europe alongside the emergence of the nation-state in the sixteenth century and a revulsion at the religious wars of the sixteenth and seventeenth centuries. Christian revelation and faith were gradually pushed to the margins of the European worldview and replaced by the supremacy of human reason, while at the political level the nation-state replaced the church as the central organizing principle of society and the source of historical meaning. The notion of progress and visions of utopia arose as secularized versions of eschatological hope and the kingdom of God. The revealed truth of the gospel, which had given rise to the best of what came to fruition in the Enlightenment, was judged defective and superstitious and set aside in favor of the truth of human reason. In some real measure, one can see this as, in part, divine and human judgment on the failures and aberrations of the church in proceeding centuries, but it was also an altogether unprecedented expression of human autonomy and rebellion against God.

The First World War and the Armenian genocide, coupled with a growing realization of the dark, soul-threatening side of industrialization, fundamentally destroyed the ideology of progress and trust in humanity, creating a terrible and terrifying void at the heart of Western civilization. This nihilism was confirmed and accentuated by the horrors of the Second World War and the genocides accompanying it. There was now no longer either God, or the myth of the gradual moral improvement of mankind through reason, to provide hope or meaning for the human enterprise. The atheist systems of racist Nazism and totalitarian Communism poured into this void with overwhelming destructive power. In our day, progress is still hanging on in the form of faith in science and technology, but the heart has gone out of it. It has deflated like a balloon. The worldwide devastation wreaked on societies and on the planet itself by exploitative materialism and the nihilistic cupidity at its core has disabused the average modern man—with the exception of the new Babel-builders, the reality-resistant, and deluded, though dangerous, transhumanists—of the utopian pretensions of the human race.

The postmodern worldview that has taken shape in the last thirty years constitutes a forceful denunciation of all ideological systems deemed to result from overarching metanarratives about reality and the way things are. All unifying worldviews such as that of the Enlightenment, not to mention political and religious ideologies that would pretend to universal truth of some kind, are critiqued as false and oppressive. All is relative, according to one's cultural and personal perspective.

While there is certainly some truth in this claim, postmodernism is itself a kind of metanarrative, claiming absolute truth for its view that there is no truth. Since it insists that there is no unifying criterion of value and unity in a given society, it opens the way for endless conflict between the myriad perspectives and interest groups jockeying for power. This power struggle is conducted on the basis of the one value that does indeed seem to be universally accepted in the post-Christian world today, human rights. The assertion of one's rights becomes the way of affirming one's human dignity, whereas in Christendom's premodern, gospel-based culture, human dignity was an ontological given—God's gift to man when he created him/her in the image of God—not something that had to be achieved by asserting one's rights. As a result, the idea of human rights risks becoming itself a new absolutist ideology, with all the dangers this entails for the gradual subversion of the very value of equality and dignity it wishes to uphold as people with this strident worldview gain power and, under the influence of human sin, begin to assert their superiority and dominate others, oppressing them and negating their human rights and their dignity, especially if they hold to a *biblical* worldview.

Moreover, the perspectival (i.e., everyone has his/her own perspective on reality and all perspectives are equal) and the politically correct ideology of postmodernism provides no moral criteria for critiquing oppressive perspectives that will inevitably arise and seek to impose a unifying imperial vision.

A further irony in the postmodern world is that under the cover of its vaunted relativism, the consumerist imperialism of the rich West, with its insatiable, greed-driven, self-justifying demand for ever-increasing production, is taking over the planet, leading to huge gaps between the rich and the poor in developing countries, rising political and economic tensions, the fierce competition for natural resources (land, oil, minerals, and water), and the ongoing devastation of the ecology of the planet and the extinction of hundreds of thousands of animal and insect species. This is war of a new kind, generating global destruction even while touting—and genuinely achieving in some real sense—development, wealth creation, and considerable social benefits for hitherto impoverished and powerless segments of humankind. The ironies are staggering. What we need to see is that this consumerist imperialism is a new kind of totalitarian ideology—soft in appearance but ruthless and global in effect—that is sweeping the world at the same time that postmodern relativism, with its radically subjective value-system, is insisting that all such unifying worldviews are false and oppressive. Indeed they are—this assessment has much truth in it—but the postmodern approach to reality is itself oppressive and has no way to counter such imperial systems when they arise.

II

Strong points about Scripture and the Christian faith that bring hope and light into our current crisis

Countless books have been written to show the historical reliability of the Old and New Testament Scriptures that provide the foundation for the church's proclamation of the gospel, and also of the enormous number of texts, some very close to the originals, that have transmitted the Scriptures down through the centuries. I shall not try to rehearse here all the evidence that is adduced. The endless production of new angles on the person of Jesus purported to be truer to his reality than the portrait in the Gospels; of new historical theories about the New Testament on the basis of some second- or third-century text (usually of gnostic origin) or of some plot, now unveiled, that supposedly subverts the orthodox Christian tradition; and of new theories of textual criticism that appear to undermine the veracity and coherence of both Testaments and of the Bible as a whole—all this is part of modernism and postmodernism, involving on the one hand the application of scientific methodology to the biblical texts (positively, this has enriched immeasurably our historical knowledge of how the Scriptures came to be; negatively, it has contributed to modern unbelief), and on the other hand the hopelessly skeptical mindset of modern man, who takes *doubt* as his criterion of knowledge, refuses all traditional authority, and, at bottom, is ever seeking new ways to discredit the gospel and avoid facing the truth of God's judgment on his own schemes and worldviews and of God's mercy in providing a way of salvation.

The *authority* of Scripture cannot be separated from the community in which it is believed. Outside of the church, it exercises no more authority than any other text. For the church, its authority is based on its witness to God's action in history to redeem mankind by the election of a particular people as the vehicle for the salvation of the human race as a whole. This salvation would come through the Messiah, the Christ, promised in numerous texts of the Old Testament as these were gathered through the centuries. The church believes that Jesus was the fulfillment of these messianic texts (such as Isaiah 11 and 53, Psalms 22 and 89, and 2 Samuel 7). It believes that he was the very Word of God made flesh and that he is ultimately, through the Holy Spirit, the author of the Old Testament texts that all together speak of God's judgment and mercy for human beings, as these were manifested supremely in Jesus's life, death, and resurrection.

The church reads the Old Testament in light of God's revelation in Christ in the New Testament, and the New Testament in light of God's messianic presence in the Old Testament, preparing the way for Christ's coming and providing the clues to understand the saving significance of his coming. These texts contain all sorts of different material and literary genres and are encompassed within an overall narrative structure. They tell a story, which is both God's story and ours. This is not a metanarrative in the sense that postmodernism uses this term, in that God's action is not intended to establish a human structure of oppressive power over the world and a unifying dogma to justify it, but rather to subvert such human power and its pretensions by judging it at the cross and defeating it by raising Christ from the dead. Since all systems of empire and oppression are based on the power of death over others held by the oppressors, Christ's resurrection confounds absolutely and eternally this pretension. The church consists of persons who do not fear death because they indwell Christ, who has overcome death, and so have the sure hope that they will be resurrected with him when he returns in glory to establish visibly his reign in a renewed earth and cosmos.

The grand story of God's creation and redemption of the world is a unified whole that encompasses, for what we call the Old Testament, all those texts considered canonical by Jewish scholars and which were finally established as the authoritative canon of God's word toward the end of the first century AD, as well as those texts that we call the New Testament which gained general acceptance in the church during the first centuries, and that, at a church council in Rome in 382, were finally declared, along with the Old Testament canon, to be the church's canon of Scripture. This unified whole is unified and authoritative only to the eyes of faith that see God acting and speaking creatively and redemptively in the texts and the events and realities they present. In these texts, God reveals himself as the Creator, Judge, and Redeemer of the world; and he reveals man as his most cherished creature, created in his own image but subject to sin and death on account of his freely willed rebellion, whom the Creator nevertheless does not abandon to destruction but redeems by becoming a man himself and making atonement himself for us.

For the eyes of faith, there is a central storyline in Scripture as God reveals his purposes and acts to carry them out. The texts carry this line forward over the centuries, developing, amplifying, and reinterpreting it to successive generations living in radically different situations. This is the story of God's people, sometimes obedient, often disobedient; all the lumps are there, the discordances, questionings, complaints, and critiques. Different interpretations of the way God acts are given as different vantage points on the human condition are put forward. If the psalms frequently suggest that the righteous are always blessed in this life, the book of Job counters this, at least in the main thrust of its narrative, and so provides a quite different angle on suffering and the testing of faith in the context of a tremendous disputation and then of an even more tremendous display of God's power in creation. There are political currents and countercurrents in the books of Samuel and Kings, showing the struggle to hear and obey God's voice within the hard realities of power. The prophets challenge the idolatry and oppressive ways of wicked kings and priests, even while speaking of God's unfailing mercy and promise of redemption to those who would heed his law and commandments. The diversity is enormous, but not limitless; always there may be heard the central storyline, for those with ears to hear.

In the New Testament, four Gospels present four perspectives on the person and work of Jesus. There are differences of detail, and the stories are told in a variety of ways, sometimes with a concern for chronology, sometimes not. Through very specific episodes and words, and with different theological emphases for each evangelist, we are given by God's providence a rounded picture of Jesus the Messiah: not a psychological portrait in the manner of a modern biography, but a picture of the unfathomable mystery of the Word of God made flesh and acting as a man-who-is-God-come-amongst-us to fulfill the Old Testament messianic prophecies and redeem mankind.

None of this is self-evidently true, for those who would look at it with a skeptical mindset. To say the Scriptures are inspired is to say something open only to the eyes of faith and within a believing community. *"My teaching,"* says Jesus in John 7:17–18, *"is not my own. It comes from him who sent me. If anyone chooses to do God's will, he will find out whether my teaching comes from God or whether I speak on my own."* We believe these texts to be inspired because the community that professes this and seeks to obey God's will is the agent of fundamental change in human vision and behavior, and declares a gospel that challenges every worldly system of power and subverts every human pretension, even while affirming the nobility and dignity of all men equally, by virtue of their ontological nature as made in God's image. The church can declare these texts to be inspired—God-breathed—as its members personally and sacramentally enter into and dwell within the Christ proclaimed therein, meeting his gracious presence and offer of salvation with trusting commitment to believe and follow him.

It is as the community called the church believes and does these things that it *has* authority and can proclaim the gospel and cite the Scriptures *with* authority. Neither the inspiration nor the authority of Scripture is an abstract entity, but rather the reality inherent in the relationship between the God revealed in Scripture and those who trust him.

In response to the charge that there is no universal truth, only local truths that are nothing more than cultural or personal beliefs, we can agree that all things human are culturally shaped and interpreted through discourse and so in a real sense relative to cultures and personal experience; but we then need to go on and point out that the Bible is speaking of divine revelation coming into the human context from outside it, with the aim of restoring the unity of mankind and uniting men and women in love, not by establishing a unifying political or economic ideological system, where a finite conviction is elevated into a dominating absolute, but by gathering those who want love and peace around Christ, who died and rose again that this might be so.

Christ is the truth; the truth is not a system, not the church, not an ideal; *he*, the person of the Savior, is the truth. We can point to his person and urge others to learn about him by reading the Bible with open minds and hearts, taking the story recounted there on its own terms, as being a particular perspective on historical reality that also claims to have universal intention and compass. We gladly admit that this is our perspective, our opinion, while arguing that the object of that perspective, of that opinion, claims universal intent, power, and truth. The postmodern mindset in principle is open to such an argument, because it is *our* argument—but we are pointing beyond ourselves and making a case, irrefutable by reason, that a loving Creator God, seeing the darkness of his world and the lostness of man, has chosen to enter the darkness and bring light and the possibility of salvation—the possibility of hope and eternal life—into concrete historical reality by living out divine love in the midst of human violence, greed, and oppression.

Furthermore, we make this argument within the plausibility structure of a community that seeks to live out this divine love within whatever social context it may find itself, through space and time, regardless of the circumstances. We are not alone in our convictions. Human beings are social creatures, and salvation, if there is such a thing, must come not to the individual soul, as if such a thing as an isolated, individual soul existed, but within the social fabric of concrete reality, which encompasses all aspects of life.

Historical particularity and universal truth both are affirmations we can make about our faith. The Bible is a unity containing enormous diversity; it is an assembly of countless perspectives over space and time, gathered into a single story by the unifying power not of a human method, as the expression of a human and hence merely finite and local design, but of God himself, the Creator of the world—and a world of such order, beauty, diversity, and within it all, unity!

And we can say that herein is our hope and the meaning of our lives and of the life of mankind—that all things should be united in God's infinite and eternal love, through Christ who has demonstrated that love within space-time, in the particularity of history, and whom God has raised from the dead so that all who believe in him may have eternal life.

All these are very powerful points to make, as long as we understand that we cannot prove them, that we hold them by faith, and as long as we make it very clear to our interlocutors that any worldview they hold is also a matter of faith. Which worldview has more explanatory power? Which deals more adequately with all aspects of human life? Which provides meaning and purpose and hope that goes beyond our individual situation and enables us to cope with misfortune, tragedy, and/or evil? These are the kinds of questions we may forcefully pose to others, even as they pose their own questions to us. And always we must be patient, respectful, with the authority that comes through humility.

Talk IV

Secularism. Islam. Influences of the Gospel on Society

It is clear that in the West we live in a post-Christian age. There are forces today, inside and outside of Western culture, that seek to eliminate the gospel and the Christian tradition, or that are largely ignorant of and/or indifferent to it, considering it a kind of fossil, a vestige from a prescientific era that has no relevance for modern life. Opposition to and persecution of Christians are increasing across the world. In the preceding talks we have looked at our contemporary social ambiance and the dominant current worldview, with a glance at how we got here. We have also tried to show some of the many strengths of the Christian position with regard to this worldview, despite the minority status of Christian faith in the developed world. In this last talk we shall try to focus the civilizational crisis we are experiencing in our day and highlight several more strengths and particularities of the gospel that can help us to live the Christian life more dynamically and defend our faith more robustly.

Secularist modern society is moving into a new paganism as it presses forward into the age of globalized communication. As in Roman society—or, in a rather different way, in Hindu societies with their pantheon of divinities—large numbers of gods are on offer, and citizens of the global consumer state are urged to take their pick as they will. These gods all operate in a circumscribed, metaphysically closed universe, and, as projections of our own desires, fears, and drives, they provide the plausibility structure for our daily lives. Production and consumption, parading under the banner of technology and serving the forces of pride, greed, and power, occupy the place of Jupiter. We live in a global supermarket with a choice among an almost infinite variety of products (in imitation of the infinite variety of creatures in God's creation), and the media and all the powers that be constantly flatter us into thinking that our identity lies in our autonomy as individuals—no transcendent law subjects us to anything—and our fulfillment is to be found in our free choice among the myriad objects at our disposal.

The problem is that the modern system of production is so vast, complex, interconnected, and global that one can almost say today that we have *no choice* but to exist inside the supermarket. In a sense, our freedom is an illusion. Even if we still insist on shopping at the corner grocery store, we know perfectly well that even *it* has, in a manner of speaking and perhaps even economically, been co-opted by the supermarket. Nor are we fulfilled through the availability of countless products to choose from—this too is an illusion. Globalized communication informs us that over a billion other persons on the earth live on less than a dollar day and are definitely *outside the benefits* of the supermarket, except insofar as the supermarket is the universal system of market production and consumption that pauperizes those who aren't equipped to profit from it. In this sense, those outside the supermarket are actually also *in* it—there are no outsiders. Globalized communication also informs us that the entire planet is deteriorating ecologically as a result of the ruthless exploitation of natural resources in the interests of production and profit. All this information disheartens us and makes us feel guilty and powerless. And to make matters worse, in terms of their own existence many citizens of this hegemonic culture that is closed to transcendence of any kind, find, despite the obvious satisfactions and benefits of material productivity, that mere production and consumption are meaningless in themselves and can provide no purpose or direction other than their own self-multiplication. The flattening out of personal and cultural specificity, tradition, and aspiration, and the breakdown of marriage and community through the linkage of the power of technology with the ideologies of individualism and profit, lead many, even among those who succeed in the terms laid down by the supermarket, to feel lonely, alienated, empty, and lost. To say this is not for one moment to decry or downplay the happiness and sense of satisfaction that may rightly accompany those able to benefit from the prosperity generated by the materialistic dynamic of our age.

As with all worldviews and ideologies shaped by fallen humankind, it is very difficult to find a viewpoint from outside the system by which to critique it. There are currently two principle forces that are attempting to do this, however—both of them, like the system itself, having universal pretensions. One is Islam, the other is the Christian gospel. They are related yet very different, despite the common tendency to make them appear similar by calling them, with Judaism, Abrahamic faiths. From a Christian standpoint, Abraham is not only the great ancestor of the faith, he points toward the fulfillment of God's saving purposes in Jesus Christ and cannot be co-opted by any post-Christian divine dictation supposedly given to Muhammad six centuries after Jesus was crucified and raised from the dead.

Authentic Christianity, as distinct from the way this term is often understood and applied by Muslims to the West as a whole and hence to the very system I have just described, is under threat today *both* from the neo-pagan supermarket and all it entails *and* from a resurgent Islam. It must be said that tensions between different religions are increasing everywhere in the world at the present time, and the Islam/Christian confrontation is by no means the only locus of religious persecution. Muslims themselves are being persecuted in parts of Myanmar, China, and India, under the pressures of Buddhist, Communist, and Hindu nationalism. The masses in all these religions would surely wish to live quietly side by side, as has often been the case in history, but the forces of nationalist, racist, and religious hatred are on the march in our day, and peaceful coexistence is becoming more and more difficult in many parts of the world.

It remains the case, however, on account of Islam's universalist vision and supersessionist doctrine with regard to Judaism and Christianity, which claims that these two religions are false and have been superseded by Islam, that the confrontation of Islam with Jews and Christians has a distinctive character and far-reaching social/political consequences. As a theistic religion, Islam is as anathema to modern secularists as Christianity, and unquestionably adherents of both these faiths should seek as much as possible to make common cause. Both will be contested, basically, where secularism prevails. But common cause with Muslims, at least where the Muslim community is in the majority, is problematical. Jews and Christians have always been considered inferior and benighted by Islam and so have suffered *dhimmitude*—second-class citizenship—in Islamic societies, Arab and non-Arab alike. Muslim tolerance toward non-Muslims, to the extent that it has existed over the centuries (as in twelfth- and thirteenth-century Spain), must be understood within this framework as a privilege granted with certain conditions by superior to inferior human beings (this is curiously parallel to the so-called tolerance of postmodernism, which is tolerant of everything except the one thing that contests its philosophy fundamentally, namely Christianity). As the Ottoman Empire unraveled in the last two centuries, and as Arab culture turned in on itself and declined, resentment toward the West—and hence toward the Christianity associated with it—replaced the earlier arrogance. In the last fifty years, this resentment has fastened onto the ultraconservative brand of Islam called Wahhabism that originated in the late eighteenth century in Saudi Arabia, and this has led, since the expulsion of Soviet Russia from Afghanistan and the rise of Al-Qaida in the 1990s and ISIS (the "Islamic State") fifteen years later, to the scourge of Islamist terrorism that the West and many other parts of the world are experiencing today.

What this means for authentic Christianity is that it is despised, at least by radical Muslims, *both* for its religious content *and* for its association with contemporary Western society, seen by many Muslims today, with a good deal of justification, as decadent, corrupt, and imperialistic. Even those many Muslims who appreciate aspects of Western culture such as democracy, human rights, and technological advance—and who have no idea that these are rooted ultimately in the Christian gospel—will tend, if pressed, to dismiss the Christian gospel as false, the result of a perversion of the biblical texts and superseded anyway by the definitive divine dictation given to Muhammad in the seventh century and written down in the Qur'an.

This is certainly not the place to attempt a detailed critique of Islam, even if I were competent to do so. At the social level, we must do everything we can to live peacefully and respectfully with Muslims, while avoiding equally the political policy often followed in our liberal Western societies, namely, never offending or criticizing Muslims in any way out of fear of causing civil unrest, even in cases when traditional Western standards of law, freedom of religion, and public behavior would warrant criticism.

I hasten to add that my position here has nothing to do with islamophobia, which we must strongly resist. In no way am I advocating intolerance toward Muslims, but rather truthfulness and clarity with respect to what we believe. At the theological level, we need to be clear about the fundamental differences between the basic tenets of the Islamic faith and ours, and we must not be hesitant to articulate these when that is appropriate, even while discerning and underscoring areas where the beliefs of the two religions are close or overlap, as in, for example, the common belief in the creation of the world by a Creator God. I want to alert us to the vital necessity for Christians today to read and learn about the Islamic religion, and this for four reasons: 1) to know what Muslims and Christians do actually believe—or are supposed to believe—on the basis of their different sacred texts, and what Jesus and Muhammad respectively said and did, so that the fundamental doctrinal claims and differences are clear in our minds; 2) to be well-informed and able to stand intelligently against the postmodern sentimentality and ignorant relativism that lumps Islam and Christianity in one basket and smilingly declares, with no historical or religious knowledge, that we all worship the same God; 3) to be able to discuss reasonably with interested Muslims the similarities and differences between our two religions and to present our own convictions in a compelling way while avoiding the pitfalls that lead to gridlock; 4) to be alert to the tactics—and in a position to contest them—being used by radical Islam, especially in traditionally Christian Europe, to infiltrate and gain political influence in every aspect of society, manipulating democratic institutions to that end and marginalizing what is left of the church's effectual presence.

Along with the unfounded accusation that the Jewish and Christian biblical texts have been falsified, the other main obstacle to dialogue with Islam is its conviction that the Qur'an was literally dictated by Allah to Muhammad, and so is inviolable. This is a very different assertion from the Jewish and Christian conviction that the numerous authors of Holy Scripture were inspired by God to write what they did. The authors were human, living within their historically conditioned situations, and each wrote with his own personality and insight. Besides what one might call the incarnational wonder of this achievement on the part of the inspiring Spirit of God, this understanding of Holy Scripture allows for the possibility of occasional factual error and of progressive revelation, through changing circumstances, of the person and purposes of God, while keeping hold of the conviction, as Christian tradition has always done, that everything needed for salvation and the communication of God's will for human beings is herein reliably set forth. Interpretation and critical study in search of the texts' possible meanings—in parallel with the observation and later scientific study of God's creation—are entirely welcome and appropriate.

The static conception of the qur'anic text, on the other hand, has resulted in a general unwillingness over the centuries, with exceptions, to consider the Qur'an critically or to imagine that it might be reinterpreted from generation to generation. One does not tamper with divinely dictated texts, which are, by definition, immutable and valid for all time. To do so is dangerous and must incur Allah's wrath. There is little wriggle room for interpretation. Inevitably, of course, interpretation and application to changing historical situations have been carried out, but the kind of historical criticism that the Bible has been subjected to for the last two centuries is hardly imaginable with respect to the Qur'an. Critical examination, for example, of the numerous historical affirmations in the Qur'an regarding biblical persons such as Ishmael, Mary, and Jesus—examination that would show these affirmations to be sheer invention with no historical basis whatsoever—is simply ruled out, on the basis of the assertion that the earlier texts have been distorted and that the qur'anic version of events provides the truth (this assertion alone can justify the obvious contradiction arising from the logical impossibility that the Angel Gabriel who, in the Gospel of Luke, announces to Mary that God had chosen her to bear a son who would be called Son of the Most High, is the same Gabriel who, in the Qur'an, is the medium for Allah's dictation of words that, regarding Jesus, say something entirely different). A closed circular argument is thus set in place that defies criticism; to make matters worse, it is topped off with frequent threats in the text that any contestation of these sacred words is forbidden, making critics liable to punishment, even death.

The key to headway in any dialogue with Muslims is the person of Jesus Christ, as he is presented in the New Testament. I believe that this is also the key to any dialogue with a postmodern Westerner. The objections we shall have to address in both cases and hopefully overcome are legion, but we must not be afraid of them. Muslims respect a person with strong faith in God, and the more we are able to show how our strong faith in God is rooted in the person of Jesus, the more they will be intrigued by Jesus. It is, indeed, by pointing to Jesus that we will be showing them *our* respect for *their* strong faith in God. Many Muslims, indeed, are finding Christ in our day as they come into contact with believing Christians. In him many are discovering God as Father, a concept unknown in Islam but lodged as a yearning deep in the human soul. Muslims will balk at first at the title "Son of God," but there is no reason to avoid this title if we explain it in terms of love within the Godhead, as an expression of that relational essence that is God and that in no way is talking about two Gods or about begetting or engendering in the human sense. The key to any such discussion is God's love and his desire to communicate it to us, which he does by his Word made flesh. Allah is not a God of love, and the biblical realities of God's covenant with mankind and his desire of personal relationship/communion with his human creatures, are altogether absent from Islam. Allah's much-touted mercy is arbitrary, unpredictable, and in any case limited to Muslims. Given Allah's remoteness, Muslims are often touched by the notion of God as Father, even though, again, this must be presented carefully, from the direction of love and with every effort to explain how this does not mean ditheism or tritheism or sexual generation within the Godhead, but speaks rather of the one Creator God who is in himself relational and who seeks to enter into personal intimacy with human beings whom he has made.

Postmodern Westerners too, in a very different way, often may be found to respect a Christian's faith, even though they will tend at first to avoid its universal implications and its summons to a reordered lifestyle by pulling out the usual relativistic stop, "That's fine for you, but of course I believe something else." It is up to us to show them the limits of their subjectivism by pointing out, for example, the absoluteness and universality of evil, against which moral relativism has no leg to stand on and is powerless.

We always need to present our case reasonably and respectfully, using rational arguments and also drawing on personal experience. We must listen carefully to what our interlocutor says, agreeing where we can, pointing out differences where necessary, receiving his/her insights where these are pertinent. Condescension of any kind must be rigorously avoided. In no way are we *superior*; the difference between us in this sense is simply that we know Jesus and point to him. Our concern is to love the other by showing genuine interest in him or her as a person. We will certainly not always have cogent answers to the questions others ask us, and we must never give the impression of being know-it-alls; but we must speak with authority and knowledge, never as from within a ghetto or elitist club, but as active members of society whose every aspect of life, personal and professional, is informed by our faith. And we must always speak with humility, as persons who have been found and loved and saved by a merciful God. We must never be ashamed, finally, of declaring our belief that Jesus is the Savior of mankind, the Christ, the Word of God incarnate, that he suffered, died, and rose from the dead, then ascended as Lord to the right hand of God the Father, from whence he will come again to judge all men and women of all times and places according to *his* truth, not according to ours.

With the Muslim, though we know that the Jesus in the Qur'an is a very different Jesus from the person in the New Testament, we can nevertheless say that since Jesus is, in principle, revered in Islam as a prophet, any Muslim ought to study the New Testament Scriptures to see what they say about this prophet. Many earnest Muslims are deeply disturbed by what is going on today in the Islamic world and are hungry to know a loving, forgiving, personal God who is with us and not remote in the heavens, even if they can't at first even entertain the notion that the Qur'an might be mistaken or that the actions of terrorists might ultimately find a warrant in the Qur'an.

We must stand up for the integrity of Scripture. The Muslim charge that the biblical texts were distorted by Jews and Christians is without the slightest historical basis, and corresponds in point of fact to precisely what the qur'anic so-called dictation does with respect both to particular texts and to the overall sense of the Old and New Testaments. With a modern Westerner holding a relativistic and skeptical worldview that excludes any possibility of divine revelation, we must point out that his or her position has no more warrant than our own and then go on to show the particularities of Jesus and the overall structure and intent of Scripture. We need to emphasize the *universal aim* of the scriptural revelation as carried through a *particular people* and as providing a way to find forgiveness for things we've done wrong and freedom from guilt, as well as victory over death and well-founded hope in a life to come in communion with a loving God.

Focusing on the person of Jesus also opens out the area of anthropology, that is, the biblical teaching about the nature of man. The revelation in Genesis 1:25–27 is, again, the key here: man (man/woman) is created in the image of God. This provides very strong arguing points for the Christian. The Muslim will at once object that any kind of imagery of God is blasphemous, and that the creature *man*, insignificant next to God, could not possibly be in the image of God. Again, rather than argue abstractly or theoretically about this, we must point to Jesus, who, as a human, is the very image of God become flesh (Col 1:15; 2 Cor 4:4; Heb 1:3) and shows us how a human being is meant to be: loving God with absolute devotion; acting with love toward all human beings equally; treating men and women and children as infinitely valuable individual persons, not as units in a larger entity, points on a graph, human ciphers, or sexual commodities; obeying the commandments of God to love God and one's neighbor as oneself; refusing to take revenge or do violence to others; welcoming little children and women and the outcasts and the destitute as having no less importance than the rich and the powerful in society; showing justice to all and respecting the freedom of persons, as these are made in the image of the Creator God, who is absolutely free; and lastly—a vital point in our day—demonstrating in his associations with women how he honored them and considered them to have the same dignity as men and to be worthy of the same respect. This is very different from Muhammad's treatment of women as we find it in the Qur'an and in Muhammad's personal sayings, the *hadiths*: women are considered to be inferior to men and must be subjected to them, while polygamy in marriage, with all that it implies about the status of women, is the norm. The kind of submission of the wife to the husband of which Paul speaks in Ephesians 5:22-33—an exhortation preceded by his commandment that all Christians be in mutual submission and respect toward each other (v. 21)—is altogether different and can only be properly interpreted if verse 25—"Husbands, love your wives, just as Christ loved the church and gave himself up for her"—is understood to be the pivotal verse in the passage with respect to the husband/wife relationship. Mutual love in and through Christ—not subjection, as in Islam according to the Qur'an—is at the heart of this text.

The question of the uniqueness of Christ is a contested issue today, but it is certainly not one we need to be afraid of. What we need to do when challenged on this is to point to the story of Christ as found in the Scriptures and the Christian tradition. There is absolutely nothing like it anywhere else in human history. Mythical gods that died and rose again there were, yes, but none that was held to be the image of the Creator himself historically incarnate in a human being, put to death on a cross, and then raised from the dead, all of this to redeem the violent human race and give us the possibility of eternal life. The Christian gospel is unique, and told in narratives that have the ring of inspired newspaper accounts! We need to make this very clear, urging our interlocutors to check out the facts about the different religions they say are all basically the same or that represent simply different perspectives such that the distinctions between them are of no objective significance. We need to help others to think these things through, and to see how absurd it is to say that everything equals everything else, especially if one is saying this with the intention of giving value to the different perspectives. It should be obvious, on the contrary, that to say such a thing takes away their value by flattening them out and making a mockery of their distinctiveness.

In pointing these things out, we will encounter resistance, because today people in the West *fear* affirmations of absolute truth, since they associate them with authoritarian ideological regimes, including—and paradigmatically—that of the church, especially the Roman Catholic Church, which, from their point of view, is indeed seen as dominating and oppressive. The modern individual, imprisoned by the ideology of autonomous freedom, recoils with a mixture of fear and indignation at any suggestion that there might be objective moral and spiritual truth outside of and beyond him- or herself and his/her own self-determinations—truth, that is, to which consideration, even obedience (!), might be called for. "Domination!" he/she cries. "Discrimination!" "Hate-speech!" "Bigotry!" The recoil is like that of a person in Jesus's day being touched by a leper.

This reveals bondage to a perverted idea of freedom. But a person reacting this way is blind to the bondage. The totalitarianism of postmodern ideology is soft, though it is hardening. We can certainly sympathize with such fears of domination as these may justifiably be associated with oppressive political or religious ideologies, and we can certainly agree that the church itself has sometimes erred and sinned greatly in this way; but we must never let the matter rest there. We need to go on to stress the fundamental difference between the truth that is in Jesus, as the Christian gospel proclaims, and the ideological truths that have functioned over the centuries as usurpers and counterfeits of the gospel. The uniqueness of Jesus is the uniqueness of the One God, who is love and life eternal, and who cherishes his beloved creature man, to the point of actually taking human form and dying for his salvation. That is a uniqueness we can declare with authority and joy. It is the very opposite of oppression and domination. It is liberation, the liberation of human beings from slavery to sin and in particular to the sin of needing to impose our will on others and dominate them; indeed, seen from this angle, it is the liberation that corresponds to and enables, for those who obey Christ, the very thing we moderns claim to prize so highly: freedom from alien domination and freedom to respect our neighbor in his/her own integrity (which respect, of course, must not entail the misguided notion that all beliefs and behaviors are acceptable and justifiable).

The modern Western person will be surprised to learn that his or her belief in the dignity of human beings, in human rights, in freedom and equality, in democracy, indeed in the separation of political and religious power that opens the way for social freedoms, derives ultimately from the Christian gospel and its long-drawn-out working through the body of Christian society over the centuries. We can admit without ado, both to the Muslim and to the Westerner, the ideological aberrations of the church that led, when it was in a position of political and social dominance, to intolerance, denigration, violence against others, auto-da-fés—all those things that mark every dominant ideology because of our human sin that distorts all truth and seeks to gain power over others—but we must make it clear that these things are not inherent in the gospel, nor are they sanctioned in any way by Jesus, nor have they been typical of normal Christian behavior over the centuries. To the contrary, they are radical distortions of the gospel, whereas violence does commonly characterize militant Islam in history and the prophet's own behavior from the period of Medina onwards, as the Muslims' relentless conquests by the sword and oppression of non-Muslims in one way or another, give evidence. Moreover, sanction and encouragement of such behavior can be found in many parts of the Qur'an, whereas nothing of the sort can be found in the New Testament or sanctioned by it. For the church to oppose what it may consider for good reason to be dogmatic heresy is necessary and perfectly legitimate, but to do this violently is in contradiction to Christ's example and commandments.

If the church has often sinned, it has also been the vehicle for the positive values of the modern world, which include a concern for equal social justice for all and a compassionate consideration for the downtrodden and the victim, whoever he or she may be—something completely unheard of in the pre-Christian world—and that has slowly worked itself into the very fiber of modern society even if, evidently, it is often denied in practice. Christians live in particular cultures and are necessarily influenced by the imperfect standards of these cultures; they are not made morally perfect by their faith, and the church has often been flawed in its actions. But the Holy Spirit, working out in society Christ's example and sacrifice through the proclamation and practice of the gospel in the church at its best, has changed billions of individual lives and human society as a whole for the better in ways unmatched by any other religion or philosophy. Repentance and forgiveness are at the heart of the gospel and are a source of constant spiritual renewal and moral transformation in the church of Christ and, through it, as in the biblical image of yeast in a loaf of bread, in society at large.

Undoubtedly one of the chief reasons for the moral decline of Western culture in the course of the last century and a half in particular, entailing alienation and internal contestation of its traditional source of moral authority, is the unbelief in the gospel that has seeped into the pores of Western man. To be sure, as I have been repeating, many of the moral aspects of the gospel have been secularized and incorporated into the mainstream of Western society, and aspects of the gospel long neglected, such as the essential goodness of the body, of sexuality, and of the whole created world of creatures, have been reaffirmed by the church and, with the exception of the nihilistic currents, by society as a whole. But the foundation for these truths is fragile if the gospel underlying them is lost or set aside, as is the case in the West today, and the church faces the task of living them out in our communities and defending them privately and publicly with intelligence and passion. Otherwise, our democracies may decay irremediably and collapse or be overthrown by forces from without.

One of the great innovations in human history, deriving from the Christian gospel, has been the care for the poor—not only one's own poor, but all poor. The emphasis on hospitals and education that gradually took form over the centuries in Christianized societies is a reflection of this. This concern for the poor (which means most people) marked out the church from the beginning and was one of the major reasons for the spread of Christian faith in the Roman Empire, as it has been ever since throughout the world. If slavery was not officially abolished in the early centuries of the church, being such an integral part of society that its official abolition was simply inconceivable, the institution was in fact fundamentally subverted by the gospel and the New Testament Epistles as being against the equality and dignity of men and women in the eyes of God (see Paul's Epistle to Philemon and Galatians 3:28). The kind of household slavery common in the Roman Empire, normally involving sexual exploitation, gradually disappeared from the early Christian communities, as the social status of women and children was enhanced through adherence to the gospel. The serfdom of feudal times that structured society in the Middle Ages up to the fifteenth century was based effectually on lord-vassal economic arrangements very different both from the earlier household form of slavery and from the later chattel slavery. As to the phenomenon of chattel slavery and the African slave trade that got underway in the sixteenth century, the church, while condemning the practice officially through papal bulls and denunciations by figures like Francisco de Vitoria, did not follow through vigorously to implement this stance until the nineteenth century, when Western society did finally abolish this unspeakable practice in the American colonies, largely through the determined opposition of committed abolitionist Christians, especially in England, France, and America, who, against great odds, fought their case on the grounds of their biblical faith and the affirmation of the equality of all human beings.

The slave trade was a horrendous aberration in Western history and arose under the influence of Arab slave trading in Africa, at a time when an expanding and economically ambitious European society was beginning to cast off its moorings in the gospel. In parts of Arab society until very recently effectual slavery in various forms has been tolerated, since this is not seen to be fundamentally incompatible with the Qur'an and with Arab tradition. In Sudan, for example, in the context of the second Sudanese civil war that began in 1983, the Khartoum military government that took power in 1989 sent murderous militias into southwest Sudan to decimate the Christian and animist Dinka and Nuer tribes. In the wake of these savage attacks, thousands of men, women, and children were abducted, enslaved, and subsequently bought and sold as chattel. The Comprehensive Peace Agreement of 2005 theoretically put an end to these frightful practices, but the continuing turbulence in Sudan and in the now-independent state of South Sudan is not reassuring. Slavery has not ended in our time, far from it. I mentioned earlier that a new form of economic slavery—the trafficking of women and children and the exploitation of migrants—is increasing in many parts of the world, including the United States. This is happening in the context of globalization. The church, in keeping with the best in its tradition, must join with civil authorities to fight this horrendous practice.

Another fruit of the gospel in Western history, one that prepared the ground for the development of modern democracy, is the separation of the political and religious powers. This reality took shape within Christendom and is rooted in Jesus's word about giving unto Caesar what is Caesar's and unto God what is God's (Luke 20:20–26). This is a subject of enormous interest and provides a talking point of the first importance when discussing the effects of the Christian gospel on society. It offers a kind of political parallel to the Jewish-Christian ontological distinction between the Creator God and his creation, which was one of the fundamental truths that opened the way for the development of modern science. The separation of the religious and secular powers in the West, and the constant vying of the two with each other through the centuries, opened the way for the modern pluralist state to emerge and gave room for the development of individual and associative freedoms within the body politic, something not paralleled in societies where all power was concentrated in the political center, or where, as in Islam, the political and religious powers were understood to be *one* and in a sense indistinguishable.

A final point to be addressed is the reality of sin and evil. Neither postmodernism nor Islam knows what to make of these realities. Original sin is absent from their worldviews, with the result that the pervasive presence of evil in human affairs is seen on the one hand as some sort of inexplicable aberration that can perhaps be redressed by education and improved material circumstances, and on the other hand as the property of infidels, those outside the faith of Islam and the qur'anic dictation. Postmodernists have scant defense against the power of sin and evil, and Muslims, inclined to identify these realities as belonging essentially to the sphere of the unconverted, have difficulty explaining the inevitable corruption and evident imperfection of the single political/religious entity that is Islam. Atonement for sin and the notion of reconciliation with God through divine forgiveness are likewise absent from both ideologies, making recovery from violence, and resistance to the impulse to take revenge and so perpetuate the violence, very problematical.

As for the gospel, it is itself the absolute opposition to evil and the definitive action against it. The Bible does not theorize about evil or seek to explain its origins, beyond pointing in several places to the figures of Lucifer and Satan—the accuser and divider—suggesting that they are one and the same, but providing no clear-cut explanation for the source in God's good creation of the emergence of evil in one of its noblest angelic creatures, other than to point to pride and jealousy of the Creator as the ultimate cause (see Isa 14; Job 1–2; Zech 5:2; the temptation stories in the Synoptic Gospels; Luke 10:18, 22:3; Rom 16:20; 1 Cor 11:14, 12:7; Rev 12:9, 20:2, 7). We are left with the terrible historical reality that raises itself up against God and the beautiful creatures he has made, seeking to usurp God's reign and pervert or destroy his creation. In response to evil, the Christian is called above all to resist and fight it, in the private and public spheres, on the basis of Christ's victory at Calvary and in the power of the Holy Spirit.

Clearly, the creation of free will in man can be seen—and always has been seen in the Christian tradition—as a risk God was taking when he made human beings in his own image. A creature with a free will and made to be like God, even though finite, can defy its maker. This is what happened, with the frightful consequences that human history in its negative mode displays. This is always the first point we must make, for ourselves and when we are responding to this objection from others. Human beings without free will would be automatons, lacking the capacity to choose, in particular to choose to love others and, ultimately, the God who made them. To those who say the good of created life isn't worth the bad, we can only say we disagree and then, praising God by faith in the midst of darkness, go about doing what we can in our own lives to counter bad with good.

Jesus came to earth to overthrow the devil—Satan—and the power of sin and death and to free those held in slavery by their fear of death (Heb 2:14–15). The resurrection from the dead is the definitive defeat of evil and opens the way for a new way of life different from anything man is capable of achieving on his own. Hope rises over the horizon, meaning appears in the midst of history, as the death that cuts short all living things and that manifests itself in the violence of the perverted human will, is itself cut down and surpassed by the victorious Christ. This is what we are called to proclaim, in words and by our actions as the community of the church and as individuals. The world and the human heart are a battleground between good and evil, as history shows. The devil is defeated, evil has been conquered, but the devil has not been destroyed yet and evil has not been eliminated. Indeed, as history moves forward toward Christ's return, the battle intensifies. We are called to be innocent as doves and shrewd as serpents; to walk with love, courage, and wisdom; and to act with authority and humility as we seek to follow Christ and do the Father's will. To do these things as faithfully as we can will constitute a persuasive defense of our faith and bring many to recognize the truth that is in Jesus Christ and the Christian gospel.

Part VI

AESTHETICS

Beauty as the Radiance of Truth

I

THE FOLLOWING ESSAY IS an approach to aesthetics within a Christian framework. It is hoped that the authority and pertinence of this framework will become evident as the essay develops. The non-Christian reader is invited to enter this house and receive my hospitality, as if he or she were in a foreign land and were invited by a native to come and dine with him. Such an attitude of openness and trust is precisely what I shall be contending for in this essay. The proof of any pudding lies in the eating, not in some prior disquisition about what constitutes an edible pudding.

The biblical revelation of the *imago Dei* provides the context for this discussion. For that context to be adequate, however, this revelation must itself be placed within a Trinitarian perspective, and this leads naturally into a variety of related issues, philosophical and cultural. It seems clear to me that any biblically based consideration of the question of beauty in its relation to truth must be situated carefully within an encompassing theological and philosophical frame. The method of this essay will therefore be to move back and forth inside these various issues, as if the discussion were taking place in a kind of labyrinth where all the interconnecting paths keep crossing each other. The systematic nature of the analysis is not to be found in any neat, linear argument, or in exhaustive analysis, but in this thematic interconnectedness.

Goodness, truth, and beauty are inseparable aspects of God's creation as depicted in Genesis 1 and 2: distinctive, correlative, co-inherent, constituting together the essential nature of *being*. I believe it is legitimate to see in them refractions of the Triune God who is love, as revealed fully in Jesus Christ. God, in the first chapter of Genesis, pronounces his creative work "good" and, at the very end of the narrative, "very good" (vv. 4, 10, 12, 18, 21, 25, 31). We may understand by this, first, that God declared his creatures to be good in that they *were*, they *existed*, they had *being*; secondly, in that each creature (animate and inanimate) was a unique particular *form of being* with its own integrity and dignity; and thirdly, in that all his creatures were manifestations of his will and order. They stood out against nonbeing and formlessness (see Genesis 1:2). Where being is, form is; forms are unique and particular, and this is good.

We may go on to understand truth as the *expression* of goodness, just as the word is the expression of God's will. Creation is the act of a Personal Being; it is not the outworking of impersonal forces. It presupposes a will, a design, a purpose, and that will expresses itself in an act of power for which the biblical author uses the metaphor of speech: *"God said"* (vv. 3, 6, 9 11, 14, 22, 24, 26). God also *"made"* (vv. 7, 16, 25, 26) and *"created"* (vv. 21, 27), so it would seem that the three verbs are coterminous. We understand speech to be the expression of a rational will whose objective is communication. Without speech, an intention cannot be known.[1] Speech communicates a prior purpose or design; it discloses and makes present something that may be in the mind of the speaker, but that is only potentially real until it is expressed. In the case of human speech, there will always be a disparity between the inchoate idea in the mind of the speaker and its actualization through symbolic expression—the two will never correspond perfectly. In the case of God, however, there can be no such disparity, for God is creating out of nothing and over against formlessness, and, being omnipotent, is able to imagine his intentions with exactitude and to actualize completely that which he imagines.

Without God's word, then, there cannot be expression. One may say that this word is the substance of God's good will, its truth, the uncovering and making known—the coming to be—of its potential reality. This is why we may speak of creation, in a way that is similar to what we say of the incarnation, as a revelation of God. The creative Word and the incarnate Word are one and the same Word, revealing and effecting, from different perspectives, God's will and purpose (John 1:1-3; Col 1:16-17; Heb 1:3; Ps 33:6). Moreover, God commits himself to the word, which is his truth, and will remain faithful to it.

But without God's breath, his word could not be spoken. God's Spirit is as essential to the *manifestation* of his goodness as is his word. By his Spirit, the spoken will of God is carried from purpose into form: it is made

---

1. With respect to human beings, I take "speech" and "word" to include, broadly, other forms of symbolic expression as well, such as painting, sculpture, architecture, mathematics, music, and dance. Each of these is unique and achieves expression in ways the others cannot. Nevertheless, the "construct of the verbal," as George Steiner puts it (*Real Presences*, 189), does seem to lie at the very center of human being, both effecting and signifying communication and semantic relationality more precisely and self-evidently than other symbolic structures.

manifest, it is revealed. *"By the word of the Lord were the heavens made, their starry host by the breath of his mouth"* (Ps 33:6).[2] The Spirit actualizes the word, bringing God's intention into being. This is as true of the redemptive Word of God in Jesus Christ as it is of God's creative Word in the primordial *fiat*. Form, effected by God's breath, completes the revelation of God's goodness encompassed in his Word. In addition, both the initial divine actualization of form, as the revelation of God's goodness, and the subsequent perception of it by rational men and women as being such a revelation, require the action of the Spirit of God.

II

This brief Trinitarian analogy has been sketched in order to provide the ground for a doctrine of God that does justice to both sides of the problematical question of how the concept of an eternal God, unchanging in his essence, omnipotent Creator of the universe and of the law that governs it, can be theoretically and positively squared with the freedom and historical action of the human creature. This is an urgent question in our day, and has a direct bearing on the subject of aesthetics, as we shall see, although at first sight this may not be readily apparent. If, on the basis of revelation (through e.g., the order and beauty of the universe, the Old and New Testament accounts of God's direct dealings with mankind, and the manifest goodness of God incarnate in Jesus Christ), we take God to be good and to be the Creator of all that is,[3] then we shall have no trouble believing that he has not determined his rational human creatures as a despot might do, to be slaves or robots, but has willed them to be free, though this has incurred risk both for him and for them, since it entailed the possibility of rebellion of the creature against the Creator, which could only lead to tragedy by distorting the creature's relation to himself, to his fellows, and to his Maker. The tension that both philosophy and theology have often perceived between

---

2. All biblical quotations in this essay are taken from the NIV translation, 1973, Ninth Impression, 1992.

3. As for the existence of evil, we may say simply that it is derivative and secondary, a perversion of the good creation. It is a privation of the good, but it is more than that; it is also willful and aggressive. Like death, it is nonbeing; but also like death, it is effectual. It is not nothing, but it partakes of nothingness and seeks to inflict it on created reality. It is a surd in the midst of being, indissociable from free will yet ultimately irrational and incomprehensible. God did not create evil, but the free will he granted to rational creatures (angels and humans), without which their rationality would have been empty of virtue and moral meaning, made them potentially capable of the sinful attitudes of pride, disobedience, and idolatry from which flow actions—those we call evil—that result in the distortion, perversion, and destruction of the created good.

heteronomous divinity and human free will is a *theoretical* dilemma—real enough on the logical plane—that fails to credit or do justice to the full-orbed biblical picture of God, of whom Jesus is presented as the very image and supreme revelation (*"Anyone who has seen me has seen the Father,"* says Jesus to Philip in John 14:9b; see Heb 1:3; John 1:1, 14; Phil 2:6–7; Col 1:19–20, 2:9).

Jesus Christ, understood to be the creative Word of God made flesh, was and certainly is the last thing from a tyrannical, oppressive figure. Indeed, his whole objective in coming to live among us was to liberate us from forms of domination and enslavement resulting from sin so that we could truly be the free creatures he fashioned us to be. Jesus reveals the fullness of what it means to say that God is love. The Creator of an ordered cosmos that exists in its objectivity and functions according to divine and unalterable law is also, precisely because he is *love*, to be understood as the Creator of human freedom—freedom which, one must not forget, can be (and has been) misused and so can lead to its opposite—disorder and enslavement. The order and law of the created universe—created by *this God*, truly revealed in Jesus Christ—is the necessary substratum for freedom and the exercise of freedom, which would be quite impossible in a context of chaos. The ultimate answer to the philosophical dilemma of reconciling the idea of an omnipotent God with the reality of human freedom lies in the concrete revelation—in the Word made flesh, the incarnation—of *who God is*.

God, as he is shown to us by revelation in the Hebraic and Christian Scriptures, is the Personal Subject who has created personal subjects in his image. As Personal Subject God is free; as personal subjects made in his image, human beings are also free. By virtue of self-consciousness, each of us is an "I," not delimited by the objective fact of his or her material body. We exist in our immediate physicality, and simultaneously we transcend space and time as God does. We imagine our way into the Creator's universe because we are at once part of it and, as spiritual beings, transcendent over it. The disclosure in Genesis that we are made in God's image shows how this can be. The cosmos can be intelligible to us through our philosophical, mathematical, and aesthetic investigations precisely because we are made in the image of its Creator and ours. The bond of brain and mind—their enigmatic oneness and distinctiveness, reminiscent once again of the divine Trinity—is a picture of this mystery.

By virtue of our free will, we may make choices of all kinds, related to every band on the spectrum of reality that comes within our cognizance. To be free is a state of being, not a quality in the strict sense. To be free is to be consciously and willingly open to the *other;* it is the opposite of self-centeredness and narcissism. It is intimately connected with love, and is inherently relational. As God is free to give himself to the *other* and to go out from himself into his creation,⁴ so human beings made in his image are free to do likewise.

This freedom finds its proper place and comes to its proper fulfillment in this world only within the overarching *objective and given* physical and moral law governing created reality. The objectivity and incontrovertability of that law point to an infinite creative Power underlying it, that is, to *Spirit* as the substratum of energy and matter. Human creatures made in the image of that Spirit are spiritual and cannot find ultimate meaning within the mere objectivity of the universe: their hearts, capable of infinity, seek to know its infinite spiritual Author. But their quest as subjects seeking union with the Subject who made them can be satisfied only as they first accept and receive the objectivity of that universe and the eternal law governing it. Neither art nor science, as subjective human enterprises, could attain to a measure of truth about the nature of being if they did not presuppose an objective reality within which they exist and to which they are responses.

The post-Enlightenment disengagement of moral from physical law, and the subsequent separation of human freedom and man-made history from nature, has had regrettable consequences and needs to be overcome if modern man is not to lose his way disastrously, like an astronaut cut loose from his capsule in space. One of these consequences has been to turn nature into an object to be dominated and controlled for autonomously determined human goals; nature has been co-opted by man-made history and reduced to mere matter to be used or overcome. The human subject no longer sees himself as standing before nature in intimate relation with it, seeking mastery of it only for the sake of survival and knowledge but without any pretension to subordinate it to his limitless manipulation; rather, he sees himself as the autocrat standing above nature and dominating it solely for what he can do with it and get out of it.

As an attitude, this instrumentalization of nature, and the perversion of agriculture by globalized monopolistic agribusiness into a market-based system of industrialized productivity, is utterly different from the wonder and awe with which all premodern peoples—pagans, Hebrews, and Christians alike—experienced the world around them and cared for it agriculturally. Pagans took nature to be a reflection or medium of divinity (however

---

4. In the light of this affirmation, we may understand the incarnation to be another manifestation of creation. The ground of this possibility is the intra-Trinitarian relations between the three persons of the Godhead, who eternally give to and receive from each other in love. We know this, of course, only by revelation as recorded in Scripture, culminating in the incarnation of the Son who reveals the Father, and through whom the Father sends the Spirit, who reveals the Son.

understood); Hebrews and Christians took it to be the omnipotent God's creation. In both cases it was experienced as the given and awesome reality in which the divine is somehow present and through which man participates in divinity and finds meaning in his life. This meaning always, at least to some degree, involves union with the sacred and eternal however this may be conceived. Nature provides sustenance, both physical and spiritual. For the Hebrews, as they expressed it in Genesis 1:26–28, mankind was understood to be the bearer of the Creator's image and the steward of his good creation, called to be its regent under God. The notion of man autonomously ransacking and exploiting nature purely for his own aggrandizement was inconceivable to the premodern mind.[5] For art and creative science, the importance of this attitude of receptivity and reverence toward nature, as opposed to the modern instrumental attitude, will inform the latter part of this essay.

The urgent need to overcome the consequences of this separation of human freedom and morality from nature should be plain to see, as the whole world plunges headlong into disarray and societal and ecological disorder even while scientists are daily discovering more about the astonishing depth and complexity of order in the physical universe. The schizophrenic dichotomy between the affirmation of laws governing the physical universe and the denial of any such laws in the moral sphere is leading to civilizational meltdown. In the absence of an objective and transcendent moral reference, the enactment of legislation and enforcement of rules as a means of stemming the tide of corruption, violence, and social disintegration is manifestly an ineffectual *pis aller*; yet without any reference to an encompassing moral order, analogous to and fundamentally part of the order of physical nature in which moral, self-conscious subjects have emerged and have their place, modern governments and judicial institutions have no other recourse, and find themselves impotent to achieve their goal.

Positive law loosed from eternal, divinely established law lacks ultimate legitimation and is powerless to prevail over human sin and wilfullness; without an absolute ground for its pronouncements, its mere subjectivity is painfully apparent and cannot carry final authority. Special interests will almost always win out over the common good. Moral relativism is inherently unstable because its affirmations, having no objective basis, can be challenged and contested at every turn. It tends to produce moral (and

---

5. This being said, it must also be pointed out that the ruthless modern desecration of nature and utilitarian contempt for it is prefigured in history by man's primordial desecration of and contempt for his own kind. Our greater technological power today simply enables us to extend to brute nature itself the violence we have always visited upon each other.

eventually political) anarchy on the one hand and legalism on the other. In any society, the proliferation of rules and regulations in order to maintain social order and define ethical conduct is a simulacrum and perversion of true law anchored in metaphysical reality. Sooner or later, it will be seen to be arbitrary.[6] Legalism always results in the opposite effect from the one intended, and invariably produces rebellion and disobedience accompanied by resentful accusation on every hand.[7] The outcome is a society of contention and acrimony, exactly the contrary of what the rule-makers hoped to achieve.

III

Theological development of Trinitarian doctrine, coupled with the outworking of its philosophical implications, can help to bring a conceptual reunion of God and human freedom and, in parallel, of nature as an *objective* reality and history as the *subjective* creation of human beings. I wish to approach that development now from the vantage point of biblical anthropology and in particular with respect to the doctrine of the *imago Dei*. This in turn will lead us finally to the implications for aesthetics of our theological discussion.

Creatures are *forms of being* intended by the Creator, and as such, they are beautiful. They manifest God's glory. Their beauty is the reflection of his truth. Their beings radiate his being. The author of the Epistle to the

---

6. The irony here is that moral relativism, perceived correctly to conduce to arbitrary ethical positions, arises in a social context that contests the absoluteness of natural or of Mosaic law on the ground that it is arbitrary simply because it is seen to emanate from God and as such is regarded as heteronomous.

7. The apostle Paul's discussion in Romans and Galatians of Mosaic law in its relation to sin, grace in Christ, and freedom, is instructive in this regard. He argues that the revealed moral law actually has the effect of exposing the defiant and deceitful sinfulness of the human heart and disclosing the incapacity of fallen human beings to submit to that law and obey it (see Romans 3:20, 21–26, 5:20–21, 7:7–25, 8:1–11; Gal 3:10–14, 19–25). The effect of this is to cause law to degenerate into legalism, with its adjuncts of self-righteousness and condemnation (of others and, frequently, of oneself), which was the endemic problem of Pharisaical religion. Natural law, as intuited in pagan societies, can produce similar effects in the form of rigid conventions and taboos that then require ritual safety valves as well as scapegoats to release the resulting inner frustrations and accusations that inevitably build up. The christological objective and central point of Paul's discussion is that Christ has fulfilled on our behalf the requirements of the law and has borne the punishment due us for our transgressions of it, so that those who put their trust in him are graciously welcomed by God and receive forgiveness and a "new heart" (Ezek 36:26). They are no longer under the condemnation of the Law; instead, as new creations under God's grace, they can live in the freedom of the Spirit, beyond the law as accuser and beyond legalism as self-defense (Rom 8:1–4; Gal 5:1, 18; 2 Cor 5:17).

Hebrews speaks of Jesus Christ the Son as being himself the very radiance of God's glory (Heb 1:3), that is, the *"exact representation"*—the icon and image—of his being. And the apostle Paul, in his Second Epistle to the Corinthians, speaks of Christian believers who, as they behold the Lord by faith, *reflect* his glory and *"are being transformed into his likeness with ever-increasing glory, which comes from the Lord, who is the Spirit"* (3:18). Jesus, the Word incarnate, *is* God's image and effulgence; human beings *made in* God's image, and in particular those who are even now being restored by the Spirit to their essential likeness to this image in Christ, *reflect* that radiance. Whatever goodness they manifest is a refraction of God's truth, and is therefore beautiful. Jesus Christ is like the sun; human beings are like the moon.

In Scripture, the word "glory" is used mainly in connection with God and connotes basically his magnificence in the sense of his revealed presence. God's glory—his *Shekinah*—shone in the Tent of Meeting and in the Temple, where he dwelt with his people (Exod 33:12–23, 34:29–35; see 2 Cor 3:7–18; Num 12:4–8; 1 Kgs 6:10–11). The word "glory" is not abstract—to the contrary. Jesus Christ is the radiance of God's glory because he is God *present to us*, God with us here and now. In him, writes the apostle Paul, *"all the fullness of the deity lives in bodily form"* (Col 2:9). This is what the apostles beheld on the Mount of Transfiguration, as Peter reports it later: *"For he [Jesus] received honor and glory from God the Father when the voice came to him from the Majestic Glory, saying, 'This is my Son, whom I love: with him I am well pleased'"* (2 Pet 1:17). And it is the power of his glory—his presence—that will defeat Satan and his minions on the last day when he comes again as the victorious Messiah: *"And then the lawless one will be revealed, whom the Lord Jesus will overthrow with the breath of his mouth and destroy by the splendor of his coming"* (2 Thess 2:8).

God is present in all his creatures in that, brought forth by his hand, every one of them reflects in some way its Author, analogously—as having being—and aesthetically—as having form. All are the work of God's Word through the breath of his mouth. But he is most especially present in and to man (man and woman), as that distinctive creature *"made in God's image"* (Gen 1:26, 27). The essential meaning of this revelation is that man is a personal being inherently—*ontologically*—related to his Creator. Creation being a deliberate, willed act, no impersonal force or idea could accomplish it. The God who creates is necessarily living and personal, even if the scope of that life and personhood is far beyond our finite experience and can only be apprehended by analogy. Hence, as creatures made in his image, we are personal beings, bound by our nature to our Maker. This is why it is actually possible for us to receive the revelation of God-as-personal.

Qualities such as self-consciousness, conscience, rationality, and free will—the moral freedom and power to determine our own course and destiny—derive from the prior reality of this ontological relationship. Efforts to determine the nature of the *imago Dei* primarily on the basis of qualitative determinations miss the point. The dignity and spiritual equality of all men and women arise from—and are guaranteed by—their status in relation to their Creator; the endowments of reason, self-consciousness, and free will are the means given by God for the development and fulfillment of that relation. It is not because of any superior gifting or intelligence or fitness for survival that we are called to treat our fellow humans with respect and to act toward them in love: it is because they, like us, are creatures made by God in his own image.

In words spoken to Noah after the flood, God discloses the significance of the *imago Dei* for relationships between living creatures in the context of the fallen world and the violence that characterizes it. *"And for your lifeblood I will surely demand an accounting. I will demand an accounting from every animal. And from each man, too, I will demand an accounting for the life of his fellow man. Whoever sheds the blood of man, by man shall his blood be shed; for in the image of God has God made man"* (Gen 9:5–6). Life is in the blood (Lev 17:11), and the life of man is infinitely precious, *because he is created in the image of God*. To kill a human being unjustly is an offense *against God*, because he/she, as created in his image, represents God in the natural world. Surely this is the chief reason why David, in his inspired prayer of repentance in Psalm 51, in which he laments the sin of having arranged for the death of his military commander, Uriah, in order to hide his adultery with Bathsheba, cries out to God in verse 4: *"Against you, you only, have I sinned and done what is evil in your sight."*

The fall, as recounted in Genesis 3,[8] did not efface the image of God in man or annul the relationship between God and man, as God's post-fall

---

8. I understand the story of the Fall in, a generic way, as an example of narrative theology. Thus it seems to me to contain a *generic* element, as pertaining to the whole human race; an *existential* element, as pertaining to the mysterious proclivity in the heart of every human being toward egotistical willfulness (the catastrophic consequences of which are suggested in Genesis 4–11); and an *historical* element, in that Genesis 3 reflects in narrative form a reality embedded in primeval history, a reality that corresponds to some event or process that happened at the dawn of the human race. The narrative addresses the imponderable enigma of how this race, emerging somehow in the course of divinely directed evolutionary development (chance by itself cannot possibly account for such an emergence) is differentiated from animals not just in its consciousness of God and of itself, but also in its capacity for evil, which can be properly construed only in terms of sinfulness and not as residual animal behavior (for an insightful discussion of these issues, see Ramm, *Offense to Reason*, chs. 4–5). The biblical texts make it clear that the human fall came in the wake of the prior angelic fall,

admonition to Noah makes evident. What it did was to *inverse* that relationship, to shift it from the positive to the negative mode. This has meant, concretely, that human beings have rebelled against being simply reflections of God—majestic destiny though this is—and have striven actually to replace him and to *be God*. Despite such folly and presumptuousness on man's part, with all the tragedy of human history that it has entailed, the Creator has not abandoned us, though we often accuse him of doing so and blame him for the misery human sin (our own and that of others) brings upon us. Our arrogant race incurs God's judgment but not his rejection. His plan of salvation for mankind working through the people of Israel and their Messiah Yeshua shows his gracious predisposition toward his rebellious creature. Human capacities of consciousness, reason, and freedom of choice remain intact,[9] even if they are now tainted and frequently misused for the glorification of man himself instead of God. The Creator, rather than enjoying the intimacy of trusting communion with his human creatures, now is the object of fear, unbelief, and idolatrous counterfeits; and men and women, instead of loving and serving their divine Maker, flee him, seek to manipulate him, or else deny him altogether.

Nevertheless, as man's very nature is in the fact of his having been made in God's image, the ontological relation between Creator and creature holds. Escape from God is impossible, as Psalm 139 affirms. Modern atheism and unbelief may incline God to fall silent in response to human

---

where a host of angels, led by Satan, rebelled against the Creator out of pride and jealousy. Jesus's temptation in the desert was a replay of Adam's temptation in Eden. This is why it had to take place after his baptism and before he began his public ministry. The Second Adam (see Rom 5:14–15; cf., 1 Cor 15:45) had to resist Satan's temptation where the First Adam had yielded to it. I take mankind's fall to be historical in that the rebellion in which it consists must by definition have involved choice and decision and cannot be construed as a merely natural development; it involved the introduction—at some point in time—of something fundamentally disordered—i.e., rebellion—into the process of creation. My own interpretation of the *imago Dei* is an attempt to shed some light on how the parameters of created human being made such an aberration possible.

9. The limitation of free will since the fall pertains to our capacity to find and choose, unaided, the true and good God who created us. As Paul and, later, Augustine and Luther, made crystal clear, we are prisoners of a rebellious orientation and have lost our spiritual freedom. In this sense it could be said that we are still morally and existentially free, but not spiritually; we can to a considerable degree discern and posit that which is good, and even adhere to it at times through the combined power of conscience, law (natural and positive), and custom, but we cannot know him who is goodness. The best of human religion and philosophy gropes intuitively toward the spiritual reality that is the Personal Creator, the God who is love, but cannot know him in the absence of his own gracious self-revelation. This separation of the moral from the spiritual, with its attendant impact on the meaning of free will, is already adumbrated in Genesis 2:9, 15–17, and 3:2–5.

self-sufficiency and indifference—he will not force himself upon us—but it cannot strip him of his reality and power, and neither can it cause him to disappear nor the relation between us and him to cease. It is evident to any sensitive observer that the fallen world is a world upside-down, where free will is often used to oppress and enslave others, and reason is often distorted into coercive ideologies and used for misguided and destructive ends. By virtue of the *imago Dei*, however, and of God's gracious determination to realize the original intention of his creation, men and women are still able to make use of the Creator's primordial gifts to the human race, although it is now beyond unaided human power—indeed, it is beyond unaided human desire and will—to know and obey the true and holy God and to enjoy full communion with him.

It is in Jesus Christ, God's very image incarnate, that the inverted image of God in man is set right. As God's Son and man's representative, he sacrificially takes upon himself on the cross the sin of mankind, including the alienation *from* God and the misrepresentation *of* God that this has produced. He consents to have our condemnation and judgment fall on him and then takes them down into death. Jesus, God's creative Word made flesh, agrees to the Father's will to make him—in a very real way—to *"be sin"* for us, so that he might be both just, in judging sin, and merciful, in opening a way for our salvation (Matt 26:36–46; Acts 2:23; 2 Cor 5:21; Rom 3:25–26). God's *creative Word* at the world's beginning thus becomes God's *redemptive Word* at the world's renewal. When Christ is raised from the grave, our whole race rises—forgiven—in him; henceforth, by pure grace, restoration to the positive mode of the *imago Dei*, and to genuine communion with the Living God, is open in principle to all. But so radical was the fall and so incapable was man of reversing it by himself, that this restoration is effectively a *new creation*. Of course, the gift must be received to be effective; it is not automatic, and it is not imposed on us. Yet, as the apostle John puts it, *"to all who have received him, to those who have believed in his name, he has given the right* [authority] *to become children of God—children born not of natural descent, nor of human decision or husband's will, but born of God"* (John 1:12–13).

To be born of God means to be born of grace, not by virtue of works or merits or of anything deriving from our own power, whether moral, intellectual, or material. The holy God sanctifies us in Christ. We appropriate this gift by faith, and so enter into that communion with God which was lost at the fall. In Christ and through Christ we discover who the true God is—the Creator God who is love—and at the same time we rediscover our own true nature as children of God made in his image: the antagonism and fear are dissipated, friendship with our Maker is reestablished. The restored trust and mutual love that now may flow between God and his human creatures open the possibility for our race of rightly using the gifts of reason and freedom in order to fulfill the mandate given to us by God at creation: to have benign oversight, as God's regents, over the earth and its creatures, including our own race, and to be fruitful (Gen 1:28). It is obvious that this mandate can be carried out properly only by free, rational persons, through love ordered by reason.

IV

As was suggested above, the right use of these gifts had not been entirely lost at the fall, however the fall is to be understood, historically speaking (see footnote 8, p. 245). God had not abandoned his creature; by the power of his word he had sustained humanity through time and limited the chaotic effects of evil, and by his Spirit he had continued to quicken human conscience and orient human development. Ethical awareness, concern with law, apprehensions of justice, technical ingenuity, and manifestations of intellectual and artistic power were all to be found in ancient civilizations as the Egyptian, Greek, and Roman cultures in particular make evident in the Western world. Indeed, our modern civilization has much to learn from the way premodern cultures understood reason and related to nature, as I shall suggest shortly.

It remains true nonetheless that before Christ, hostility and warfare between "nations" (clans, tribes, ethnic groups) were the norm, even if, within the boundaries of these groupings, orderly societies were established and maintained. There was no exception or possible exception to this state of affairs.[10] Power, jealousy, ambition, and revenge were the dominant operative principles in human relationships, which were structured, broadly, in terms of masters and slaves, while fear and manipulation determined the way men related to their gods. The experience of guilt was universal, as was the practice of propitiatory sacrifice in response to it. Polytheism, even as it deified natural forces, did evidence intimations of the personal nature of the divine, but the true God, the one and only God, whose nature was

---

10. It is obvious that since Christ this has also continued to be the case, within societies touched by the Christian gospel as well as others. But since Christ, a completely new possibility of living has also been open to men and women, a heavenly leaven working within the lump of violent humanity that has profoundly altered the shape of human history and brought self-sacrificial love and true, well-founded hope within its scope. This has significantly affected ethics within societies reached by the gospel, opening up perspectives of change and improvement of the human condition in this world and the liberating expectation of eternal life with God beyond the grave.

holiness, love, and purity, was unknown, although, significantly, modern anthropology has disclosed traces, especially among certain African and North American peoples, of what might be called tribal memories of such a being, still perceived dimly as the Creator, as well as hopeful intuitions of a coming Redeemer of some kind.

The Greek philosophers, believing the universe to be under the rule of reason, rationalized the mythology of their forebears, even while a multitude of gods continued to fill the popular imagination. The philosophers were concerned to purge religious beliefs and practices of their cruder anthropomorphic elements;[11] but as Etienne Gilson has pointed out, in Greek thought, principles are not simply substitutes for gods as such.[12] Principles and deities coexist, even in Aristotle and later thinkers, the one corresponding to the rational attempt to understand the world as a world of things, the other corresponding to existential and religious needs. It is the coordination of these two spheres that the philosophers are unable to determine clearly. Indeed, within the compass of Greek experience and understanding, no solution to this problem was ever found or could have been found because of the radical separation in their thinking between the transcendent, eternal realm and the physical, transitory (and therefore ultimately meaningless) realm of human activity.

In Greek philosophical thought, the reflection—distorted but real—of the *imago Dei* of which Genesis speaks was to be found in the conviction that the cosmos is a rational system in which man, as the possessor of a rational soul, participates. Plato's Good, as the highest form of reason and the source of the intelligibility of the objects of knowledge, and Aristotle's Unmoved Mover, as the pure actuality of thinking and the metaphysical magnet attracting, by the force of *eros*, all things having being, were, in essence, divinized rational principles, with which humans, being rational, had a special and indefeasible relation. The God of which these thinkers spoke, and the divine mind that they conceived of as ordering the universe, were impersonal ideas expressive of the reason that was thought to govern reality.[13] Theology was identical with cosmology, with the cosmos understood as

---

11. See e.g., Plato, *The Laws* X, 884–910; *Republic* II:376—III:412.

12. Gilson, *God and Philosophy*, ch. 1.

13. Plato's demiurge in the *Timaeus* is no exception to this, despite its characterization by the philosopher as "the maker and father of the universe" (*Timaeus* 28c). This personified figure may be construed as a religious rational principle or philosophical myth used to explain the efficient cause of becoming. As such, it is to be distinguished from the Platonic Forms, which are pure metaphysical principles. Plato conceives of the demiurge as a primordial organizing principle that fashions eternally preexistent matter according to an eternally preexistent pattern.

divine, eternal, and unchanging. The divinities were seen as agents only in that they were taken to be principles that gave intelligibility to the cosmos. Their causal functions were notional, not active. The conception of God as personal Creator and absolute Source of all that is, was absent. Such an understanding of divinity—of a God who *is* (not who *is something*), whose essence is identical with his existence—cannot be the product of speculation, but only of revelation.

Only such a God as this, a personal Creator, can bind together what for the Greeks were the irreconcilable spheres of the divine and the earthly: reason and action, the eternal and the transitory.[14] In the case of highly developed pre-Christian cultures, the historical realm held little interest. Plato's conception of time as "the moving image of eternity"[15] gave philosophical expression to a general understanding among ancient peoples that change and death made all things under the sun unreal in a fundamental sense, and that only the heavens, considered to be eternal and changeless, were truly real. The Greek thinkers labored, however, to find connections between the two realms, and this, again, may be understood to be a reflection in the human soul of the *imago Dei*, expressing itself in a culture under the sway of the fall (that mysterious primeval turning away from the living God) and lacking direct divine revelation. Plato's doctrine of forms, with its notion of time and the things in time as being copies or shadows of eternal ideas, is a complex dialectic of transcendence and immanence. Human beings, according to Plato, contain an immortal principle within them, the rational soul, which strives against the body of corruption in which it is imprisoned, in order to discipline the irrational passions by reason and progressively to shake loose the material world of succession and decay and lay hold on immortality.[16] In Hellenic thought, reality was that which lay open to the intelligible, and the intelligible was accessible by reason and by reason alone. Rationality and immortality were indissolubly linked.

As I have suggested, there is here an intimation of the truth that is revealed fully in Christ, the creative Word made flesh, in whose image rational human beings are fashioned. The Logos—that later Stoic permutation of the classical Greek understanding of the cosmos as permeated by order—takes human form in Jesus of Nazareth in order to save man and bring him back to the knowledge of his Creator.[17] Thus it is revealed to men and women

14. In our own day, the same holds true with regard to the perceived opposition between divine omnipotence and human free will, as suggested above.

15. Plato, *Timaeus* 38b, 37d.

16. For a discussion of Plato's anthropology, see Nygren, *Agape and Eros*, 168–75.

17. It is the Gospel of John, of course, that most explicitly develops this Logos perspective.

that the ordering Logos/Word governing reality is reason, yes, but is far more than reason —that *he* is that which is more fundamental than reason and which encompasses reason, namely a Personal Being. By virtue of the *imago Dei*, the Greeks—and indeed all premodern peoples to one degree or another—*participated* in the order of the cosmos, the divine order. This was (and *is*, as I shall be arguing) a correct apprehension of that to which man is called and without which he cannot be fully human. Having no knowledge of God by direct revelation, they could not grasp this participation in any terms other than those of reason. The *personal* dimension of participation in divinity, involving the whole human person and thus including all that appeared in a human being to be ephemeral, was inconceivable for the Greeks. But their openness to the world, their receptivity to the order of nature, their wonder before being, were authentic expressions of human beings as created in the image of God, and indeed were far more *personal* responses than they themselves were capable of grasping intellectually.

V

This is the chief reason, in my view, why beauty played such a pivotal role in Greek culture. The awareness of beauty, as we shall suggest below, arises from the contemplation of form, which is the translation of being itself into concrete manifestations. To the Greek mind, this awareness both pointed to and was underpinned by the glory and the changelessness of the heavens, which seemed the very image of eternity. Here is the source of the Platonic ideas. In *form*, something eternal was intimated, and this meant something rational. To the Hebraic and Christian mind, as the beneficiary of divine self-revelation, this intimation was, as it were, *fleshed out* and taken to a more comprehensive level: a beautiful form is seen to be an expression of the rational God's creative Word, its beauty a radiant reflection of the truth of personal being, that is, of the fundamental nature of reality, which is that God is love.[18]

For the modern mind, mired in positivistic skepticism like a seagull trapped in an oil spill, the idea of participation in metaphysical reality through the contemplation of being is unintelligible. Reason in today's world has lost all contact with the metaphysical; indeed, the very word "metaphysical" connotes for modern men and women something intrinsically irrational. The instrumentalization of nature referred to above is in fact rooted in the instrumentalization of reason. We look upon reason as

---

18. I John 4:8; John 3:16; Rom 5:8. It is in Jesus and his redemptive work that God's nature as love is made manifest. In him, we see who God truly is (John 14:8-11).

that utilitarian power by which our wills penetrate, control, and manipulate reality, to the point of reinventing it. Our rational power, far from waiting on reality to intuit its nature and ground and to gain wisdom, aims to wring from it knowledge by analysis and experiment and then use that knowledge to alter it in ways we see fit. Clearly this approach to the physical world has been immensely productive in the last 400 years and has freed man practically, if not ontologically (as the transhumanists would wish it), from the subjection to nature that characterized premodern societies. But the disappearance of the sense of the mystery of being and the loss of the contemplative spirit have been a high price to pay for these cognitive and material gains, as has been the case with, at another level, the ecological chaos the planet is now experiencing directly as a result of our heartless exploitation of nature. This is nature's revenge. Modern man tends to see only appearances and surfaces in the natural world and hence is unable to find in nature a source of meaning. The instrumentalist attitude has co-opted and emasculated the symbolical imagination.

This attitude is not identical with that properly critical attitude toward reality that has characterized Western thought since the Greeks. The capacity to critique the *other*, to draw back from a being different from ourselves and observe and analyze it with a measure of objectivity, is integral to a full and proper use of the faculty of reason. This critical capacity as it has developed in the West extends, of course, to one's self, to the human person or persons exercising reason, as being themselves objects of analysis for the Greeks and objects of judgment and salvation for the Hebrews. Both the philosophical imagination of the Greeks and the theological imagination of the Hebrews contributed to the emergence of critical reason as a fundamental characteristic and one of the glories of Western civilization. These traditions combined to put Western man at a remove from nature and so in a position to analyze, know, and transform it. The critical spirit, as a form of reason, de-divinizes the world.

This does not mean, either for the Greeks or Hebrews, that the divine is not active and present *somehow* in the material world, but it does mean that the material world is not *itself* divine, although for the Hebrews the forces of nature, as realities created by the will of God, are certainly under God's ultimate control and governance. For the Greeks, it was the transitory nature of the material world and its proneness to change that opened the way for extruding divinity from its essence and operations; for the Hebrews, it was the belief, consequent on God's self-revelation to them in word and power, that the world was his *creation* and that he was altogether transcendent and sovereign over it. Thus to divinize any aspect of it was seen to be idolatry and a transgression of the first commandment to have no other gods but Yahweh himself (Exod 20:3; Deut 5:7).

The instrumentalist and utilitarian attitude toward reason began to emerge with the rise of modern, post-Aristotelian scientific thought in the early seventeenth century,[19] when the Hebraic and Christian perception of God and of his relation to the world began itself to be criticized and called into question. The rise of deism led to the gradual evaporation of belief in God's presence in or even near the world. Critical reason, as a means to knowledge, began to become an end in itself, subject to no constraint higher than its own theoretical and practical power. With Descartes, Hume, and Kant, from different perspectives, the metaphysical realm was put beyond the reach of certain knowledge, at least for theoretical reason.[20] If Kant's argument for religion within the limits of reason alone did not by any means exclude the possibility of divine revelation as a reality having its origin outside of man himself, it appeared at first glance to do so and led inevitably to the general collapse of belief in both creation and incarnation as being the two fundamental expressions of divine revelation in the biblical tradition. Then, with the world-shaking events of the American and French Revolutions, and subsequently with the Romantic sensitivity to change and the philosophical work of Hegel, Marx, and Nietzsche, the conception of time as history and of reality as endless becoming came to dominate Western thought.[21] As the twentieth-century framework for the understanding of reality, this conception went hand in hand with a worldview driven by scientific discovery and constant technological innovation.

The modern ideology of relativism is rooted in this insight. It implies that there is nothing permanent in human beings or in any part of nature. Henceforth, not only is the transcendental realm unknowable and therefore arguably a mere fiction, but the entire material realm is subject to constant change and is therefore also, in a sense, unknowable. It is continually being reinvented, *ad infinitum*. The only thing permanent is change itself. The classical understanding of rationality in the pursuit of truth, in the conviction that there is such a thing and that it is certain and absolute and not

---

19. Francis Bacon famously spoke of the need to "twist the lion's tail" in order to make nature yield her secrets. But the great scientists of this period—Copernicus, Galileo, Kepler, Harvey, Newton—were all strong Christian believers whose revolutionary scientific vision was inspired by their faith.

20. Descartes's innate idea of God as the conceptual means by which to overcome his epistemological skepticism could not survive Locke's empiricist criticism, not to mention Hume's; innate ideas in themselves, and all the more as an epistemological tool to establish any kind of knowledge, were henceforth ruled out of the philosophical court.

21. For an incisive discussion of this development, see Grant, *Time as History*.

subject to change and mutation, is consequently undermined, and reason is reduced to the status of a tool by which to gain power over material reality.

During the nineteenth century, the nihilistic implications of this vision were held at bay by an optimistic faith in progress that vindicated at least a belief in rationality as progressive, as something intrinsically good that was pushing back obscurantism and evil. Few people apart from far-sighted thinkers like Marx noticed the deep rifts that industrialization was making in the social fabric of Western societies and, through exploitative colonialism, in non-Western societies as well. Fewer still saw the storm clouds gathering, even if, by the end of the century, a sense of decadence and civilizational decline was widespread. Again, political liberalism, movements of social reform, and an overall increase in technological ingenuity and wealth offset the rising malaise and sense of menace pervading European culture. It is not difficult to see parallels with our own early twenty-first century period.

Then came the twentieth century, with its parade of unimaginable and irrational horrors, its fratricidal wars, genocides, global destruction, and unspeakable barbarism. All this led to the collapse of the ideal of progress as the means to alleviate human misery and of belief in the power of reason to achieve this end. In the face of evil and the overwhelming power of oppressive ideologies, existentialism and the philosophy of the absurd came to dominate continental thought, while in Britain, philosophy confined itself to the analysis of linguistic logic. The only recourse remaining to rationality conceived as a still believable, useful, and broadly applicable tool of human activity appeared—and appears—to be scientific/technological reason; but even this—the *ultimate* instrumentalization of reason—is equivocal, since science and technology have so manifestly served the cause of evil quite as much as the cause of good.

Without question, science and its practical-minded twin, technology, have brought inestimable material benefits to humankind and opened vast horizons for investigation and development in every area of life. The traditional society of scarcity is almost extinct. Education and literacy are widespread, medical science is making physical pain more bearable, eradicating many diseases, and extending the span of human life, and a measure of material comfort, leisure, and personal flourishing is increasingly a goal for the masses as well as for an elite. Individual freedom to pursue goals one has set for oneself is becoming a normative aim in many parts of the world, for women as well as for men. In a certain sense, then, freedom and reason, those qualities built into man-as-*imago Dei*, can be said to be functioning effectively in late modern society, despite the abyssal depths into which mankind plummeted in the twentieth century.

But at the same time, the superficiality, greed, ugliness, selfishness, and incivility of modern societies are increasingly the source of deep malaise and dissatisfaction. Societies of scarcity, while lacking commodities, were in many essential ways, such as those having to do with family and community, more satisfying than commodity-saturated societies like our own. Industrialization tends almost invariably to uproot people from the land and household economies and alienate them in vast, noisy, polluted urban agglomerations where their senses of inner identity and historical community are largely lost. Television, computer games, and proliferating gadgets replace conversation and genuine relationship. Men and women are driven to live more and more as self-focused units rather than as persons-in-relationship, and even the most intimate ties of family are inclined to grow superficial and strained as the exploitive industrial and commercial forces press in from outside. Even the increased longevity of life is a mixed blessing, to the degree that modernity, while extending the life-span, does not accompany this feat with any increased sense of meaning or purpose to the longer life one may now lead. To the contrary, technological society, cut off from transcendence, provides no meaning to life beyond the acquisition of more money and ease.[22] This state of affairs does not correspond to the deeper needs of human beings made in God's image, and profound dis-ease, frustration, and often despair and rage accompanied by violence, are the result.

Technology is experienced by more and more people as an all-encompassing web, a kind of second man-made creation, which enslaves and circumscribes human beings and the planet they live on quite as much as it liberates them. Modern man, for all his cumulative knowledge, seems flat, distanced from himself like a spectator looking at a screen. He seems to walk beside life, handling it as from the outside, with machines always interposed between himself and reality. The abstract and the virtual have more place in his life than the concrete and the immediate. His sense of time and space have become atrophied and emptied of meaning precisely to the degree that permanence and location have been superseded in his experience by the increasing velocity and ephemerality of every aspect of life and by constant geographical displacement of an abstract, disembodied sort, where for hundreds, even thousands, of miles, in cars, planes, and trains, his body hardly makes contact with the ground or comes to rest at a *place*. Life is a series of points on a graph, scarcely connected with each other at all. It is lived as in a vacuum, under the conditions of a laboratory experiment.

---

22. For an incisive and deeply felt analysis of the modern predicament, see Berry, *Art of the Common Place*, especially part II.

Indeed, the comparison of their lives with those of rats undergoing tests in a maze is one readily made by people living in large cities today.

Time and space themselves have been instrumentalized. Increasingly, our experience of the present is like a dot in the middle of a blank sheet. The future, lacking any divine dimension for the average modern person, is empty of real hope, and the past, rendered to a large extent obsolete by the relentless technological drive forward, serves mainly not as a source of wisdom or identity, with strength to stabilize and orient the present, but as a mine for the extraction of scientific knowledge about other epochs. The enormous effort to know and salvage the past is a mirror image of the effort to fathom the natural world and the cosmos—it is interesting, exciting, and useful in certain ways, but the knowledge it yields seems, again, to be appropriated as from the outside and to lead, generally speaking, not to wonder or silence, but to a sense of power, clamorous intellectual cacophony, and an obsessive thirst for still more knowledge. The quest for knowledge as a source of truth and means to wisdom, one of the great pillars of Western civilization, has long since yielded to a self-serving hunger for information and data as a source of power.

To live truly in the present is very different from living in the split second of the now. It cannot be done without an organic anchorage in the past, in some tradition and sense of continuity; and it cannot be done without some way of anticipating the future with hope—not only our own future beyond our own death, but also the future of our society and race, of the collective we belong to. Lacking such hope, we lack purpose, and without purpose, for ourselves and our race, we are less than fully human. This is surely one of the chief reasons why modern man, strangely suspended in space, abstracted from earth and orbiting it like an astronaut, seems somehow two-dimensional, hollow-chested. If he stops to pause and think and contemplate the other-than-himself—the other-for-itself-and-not-for-himself—he is immediately out of his depth and lost, for the *other*—whether person or object—as a reality of being beyond his reach and will-to-power, is alien; it is knowable only to the receptive heart and the participative spirit.

But modern men and women have no time to wait on nature, to contemplate, to reflect quietly. Time and space and everything contained within them have been made functions of utility and, increasingly, of *commercial* utility. Indeed, unadulterated nature, free of human footprints, is nowhere to be found anymore. Wherever he goes today, man finds his own, often mocking, face staring out at him. He lives in a huge house of mirrors that reflect at every turn his sad, soft, sallow face, with its slightly empty expression, distraught and anxious.

The flattening of the modern soul and the inherent narcissism of technological man are also manifest at the economic level. The commercialization of all reality has totalitarian consequences that are rarely called by that name, but should be. It is scandalous that, despite an overall increase in the world's wealth, the rich, technically competent nations are growing richer and more technically competent, while other nations, especially those in Africa, are falling farther and farther behind, materially speaking. The freedom and opportunity so vaunted in the West are precisely what billions of people in other parts of the world are being deprived of by that same West. Our continued economic exploitation of underdeveloped but resource-rich countries is an iniquitous extension and expression of the colonial policies of the nineteenth and twentieth centuries, hidden under a deceptively more benign exterior. The unscrupulous manipulation of markets for their own benefit by technologically advanced democracies, resulting in the impoverishment and virtual enslavement of millions of people, reflects the hypocrisy and moral shallowness of these democracies, even as they trumpet the quality of life their own citizens are said to enjoy. As the Second World War ended the first phase of modern colonialism, it is not difficult to imagine a Third World War ending the current phase.

Many of the exploited nations find themselves caught between different cultural realities that they cannot reconcile. They are losing their old cultural identities without being able to replace them with new ones. The mythical apprehension of the world characteristic of primitive societies, where organic participation in natural cycles and processes gave life meaning, is no longer a possibility in our day; but for non-Western peoples lacking the cultural infrastructure that makes science possible, the scientific rationality of modernity is also out of reach and can loom as a terrible menace, a mountain impossible to climb. The resulting loss of the old identity, coupled with the loss of hope in the possibility of acquiring a new identity, creates an essentially tragic dilemma and can lead to despair and cultural suicide as uprooted peoples, feeling under threat, fall back on ethnic, tribal, religious, or national identities and defend them violently, sometimes to the point of seeking to annihilate other threatened peoples. This is one of the most terrible consequences of modernity and its all-encompassing technological, instrumentalizing ethos.

VI

But freedom is not simply being lost by many populations in the developing world. In the midst of the flurry of opportunities and possibilities of all kinds that the modern culture of production and communication sets before us, we are losing our freedom *to be*. So insistent is the pressure *to do and to make, to choose and to have,* that the very capacity *to be* is atrophying, actually disappearing from the life of civilized man, even as the sixth sense (and so much lore and skill with it) possessed by primitive peoples living in intimate proximity with nature, has long since disappeared. One recalls the psalmist's exhortation, *"Be still and know that I am God"* (Ps 46:10a). This has become almost impossible for us today. The depth of existence—of *our* existence—is flattening out, at the very moment, ironically, that we reach into the depths of space with our telescopes, to the bottom of the sea with our bathyspheres, into our brains with laser beams, and into our minds with psychological instruments, theoretical analysis, and meditative techniques (always *techniques*—we scarcely know how to function in nontechnical terms, that is, in terms that seek *not to control* but to *relate to* the objects of our consideration).

Even the abundance of choice in Western societies can contribute to this flattening out as, solicited on all sides and at every moment by countless voices and words and items, we are drawn to flit from thing to thing, from product to product, unable to linger on any or be satisfied with any. Furthermore, though we may understandably exult inside a well-stocked supermarket before the limitless choice at our disposal, the very limitlessness can actually be suffocating; and—perhaps more importantly—we may not even notice that the supermarket culture *itself*, as a basic aspect of modern technological society and as representative of that society, for better but also for worse, is increasingly *imposed* on us, leaving us little if any room for maneuver. The example of the supermarket may stand as a metaphor for our situation in consumerist modern societies. Our freedom of choice and action is much more ambiguous than we usually suppose.

We hardly know any longer how to be still and receive from the *other*, whether it be an object, a person, or God himself. We see with our scientific probes and our endless critical analyses of everything only what our own instruments tell us. They tell us a great deal, undoubtedly, and a great deal about the actuality of the objective world out there and even about the connection between it and our own subjectivity. But they involve us in that connection only on our own terms, functionally. We consider the world *from the outside*; the connection does not become a *relation*.

Now this yields immensely interesting, exciting, and useful information about all kinds of things; but it also masks a tragic reality. Any sense of the mystical that might graze our consciousness as we observe some aspect of reality, we instinctively take to be a purely subjective and unreliable emotion. This has effectively become an instinct, replacing the sixth sense of primitive peoples and the sense of mystery before the sheer *presence* of the world—of *being*—that characterized all premodern cultures, most notably that of the Greeks. We have forfeited the capacity to look *into* that reality, to be drawn by it into its particular *form* of being and, beyond that, into its *very being*. We look *at* objects, not *into* them. We have the greatest difficulty in actually *receiving* anything from the world that is not solicited by ourselves, anything that might come to us from an object itself as we stand before it and simply take in its givenness, its existential reality. We have lost the sense of wonder and, with it, something essentially human. In a word, utilitarianism is shrivelling the human capacity to *love*.

I have written about the progressive distortion and, finally, the loss in Western culture of the biblical teaching on the *imago Dei*, with the result that our ethics, including our admirable emphasis on human rights, lacks both a transcendent reference and a solid foundation. In the constantly shifting sands of our technological age, where all ethical and philosophical speculation other than that of the most utilitarian and empirical variety is extremely difficult to sustain, the absence of any rock on which to build bodes ill for democracy's future. It is impossible for a democratic society to hold together peacefully for long, especially in a culture driven by technical innovation and the cult of efficiency and productivity, if a truly universal ethic, assented to by all, has been shattered into the countless private and competing value systems of the citizens who make up the society, each stressing the primacy of the desires, goals, and rights of the individual—indeed, of *this particular individual* holding *this value system*—over against any absolute and transcendent norm.

As made in God's image, men and women will continue to manifest freedom and reason in a variety of ways, but the field of action and the content of these God-given capacities will steadily shrink, while the ontological core of the *imago Dei*, having to do with our indefeasible relation to the divine, will continue to be perverted into multiple idolatries of a speciously spiritual or religious nature, most commonly of a dualistic or gnostic sort that presses the "lord" of our modern materialistic pantheon—*technology*—to be wedded to some kind of spiritual consort (i.e., *system*) in order to wear a more human face. In this way, one or another aspect of human culture is and will be absolutized by being linked with spirit, and man himself is and will be indirectly divinized. All reference to a personal God who creates and redeems, or to a moral absolute beyond the ever changing values of humankind—an absolute expressive of a natural law ordained by a Creator—is and will be carefully avoided.

Certainly there are many voices speaking out against this overwhelming thrust of the modern world with its scientific/technological worldview and associated varieties of religiosity and paganism which, while vaunting (rightly) the ideal of liberty and human rights, in fact, at the same time, also undermines them. God has not abandoned his world, and in man himself, made in his Creator's image, the aspiration toward the good, the true, and the beautiful is forever reasserting itself.

Having provided several perspectives on the *imago Dei* in our modern context, I shall now turn to the God-given mandate that accompanies God's creation of human beings. This will lead us to aesthetic considerations and a closer analysis of beauty.

VII

Genesis 1:28 is an integral part of the revelation that man is created in the image of God. Men and women are commissioned to be caretakers of God's world, stewards and guardians of his created Earth. As the Creator's personal representatives and agents/stewards, they are to exercise benevolent and fruitful leadership over it. Although, in God's purpose, they must not plunder or desecrate the natural world, they are called to nurture and develop it. Physical creatures themselves, made of dust and so akin to all things material, but also spiritual beings like God himself and the angels, endowed with reason and moral freedom, they are eminently equipped to carry out this mandate. They are of both the natural and the spiritual worlds. Being responsible to God, they are responsible to his creation. As spiritual beings endowed with reason, they are called to tend, use, embellish, and transform the raw material of the natural world. God has contracted it out to them, and they are called to rule over it. To do this, they must exercise kingly power, but this power is to be a reflection of the divine wisdom by which the world was made (Prov 8:22–31; Ps 104:24). It is not to be capricious, arbitrary, or rapacious. *Homo fabiens* is called to work out the destiny of *Homo sapiens*.

In Genesis 2:19–20, we find the key to the application of this mandate: God brought before Adam the creatures he had formed from the ground *"to see what he would name them."* However Christians in different traditions understand this text, it carries an incontrovertible meaning. All created things, organic and inorganic, not just the beasts of the field and the birds of the air, are to be named. That naming is performed by Adam, not Eve, because it is an exercise of the masculine authority granted to the human race, as distinct from the feminine power of nourishing life. Although this masculine authority and this feminine power are to be found in both men and women, the primary repository of the former is in the male and that of the latter is in the female. So, on this understanding, it is *Adam* who is called by God to name.

Here we have the creative power of the word, as exercised by man made in the image of God, that is, in the image of the Word by whom the worlds were bodied forth. As the Creator by his word brought form out of formlessness and light into darkness (Gen 1:2–3), so his representative on earth will bring civilized order into nature. It is by the creative power of the word that God's commission to his human creature to subdue and care for the world will be carried out.

Naming presupposes prior relationship. Man is not identical with the rest of creation, he is above it; but he is bound to it intrinsically—ontologically—just as he is bound ontologically to God. Naming of the other brings about objective knowledge that is only possible because of and on the basis of the prior subjective, tacit *relation* to the other that is constitutive of human being. The order of being precedes and makes possible the order of knowing. Naming mediates between being and knowing; it calls form and particularity out of being into intelligible existence.

The word does not replace the object named. To name the other does not mean to appropriate the other; it is not a possessing, not a destroying of the other's integrity. It does no violence to the other. It is a symbolic identification of the other by a rational human being that enables the primordial kinship between man and other creatures to enter into the epistemological sphere, the sphere of civilization, and so to become capable of development.

An important nuance must be added here, lest one think that outside the act of naming we have no knowledge of the world. Even the subjective, tacit relation of human beings to the other is a kind of knowledge—but it is a visceral and spiritual knowledge, not an intellectual one. This is the part of truth to be discovered in the animistic beliefs often found among primitive peoples, whatever demonic perversions these may also enshrine. The human creature, ontologically integrated into the material world God has commanded him to oversee, can know—not by intellect but by the penetration of his spirit—all other created objects, both organic and inorganic. The word penetration is apt: this knowledge is of an erotic kind; it consists in the going into the other in love and the receiving of the other in love. To love and know a rock in this sense, for example, involves the consideration with wonder of its existence as over *against* and as over *before* oneself, in such a way that I, the human subject, go out toward (i.e., appreciate/penetrate/*love*) the object—this rock—thus uncovering its beauty and becoming the recipient of its created splendor. Investing the rock through my attentive and respectful awareness, I become the beneficiary of its radiance; giving myself to it contemplatively, I find that I am receiving back from it its own singular reality. Desire is basic to this movement. The physical may of course also play a part, if I am able to touch and know with my hand—my body—the object of my attention.

The aesthetic component of this God-determined relation of a human subject to an inanimate rock, a *relation* that turns into a *relationship*, an *encounter*, by virtue of my freely offered human appreciation, becomes evident at this point and will be developed shortly. Suffice it to say here that the rock's beauty, which radiates out to me as I consider the peculiar object that it is, is the expression of its truth, that is, of its existence precisely as this created form, as this unique rock. My experience of beauty arises from the erotic interplay of my subjectivity as a human person made in God's image and the rock's objectivity as a created form with its own identity and autonomy.

To return to the matter of naming, we may say that the name granted to anything in a given language is contingent and subject to change; but this does not mean that the link between language and object is arbitrary and merely a matter of custom. On account of the *imago Dei*, understood to be inclusive of the mandate given to men and women to oversee, both the word and the bond with the other are inherent in human being. It follows that naming is fundamentally meaningful and establishes *effectively* the relation already existing between the namer and the object named. As the primordial manifestation of reason, naming brings the other into the realm of intelligibility. The very possibility of this is cause for wonder and arises from the peculiar position that the human being as *imago Dei* occupies in the created universe: essentially bound to it and also essentially transcending it.

The enterprise of science, which we shall be discussing later in this connection, is a notable focusing, within a particular area of inquiry, of this correspondence between human reason and the objective world in which humanity has his place. Nature is intelligible to rational investigation, just as an object becomes intelligible when we name it. It is impossible to make sense of this remarkable state of affairs outside of the revelation and doctrine of the *imago Dei*.

Because giving a name to an object does not replace the object but makes a rational bridge between the namer and the object—an achievement made possible on the one hand by the God-given power of human reason, and on the other hand by the fact that both namer and object are created beings standing on the same ground—the two, as autonomous creatures, will forever stand *over against* each other and, at the same time, *before* each other, face to face. That I can know an ant or a tree by naming it in no way deprives the ant or the tree of its autonomy before me and before God.

My naming opens the path to natural knowledge of the other. Yet, as we have seen, there are other kinds of knowledge. Natural knowledge, made possible through naming, teaches us about the *form* of the being of the other; it teaches me nothing about its being *per se*. Knowledge of the *being* of the other is mystical and arises not out of the word but out of silence. It is spiritual, the fruit of communion. In the manner suggested above in our discussion of the rock, it starts with *eros* but moves *through* it, *through* desire, *through* beauty itself, to a contemplation of the ultimate truth of which beauty is the radiance; and this truth is not impersonal being, it is not an idea—it is rather the *Personal Being who is the Triune God*, the *Creator of all that is, by the power of his Word and breath*. Here the primordial, preverbal relation between man and God on the one hand and between man and other creatures on the other, is actualized, not as conceptual construct but as *ontological presence*. Here man has nothing to say or do—he has only to wait, to be still, to receive. Here is silence.

It is precisely in silence that God speaks. In him, silence and speech are one; through them together, he manifests his *glory*, he makes himself *present*. Sound, music, language—these only have meaning, and can only be understood, within and against the backdrop of prior and primordial silence. One of the most flagrant manifestations of our modern alienation from both God and the natural world is the unwillingness and incapacity of so many today to endure silence, much less enjoy it. Homeless, they seek security in noise and babble, rather than finding peace in the silence of the Word, their ultimate Source and home.

VII

We have seen that naming, as the primary exercise of reason, is the means provided by God for men and women to carry out their mandate to rule, tend, and nourish the world. The process of naming involves two fundamental kinds of activity: science and art. In these ways, man *knows* the world.[23] A third kind of activity, which, as I have suggested, we may call mystical contemplation, goes beyond naming into the wordless realm of the knowledge of being itself and of being himself. No hard-and-fast boundaries separate these three activities—reason, intuition, and contemplation

---

23. I am taking science here to be, in a basic sense, an extension of classical philosophy, insofar as both involve investigation of some kind into the nature and structure of given reality. I am not here making distinctions between the very different Greek and modern conceptions of science.

play a part in all of them. At this point we shall examine the first two, giving special emphasis to art and the nature of the beauty it reveals.[24]

In both science and art—the two basic modes of naming and so of knowing the world—analysis, intuition, and mathematics are active. There is much overlapping. Yet for all that, the two approaches to knowledge are very different. The one is essentially analytical and, by extension, practical: it investigates what is; it dissects, abstracts, calculates; it devises theories and tools; it divides things and breaks them down into their constitutive parts in order to understand how they function and to find underlying general laws governing their behavior. Modern science, combining theory with observation and experimentation, as it has taken shape since the late sixteenth century, seeks to know and thus to master the materiality of the world, which is why technology must be seen as a logical extension of it and not as something inherently different because it is practically oriented.

Mathematical language assumes increasing importance in the history of culture, doing things verbal language cannot do with respect to the mastery of materiality. It is an abstract language, a specialized language, that permits us to penetrate, know, and articulate the world of matter, the world of laws and forces, in their visible and invisible reaches and connections. By its kind of naming it penetrates reality to understand how things work; its apprehension of the forms of being is essentially cognitive, even if *eros*, the desire to know and to pierce, is the driving force behind it, as in the case of the kind of naming/knowing we considered above in our discussion of the rock. A relationship between knower and known is established here too, although it is cooler, more distant, than in the case of art. But in both modes, the knowing is relational, arising out of the inherent bond between subject and object.

The other way of naming is intuitive and concerned with meaning, with sense, with the spiritual aspect of the invisible and visible. This is the way of art, poetry, drama, novels, paintings, sculptures, music, and films, along with architecture—which is a product of both science and art—occupying a kind of bridge position. Art aims to represent the world—across

---

24. I am using the word "art" in the broadest sense to include all the main forms of the fabricating imagination (as distinct from the investigating imagination): poetry, drama, the novel, painting, sculpture, music, architecture, film, dance. This being said, we must immediately add that the two kinds of imagination are, in some sense, the same imagining viewed from different perspectives, and constantly overlap or interpenetrate each other. Any artist knows that what he or she makes is also somehow a discovery; and any mathematician knows that his or her discoveries are in some sense also inventions. This interactivity of the subject and object, which has become essential to modern physics and to enlightened modern discourse in general, finds its possibility and explanation in the revelation of the *imago Dei*.

the whole range of the artist's experience of it—in some essential and meaningful way, to master it by gathering together numbers of its elements and focusing them, condensing and transforming them by the power of imagination, into a synthetic work that has the value of a symbol, a sign, and in a certain sense (as we shall see), of a sacrament.

Art is essentially intuitive and synthetic, not analytical. Whereas mathematics represents the world abstractly, art represents it through the medium of concrete particulars: words, notes, pigments, lines, stone, wood, movement, images on celluloid. Both modes of knowledge and mastery have universal import, but in entirely different ways. Through material and concrete means, art penetrates the spiritual dimension of material reality, the breath within it, one might say. From within materiality, and using, as a means to its end, natural laws and techniques which themselves may have been discovered scientifically, through analysis and experimentation—laws of perspective, say, proportion, tonal relations, or spatial composition—art works by tapping into the order of the spirit, finding or making meaning and significance. The aim of art, unlike science, is not to discover the fundamental laws and structures of the universe for their own sake, even though, of course, it uses natural laws for its own purposes. Scientific knowledge and praxis—action—are not its objectives. Science, by contrast, enables us to grasp reality by knowing its inner mathematical workings, but it does not enable us to know its meaning or express its spiritual mystery.

These two modes of knowing complement each other. We are less than human if we lack either. Both convey order to us; both make reality intelligible.

It is my contention that we have this capacity, this power, to find and to make order—both—by virtue of our being created in the image of God who, as Creator of all that is, is the great orderer. Order in its full sense is the work of reason, of course—but of reason *as an expression of love*, of reason *ordered to love*. Both law and contingency are essential to it. Order as I am using it, both divine and human, is at the farthest possible remove from legalism and uniformity, and also from chaos. What we find here is infinite diversity and development, but within an overarching frame and vision, coherent and dynamic. This is the opposite of chaos. Chance and contingency have their role in such a universe, certainly, and a very important one—but *within the overarching frame,* within the *divine*—or by extension, the *human*—decree. There is no place in this decree for chaos in the strict sense of the word. Here we are, in fact, in the realm of truth, of *reality as it is*, and we might call this truth the *structure* or expression of goodness, or, equally, the *manifestation of being.*

Beauty of whatever sort—whether physical, moral, or spiritual—is the *radiance*—the outshining *splendor*—of this truth. Goodness, truth, and beauty together are modes of love, as the Father, Son, and Holy Spirit are the distinct personal modes of the Godhead, of the One God-who-is-love, who has been revealed supremely in Jesus Christ to be love. Both science and art, as human expressions of truth, radiate beauty, more or less resplendently according to the nature of the achievement.

Two points must be made here before more can be said about beauty. First, we need to note that the context for the mandate to rule the world, which in turn involves and requires the work of science and art, is patently *theological*. Having created humankind and equipped his human creatures, God proceeds to give them a task. Science and art are the means of carrying out that task, within whatever social and political orders where groups of human beings may find themselves. In order for science and art to bear healthy fruit in any given culture, to enhance sociability, knowledge, and wisdom and to provide fundamental meaning to life, the transcendent reference must be maintained. This reference points to a reality invisible to our eyes, beyond our mastering reach, greater and more lasting than earthly human life. The cords binding the invisible and visible realms are composed of strands of goodness, truth, and beauty, and their strength is eternal.

In earlier stages of human culture, science and art were, of course, intimately linked to the sacred. In the West, this remained the case, broadly, well into the seventeenth century, even though direct reference to the sacred—to biblical themes in art, and to divine law and causality in philosophy and science—declined progressively from the first quarter of the sixteenth century and markedly from the period beginning a century later. Nevertheless, transcendent reality—the realm of the divine and the spiritual considered to be objective—remained unquestionably the broad backdrop of creative human enterprise in the West until the last third of the eighteenth century. From then on, this backdrop began to fade.

With modernity, as suggested earlier from a different perspective, we have entered a new stage of human development, which has seen both art and science progressively severed from their unifying theological frame and root, in keeping with the movement of Western culture as a whole. I believe this is why they have increasingly lost their balance, direction, and mutual rapport in the course of the twentieth century, and no longer serve today as bulwarks and sources either of authentic protest or of authentic hope. A central thrust of the great period of modern painting, sculpture, literature, music, and architecture that gathered momentum from the last quarter of the nineteenth century in Europe[25] and extended into the 1960s has been, in reaction against the materialism of the age, the quest for some kind of spiritual/metaphysical dimension—even if it be, misguidedly, as it has sometimes been, the perverted spirituality which is gnostic nihilism—to replace both the eroded Christian heritage as it existed at the end of the nineteenth century and the collapsed faith in Enlightenment reason in the wake of the unimaginable savagery of world wars and genocide and, paradoxically, during the same period, of astounding scientific discoveries about the material world. Few of the protagonists in this stunning explosion of creativity were overtly Christian believers, far from it, but their quest through the arts for a new, authentic apprehension of the nature of man (man/woman) and for a fresh vision of the absolute may arguably be understood as a tumultuous expression of man-made-in-God's-image, tragically alienated from his Creator (the *imago* inverted) but hungering for salvation, for union with the divine, even while resisting, for the most part, the call of the risen Christ. This formidable revolution in the arts has found a variety of avenues, such as a recasting of myth; or a loosening and dislocation of poetic forms and literary techniques; or a primitive, expressionistic vitalism; or an upwelling of the subconscious; or a consummate projection of subjectivity in the form of abstract art; or a powerfully imaginative reconfiguration of pictorial space; or a fresh apprehension of form, matter, light, color, musical tonality, and indeed of speech itself as having, in the first place, value in their own right apart from any figurative content they display, and as being, secondly somehow, bearers of meaning and order and perhaps pointers toward something sacred and metaphysical.[26]

25. A representative, admittedly arbitrary and limited, sample of such painters and sculptors in Europe and America would include Manet, Monet, Munch, Bonnard, Rodin, Seurat, Van Gogh, Gauguin, Cézanne, Matisse, Picasso, Braque, Kandinsky, Chagall, Klee, Rousseau, Rouault, de Chirico, Giacometti, Morandi, Dali, Duchamp, Mondrian, Malevitch, Hartung, Soulages, Nicolas de Staël, Moore, Hepworth, Arp, Brancusi, Chilida, Calder, David Smith, Pollock, Rothko, and Newman. One might name dozens of others, of course. On the negative side of the modernist movement, a strong thrust toward nihilism was also very evident.

26. In the sphere of Western literature, one could cite, as a sampling from broadly the same period, Gerard Manley Hopkins, Baudelaire, Laforgue, Rimbaud, Mallarmé, Valéry, Claudel, Péguy, Apollinaire, Conrad, Ford, Joyce, Wolff, David Jones, Beckett, Lawrence, Ibsen, Mann, Broch, Proust, Bernanos, Mauriac, Saint-John Perse, Cendrars, Éluard, Aragon, Ponge, Bonnefoy, Yeats, Eliot, Pound, Auden, Stevens, William Carlos Williams, Frost, Lowell, Roethke, Nemerov, Bishop, Plath, Tranströmer, Rilke, Kafka, Blok, Celan, Mandelstam, Akhmatova, Pasternak, Lorca, Faulkner, Hemingway, Steinbeck, Dos Passos, O'Connor, Nabokov, O'Neill, Borges, Fuentes, Marquez, Machado, Neruda, Seferis, and Milosz, among others. In the realm of classical music, a few preeminent examples are Debussy, Ravel, Bruckner, Mahler, Strauss, Stravinsky, Shostakovich, Vaughan Williams, Schoenberg, Britten, Bartok, Berg, Sibelius, Webern,

But it seems to me that this great movement, of which the last genuinely innovative phase in painting, in my view, was the American Abstract Expressionists and Minimalists of the 1960s and 1970s, has run out of creative energy. The nihilistic streak in it—a modern form of gnosticism—reflecting despair about humanity and the material world and entailing a rejection or mockery of both, appears to me to be threatening the positive quest in modernism to affirm, somehow, a renewed transcendental vision without, at least overtly, the trappings of Christian faith. That there is in fact today a genuine renewal of art in the Christian community is undeniable, but that is not the point I am making here. The roots nurturing Western civilization—namely, the Hebraic-Christian tradition—had already been pulled up and repudiated by a majority of the thinking classes before the revolutionary modernist movement began in the early twentieth century, and the sap of vital faith had already more or less dried up in the old forms by which it had been known in European history. This is precisely why the foremost modernists saw the need for a complete overhaul of artistic conceptuality and practice.

But if the roots of a tree are dying, eventually the trunk and branches must die as well. I wonder if this is not happening. There is no longer any integrating transcendental vision to sustain or energize Western culture, with the result that every individual artist must fabricate his or her own picture of reality. Original work may come out of this, of course, but that is not the same thing as a civilizational dynamic vision. There is, in a word, nothing to replace the rejected Christian faith and worldview.

The amazing scientific discoveries of the last 100 years, while affirming the power of human rationality, cannot by themselves provide a metaphysical worldview which satisfies the human spirit created in the image of God. What remains is materialism and consumerism, with nihilism and boredom at their core. In this context, the gnostic drive, in its characteristic quest for redemption by escaping/overcoming mankind and the material world as presently constituted (both of which it sees as contemptible), is developing new strength and attractiveness in Western society and now takes the novel form of transhumanism, which aims not, as in earlier expressions of gnosticism, to flee the abhorred human condition via *spiritual* knowledge—*spiritual* gnosis—but rather to transform and surpass this human condition via *technological* knowledge—*technological* gnosis. This objective, which goes way beyond the notion of augmentation, is intended to issue in a new creation, an ideal which, for anyone with eyes to see, is evidently an

---

Messiaen, Pärt, and, of course, in the midst of this musical revolution, there was the tremendous explosion of jazz.

imitation of the redeemed new creation in Christ. I do not see true creativity in this gnostic drive, only illusion and destruction.

This current state of affairs has led, in the sphere of art, to what looks to me to be a kind of artistic anarchy and flashiness, with an attendant commercialization of the artistic scene and, often, the substitution of banal novelty or sheer ugliness for authentic creativity. I do not deny for a moment that truly creative work is being done today in the various fields of art, but it appears to me that there has been a falling off of genuine creative vision relative to the earlier generations of the modernist movement. Certainly fine novels, poetry, music, drama, films, and modern dance are being written and performed with great technical competence, experimental sculptures and paintings are being produced, and remarkable buildings and innovative urban realizations are being erected. Technology itself is undoubtedly opening up all kinds of new artistic possibilities, and it is clear that many people today, yearning for spiritual substance to their lives, are looking in the direction of art to fill their needs. A powerful ecological vision is clearly impacting the creative arts and may turn out to be the carrier of a potent new modernism, with an authentically spiritual dimension, as nature, with its inherent implication of creation and, hence, of a Creator, is rediscovered and embraced. I very much hope so. The fact is that my own knowledge of this current work in the various arts today is very limited, so I mustn't presume to discuss it further. I can only hope that my negative conjectures may prove less accurate than my positive ones.

Concomitantly with the modernist project in the arts and the phenomenal development of the sciences in the twentieth century, the church itself, in all its different expressions, was also undergoing renewal in Europe and elsewhere. But the full impact of this renewal would not be felt until the second half of the twentieth century, and even now, in the early twenty-first century, is hardly recognized by those same thinking classes that for the most part have long since put paid to the Christian religion and who only have eyes to see the decline of Christian faith in Western society. Vatican II and ecumenical *rapprochement* between the Christian denominations/confessions are signal institutional examples of this renewal, as is the massive shift of the Christian center of gravity from Europe and America to Africa and to a lesser extent to South America. At the popular level, the outpouring of the Holy Spirit associated with the Pentecostal movement that began in the early twentieth century and has spread throughout the world has had an enormous, mostly positive, impact on Christian faith and practice; one of its expressions, the charismatic movement, has powerfully impacted the church worldwide and generated countless influential local Christian communities. Another significant development is the rise of messianic Judaism, a current within Judaism that is concerned with bringing Jews to discover in Jesus their Messiah. This movement, which sees itself as preparing the way for the return of the Messiah in glory, is gathering strength, especially in America and Israel. A last example, at the theological level, has been the "rediscovery" of the doctrine of the Holy Trinity associated initially with the innovative work of Karl Barth, Karl Rahner, and Thomas Torrance. The importance of this development, coupled with the "rediscovery" of the Holy Spirit, cannot be exaggerated. Underneath the radar screen of the media, there is much-needed purification and deep renewal going on in the church in our day, accompanied, inevitably, by persecution. I see this as a providential counterweight to the powerful anti-Christian forces at work today, not least in the West, intent on destroying forever the witness to Jesus Christ.

As an illustration of these anti-Christian forces, one notes that in the contemporary postmodern period in Western society as a whole, beginning in the 1970s, reference to an objective transcendent reality is simply absent from most scientific and artistic activity and from intellectual discourse in general. Indeed, as George Steiner points out, absence itself—the *absence* of a transcendent reality—is a central preoccupation of late twentieth-century art and literature.[27] The silence of which I spoke earlier, as the context of the eternal Word, has been turned inside out and become the *silence of absence*. Relativism—our modern creed—and the wars and genocides of the last century, have undermined belief in absolute truth of any kind and replaced it with the counterfeit absolute of ideology, with the result that a *potpourri* of individualized, subjectively derived beliefs has crowded out even the residue of genuine, albeit vague, spirituality and the search for a kind of transcendence to be found in the classical period of modernism.

Having closed off God's word in our thoughts and actions, we are paying a terrible price and find that, for us in our self-enclosed finitude, there is no *word* coming our way from what we perceive to be the infinite void. As a result, evil has had, and continues to have, a field day. Murderous ideologies have flourished and are flourishing because genuine, dynamic Christian faith, with its transformative ethical consequences and its construction of community, is in short supply and mocked by the majority of opinion-makers in contemporary Western culture. We have filled and continue to fill the void in which we twist and turn with narcissistic self-indulgence, with a variety of humanistic and philosophical projections such as Hegelian idealism, with its dialectics of history and Spirit, romantic imagination, Nietzschean will-to-power, evolutionism (everything out of nothing),

---

27. See Steiner, *Language and Silence*; Steiner, *Real Presences*; Steiner, *Grammars of Creation*. Samuel Beckett, Paul Celan, John Cage, Alban Berg, and Casimir Malevitch can be cited in this connection, among many possibilities.

Heideggerian being, Sartrean existentialism and nothingness, aesthetic pantheism, New Ageism, satanism, and the apotheosis of gnosticism which is transhumanism.[28]

All such projections operate today, of course, in the modern context of a hypertrophy of technology and media, fueled by scientific discovery, and resulting in unabashed utilitarianism and the commercialization and quantification of everything. The key point here for my purpose in this essay is that philosophy, science, and art, abstracted from the metaphysical context that has always given them meaning and direction, must eventually lose their moorings, inner purpose, and coordination, and end up by fragmenting the culture of which they are a part and breaking it down instead of unifying and constructing it. This goes far to explain, fundamentally, the *disorientation* of modern Western culture.

VIII

We come now to the question of beauty as we find it in nature and in art. The reality of our human relation to other creatures is what points us in the direction of our relation to the Creator. Neither brute nature, nor speculative philosophy, science, or art can in themselves reveal to us the true God in his full and personal reality; but all of them can and do give intimations of his presence; they can and do *point toward him*. They are tracers, signals, signs, like lightning in the night. As signs of God's presence, they are signs of hope. It is in this connection that we may speak of beauty as a source of hope, as it points us through and beyond its object to the unseen Source of the object.[29] Beauty, truth, and goodness, as we encounter them here and there, now and then, fill us with a yearning, a longing. They satisfy us without satisfying us. This is true both in nature and in art. A magnificent night sky laden with stars fills us with wonder, and also with an ache; so does Van Gogh's *Starry Night*. But they are very different, obviously. What exactly is going on here?

---

28. In this connection, see Denis Donoghue's incisive discussion of Stevens and Eliot in Donoghue, *Words Alone*, ch. 9.

29. A citation from Gregory of Nyssa, *Life of Moses*, paras. 231–32, is apt here: "Such an experience seems to me to belong to the soul which loves what is beautiful. Hope always draws the soul from the beauty which is seen to what is beyond, always kindles the desire for the hidden through what is constantly perceived. Therefore, the ardent lover of beauty, although receiving what is always visible as an image of what he desires, yet longs to be filled with the very stamp of the archetype. And the bold request which goes up the mountains of desire asks this: to enjoy the Beauty not in mirrors and reflections, but face to face."

Beauty, wherever found, both attracts and radiates. It both draws us to itself and comes out toward us; it takes us over, to a greater or lesser degree. Its form, revealed by light or sound, is overpowering, yet intimate. We are drawn into a relation to the beautiful object, made of rock or earth, cloud, water, flesh, or, in art, of words, notes, paint, stone, choreographed movement, etc. Beauty can also enslave, but only if our relation to reality is unhealthy, only if we are moving in the orbit of idolatry, if aestheticism becomes an end in itself, a god with a small "g", a substitute for truth, as is commonly the case today and indeed as has been the case increasingly since the dawn of romanticism two centuries ago. Moreover, we can appropriate beauty for evil purposes, in which case it is no longer beauty but merely the appearance of beauty, for beauty disconnected from truth has lost its inner reality.[30]

When our relation to the beautiful object is healthy, and we take the time to pause and contemplate it, beauty brings us face to face with the very *being* of the other. First of all, we enter into the mystery of the other's sheer *presence* by virtue of its qualities, its properties, its peculiar, unique, material, or musical, form. Its form and matter are inseparable, and its truth, made radiant in beauty, is lodged precisely here in this specific materiality or musical expression. Its truth is not behind or beyond itself, as it were, in some Platonic *idea* of it, distinct, greater, more perfect than itself; no, its truth is here and now, in *this* object having *these* qualities. *And yet*, the sheer *being* of the object, its hereness and nowness, its existence before us, autonomous yet mysteriously connected to us, attracting and radiating like a star, *points us beyond itself*.

For those to whom God has revealed himself in Jesus Christ, that beyond is no Platonic idea; it is the personal and holy Creator of all reality. He is the truth, the ultimate reality: *"I am the way, the truth, and the life,"* says Jesus, the incarnate Son of God (John 14:6a). And he who is truth is love. He is being-in-communion, the One in whom ontology and ethics (understood as relations-in-love) are one. To stand before being as manifest in a beautiful object, from a particle of matter seen through an electron microscope all the way up the ladder to a human person, is to stand before love and to be irradiated by it. The Creator called his creation good when he fashioned it by his Word; and the incarnation of that same Word in Jesus of Nazareth

---

30. One is reminded here of the great text in Ezekiel 28 about the King of Tyre, often thought to represent the figure of Lucifer: "You were the model of perfection, full of wisdom and perfect in beauty. You were in Eden, the garden of God . . . You were blameless in your ways from the day you were created till wickedness was found in you . . . Your heart became proud on account of your beauty, and you corrupted your wisdom because of your splendor" (vv. 12b, 13a, 15, 17a).

is an affirmation of the goodness and intrinsic value of the material world. At the same time, by his self-sacrificing work of grace, Jesus redeems that creation, fallen as it is because of human sin, and, as a result, mired in hatred and violence.

Art, in whatever medium, is a representation of the artist's experience of nature—of given reality—as that reality has been digested, internalized, intensified, concentrated, focused, recast into new form, or transfigured, according to the peculiar means of the medium and the imaginative power of the artist. It is not creation in the primal sense. That is a divine prerogative, not a human one, and the pretensions to divine power that some artists have claimed are simply hubris, quite ridiculous, what philosophers might call a confusion of categories. The artist does not, strictly speaking, imitate or copy, no matter how descriptive or naturalistic his or her style. That is impossible, logically speaking. Creatures, even if they be human beings made in God's image, are on an absolutely different level of being from the Creator. Rather, the artist *selects, abstracts, reconfigures, transforms;* he/she gathers original forms into new forms by virtue of their power to do so as beings themselves, fashioned in the image of God with the mandate to rule over creation, to shape, guide, rework it. By this means, artists—to a limited extent, of course—*know* nature, they *penetrate* and appropriate it for themselves and for the benefit of those who appreciate their art. This art is the expression of their knowledge, of their response to created reality, of their relation-in-love to the world. In a very real sense, as God's agent and co-worker in creation, the artist adds to the plenitude of *being*, though not, strictly speaking, to the plenitude of *creatures*; his/her work is *analogous* both to creation and to re-creation—that is, to redemption—while actually being neither.

This is why it may be possible, if great care is used, to speak of art as being, in a sense, sacramental. Its representation of original material elements in a way that brings before us the inner meaning of those elements in a fresh, formal unity that stands on its own, in the integrity of its own being, is operating, with respect to the original material, something similar to what the Jewish Seder celebration, or the Christian celebration of the Eucharist, are doing with respect to the Exodus from Egypt or to Christ's death on the cross. It has in itself no *primal* creative or redemptive power, but it points analogously and, in a certain sense, sacramentally, to primal creation and redemption. And in doing so, it renews us, it clarifies our thoughts and reinvigorates our hearts. It brings us life. In its apprehension of form, order, and the mystery of being, art lifts us toward the Source of being itself, who, by love, has created all that is and has structured it by his truth; and, by virtue of its own beauty, which is a reflection of beauty itself—beauty *himself*—art actually makes God the Source of being present to us in a certain sense, albeit a quite different sense from the eucharistic celebration, in which the personal presence of Christ is actualized by the Holy Spirit.

Scripture speaks of that truth of which beauty is the radiance, as God's Word incarnate in Jesus Christ, by whom the world was made and redeemed. As God's Word gives voice to the silence of the void, as it shapes space and measures time, so poetry and the arts do likewise, within the framework of the creation and the primal matter of being. Artistic creation, or recreation, reflects and echoes original creation, within a particular culture and society and at a specific moment in historical time. It enables us to hear, as it were, sounds that evoke primal reality, as astronomers, by their detection of radio waves billions of years old, claim to be hearing cosmic noise that harks back to an early phase of the universe.

But I am convinced that art, in another sense, also points forward to the end, that is, to the fulfillment in God's kingdom of the purposes and glories of creation. It echoes heaven as it echoes paradise; and the two indeed are resonant of each other. We find this theme in T. S. Eliot and C. S. Lewis (and see footnote 29, p. 271). We may discern a similarity between certain processes and functions of memory and of art. Each involves a distilling process, a perfecting and condensation of material, to reveal inner truth. Both are like geodes: there is the rough matter, but pressure has transformed the minerals inside the rock into jewels. I am thinking here in particular of memories of joy, frequently but not necessarily associated with childhood and with experiences of love or peace or natural beauty. These are pointers, I believe, to the fullness of joy that we shall know in heaven, in unbroken communion with our Creator and Lord. Just so, I have argued, are works of art that radiate beauty. By words, paint, stone, wood, notes, rhythmic gesture, etc., they articulate space and measure time, and precisely by shaping and transfiguring the God-given forms of material reality into concrete, man-made forms, they lift us who are made in God's image into the timeless sphere of spirit, where all that has been and is beautiful, true, and good in human history is gathered into God's eternal, vibrant present.

IX

It is important here to reflect briefly on light. Jesus calls himself the light of the world (John 8:12)—but let us not forget that he also calls his *disciples* the light of the world (Matt 5:14). He says that those who follow him will not walk in darkness but will have the light of life (John 8:12); and in Psalm 36:10, the psalmist likewise associates light and life: the Lord is the source of life, and in his light we shall see light. We are made in the image of God; the more we are conformed to that image—that is, to Jesus—the more we will reflect light in all we do. We will become vessels of light, *"being transformed into his likeness with ever increasing glory,"* as Paul puts it in 2 Corinthians 3:18.[31] *"This comes from the Lord,"* he adds, *"who is the Spirit."*

We must not forget that in an individual or in a culture, light received can become darkness. *"If then the light within you is darkness, how great is that darkness!,"* exclaims Jesus in Matthew 6:23b. I think that is happening to us in the West, to the extent that we are repudiating him who is the light of the world and so losing contact with transcendent reality, the Source of life and hope. For there is no other source of hope—of *true* hope—than the One who made us and redeemed us, and so opened a home for us beyond death.

As God, who is Spirit, is light, it is not surprising that the physical substrata of the universe he has created—its energy—is light, or that this energy, in the physical and visible universe, is what most resembles what we call spirit, or that the chief metaphor for truth and revelation—certainly in the Judeo-Christian tradition—has been light. By him who is light, that which is exists; and by virtue of *created* light, that which exists is revealed to us who have been made in God's image and so have eyes, both physical and figurative, to see.

All this is immensely relevant to art. The history of art—certainly of Judeo-Christian art, both Western and Eastern—could be described as so many changes rung on the appropriation of light. It is light that reveals the form and color of objects in the physical universe. Furthermore, it is *focused* light, or intensely clear light, that reveals the effulgence of objects, and transfigures them from mundane shapes or lusterless tones into brilliant, colorful forms. Art, whatever the medium, is concerned to duplicate—working, of course, with already given matter—this process of luminous intensification. A painter, for example, is *directly* involved in this way with objects; a poet's involvement with light is *metaphorical*. Both these artistic activities provide analogies with the *spiritual* experience of a Christian disciple, who seeks to allow the Holy Spirit to do to his soul what a beam of light focused through a window or through a parting in the clouds does to an object in its path.

---

31. One thinks here of the first two verses of George Herbert's poem "The Windows" in his great work *The Temple*: "Lord, how can man preach thy eternal word?/ He is a brittle crazie glasse:/Yet in thy temple thou dost him afford/This glorious and transcendent place,/To be a window, through thy grace./But when thou dost anneal in glasse thy storie,/Making thy life to shine within/The holy Preachers; then the light and glorie/More rev'rend grows, & more doth win:/Which else shows watrish, bleak, & thin" (Hutchinson, *Works of George Herbert*, 67).

As we engage with light in these different ways, we find that time and place themselves are transcended. It is not just that an instant in time has been frozen, as is often said rather misleadingly about photographs in particular. It is that the present has been expanded or deepened into the eternal. A work of beauty actually gives us a glimpse of eternity—not through its subject matter necessarily, but by virtue of the artistry with which the subject matter is portrayed. Mysteriously, this transcendence of temporal reality is accomplished precisely through the illumination of the object in its particularity and its concrete *place and context* in time and space. But the viewer, or reader, must appropriate this experience for him- or herself, just as the artist has appropriated his or her experience of given reality in making the artistic work. This is done through contemplation, through *time*—time consecrated to the work in question. Paradoxically, the interiorization of beauty—in nature or in art or in the appreciation of art—leading us through and beyond the moment into the eternal, can only be accomplished in and with time.

It is here that art can, quite precisely, throw light on the nexus of creation and redemption in which human history is lived out. It is by light, as the first word spoken by the Creator, that the universe was created; and by that same light of truth, the same word—spoken into the created world in the incarnate Christ—redeemed it from darkness. In a piece of art, analogously, the object transfigured by light, made luminous and beautiful, is a created object; and by the power of the artist's imagination, that object is re-presented, transformed, revealed in its truth—in a certain sense, *redeemed* (though not in a salvific sense, of course).

I believe we can see art here as a metaphor—certainly as an analogy—for God's creation and redemption of the world. Light is the expression of grace—both common and special. What God has made, especially humankind, is forms of grace. It is by grace that fallen humanity is saved. Fashioned in God's image and recalled to the fullness of that image in Jesus Christ, we participate knowingly in the community of grace. As the order of primal creation is the work of reason ordered to love, so, by analogy, is the order of art. Light—whether physical or metaphorical—is art's very medium. It brings clarity, it expresses truth. And light is the quintessential form of grace, the very expression of love, manifest in beauty. So we may conclude by saying that in its immediacy to our senses in space and time, revealing the beauty of actual objects and persons, light—in nature and *also in art*—points us backward and forward to our Source and End, to creation and to eschatology, to the Alpha and Omega in whom we live and have our being, in whom we are called to live and have our being *forever*.

Talk on Poetry

(Conference, Canterbury)

I SEE MY TASK today as an attempt to discuss my own vision as a Christian who is a poet, and by that means to open up wider issues to do with aesthetics and beauty. I believe this matter to be of the greatest importance today, in general but also in particular for those who profess the Christian faith in our secular age. Art in our time, when it is authentic and not just kitsch or nihilistic desecration, has become a chief vehicle for presenting to our neo-pagan society an intuition of transcendent reality, which the materialist worldview rules out by definition. Public interest in art from the past, and from all cultures, has never been greater. People pour into the exhibitions at museums. The materialist worldview, sustained by science understood in a positivist way, and by what I call technology-as-ideology, is being challenged today on many fronts, not least by the refusal of religious faith, Christian and other, to go away, as many modernist thinkers expected it to do.

The hunger that we find today for every kind of art is not just a spiritual substitute or counterfeit, as some Christians might think; it is that sometimes, but it is also much more than that. It expresses, for many, a genuine search for meaning and spiritual reality, in the perceived absence of any *other* vehicle *for* or access *to* such reality. While relativism and an intellectual resistance to the notion of truth in any absolute sense may be what many people claim to believe in today, at the deeper level of their heart these same people—who are made, as Christians believe, in the image of God even if they don't know it—may well be aching for the transcendent reference and value that could give real *significance* to their lives.

Within the compass of modern life, bewildering and seemingly pointless to many thoughtful people, with its depersonalization at so many levels, its violence, and its perceived closure in death without remainder, the conviction that life—and our own lives in particular—really have significance and enduring value is hard to come by. The church, as most of you are aware, is more or less scorned or ignored by many in our Western society who, for a number of reasons, some entirely understandable, consider it outdated, irrelevant, and lacking credibility. Yet these same people may well be attracted by art in some form, and indeed by developments within the church, of which there are many, such as the so-called Emerging Church movement, that put strong emphasis on art. Why is this? What does this attraction mean, and what is the basis for it? I want now to consider these questions, which are vital for us as Christians to try to understand.

That is our backdrop. Let me now move to a more personal note, to suggest the pertinence of these thoughts to art as I understand it, and to my own work as a poet. The Lord found me at the age of twenty-nine. At the time I was living in New York and writing a novel—in effect I was looking for God through art, though I didn't know that this was what I was doing. My conversion, which was radical, presented me almost immediately with a major dilemma. I was a *new creation*, by the grace of God: forgiven, cleansed, ushered into the realm of the Spirit and a relation with the true God—God the Father of the Lord Jesus Christ. From being upside-down, my world turned right-side up. I saw everything *fresh* and *new*, as if waking to the first morning. I had been blind, lost in modernity, like those lonely stick figures the Italian sculptor Giacometti used to make—and now I *saw*! Meaning flowed into my life. Things fell together that before had been disparate, unconnected, incoherent. And things found their proper names, which before had been at best concepts or sheer phenomena, lacking the transcendental reference—God—that alone could give them meaning: sin, evil, death, redemption, hope. The Bible, hitherto opaque, became my joy and guide. From an unreadable book, it became God's word to me personally, and I found, first, my fundamental identity as God's adopted son through Jesus Christ, the Eternal Son; and then, secondly, my place in God's corporate people, in a long historical tradition with its source in ancient times, an imperative and dynamic for present living, and an eschatological end, an end beyond this life in a fullness of communion with the Creator and with others who love him. I was no longer alone! I was no longer a stick figure! I was loved! God, through Christ and by the Holy Spirit, had become real, knowable, loving, present, in his Creation and in the body of his Son, the church. He was my Father and his Son was my Savior and Lord. Hallelujah!

But the artistic problem was real. How to situate this new creation, both personal and corporate, that I experienced myself as being and as participating in, living henceforth in the realm of the Spirit and not simply in the realm of natural phenomena—how to situate this new creation in relation to the person I had been for twenty-nine years? How to write my novel, now that my whole perspective on reality had been turned upside-down? I won't go into the details of what happened in the next years as I struggled with this question, except to say that, for a number of reasons, I did lay aside the novel two years later, upon the hard-won realization that I was not gifted as a novelist. Following that, I did no creative writing in the strict sense for ten years, until one day the Lord abruptly returned my writing gift to me, now in the form of poetry. I had written a lot of poetry as a young man, but I had not been thinking about taking up that practice again—and then suddenly, in 1982, I was moved to write a poem, for the first time in twenty years. This had not been a subject of prayer or even of any conscious longing. God simply and graciously gave poetry back to me as a gift, out of the blue. I haven't stopped writing since, whenever I can, whenever I have the time and inspiration, and I do everything in my power to study literature and the literary tradition, to refine my understanding of what poetry is, and to hone my own poetic vision and style.

Here are some of the things I've learned. The puzzle of living out, in the artistic dimension, this new creation that I am, as an individual and as a member of Christ's body in space and time, this new creation that is in the world but not of it—this puzzle is parallel to the challenge to all of us who are Christians, as we go about living our daily life as citizens both of heaven and of some political entity in this fallen world. Poetry is about experience, and the challenge to a poet who has experienced redemption in Christ is how to express and convey that experience in terms that are understandable, at least partially, to people who have not had that experience. This is all the more difficult today, in the overwhelmingly secular climate of our age. The language of Christian faith is increasingly unknown in our society. How can the Christian artist communicate to such a society the new reality that informs his or her whole existence? What language can we find adequate to the task?

The Christian poet, by virtue of incorporation into Christ's death and life, is living, one might say, in a world of color and, as a poet, is trying to express his or her experience of a colored world and make this world somehow real to people who only see in black-and-white and who may be inclined to think that no colored world exists or, from a politically correct angle, that for anyone to claim that it does exist and to write accordingly is to discriminate against those who don't believe that way. I am not talking here about evangelism, or about explaining the gospel to unbelievers, but simply about the poet who is a Christian writing out of who he is, who she is: this poet is a *new creation*, the member of a community that is a *new creation*, and this new creation is his or her inner *identity*, so that to ignore or avoid this truth in the interest of, say, having one's work be easily acceptable to a wider audience, or on the pretext that the question of inner identity doesn't make any difference at the aesthetic level, would be false and would lack artistic integrity.

So how can this artistic act of communication be accomplished? There is no recipe, obviously. But there are helpful guidelines. Let me approach this from several perspectives: personal, technical, and theological.

At the personal level, a poet must find his or her own voice. He/She must let a style develop in accordance with what comes naturally, allowing influences from other poets to do their work but being diligent to move through each influence until somehow a distillation has set in and taken hold, an inner assurance of one's own vision and manner of composing. As the poet who is a Christian gradually coordinates, in cooperation with the Holy Spirit, the new being that he/she is, with the fallen world in which he or she lives, that personal voice will begin to emerge.

What is it that moves me most intensely? What deep beauty in human beings or in nature do I want to find words to express? What mysteries do I want to intimate? In one sense, of course, I can't know what I want to say until I'm trying to say it, until I'm actually putting words down. The words will lead me, they will point me to what it is I crave to bring up from my heart. But underneath that effort, that activity, there is emotion inflected by thought, there is a fire that wants to burn. This fire will push out the words, as the words will express the fire. There's a circular process going on here between the emotion and the words.

Poetic inspiration is mysterious. In my case, I experience an unsolicited emotion that may come through a word, a rhythm, a sensation, a shock of insight, a sensory detail that arrests me. What is inexplicable is that one may have had similar experiences at other times, without their having generated an inspiration. Be that as it may, the triggering emotion that demands to find a form may be linked to a story, an event, a personal encounter, a landscape; it may be rain on the roof, bringing back memories; it may be leaves floating on a river; it may be anger at injustice; it may be an experience of love or of loss. The poem is an attempt to bring order into that emotion, to find out and give verbal shape to what it is that is burning inside oneself.

The poet is a sculptor, doing through words what the sculptor in stone or, differently, the sculptor in clay or, again differently, the sculptor-as-constructor does with his own material. The content and the form are indissolubly bound together. The meaning of the poem is *this* content in *this* form; its meaning cannot be detached from the poem itself, it cannot be paraphrased as if it were a separate entity. The poem may be bad, it can be the object of critique and judgment; but its meaning is inherent in the entity that it is.

No work of art in any medium is worth anything if it is not brought forth with passion. For all that it is obviously a contingent product, a poem is also the result of an inner necessity. In some way, it is the product of an eruption, of a telluric pressure, a geological thrust. Reason and intellect operate on magmatic material. That material must be channeled, formed; but this too is the work of passion, what I might call *intellectual* passion. A good poem comes up from the depths of the soul, from the unconscious, from memory, where all kinds of combinations occur outside the reach of the shaping intellect; but then the shaping intellect must gather these into a coherent whole, into a work of art, a *poem*.

Here we move into the technical domain. As with any art, technique is critical. Art is something we make, and we make it with tools that we wield more or less skillfully. Meter, which gives a regular beat to rhythm; rhyme, when a chosen form requires it or may be enhanced by it; alliteration, assonance, imagery, metaphor, simile—all these are tools the poet needs in order to do his shaping of the raw material. Poetic language, whether contained in strict classical forms like the sonnet or the villanelle, for example, or expressed in free verse, is more intense, more compact, than ordinary prose. It says a great deal succinctly, with the concentrated coordination and movement one might associate with a performing acrobat or professional athlete. It is like an essence, or, as in cooking, a reduction. Yet it is always concerned with the particular, the concrete, the unique. If an abstract idea or a concept crosses its horizon, that idea or concept must find an image or a concrete corollary to be expressed.

Poetic language is multidimensional, its words may have multiple senses. They *con*note as well as *de*note; the way they are put together, the connections between them, create echoes and resonances that sound and reverberate within the poem and beyond it. The sound of the words is absolutely critical. By their sounding and by their cadence, they create an effect akin to music, with the fundamental difference that they carry semantic meaning. But, and I repeat myself here, that meaning and the form that carries it are inseparable; the form and the content cannot be pried apart.

True art offers us, for our delight, the world in its concrete thickness and beauty. It renders the particular and unique. Yet by virtue of the order it achieves, the beauty it fashions, it intimates, through the particular, the universal. A good poem engages all the faculties of the poet and also of the reader or hearer: the senses, emotions, imagination, and intellect. This is enormously important in today's one-dimensional, information-obsessed culture. The poet's aim and job are to communicate *experience*, not information. If information must be conveyed, a way must be found to do this poetically through, again, the choice of words, meter, imagery, and/or rhetorical ingenuity. Again, *intellectual passion* will be important in achieving this.

A poem, and any work of art in any medium, is the fruit of an encounter between the artist and the world *out there*, as he or she experiences it. The poet's *subjectivity* encounters the world's *objectivity*. It is this encounter, this coming-into-relation, that generates the work of art.

Let me conclude by suggesting what I take to be the theological underpinning of this phenomenon, which I will also develop this afternoon. Genesis 1:27 and 28 reveal—and it *is* a revelation—that man/woman is made in the image of God and has the mandate to master and care for God's creation. In our very being, we are *bonded* to the transcendent, to the divine, and also gifted with the means to tend, groom, and domesticate the garden of the world. We are *by nature* in relation to God and cannot help but aspire to communion with divinity. Now, since God is free to act by his own will, we who are made *in his image* are also free to determine how we will relate to the reality in which we find ourselves. Hence by virtue of our moral freedom we can turn our created *positive* relation with our Creator into a *negative* relation and aspire to set God aside and to claim his divinity for ourselves. This is what original sin is all about, as portrayed in Genesis 3. It falsifies our relation to God, to our fellow human beings, and to the creation. The ecological and social crises we are experiencing today are a manifestation of that falsification. For our purposes here, however, the point is that relation to divinity is intrinsic to human nature, whether that relation be in the positive or the negative mode.

True art, whatever the religious or cultural milieu from which it emerges, points to and in some way reflects the divine, the transcendent. Beauty, wherever it be found, is a timeless universal that expresses God's glory—and we humans can participate in it and display it in our art and our science, precisely because of our inherent bond with God the Creator, the *imago Dei*. This is the case whether or not we are new creations in Christ. Great art is by no means a possibility uniquely available to Christians. The fall, as Christians understand it, does not eliminate from human nature all positive contact with the goodness, truth, and beauty that are reflections in the world of the divine nature, of which we bear the image. Art is possible because of that residue of positive contact with the divine. Our rebellion gives rise to idolatry, yes, but not *only* to idolatry. God preserves us by his grace, and the impulse to know him truly remains embedded in our being, even if the *full knowledge* of who he is is revealed, as Christians believe, only through Jesus Christ.

True art, by pointing to and somehow participating in divine life, actually transforms concrete, material elements into human creations that shimmer with transcendent reality. True art and the sacred are closely linked. This very dynamic of transformation reveals what I might call the *sensed need*, common to our race, for redemption. This, I think, is what explains the contemporary hunger for art of every kind that we observe today among Western populations starved for spiritual food, meaning, and, I dare to say, redemption.

Let me conclude with this simple observation. We as Christians must respond to this hunger by exploring ways in which the Holy Spirit wishes to reenergize the church. It is my conviction that one of the most important ways we can do this will be to raise up and call forth artists of the first rank, who will seek to create beautiful works and who, in whatever medium, can find the language to glorify God through their artistic productions. Art itself, of course, cannot convert people to Christ; only the Holy Spirit, through God's word, can do that. But true art, by radiating in some way the truth of *being*, whose Source is God, can touch the human spirit and dispose the heart to be open to receive the good news of Jesus Christ, Savior and Lord.

Notes for Short Talk on Beauty and Truth

(Church of the Redeemer, New York City)

Let me start off by making a few remarks about the subject of beauty, before placing them in the context of the biblical doctrine of the *imago Dei*, based on Genesis 1:27: *"So God created humankind in his own image, in the image of God he created them, male and female."*

When we take in an object (or hear a sound) that we consider to be beautiful (I include here all objects, natural and man-made, organic and inorganic), several things are going on that we may not be aware of. First of all, the object attracts us toward itself—it is *attractive*. Secondly, it exudes vitality—it *radiates outward*. The object both draws us into itself and comes out toward us. We in turn respond by being attracted to it and by receiving its beauty into ourselves.

While we find ourselves responding on many qualitative levels—aesthetic, emotional, intellectual—what is actually most important in the encounter is its substratum, which is not a matter of qualities at all. Nor is it quantifiable, certainly. It is a mystery. We are discovering an object that is over against us, *out there*, autonomous, and yet we make this discovery precisely as we respond to the object, that is, as we connect to it, as we *enter into a relation* to it. Whether the object is natural or man-made, it has *being*, it *is*, and this being *is not the same thing as the sum of its qualities*. We find ourselves standing in its presence, before its very being. Both it and we are unaccountably *there*, and the relation between us is a mystery.

The presence to us of this beautiful object-that-is, attracting and irradiating us, is thus dynamic and relational. It cannot be analyzed with pure objectivity, as if it were outside of its relation to us. The principle here is the same as with any interpretation: there is no purely objective interpretation of an event or a text, since the interpretation is being made by an individual with a particular perspective. In the case of a beautiful object present to us, however, we are talking about something more profound than an interpretation. The relation between us and the radiant object is a reality beyond both *its* objectivity—its autonomous existence—and *our own* subjectivity. We too have being, let us not forget. Even if all our qualities could be enumerated, including every atom that constitutes us, neither our sheer being nor our particular form—that is, our identity that persists through the ongoing renewal of the matter our bodies are made of, and that informs and integrates that matter—would be thus comprehended or defined. Our being and our form are of another order than the qualitative or the quantitative. Like the beautiful object we are confronted with, we too are mysterious. Our existence is rationally unfathomable. Two beings, then, at least one of which is human and personal and is responding personally to beauty, are connecting with each other. In some sense—with a depth of engagement varying according to the nature of the object—they enter into community. This is the heart of the mystery involved in the recognition by a person of a beautiful object. The mystery precedes and underlies any qualitative apprehension of the object before us.

It is important to note that the initiative, as it were, comes from the object, not from us. Its beauty calls forth our response. The object and its beauty are one, they cannot be separated; and when we see this beautiful object, we are caught up by it, *won over* by it.

We may call this response love, *eros*. *Love* is the name of the relation established between us and the beautiful object.

Clearly, there are qualitative elements involved in the recognition of an object as beautiful: form, proportion, the harmony of parts (including color if it is present), luminosity, rhythm, balance, to name a few. If the object is a human person, moral and spiritual qualities are involved as well. We will be attracted by what is true and good. Raphael and the Italian High Renaissance spoke of grace—gracefulness—a kind of mixture of offhanded naturalness and elegance. They applied this to art, understood as the expression of the highest laws of being. We will speak of art shortly.

Beauty is the radiance of truth, which itself is an expression of goodness. Truth is the real, the authentic, that which has integrity and is not *deformed*. It expresses the good. Its radiance, in a material object or a person, is beautiful.

The mystery involved in the perception of beauty, which inheres in the relationship between two beings, the human observer and the beautiful object, points back to an ineffable Source of being and suggests that the mystery at the heart of being itself is relational and may be named love. Human persons, capable of responding to the beautiful, logically cannot emerge out of the ultimately impersonal. However one understands the dynamics of evolution, leading up to the personal/rational being that is man (man/woman), metaphysical reflection makes clear to us, regardless of what materialists may say, that a directing, personal power behind that dynamism, informing matter, is necessary. This points to the presence behind, underneath, in a sense *within*, human persons of a divine being who is personal and who has created human persons as well as all other beautiful objects which those persons are able to connect to and call beautiful. That which is, is good; what is true expresses it; it is manifest in beauty.

Speaking as a Christian theologian, I approach these issues from within a biblical framework. Two central aspects of this framework concern the nature of humankind, as created in the image of God, and the nature of God, as being three divine Persons—or three personal modes of divinity—in one divine being. Both of these truths, as I take them to be, are revealed fully and fulfilled in Jesus Christ, the Word of God incarnate. The revelation about man (man and woman) as made in God's image (*imago Dei*) is given in Genesis 1. The *imago Dei* must be understood as an *ontological* reality, not simply as a *qualitative* one. What we are being told is that humankind, and each individual person, is constitutionally bound to God the Creator; that is, it is the *very nature of human being* to be in relation to God. With what the Bible portrays as the fall of man—the self-assertion of man as over against his Creator—that relationship was not destroyed, rather it was *inversed*, turned from the positive to the negative pole.

Now the Christian tradition, from Irenaeus in the second century, has tended to talk of the *imago Dei* in terms of ontic—inherent—qualities, especially rationality and freedom, which characterize both God and human beings, at the expense of the more fundamental reality that I have indicated, namely, the ontological/relational one. This tendency, unfortunately, prepared the way for a gap to open up in Western man's self-understanding between his intrinsic connection to God and his natural human capacities. Starting in the eighteenth century, faith and reason were progressively set in opposition. As Christian faith, for complex reasons, weakened in Western culture, the God side of the equation dropped away and the notion of man as a rational, autonomous being came to occupy the whole conceptual stage.

Such a view, dominant in today's secularized West, makes it difficult to understand what is going on in our spontaneous reaction to beauty that I described earlier. Whatever human self-understanding a given culture may have (such as the modern Western view just noted), it cannot, of course, alter the fundamental reality created by God. The heart of that reality is connectedness, relationship. In the Genesis text, with respect to the *imago Dei*, it is revealed that, in addition to the built-in bond to the Creator, humankind has a mandate to be God's representative in the creation and to care for it. In Genesis 2, the account of the naming of the animals by Adam symbolizes this responsibility and demonstrates the authority and intimacy it presupposes.

It is here that we come to the crux of my approach to the question of beauty. As we behold any object of God's creation, or any beautiful object of man's confection, we need to understand that a prior relation exists already between it and ourselves. All being is the Creator's work and as such bears his mark. Human beings, as made in God's image, bear this mark in the ontological way I have indicated. With other beings we have our creaturehood in common, and with respect to them, furthermore, we have our God-given mandate to care for them. As God's image and representative in the world, we are to love the world as he loves it. As between us and our Creator, so between us and the objects of his created world, starting with ourselves, there is a spiritual bond. Man-in-sin, man-in-revolt-against-God, experiences the inversion of this, but the bond itself cannot be obliterated, even if—whether unconsciously, or through overt indifference or hostility—we deny its existence and the existence of God altogether.

Since the *imago Dei* is *inversed* by the fall, instead of love, there is enmity: between human beings and God, between ourselves, and between ourselves and the rest of creation. That inversion is in turn upended by manifestations of love, of which the supreme example is the incarnation of the Son of God, Jesus of Nazareth. Through Jesus Christ, God has accomplished, and in principle made available to all men and women, the reconciliation to himself of humanity and of the rest of creation. Through and in him, the spiritual bond-in-love is restored. Jesus, by his atoning work, is the fulfillment of all the bits and pieces, all the occasions, of love scattered through his world. Toward him, the creative and redemptive Word, they all point and have always pointed.

I conclude with this thought. In beauty, love shines forth. Beauty, truth, and goodness cannot be separated, even if they can be distinguished. Like the Persons of the divine Trinity, they interpenetrate and co-inhere. They are dimensions of love. Speaking in Trinitarian terms, one could suggest that goodness, analogous to God the Father, is the primordial ground of love; that truth, analogous to God the Son, the creative Word spoken by the Father, is the bringing forth of love in the forms of created reality, expressive of God's goodness; and that beauty, analogous to the Holy Spirit, is the effulgence of love in these created forms.

Bibliography

Avis, Paul. *Ecumenical Theology and the Elusiveness of Doctrine*. London: SPCK, 1986.
Baillie, Donald M. *Theology of the Sacraments*. London: Faber and Faber, 1957.
Banner, Michael. *Christian Ethics and Contemporary Moral Problems*. Cambridge: Cambridge University Press, 1999.
Beckwith, Roger T. *Priesthood and Sacraments*. Abingdon, UK: Marcham Miner, 1964.
Behe, Michael J. *Darwin's Black Box*. New York: Touchstone, 1996.
Berry, Wendell. *Art of the Common Place*. Washington, DC: Counterpoint, 2002.
Bridge, Donald, and David Phypers. *Meal that Unites?* London: Hodder and Stoughton, 1981.
Brooks, David. *Second Mountain: Quest for a Moral Life*. New York: Random House, 2019.
Bruneteau, Bernard. *Siècle des Génocides*. Paris: Armand-Colin, 2004.
Cavanaugh, William T. *Theopolitical Imagination*. Edinburgh: T. & T. Clark, 2002.
Clark, Neville. *Approach to the Theology of the Sacraments*. London: SCM, 1956.
Condon, Guy, and David Hazard. *Fatherhood Aborted*. Wheaton, IL: Tyndale, 2001.
Danielson, Dennis Richard, ed. *Book of the Cosmos*. Cambridge, MA: Perseus, 2000.
Davies, Paul. *Mind of God*. London: Simon & Schuster, 1992.
Delsol, Chantal. *Éloge de la Singularité*. Paris: La Table Ronde, 2000.
Dillistone, Frederick W. *Christianity and Symbolism*. London: Collins, 1955.
Donoghue, Denis. *Words Alone: The Poet T. S. Eliot*. New Haven: Yale University Press, 2000.
Ellul, Jacques. *Trahison de l'Occident*. Paris: Calmann-Lévy, 1975.
Gilson, Etienne. *God and Philosophy*. New Haven: Yale University Press, 1941.
Grainger, Roger. *Language of the Rite*. London: Darton, Longman and Todd, 1974.
Grant, George. *Time as History*. 1969. Reprint. Toronto: University of Toronto Press, 2001.
Gregg, David. *Anamnesis in the Eucharist*. Grove Booklet, series on Liturgy, No. 5. Bramcote, UK: Grove, 1976.
Gregory of Nyssa. *Life of Moses*. The Classics of Western Spirituality. New York: Paulist, 1978.
Hanson, Anthony, and Richard Hanson. *Reasonable Belief*. Oxford: Oxford University Press, 1981.
Hobson, George. *Episcopal Church, Homosexuality, and the Context of Technology*. Eugene, OR: Pickwick, 2013.
———. "Towards a Doctrine of Providence: A Response to Contemporary Critiques." DPhil diss., Oxford University, 1989.

Hutchinson, Francis E., ed. *Works of George Herbert*. Oxford: Clarendon, 1941.
Keck, David. *Forgetting Whose We are*. Nashville: Abingdon, 1996.
Kirkpatrick, Dow, ed. *Doctrine of the Church*. New York: Abingdon, 1964.
Küng, Hans. *Why Priests?* Translated by John Cumming. Glasgow: Collins, 1972.
Leenhardt, Franz J. "This is My Body." In *Essays on the Lord's Supper*, edited by Oscar Cullman and Franz J. Leenhardt. Translated by John G. Davies. Atlanta: John Knox, 1958.
MacIntyre, Alasdair. *Whose Justice? Whose Rationality?* London: Gerald Duckworth, 1988.
Mascall, Eric L. *Corpus Christi*. London: Longmans, Green, 1953.
———. *Whatever Happened to the Human Mind?* London: SPCK, 1980.
Micklethwait, John, and Adrian Wooldridge. *God is Back: How the Global Revival of Faith is Changing the World*. New York: Penguin, 2010.
Moule, Charles F. D. *Sacrifice of Christ*. London: Hodder and Stoughton, 1956.
———. *Worship in the New Testament*. Grove Booklets, series on Liturgy, Nos. 12 and 13. Bramcote, UK: Grove, 1977, 1978.
Nygren, Anders. *Agape and Eros*. London: SPCK, 1982.
Pearcey, Nancy R., and Charles B. Thaxton. *The Soul of Science: Christian Faith and Natural Philosophy*. Wheaton, IL: Crossway, 1994.
Pedersen, Johannes. *Israel: Its Life and Culture, Vol. 1*. 4 Vols. London: Oxford University Press, 1926.
Polanyi, Michael. *Personal Knowledge*. London: Routledge, 1958.
Polkinghorne, John. *Belief in God in an Age of Science*. New Haven: Yale University Press, 1998.
———. *Quarks, Chaos, and Christianity*. New York: Crossroad, 2006.
———. *Science and the Trinity*. New Haven: Yale University Press, 2004.
Ramm, Bernard. *Offense to Reason: A Theology of Sin*. Vancouver: Regent College Press, 2000.
Ramsey, Michael. *Christian Concept of Sacrifice*. Oxford: Sisters of the Love of God, 1974.
Ruse, Michael. *Darwin and Design: Does Evolution have a Purpose?* Cambridge: Harvard University Press, 2003.
Sherrard, Philip. *Eclipse of Man and Nature: An Enquiry into the Origins and Consequences of Modern Science*. West Stockbridge, MA: Lindisfarne, 1987.
Sloterdijk, Peter. *Essai d'Intoxication Volontaire*. Paris: Calmann-Lévy, 1999.
Staune, Jean. *Notre Existence a-t-elle un Sens?* Paris: Presses de la Renaissance, 2007.
Steiner, George. *Grammars of Creation*. New Haven: Yale University Press, 2001.
———. *Language and Silence*. New York: MacMillan, 1967.
———. *Real Presences*. London: Faber and Faber, 1989.
Strobel, Lee. *Case for a Creator*. Grand Rapids: Zondervan, 2004.
Temple, William. *Christus Veritas*. London: Macmillan, 1925.
Tillard, Jean M. R. *What Priesthood has the Ministry?* Grove Booklet, series on Ministry and Worship, No. 13. Bramcote, UK: Grove, 1973.
Tresmontant, Claude. *Sciences de l'Univers et Problèmes Métaphysiques*. Paris: Seuil, 1976.

Volf, Miroslav. *A Public Faith: How Followers of Christ Should Serve the Common Good.* Grand Rapids: Brazos, 2013.

Volf, Miroslav, and Matthew Croasmun. *For the Life of the World: Theology that Makes a Difference.* Grand Rapids: Brazos, 2019.

Whitehead, Alfred. N. *Symbolism.* Cambridge: Cambridge University Press, 1927.

Williams, Rowan. *Eucharistic Sacrifice: Roots of a Metaphor.* Grove Booklet, series on Liturgy, No. 31. Bramcote, UK: Grove, 1982.

www.ingramcontent.com/pod-product-compliance
Lightning Source LLC
Chambersburg PA
CBHW071233230426
43668CB00011B/1419